THE PARISH IN ENGLISH LIFE, 1400–1600

THE PARISH IN ENGLISH LIFE
1400–1600

edited by
Katherine L. French, Gary G. Gibbs, and Beat A. Kümin

MANCHESTER UNIVERSITY PRESS

MANCHESTER AND NEW YORK

distributed exclusively in the USA by St. Martin's Press

Published by Manchester University Press
Oxford Road, Manchester M13 9NR, UK
and Room 400, 175 Fifth Avenue, New York, NY10010, USA

Distributed exclusively in the USA by
St. Martin's Press, Inc., 175 Fifth Avenue, New York, NY10010, USA

British Library Cataloguing-in-Publication Data
A catalogue record for this book is available from the British Library

Library of Congress Cataloging-in-Publication Data applied for

ISBN 0–7190–4953–9 *hardback*

First published 1997

01 00 99 98 97   10 9 8 7 6 5 4 3 2 1

Typeset by Carnegie Publishing, Preston
Printed in Great Britain by Biddles Ltd, Guildford and King's Lynn

CONTENTS

LIST OF ILLUSTRATIONS

Plates

Figures

LIST OF TABLES

NOTES ON CONTRIBUTORS

Margaret Clark has completed a thesis on the Reformation in Cumbria at Trinity College, Bristol. She is now working at the University of Central Lancashire, Preston, on a local history project.

Will Coster is Lecturer in History and Director of the Institute for the Study of War and Society, De Montfort University, Bedford. His publications include *Kinship and Inheritance in England: Three Yorkshire Parishes* (1993).

Eamon Duffy, Reader in Church History at the University of Cambridge, is a fellow of Magdalene College and author of *The Stripping of the Altars: Traditional Religion in England c. 1400–c. 1580* (New Haven and London, 1992).

Ken Farnhill is writing a Cambridge University thesis on the religious gilds and parishes in late medieval East Anglia. He is the author of 'The religious gilds of Wymondham 1470–1550', *Norfolk Archaeology* (1996).

Judy Ann Ford is Assistant Professor of History at East Texas State University; she has published 'Art and identity in the parish communities of late medieval Kent' in vol. 28 of *Studies in Church History*.

Andrew Foster is Principal Lecturer in History at the Chichester Institute of Higher Education and author of *The Church of England 1570–1640* (London and New York, 1994).

Katherine French is Assistant Professor of Medieval History at the State University of New York at New Paltz. She is the author of 'The legend of Lady Godiva and the image of the female body', *Journal of Medieval History* (1992).

Gary Gibbs is Assistant Professor of History at Roanoke College, Salem, Virginia. He is the author of 'Child marriage in the diocese of Chester 1561–65', *Journal of Regional and Local Studies* (1988).

Alexandra F. Johnston is Professor of English at the University of Toronto. She is founder and director of *Records of Early English Drama* and co-edited the first collection in the series, the records of York.

Beat Kümin is a research fellow of Magdalene College, Cambridge, and author of *The Shaping of a Community: The Rise and Reformation of the English Parish c. 1400–1560* (Aldershot, 1996).

Caroline Litzenberger is Assistant Professor at the Department of History of West Virginia University; her publications include the edition of *Tewkesbury Churchwardens' Accounts 1563–1624* for the Gloucestershire Record Series (1994).

Sally-Beth MacLean is Executive Editor of *Records of Early English Drama* at the University of Toronto. She has co-edited *Power of the Weak: Essays on Medieval Women* (Champaign, 1995).

Claire S. Schen is Assistant Professor of History at Wake Forest University and currently working on a manuscript on charity and poverty in London in the sixteenth and seventeenth centuries.

John Schofield is Academic Editor at the Museum of London Archaeology Service. He is the author of *Medieval London Houses* (New Haven and London, 1995) as well as of other monographs on urban archaeology.

PREFACE

This book originated at the First International Medieval Congress, held at Leeds, where a joint session by the editors revealed a great deal of interest in the parish. Clive Burgess, Virginia Bainbridge, and Beat Kümin had already been running a very successful parish seminar at the Institute of Historical Research in London, and the time seemed right for a volume dedicated to the diversity of work on this subject.

In putting together this collection we have accumulated a large number of debts. Specifically, we would like to thank Alec McAulay for his early encouragement and the history departments of Roanoke College in Salem, Virginia, the State University of New York at New Paltz, Lawrence University in Appleton, Wisconsin, and Magdalene College, Cambridge, for their support as we e-mailed, faxed, and snail-mailed each other over the course of this collaboration. Karen Harris at Roanoke College was especially helpful in getting us through last minute deadlines and the inevitable crises, Michele Slate helped to compile the index, while J. S. Johnston and Subash Shanbhag kindly agreed to draw the maps. The contributors' ready co-operation made our work much easier and – for very different reasons – we are particularly indebted to Andrew Foster and Claire Schen. Several people and institutions provided important financial help at various stages of the project: Roanoke College, the New Paltz Foundation, Kenneth Garren, the Dean of Liberal Arts at Roanoke College, David Kline, the Dean of Liberal Arts at SUNY-New Paltz, Michael Barone, Father Edward Jackman OP and the Jackman Foundation, as well as Magdalene College's Morsehead-Salter Fund. Finally, the editors want to thank their long-suffering students, who put up with our tardiness in returning their essays, blankness in our eyes as they tried to talk to us, and vagueness in our responses to them.

K.L.F., G.G.G., B.A.K.

LIST OF ABBREVIATIONS

BL	British Library, London
CKS East	Centre for Kentish Studies, Canterbury
CKS West	Centre for Kentish Studies, Maidstone
CUL	Cambridge University Library
CWA	Churchwardens' accounts
DNB	*Dictionary of National Biography*
EHR	*English Historical Review*
f., fos	folio, folios
GDR	Gloucester Diocesan Records
GL	Guildhall Library, London
GMR	Guildford Muniment Room
GRO	Gloucestershire Record Office
JEH	*Journal of Ecclesiastical History*
LDA	Leeds District Archives
LP	*Letters and Papers, Foreign and Domestic, of the Reign of Henry VIII*, ed. J. S. Brewer, J. Gairdner, and R. H. Brodie (36 vols, London, 1862–1932)
MDCLW	Metropolitan and District County Library, Wakefield
MS(S)	Manuscript(s)
NCC	Norwich Consistory Court
NS	New series
NYCRO	North Yorkshire County Record Office, Northallerton
OA	Oxfordshire Archives
OS	Old series
PaP	*Past and Present*
PRO	Public Record Office, London
REED	Records of Early English Drama, Toronto
RO	Record Office
SCH	Studies in Church History
TBGAS	*Transactions of the Bristol and Gloucestershire Archaeological Society*
TCWAAS	*Transactions of the Cumberland and Westmorland Antiquarian and Archaeological Society*
TRHS	*Transactions of the Royal Historical Society*
VCH	The Victoria History of the Counties of England
YPRS	Yorkshire Parish Record Society

PART I

Contextualising the parish

Introduction

Why the parish? Because of its importance in the religious, political, and cultural life of English society. It was the level of most collective social behaviour. Poor relief, religious worship, neighbourhood and village celebrations, the collection of taxes, and a myriad of cultural interactions and negotiations were all organised and conducted within this fundamental unit. English society and culture between 1400 and 1600, two centuries at the watershed between the medieval and early modern periods, simply cannot be understood without taking the parish into account. This, in brief, is the *raison d'être* of this volume; it contains fourteen essays by scholars working in the British Isles and North America. Together they represent a variety of approaches, methods, disciplines, and sources. The authors also advance a wide range of new interpretations and propose areas of further research.

I

The collection is arranged in four parts to highlight a number of issues that transcend chronology and allow the parish to be seen in a comparative perspective. Part I places the subject matter in two larger contexts: a historiographical one and a geographical one. Each issue is dauntingly complex. The former, historiography, is important as it supplies the basic assumptions, approaches, and methods that the current generation of students carries into the archives. A large part of this introduction offers an assessment of the trends and issues that have dominated previous scholarly work on the parish. The second context is a geographical one. The English parish was part of a universal institution. All of Christian Europe was divided into similar units, as indeed were the colonies in the New World. English parishioners shared many of the same challenges and concerns as their counterparts throughout Christendom. The greatest deficiency in the historiography of the English parish is the tendency to view it in isolation. Beat Kümin attempts to break out of that pattern and to identify some of the larger paradigms that would have been so familiar to the people at the time. One is reminded of the way Margery Kempe experienced her pilgrimages to Rome, Danzig, and Santiago; more often than not she found succour and communion in the familiarity of a parish church.[1]

1 S. B. Meech and H. E. Allen (eds), *The Book of Margery Kempe*, Early English Text Society (London, 1940); Clarissa Atkinson, *Mystic and Pilgrim: The Book and World of Margery Kempe* (Ithaca, 1983).

Part II addresses the variety of available records, their relative merits and limits. All students of parish history have had to confront the vagaries and limitations of their source materials. What type of evidence survives constructs and defines our image of a subject or region. For those who examine the northern part of England, like Margaret Clark and William Coster, surviving parochial records are few and far between. The border parishes in particular had some unique qualities that stretch the very concept of an 'English' model. Clark's research on Cumbria identifies the ways in which individual leadership, clan remnants, and scattered settlement helped to create a parish culture that was quite different from the nucleated southern communities.[2] Andrew Foster's analysis of the geographical distribution of surviving churchwardens' accounts shows the degree to which the genre manifests a bias both in terms of parish wealth and location. His chapter is the first comprehensive methodological approach to the diversity of source survival in the post-Reformation period, and a further reminder that historians have to be careful not to assume that certain trends apparent in records surviving from the south and east set some sort of national pattern; they may or may not. The Tudor Reformations changed the range and purpose of most local records. William Coster explores parish registers from northern England, developing an interesting method of 'reading' lists of baptisms, marriages, and deaths. His conclusions suggest that the sources offer more than just official demographic information; they could express religious preferences and larger community values, but individual clergymen also saw them as a place to explore their own curiosity, moral concerns, and sense of community. Yet written evidence represents only one type of parish material. Physical remains abound in the form of artefacts and parish buildings, especially the church itself. John Schofield introduces historians to some recent excavations in the City of London. With few exceptions the Great Fire of 1666 destroyed most of the capital's churches. Their secrets now lie hidden below mud, streets, and more modern foundations. Archaeology can unlock some of those secrets and inform us about the evolution and development of the parish system in the City.

Part III looks at the range and form of community actions and expectations. The issue of 'community' in the late Middle Ages has become quite controversial recently. Some scholars have questioned the very use of the term, arguing that it has been far too laden with notions of utopian social relations or egalitarian local associations.[3] 'Romanticising' the lost

2 Cf. C. Haigh, *Reformation and Resistance in Tudor Lancashire* (Cambridge, 1975).
3 Miri Rubin, 'Small groups: identity and solidarity in the late Middle Ages', in
   J. Kermode (ed.), *Enterprise and Individuals in Fifteenth-Century England* (Stroud,
   1991), pp. 132–50; Christine Carpenter, 'Gentry and community in medieval
   England', *Journal of British Studies*, 33 (1994), 340–80; Maryanne Kowaleski,
   'Introduction (to 'Vill, guild, and gentry: forces of community in later medieval
   England'), *ibid.*, 337–9.

culture of the Middle Ages has clearly been an enticing perspective for many historians. The nature of many parochial sources facilitates this tradition, as they record completed actions rather than the difficulties, tragedies, and squabbles that accompany any group effort. Nonetheless, collective actions and expectations made up a significant portion of parish life. Katherine French's study of Somerset parishes reveals a complex and colourful set of fund-raising strategies. These efforts represent a level of religious action that was at once local, communal, participatory, and as real to the parishioners as the liturgy of the Church. Shared actions and shared beliefs helped express and maintain a parish sense of obligation and belonging. French's chapter also provides further evidence of the practical 'services' offered by the ecclesiastical community and the subtle differences between rural and urban surroundings.[4]

Cultural attitudes also found expression in rituals and devotional art, the focus of so many controversies in the Tudor era. Three chapters bring us face to face with the cultural struggles of the sixteenth century. Eamon Duffy studies the rood screens, the architectural devices that separated the nave from the chancel. The chapter illustrates lay involvement in the creation and maintenance of 'sacred space', and demonstrates how even individual bequests by rich patrons could have 'communal' dimensions. Yet these richly decorated treasures became objects of state-sponsored removal as part of successive campaigns against images and Catholic relics. As William Harrison wrote in 1587, 'there was wont to be a great partition between the choir and the body of the church, now it is either very small or none at all and, to say the truth, altogether need-less ...'.[5] Alexandra Johnston and Sally-Beth MacLean examine dramatic performances in the Thames and Severn river valleys. Parish-sponsored religious plays were sources of entertainments as well as religious instruction in the late Middle Ages; and they generated financial support for many communities. The evidence of biblical plays, moreover, undermines the old cliché of an unscriptural pre-Reformation religious culture. The authors show that many of these activities continued well into Elizabeth's reign. In fact, the more local control and independence a parish possessed, the more likely the survival of dramatic performances. The position of the parish within larger society underwent similar transformations in the sixteenth century. Gary Gibbs's study of London churchwardens' accounts illustrates how parish priorities changed to meet new needs and new religious sensibilities. The nature of these changes suggests that communities redefined themselves, jettisoning obligations to help ancestors out of purgatory and negotiating new responsibilities to the ever-increasing

---

4 See C. Burgess and Beat Kümin, 'Penitential bequests and parish regimes in late medieval England', *Journal of Ecclesiastical History*, 44 (1993), 610–30.
5 William Harrison, *The Description of England*, ed. George Edelen (Washington, 1994), p. 36.

numbers of 'wandering poor'. Furthermore, Gibbs provides solid evidence of more contact and interaction between parish officials and outside authorities.

Part IV looks at particular groups. Far from parishes being egalitarian communities, factors such as gender, ethnicity, and status delineated how one participated in their affairs. The ability of church-wardens and local elites to guide and protect their fellow parishioners through the Tudor upheavals is examined in two chapters. Caroline Litzenberger studies the valiant efforts of the leading members of St Michael, Gloucester, to conform to all the various mid-century directives to keep the community together. In contrast Ken Farnhill – in a pion-eering, in-depth analysis of rural parish landholding and 'management skills' – identifies clear evidence that the parish officials of Cratfield in Suffolk concealed lands from Crown officials in open defiance of govern-ment instructions.

The remaining two chapters tackle the fate of specific segments of parish society. Judy Ann Ford studies the lives of foreigners in the town of Sandwich. She finds that the avenues of acceptance and assimilation that had existed in the fifteenth century were largely gone by the seven-teenth. Claire Schen writes on women's religious and social lives in London, where the Reformations are found to have limited the scope for female opportunities and involvement in the parish. Both groups were clearly unique, but they shared a common marginal experience within their towns and villages. The chapters in this last part underline how any sense of the parish as a community must be mitigated by a recognition of gender and status and the opportunities and constraints they brought to parish involvement.

II

It is difficult to construct a linear narrative about the historiography of the English parish that would do justice to the varied influences on the work included in this volume. First, despite some overlap, medieval and early modern historians do not share the same canon. Second, important neighbouring disciplines such as archaeology, art history, and the study of drama have a largely independent scholarly tradition. Third, about half the contributors are from a non-English background and tackle the subject with a set of very different national traditions and approaches. There are thus differences in methodology and historiography to be found in just about every chapter. Taken together, however, they illustrate the variety and complexity of the issues.

The sources, of course, provide the starting point for any historical enquiry. Here we are indebted to the endeavours of local record (and other learned) societies, whose members have provided an incessant supply of editions of gild certificates, wills, parish registers, vestry minutes,

and a myriad of other ecclesiastical records.[6] Churchwardens' accounts
in particular continue to be transcribed in large numbers.[7] In addition,
there were innumerable individual efforts, often by members of the
clergy with an interest in the history of their own benefice.[8] From an
early stage, lists were drawn up, and periodically updated, to facilitate
the search for appropriate sources, although no compilation can ever
hope to be final.[9]

A historiographical survey can start with the Tudor period itself, for
instance with Roger Martyn's famous reminiscences of parish life in Long
Melford, and should pay tribute to the countless antiquarian efforts of the
succeeding centuries.[10] Two pioneers, however, dominated the beginning
of modern parish studies: J. Charles Cox and Cardinal F. A. Gasquet.
Cox's descriptions of parish accounts and church interiors remain useful
to anyone new to the subject, while Gasquet's sympathetic portrayal of
late medieval ecclesiastical life is experiencing something of a renaissance.[11] Their work focused on a collection of anecdotal material and an

6 Among those still invaluable today is L. Toulmin Smith (ed.), *English Gilds:
   Original Ordinances of more than 100 Early English Gilds of the Fourteenth and Fifteenth
   Centuries*, Early English Text Society, OS 90 (London, 1870).
7 Early examples include Thomas Wright (ed.), *Churchwardens' Accounts of the Town
   of Ludlow, in Shropshire, from 1540 to the End of the Reign of Queen Elizabeth* (London,
   1869); recent editions by Caroline Litzenberger (ed.), *Tewkesbury Churchwardens'
   Accounts 1563–1624* (Stroud, 1994), S. Doree (ed.), *The Early Churchwardens'
   Accounts of Bishops Stortford 1431–1558* (Hitchin, 1994), and C. Burgess (ed.), *The
   Pre-Reformation Records of All Saints, Bristol* (3 vols, Bristol, 1995–). Forthcoming
   sets will include Thame in Oxfordshire (J. Carnwath) and Mildenhall in Suffolk
   (J. Craig).
8 J. Brooke and A. Hallen (eds), *The Transcript of the Registers of the United Parishes
   of S. Mary Woolnoth and S. Mary Woolchurch Haw, in the City of London, from their
   Commencement 1538 to 1760. To which is prefixed a short account of both parishes, list
   of Rectors and Churchwardens, chantries, etc., together with some interesting extracts
   from the churchwardens' accounts* (London, 1886).
9 E. Philipps, 'A list of printed churchwardens' accounts', *EHR*, 15 (1900), 335–41;
   R. Hutton, *The Rise and Fall of Merry England: The Ritual Year 1400–1700* (Oxford,
   1994), pp. 263–93; A. Camp, *Wills and their Whereabouts* (4th edn, London, 1974);
   N. Tanner, 'Sources for popular religion in late medieval England', *Ricerche di
   Storia Sociale e Religiosa*, 48 (1995), 33–51; for parish registers see the notes in
   Chapter six below.
10 Martyn's nostalgic remarks about the pre-Reformation period have been re-
   edited in D. Dymond and C. Paine (eds), *The Spoil of Long Melford Church*
   (Ipswich, 1989), and inspire the prologue to C. Haigh, *English Reformations*
   (Oxford, 1993); R. Newcourt (ed.), *Repertorium ecclesiasticum parochiale Londiniense*
   (2 vols, London, 1708–10) remains an essential source for London parish history.
11 J. C. Cox, *Churchwardens' Accounts from the Fourteenth Century to the Close of the
   Seventeenth Century* (London, 1913); J. C. Cox and C. B. Ford, *The Parish Churches
   of England* (London, 1934 plus successive edns); F. A. Gasquet, *Parish Life in
   Mediaeval England* (London, 1906); see also A. Jessopp, 'Parish life in England
   before the great pillage', *Nineteenth Century*, 43 (1898), 47–60, 431–47; for
   pioneering work on a subparochial institution see H. F. Westlake, *The Parish
   Gilds of Medieval England* (London, 1919).

illustration of 'peculiar' features, but it did a great deal to stimulate interest in the topic.

More systematic and analytical approaches were first applied to studies of the parish's secular dimensions. Post-Reformation poor relief and administrative duties took centre stage in volume 1 of the Webbs' seminal analysis of English local government and in W. E. Tate's discussion of the wide range of relevant parochial sources.[12] Moving back in time, George C. Homans explored the overlap between parochial and manorial experience in a book on medieval English villagers, whose final chapters examined the parish as one of the main *foci* of rural everyday life. He set the vigour and richness of communal religious activities in stark contrast to the more oppressive aspects of peasant reality.[13] Elaborating on a similar theme, Warren O. Ault identified a large number of overlaps between the secular and ecclesiastical sphere in the late Middle Ages: the appearance of churchwardens in the lord's courts, agricultural by-law fines allocated to the local church, and the role of the rector's glebe in the local economy. Whatever its religious goals, the parish always played its part in the manor and wider civil society.[14] As for the role of gentry and nobility within the community, historians disagree: Colin Richmond's claim about a gradual withdrawal of local elites clashes with Christine Carpenter's emphasis on their continuing involvement.[15]

The fundamental research into English canon law is associated with the name of Charles Drew, to whom we owe the standard work on the origin of lay duties and the emergence of the office of churchwarden. In the wake of the Fourth Lateran Council of 1215, successive episcopal councils and synodal decrees charged the laity with the repair of nave and churchyard, as well as with the provision of certain ornaments and

---

12 S. and B. Webb, *English Local Government from the Revolution to the Municipal Corporations Act: The Parish and the County* (London, 1906); W. E. Tate, *The Parish Chest: A Study of the Records of Parochial Administration in England* (Cambridge, 1946); see also J. Toulmin Smith, *The Parish* (London, 1857).

13 G. C. Homans, *English Villagers of the Thirteenth Century* (Cambridge, Mass., 1941).

14 W. O. Ault, 'Manor court and parish church in fifteenth-century England: a study of village by-laws', *Speculum*, 42 (1967), 53–67, and 'The village church and the village community in mediaeval England', *ibid.*, 45 (1970), 197–215; the secular dimensions of parish life are highlighted in B. Kümin, *The Shaping of a Community: The Rise and Reformation of the English Parish c. 1400–1560* (Aldershot, 1996), ch. 2.3.

15 C. Richmond, 'Religion and the fifteenth-century English gentleman', in R. B. Dobson (ed.), *Church, Politics, and Patronage in the Fifteenth Century* (Gloucester, 1984), pp. 193–208, and his 'English gentry and religion *c.* 1500', in C. Harper-Bill (ed.), *Religious Beliefs and Ecclesiastical Careers in Late Medieval England* (Woodbridge, 1991), pp. 121–50; Jeremy Catto, 'Religion and the English nobility', in H. Lloyd-Jones, V. Pearl, and B. Worden (eds), *History and Imagination* (New York, 1981), pp. 43–55; C. Carpenter, 'The religion of the gentry of fifteenth-century England', in D. Williams (ed.), *England in the Fifteenth Century* (Woodbridge, 1987), pp. 53–74, and her 'Gentry and community'.

liturgical items.[16] Given the high level of tithes and other customary dues payable to the clergy, this amounted to another, potentially crippling, burden on parishioners.[17] And yet by 1350 collective obligations, combined with a fair amount of grass-roots initiative, had helped to boost communal control and lay participation. From the first accounts surviving from this period, elected churchwardens raised and spent considerable funds, appeared as the parish's legal representative in both secular and ecclesiastical courts, and carried out a wide range of additional local responsibilities.[18]

It was the debate on the English Reformation, however, which nurtured a new boom in parish-related research. Challenging the conventional interpretation which explained the religious changes as an act of state, A. G. Dickens – following John Foxe's tradition – pointed to late medieval roots and early support for Protestantism among the population at large.[19] Much of his pioneering work in the 1960s drew on heretical and anticlerical behaviour emerging from court records and on testimonies of individual beliefs extracted from wills. The approach came to dominate the debate over the next two decades, with scholars devising increasingly sophisticated analytical tools, but also pointing to serious methodological problems. Wills alone now seem riddled with too many questions to allow an unrestricted window into people's souls or to enable us to assess the attitudes of entire local communities.[20] Historians thus started to integrate less individualistic, everyday evidence such as the flourishing subparochial institutions and the great wealth of administrative records. They soon found the Dickens model wanting and some concluded that 'the English people did not want the Reformation'.[21] This 'revisionist'

16 Charles Drew, *Early Parochial Organisation in England: The Origins of the Office of Churchwarden*, St Anthony's Hall Publications 7 (York, 1954).
17 E. Mason, 'The role of the English parishioner 1100–1500', *JEH*, 27 (1976), 17–29.
18 R. N. Swanson, *Church and Society in Late Medieval England* (Oxford, 1989), ch. 6; J. A. F. Thomson, *The Early Tudor Church and Society* (London, 1993), ch. 9.
19 A. F. Pollard, *Thomas Cranmer and the English Reformation* (London, 1904); A. G. Dickens, *The English Reformation* (London, 1964; 2nd edn 1989). For detailed historiographical surveys see P. Heath, 'Between reform and reformation: the English church in the fourteenth and fifteenth centuries', *JEH*, 41 (1990), 647–69, and R. O'Day, *The Debate on the English Reformation* (London, 1986).
20 A discussion of recent (quantitative) approaches in 'Wills, inventories and the computer', a special issue of *History and Computing*, 7 (1995); methodological concerns e.g. in C. Burgess, 'Late medieval wills and pious convention: testamentary evidence reconsidered', in M. Hicks (ed.), *Profit, Piety and the Professions* (Gloucester, 1990), pp. 14–33.
21 J. Scarisbrick, *The Reformation and the English People* (Oxford, 1984), p. 1 (quote); the challenge to Dickens's interpretation was first formulated in C. Haigh, *Reformation and Resistance in Tudor Lancashire* (Cambridge, 1975), and is perhaps most imaginatively put in E. Duffy, *The Stripping of the Altars: Traditional Religion in England 1400–1580* (New Haven, 1992), Part I.

view owed a lot to a fresh examination of fraternities, chapels, and chantries which – although they resulted from independent 'voluntary' initiatives – no longer appeared as fundamentally incompatible with the 'compulsory' parish. Instead, all these local institutions promoted belief in purgatory, they offered complementary forms of religious activities, more specialised forms of social association, and shared the same pool of officeholders and resources.[22] Churchwardens' accounts formed another (very eclectically used) pillar of this enquiry, for it was here that religious change in the localities could be most easily dated. More or less everywhere, however, late medieval vitality did not prevent rapid enforcement of the new official directives. Saints, altars, and screens disappeared quickly, rather too quickly in fact for the revisionists' liking.[23]

At the same time impulses came from new approaches in cultural history, the French *Annales* school, anthropology, and a number of other neighbouring disciplines. The exploration of ritual and ceremonial customs, for instance, yielded important insights into the ways in which members of past societies expressed their civic identities.[24] The local ecclesiastical community played an important part in this process: occasions such as the parish mass or Corpus Christi processions offered a platform for reconciliation as well as for the display of social inequality.[25] The sixteenth century again appears as a watershed. National elites attempted to impose more order, sobriety, and outside control over ceremonial customs, aiming at a

22 Scarisbrick, *Reformation*, chs 1–2; B. Hanawalt, 'Keepers of the lights: parish guilds in medieval England', *Journal of Medieval and Renaissance Studies*, 14 (1984), 21–37; C. Barron, 'The parish fraternities of medieval London', in C. Barron and C. Harper-Bill (eds), *The Church in Pre-Reformation Society* (Woodbridge, 1985), pp. 13–37; B. McCree, 'Religious gilds and the regulation of behaviour', in J. Rosenthal and C. Richmond (eds), *People, Politics, and Community in the Late Middle Ages* (Gloucester, 1987), pp. 108–18; G. Rosser, 'Communities of parish and guild in the late Middle Ages', in S. Wright (ed.), *Parish, Church and People* (London, 1988), pp. 29–55, and his 'Parochial conformity and voluntary religion in late medieval England', *TRHS*, 6th Series 1 (1991), 173–89 (esp. on chapels); K. Wood-Legh, *Perpetual Chantries in Britain* (Cambridge, 1965); A. Kreider, *English Chantries* (Cambridge, Mass., 1979); C. Burgess, '"For the increase of divine service": chantries in the parish in late medieval Bristol', *JEH*, 36 (1985), 46–65.

23 R. Hutton, 'The local impact of the Tudor Reformations', in C. Haigh (ed.), *The English Reformation Revised* (Cambridge, 1987), pp. 114–38; R. Whiting, *The Blind Devotion of the People: Popular Religion and the English Reformation* (Cambridge, 1989); for an attempt at a more comprehensive long-term examination of CWA see Kümin, *Shaping of a Community*.

24 Richard Trexler, *Public Life in Renaissance Florence* (New York, 1980); Edward Muir, *Civic Ritual in Renaissance Venice* (Princeton, 1981); C. Phythian-Adams, *Local History and Folklore: A New Framework* (London, 1985); Mervyn James, 'Ritual, drama and social body in the late medieval towns', *PaP*, 98 (1983), 3–29.

25 John Bossy, 'The mass as a social institution 1200–1700', *PaP*, 100 (1983), 27–61; Miri Rubin, *Corpus Christi: The Eucharist in Late Medieval Culture* (Cambridge, 1991).

reformation of manners and encouraging a change from religious/ communal to more hierarchical symbols.[26] Rural historians, meanwhile, paid increasing attention to parishes as units of social and political organisation.[27] In their influential study of early modern Terling in Essex, Keith Wrightson and David Levine illustrated how post-Reformation English governments expected parochial officers to exercise an increasing range of administrative and regulative duties. Confronted by socio-economic pressures, a perceived threat from the lower sorts, and inspired by a Puritan mission, village elites – to summarise a by no means uncontroversial argument – aligned themselves with external moral values rather than with those of their poorer neighbours. Social polarisation was the inevitable result.[28] The parish, however, was not breaking down. Ian Archer's scrutiny of London vestry minutes – an otherwise unduly neglected source – reveals just how important it remained for the preservation of at least some sort of social stability. The reciprocity between deference from below and relief from above, an intriguing continuity of the medieval exchange of alms *v.* prayers – ensured that neighbourhood values did not disappear completely.[29] Communal life, of course, had never been entirely harmonious and parishes socialised their members in various ways. Barbara Hanawalt's work on status, gender, and stages in the life cycle demonstrates how heterogeneous medieval communities were.[30]

Debates about the character of 'popular religion' and its relation to pagan or magical practices have also proved very fruitful. Ever since Antonio Gramsci applied the term to what most of his contemporaries called folklore and superstition, scholars have struggled to develop a methodology to arrive at reliable assessments about the religious world

26 Peter Burke, *Popular Culture in Early Modern Europe* (New York, 1978); William Beik, 'Popular culture and elite repression in early modern Europe', *Journal of Interdisciplinary History*, 12 (1980), 97–103; C. Phythian-Adams, 'Ceremony and the citizen: the communal year at Coventry 1450–1550', in P. Clark and P. Slack (eds), *Crisis and Order in English Towns 1500–1700* (London, 1972), pp. 57–85, Michael Berlin, 'Civic ceremony in early modern London', *Urban History Yearbook* (1986), 15–27, Hutton, *Merry England*.

27 See the essays by De Leeuw, Goering, and Johnston in J. A. Raftis (ed.), *Pathways to Medieval Peasants* (Toronto, 1981), pp. 311–38.

28 K. Wrightson and D. Levine, *Poverty and Piety in an English Village: Terling 1525–1700* (New York, 1979; 2nd edn 1995); see the postscript to the 2nd edn for an evaluation of the critical response. Discussions of the office of churchwarden in Kümin, *Shaping of a Community*, ch. 2.2.2, and J. Craig, 'Co-operation and initiatives: Elizabethan churchwardens and the parish accounts of Mildenhall', *Social History*, 18 (1993), 357–80.

29 For the essentially non-separatist, parish-going character of Elizabethan and Jacobean Puritanism see P. Collinson, *The Religion of Protestants: The Church in English Society 1559–1625* (Oxford, 1982); I. Archer, *The Pursuit of Stability: Social Relations in Elizabethan London* (Cambridge, 1991).

30 Barbara A. Hanawalt, *The Ties that Bound: Peasant Families in Medieval England* (New York, 1986), and her *Growing Up in Medieval London: The Experience of Childhood in History* (New York, 1993).

of the lower classes.[31] Some, including Mikhail Bakhtin and Carlo Ginzburg, have argued that differentiations between popular and elite views became increasingly significant in the early modern period. Many a fascinating account has since broadened our understanding of the nature of heresy, the persistence of unorthodox ideas within the local community, and the cryptic facets of popular subcultures which only rarely emerge to the surface.[32] The concept of the 'Christian Middle Ages', for example, has been questioned by a number of historians, for whom only the catechetic efforts of the (Counter-) Reformation ensured a significant penetration of the population at large.[33] Most recently, however, the pendulum has swung the other way. For both England and the Continent, parish-based research has yielded a wealth of support for the very real impact of official, traditional religion both before and after the religious changes. In any case, late twentieth-century scholars no longer associate 'religious history' with Church or theology alone and they are increasingly sceptical about too simple an elite/popular division.[34]

All these questions, ranging from Reformation change to microhistorical case studies, cannot really be tackled without a closer look at the parish. A pioneering, if somewhat unfocused, collection of essays provided a first survey of the subject in 1988 and a great number of relevant doctoral works are now coming to fruition.[35] Popular attitudes

31 Antonio Gramsci, 'The study of philosophy and of historical materialism', in *The Modern Prince and Other Essays* (New York, 1980), pp. 58–75; Natalie Zemon Davis, 'Some tasks and themes in the study of popular religion', in C. Trinkaus and H. Oberman (eds), *The Pursuit of the Holy* (Leiden, 1974), pp. 314–26, and her 'From "popular religion" to religious cultures', in S. Ozment (ed.), *Reformation Europe: A Guide to Research* (St Louis, 1982), pp. 321–41.

32 M. Aston, *England's Iconoclasts* (Oxford, 1988); R. G. Davies, 'Lollardy and locality', *TRHS*, 6th Series 1 (1991), 191–212; M. Bakhtin, *Rabelais and his World*, trans. Helene Iswolsky (Cambridge, Mass., 1968); E. LeRoy Ladurie, *Montaillou: Cathars and Catholics in a French Village 1294–1324*, trans. B. Bray (London, 1978); Carlo Ginzburg, *The Cheese and the Worms*, trans. John and Anne Tedeschi (New York, 1982).

33 J. Delumeau, *Catholicism between Luther and Voltaire* (London, 1977); Robert Muchembled, *Popular Culture and Elite Culture in France 1400–1750* (Baton Rouge, 1985).

34 Duffy, *Stripping of the Altars*; C. Burgess, '"A fond thing vainly invented": an essay on purgatory and pious motive in later medieval England', in Wright (ed.), *Parish, Church and People*, pp. 56–84; W. Christian Jr, *Local Religion in Sixteenth-Century Spain* (Princeton, 1981); P. Blickle, 'Communal Reformation and peasant piety: the peasant Reformation and its late medieval origins', *Central European History*, 20 (1987), 216–28 (esp. section on 'Christianisation').

35 S. Wright (ed.), *Parish, Church and People: Local Studies in Lay Religion 1350–1700* (London, 1988) with a very valuable introduction by David Palliser; for recent doctoral work see the contributions in this volume and J. Carnwath, 'The churchwardens' accounts of Thame *c.* 1443–1524', in D. Clayton *et al.* (eds), *Trade, Devotion and Governance* (Stroud, 1994), pp. 177–97; A. Brown, *Popular Piety in Late Medieval England: The Diocese of Salisbury 1250–1550* (Oxford, 1995); V. Bainbridge, *Gilds in the Medieval Countryside* (Woodbridge, 1996).

towards death and the division of sacred space also attract increasing attention.[36] One of the most important projects involving parochial sources is the collection of 'Records of Early English Drama' (REED). Started at the University of Toronto in 1976, it seeks to locate and record – county by county – all references to English drama up to 1642, when the Puritans closed London's public theatres.[37] The early Stuart decades, particularly the troublesome enforcement of Arminian ideas about the 'beauty of holiness' and the resilience of the parish during the English Revolution, provide yet more areas of lively and by no means completed enquiry.[38] It seemed timely to take stock by assembling a wide spectrum of these different approaches.

III

So where do parish studies go from here? The chapters of this volume suggest that we can speak of parochial 'conformity' only with the greatest reservations. Religious and secular reform was not simply imposed, but negotiated and modified in accordance with local concerns. Resistance could take the form of outright rebellion, but more often it involved subtler strategies of adaptation, evasion, or concealment. Religious preference and individual beliefs reveal only parts of the story; communal priorities and the quest to preserve one's heritage were of equal importance. Change, however, is not the only issue worth pursuing, nor can we understand past societies without looking at them from above as well as below. Parish identity, the complex matrix of religious, secular, and cultural factors contributing to the idiosyncratic character of some 9,000 local communities, is no doubt one of the most promising areas of future research.[39]

36 Vanessa Harding, 'Burial choice and burial location in late medieval London', in S. Bassett (ed.), *Death in Towns: Urban Responses to the Dying and the Dead 100–1600* (Leicester, 1992), pp. 119–35; R. Dinn, '"Monuments answerable to men's worth": burial patterns, social status and gender in late medieval Bury St Edmunds', *JEH*, 46 (1995), 237–55; Margaret Aston, 'Segregation in church', in W. J. Sheils and D. Wood (eds), *Women in the Church*, SCH 27 (Oxford, 1990), pp. 237–94; R. Morris, *Churches in the Landscape* (London, 1989).

37 Numerous volumes and articles (cf. Chapter ten below) have already appeared; for current information see the *REED Newsletter*.

38 J. Fielding, 'Arminianism in the localities: Peterborough diocese 1603–42', in K. Fincham (ed.), *The Early Stuart Church* (Basingstoke, 1993), pp. 93–113; A. Foster, 'Church policies of the 1630s', in R. Cust and A. Hughes (eds), *Conflict in Early Stuart England* (London, 1984), pp. 193–223; J. Morrill, 'The Church in England 1642–9' in his *Reactions to the English Civil War* (London, 1982), pp. 89–114.

39 See in particular Chapters four, six, ten, and twelve below; even Litzenberger's 'conformity' is informed by local considerations. For the complexity of the matrix cf. K. Wrightson, 'The politics of the parish', in P. Griffiths, A. Fox, and S. Hindle (eds), *The Experience of Authority in Early Modern England* (London, 1996), pp. 10–46.

A second must be the attempt to transcend the barriers between late medieval and early modern historians as well as between English, European, North American, and other scholarly traditions. Reformation specialists cannot understand local responses to sixteenth-century change without considering the medieval foundations. Likewise, medievalists need to be aware of the early modernists' concerns if they wish to highlight the relevance of their findings. The complexity and diversity of parish experience should warn us against extrapolating from regional samples or conclusions based on merely one source, and the overlap between the religious and secular dimensions must prohibit any 'reductionist' explanations of the success or failure of the Reformation. Parishioners, finally, were individuals as well as community members; they were locals, strangers, males, females, adults, or children. The methodology to do justice to all these factors remains to be drafted. To acknowledge their existence, however, is an important first step.

The English parish in a European perspective

Historians of the fifteenth and sixteenth centuries are offering ever more detailed insights into English parish life.[1] Both local peculiarities and national trends start to emerge from the sources, with secular and social aspects attracting increasing attention alongside religious developments. What has not yet been addressed, however, is the potential for wider geographical comparison, perhaps owing to the formidable quantity of domestic material still waiting in the archives. This chapter attempts to assess the English evidence from a European perspective, with particular emphasis on the institutional and communal dimensions. It cannot hope to do justice to the vastly heterogeneous experiences of parishioners throughout the Continent, but seeks to establish a basis for future reference and differentiation.

There is as yet no comprehensive introduction to the subject for our period.[2] Most of the information has to be collated from a wide range of 'national' surveys (however anachronistic modern boundaries may be) and an almost unmanageable wealth of more specialised studies.[3] The expansion of interest in the topic is clearly a Europe-wide phenomenon

1 I am grateful for suggestions received at the First International Medieval Congress at Leeds, the Chichester Centre for Ecclesiastical Studies, and the Birmingham Medieval Society in the course of 1994. For a discussion of recent studies on the English parish cf. Chapter one above.
2 For particular aspects see S. Reynolds, *Kingdoms and Communities in Western Europe 900–1300* (Oxford, 1984), esp. pp. 79–100, L. Genicot, *Rural Communities in the Medieval West* (Baltimore, London, 1990), ch. 4, *Communautés rurales*, vol. 4: *Europe occidentale* (Paris, 1984), K. S. Bader, 'Universitas subditorum parochiae', in K. Obermeyer and H. Hagemann (eds), *Festschrift für Hans Liermann zum 70. Geburtstag* (Erlangen, 1964), pp. 11–25, A. Paravicini Bagliani and V. Pasche (eds), *La parrocchia nel medio evo* (Rome, 1995), R. Swanson, *Religion and Devotion in Europe* c. *1215–1515* (Cambridge, 1995), and – for bi-national comparisons – P. Prodi and P. Johanek (eds), *Strutture ecclesiastiche in Italia e in Germania prima della riforma* (Bologna, 1984), and R. Brentano, *Two Churches: England and Italy in the Thirteenth Century* (Berkeley, 1988).
3 National surveys in *Pievi e parrocchie in Italia nel basso medioevo (sec. XIII–XV)* (2 vols, Rome, 1984), *L'encadrement religieux des fidèles au Moyen Age et jusqu'au Concile de Trente*, vol. 1 (Paris, 1985), and B. Kümin, *The Shaping of a Community: The Rise and Reformation of the English Parish* c. *1400–1560* (Aldershot, 1996). Only the smallest fraction of primary and secondary works can be touched upon here; for bibliographical guidance see J. Coste, 'L'institution paroissiale à la fin du Moyen Age: approche bibliographique', *Mélanges de l'Ecole Française de Rome: Moyen Age*, 96 (1984), 295–326, and H. R. Schmidt, *Die Konfessionalisierung im 16. Jahrhundert* (Munich, 1992).

and scholars are identifying further research priorities all the time.[4] Even the most cursory of glances at this material reveals a complex combination of similarities and differences between the English and Continental contexts. The same, however, could be said of any other national Church. The *ecclesia anglicana* is no more 'peculiar' than its French, Italian, or German counterparts. Some characteristics correspond to contemporary norms, others are modified by specific local circumstances. Western Christendom offers a truly mesmerising range of structures and strategies; in what follows, we will focus on just one of its many institutional varieties.

An important caveat, the vagaries of source survival, should be addressed right at the start. The great wealth of episcopal and parochial records surviving for England is clearly 'unusual' and corresponding information for Italy, for example, has to be retrieved from scattered notarial records.[5] The range of documentation for any one region reflects a great number of variables: patterns of literacy and education, familiarity with more advanced business practices, the relationship between oral and written culture, storage facilities, losses caused by wars and revolutions – to name but a few. Scholarly assessments must thus be interpreted with a view to their empirical foundation. Studies based mainly on legal evidence and complaint literature, for instance, provide us with a more selective perspective than those supplemented by information on everyday religious life. Our impression of the relative strength and vitality of the late medieval and early Tudor English Church may owe a lot to the comprehensiveness of its archives.[6]

And yet, whatever the quality of record survival, there were many notable differences. Starting at the top of the ecclesiastical pyramid, it is evident that the Roman *curia* had much greater influence on the Italian peninsula than elsewhere, while the powerful rulers of late medieval Spain, France, and England managed to create embryonic 'national Churches' well before the Reformation.[7] The number and size of bishoprics was an

---

4 'Il y a encore beaucoup à dire sur la paroisse médiévale': J. Avril, 'La paroisse médiévale', *Revue d'Histoire de l'Eglise de France*, 74 (1988), 113.
5 The lack of bishops' registers in Italy is particularly striking: D. Hay, *The Church in Italy in the Fifteenth Century* (Cambridge, 1977), pp. 5 (quote), 49–50; Brentano, *Two Churches*, ch. 5. 'L'Angleterre est ... un terrain privilégié d'observation, grâce à la richesse des archives épiscopales': N. Coulet, *Les visites pastorales* (Turnhout, 1977), p. 23.
6 The availability or absence of CWA, illustrating a wide range of orthodox and communal activities, seems particularly important (cf. section III below); summarising for the English situation: C. Harper-Bill, *The Pre-Reformation Church in England* (London, 1989).
7 'Il n'éxiste pas d'histoire de l'Eglise italienne, celle-ci étant toujours confondue dans l'histoire de la papauté': E. Delaruelle *et al.*, *L'Eglise au temps du grand schisme et de la crise conciliaire* (Paris, 1962), i. xviii; F. Oakley, *The Western Church in the Later Middle Ages* (Ithaca, London, 1979), pp. 71–9 (quote).

equally distinctive factor: England numbered some seventeen dioceses, Ireland thirty-four, the German-speaking Church fifty-nine, and France 131, while mainland Italy contained no fewer than 253.[8] Some of the German bishops were princes in their own right, with a share in the election of the Emperor, and, like their English colleagues, substantial landed property. The latter, however, exerted political functions only as civil servants of a more centralised monarchy, while many of their Italian counterparts were caught up in the power games of the expanding city states or – if they happened to be based in the very south – endowed with so small a territory and endowment that they were hard to distinguish from, say, a Lancashire parish rector.[9]

On the whole the English Church appears to have been an 'exceedingly rich' institution.[10] It held perhaps a third of the landed wealth in the country and maintained a very large number of clergymen. In sixteenth-century Castile there were on average forty-two households per secular priest, in the pre-Reformation diocese of Geneva twenty-eight, but in England just twenty-four.[11] The German towns of Braunschweig, Rostock, and Hamburg contained four parishes each, Cologne twelve, Toledo in Castile twenty-eight, and Verona fifty-two, but London no fewer than 110. This worked out at one parish per 450 inhabitants for the English capital, while Toledo incumbents looked after some 1,800 souls.[12] The average number of parishioners for England as a whole has been estimated at 300, but – as everywhere – the figures varied greatly from place to place and small flocks were certainly no English prerogative.[13] The nature of the secular framework mattered too. It will be argued below that areas with strong feudal lordship differed significantly from those governed by the peasants and townspeople themselves. As for ecclesiastical jurisdiction, in England it developed comparatively late and under the watchful eye of a strong monarchy, while the fragmented German political landscape allowed spiritual courts to operate much more freely. On the eve of the Reformation, they became an important

8 Figures in Hay, *Church in Italy*, p. 10, and P. Johanek, 'La Germania prima della Riforma: una introduzione', in Prodi and Johanek (eds), *Strutture*, p. 31.
9 Hay, *Church in Italy*, pp. 60–1.
10 Harper-Bill, *Pre-Reformation Church*, p. 44.
11 Rough estimates based on W. A. Christian, *Local Religion in Sixteenth-Century Spain* (Princeton, 1981), p. 14, L. Binz, *Vie religieuse et réforme ecclésiastique dans le diocèse de Genève 1378–1450* (Geneva, 1973), pp. 474, 499, and R. Swanson, *Church and Society in Late Medieval England* (Oxford, 1989), p. 30.
12 Figures in B.-U. Hergemöller, 'Parrocchia, parroco e cura d'anime nelle città anseatiche del basso medioevo', in Prodi and Johanek (eds), *Strutture*, p. 144, Christian, *Spain*, pp. 8, 11, 149, and S. Brigden, *London and the Reformation* (Oxford, 1989), pp. 24–5.
13 J. Moorman, *Church Life in England in the Thirteenth Century* (Cambridge, 1945), p. 92; in the French diocese of Chartres the average may have been as low as ninety-seven: Genicot, *Rural Communities*, p. 94.

reason for the stronger resentment of the Church's secular powers in Central Europe.[14]

On the other hand, common European features are probably even more striking. The whole of the Western Church, for instance, had been affected by the Gregorian reform and 'the medieval parish, with its fixed territorial boundaries, its incumbent with tenure of position, its patron with a right to choose the incumbent, its fixed sources of revenue, and its generally secure canonical status' was one of its most significant results.[15] The fight against excessive lay powers associated with the preceding *Eigenkirche* system, however, had encouraged incorporations. In Scotland, the quota of appropriated parishes reached a staggering 85 per cent by the end of the Middle Ages, in England well over a third. In all these cases, rectorial revenues, and especially tithes, were redirected to extra-parochial recipients such as colleges and monasteries which delegated pastoral duties to poorly paid vicars and curates.[16] Bishops and ecclesiastical institutions also tended to accumulate the lion's share of parochial patronage. This was true in 45 per cent of North Brabant parishes, in eleven out of sixteen churches from a sample of five Hanseatic cities, and in 60–86 per cent of English case studies.[17]

There were further shared characteristics. Every parishioner in Western Europe was – at least in theory – subjected to the legislation of provincial and diocesan synods, as well as the moral and religious supervision of episcopal visitations.[18] Similarly, lay fraternities became a key feature of local religious life. They involved both men and women, townspeople and peasants, with a particular 'middling sort' appeal to 'artisans

---

14 P. Kirn, 'Der mittelalterliche Staat und das Geistliche Gericht', *Zeitschrift für Rechtsgeschichte: kanonische Abteilung*, 15 (1926), 197; H. Cohn, 'Reformatorische Bewegung und Antiklerikalismus in Deutschland und England', in W. J. Mommsen (ed.), *Stadtbürgertum und Adel in der Reformation* (London, 1979), pp. 303–30.

15 R. E. Rodes, *Ecclesiastical Administration in Medieval England* (Notre Dame, London, 1977), p. 19.

16 R. Fawcett, *Scottish Medieval Churches* (Edinburgh, 1985), p. 25, Swanson, *Church and Society*, p. 44; again, there were substantial variations within one country: only 6 per cent of parishes were appropriated in Exeter, but 37 per cent in Bristol: M. Skeeters, *Community and Clergy: Bristol and the Reformation c. 1530–70* (Oxford, 1993), p. 101.

17 A.-J. Bijsterveld, *Laverend tussen Kerk and wereld: de pastoors in Noord-Brabant 1400–1570* (Amsterdam, 1993), pp. 394–400, and Hergemöller, 'Parrocchia', p. 157; English evidence in J. Oxley, *The Reformation in Essex to the Death of Mary* (Manchester, 1965), pp. 263–4, P. Marshall, 'The dispersal of monastic patronage in East Yorkshire 1520–90', in B. Kümin (ed.), *Reformations Old and New* (Aldershot, 1996), p. 127 and N. Tanner, *The Church in Late Medieval Norwich* (Toronto, 1984), pp. 173–8. In Normandy, however, the majority of livings remained in lay hands: Genicot, *Rural Communities*, 101.

18 Genicot, *Rural Communities*, p. 119; for a comparative discussion of visitation evidence see Coulet, *Visites pastorales*, for variations in diocesan government: Avril, 'Paroisse', 100–3.

indépendants et ... commerçants'.[19] Whatever charitable, convivial, or professional activities they developed, they retained a primary focus on prayers for the dead and funeral provisions. The emergence of voluntary associations with members from within and without the parish was somewhat at odds with the established ecclesiastical framework, but on the whole 'it seems unlikely that [they] were created or used against the institutional church'.[20] Structural similarities, however, did not preclude differences in quality or emphasis. Rural fraternities tended to be less elaborate and more 'comprehensive' than urban institutions, Western European gilds are seen as predominantly traditional and ritualistic in character, while groups like the *laudesi* in northern Italy promoted more contemplative forms of lay devotion and spirituality.[21]

As for pastoral provision, complaints about pluralism, excessive financial exactions, and the personal shortcomings of parish clergymen could be quoted from Kent, the Upper Rhine, Switzerland, Tuscany, and many other places.[22] The existence of varying degrees of 'anticlericalism' should thus not be ignored, but it is important to distinguish between personal, institutional, and financial conflicts on the one hand, and challenges to the spiritual and pastoral role of the clergy on the other. In the late medieval Church, judging from an ever more widely shared historiographical assessment, the latter were few and far between.[23] Non-residence was a universal problem, but it varied in extent. It seems to have affected just one-sixth of pre-Reformation English benefices, but perhaps one in two in France, two-thirds of German parishes, between 60 and 70 per cent in certain areas of the Netherlands, and up to 80 per cent in the diocese of Geneva. The observation, therefore, that visitation records from the diocese of Lincoln imply a relatively high satisfaction quota among the local laity, while complaints from the parishioners of Hanseatic parish communities,

---

19 A. Vauchez, *Les laïcs au Moyen Age* (Paris, 1987), pp. 115–16.
20 Genicot, *Rural Communities*, p. 103; a similar conclusion in G. Rosser, 'Communities of parish and guild in the late Middle Ages', in S. Wright (ed.), *Parish, Church and People* (London, 1988), pp. 29–55.
21 F. Rapp, 'La paroisse et l'encadrement religieux des fidèles du XIVe au XVIe siècle', in *L'encadrement religieux*, pp. 37; Vauchez, *Laïcs*, pp. 119–20.
22 P. Johanek, 'Vescovo, clero e laici in Germania prima della Riforma', in Prodi and Johanek (eds), *Strutture*, pp. 104ff; Hay, *Church in Italy*, pp. 49–57; C. Pfaff, 'Pfarrei und Pfarreileben', in *Innerschweiz und frühe Eidgenossenschaft* (2 vols, Olten, 1990), i. 210ff; Genicot, *Rural Communities*, p. 98, and see the contributions in P. Dykema and H. Oberman (eds), *Anticlericalism in Late Medieval and Early Modern Europe* (Leiden, 1993).
23 English revisionists have argued this case for some time; B. Moeller, 'Die Rezeption Luthers in der frühen Reformation', in B. Hamm *et al.*, *Reformationstheorien* (Göttingen, 1995), pp. 23–4, and F. Häusler, 'Von der Stadtgründung bis zur Reformation', in P. Meyer (ed.), *Berner–Deine Geschichte* (Wabern, 1981), p. 98, make similar points about German-speaking areas. The balance between conflict and harmony in lay-clerical relations is stressed in Y. Grava, 'Paroisses villageoises et communautés d'habitants', in *L'encadrement religieux*, pp. 197–210.

to take but two examples, were plentiful, may reflect more than just un-equal record survival.[24] Furthermore, a comparative look at clerical education confirms the somewhat better – or less dramatic – state of affairs in the *ecclesia anglicana*. In Italy, there may have been more than a dozen universities by the fifteenth century (compared with just two in England), but they did little in the field of clerical training, and seminaries were not established until well after 1500. A similar picture has been drawn for the German empire, but in the diocese of Lincoln the graduate quota among parochial incumbents was a considerable 14 per cent in 1400 and an even more impressive 30 per cent in 1500. Recent quantitative work suggests that our impression of a poorly educated clerical proletariate may be in need of revision for other areas, too. By about 1500 at least 50 per cent of North Brabant rectors and vicars had attended a university, as had a third of the chaplains. These figures remained more or less stable well into the seventeenth century, despite a long-standing historiographical claim of a post-Reformation 'educational revolution'. Whether university training for the clergy had an immediate influence on the level of Christianisation among the laity is of course another question. In the parishes visited by the bishops of Geneva, at least, there may have been few actual graduates, but two-thirds of all priests were judged to be 'competent' anyway.[25]

Adequate spiritual guidance became a high priority for ecclesiastical reformers. Particularly after the Fourth Lateran Council in 1215, the Church embarked on an energetic pastoral offensive. Annual confession and communion, the attendance of mass on Sundays and major feasts, the knowledge of the *Pater Noster*, *Ave Maria*, and the *Credo* emerged as minimal requirements throughout the Continent. What mattered was not yet broad scriptural knowledge, but a basic canon of prayers and ritual activities.[26] Equally ubiquitous were examples of individuals who failed to meet even such humble standards, but perhaps again more often in badly provided-for Italian parishes than in northern Europe.[27]

---

24 Hergemöller, 'Parrocchia', p. 164; Harper-Bill, *Pre-Reformation Church*, pp. 47, 50; A.-J. Bijsterveld, 'Reform in the parishes of fifteenth- and sixteenth-century North Brabant', in Kümin (ed.), *Reformations Old and New*, p. 25; Binz, *Vie religieuse*, pp. 302–3.

25 D. Hay, *Church in Italy*, pp. 52, 56, and his 'Il contributo italiano alla riforma istituzionale della Chiesa', in Prodi and Johanek (eds), *Strutture*, p. 43; Johanek, 'Vescovo, clero e laici in Germania prima della Riforma', in *ibid.*, pp. 121–2; J. Lander, *Government and Community* (London, 1980), p. 131; Bijsterveld, *Lave-rend tussen Kerk en wereld*, pp. 383–4; Binz, *Vie religieuse*, p. 340.

26 E. Duffy, *The Stripping of the Altars* (New Haven, 1992), p. 54; M. Aubrun, *La paroisse en France des origines au XVe siècle* (Paris, 1986), p. 172. Vauchez, *Laïcs*, pp. 133–43, speaks of the 'tournant pastoral du XVIIᵉ siècle'.

27 There is, however, little firm evidence for such claims: 'Italian ignorance and superstition, if they seem more noticeable than in northern Europe, may be so . . . in large measure because much of the peninsula is mountainous and difficult of access'; Hay, *Church in Italy*, p. 64.

Against the background of this complex mixture of similarities and differences, four crucial aspects of European parish life will now be examined in some more detail: (I) differences in the formation of the parochial network and the appointment of incumbents, (II) evidence for overlaps with secular local communities, (III) the expansion of lay institutions and parish activities in the later Middle Ages, and (IV) the experience of sixteenth-century change.

I

The *raison d'être* of the local ecclesiastical network was to ensure an adequate administration of sacraments. Baptism and burial stood out as crucial parochial rites, with the cult of the dead often seen as the main spiritual focus of the community.[28] The chronological development of the parish system differs considerably from place to place. The origins in England date back to the seventh and eighth centuries, when royal and episcopal initiatives established a number of collegiate 'minster' churches with a large territory. Following a rapid proliferation of private seigneurial chapels between the tenth and twelfth centuries, these proto-parishes gradually fragmented into smaller units centred on newer and more accessible churches. The final network was completed by the thirteenth century and not fundamentally rearranged until the nineteenth.[29] Looking across the Channel, one finds that the multiplication of localised parishes may have occurred somewhat earlier, as in France, where most studies point to the period between the eighth (Carolingian initiatives) and late eleventh centuries, or considerably later, as in northern Italy, where some minster or *pievi* churches survived well beyond 1400.[30]

On the whole, the expansion of parochial provision is attributed to the 'lords', who in turn acquired control over local religious life and clergy under the system of the privatised *Eigenkirche*.[31] But there were alternatives such as the 'communally owned churches' in some areas under Germanic law, particularly in Scandinavia but also in Frisia and elsewhere. To take the Norwegian example, from about 1000 every legal district erected one central church, often on an old pagan cult site, and several neighbourhood

28 The role of the cemetery, the cult of ancestors, and the importance of altar relics are stressed by many French historians: H. Platelle, 'La paroisse et son curé jusqu'à la fin du XIIIe siècle', in *L'encadrement religieux*, p. 16, R. Fossier, *Peasant Life in the Medieval West* (Oxford, 1988), ch. 2.

29 J. Blair, 'Introduction', in his (ed.), *Minsters and Parish Churches* (Oxford, 1988), p. 1. There is, however, some evidence for earlier 'local' churches, and the odd hint of 'communal' (rather than seigneurial) foundations. (I owe this information to Dawn Hadley.)

30 Aubrun, *Paroisse*, pp. 33ff, 70ff; C. Violante, 'Sistemi organizzativi della cura d'anime in Italia tra Medioevo e Rinascimento', in *Pievi e parrocchie*, i. 21ff.

31 Genicot, *Rural Communities*, p. 91.

churches, all under communal government. Besides providing furnishings, ornaments, and bells the inhabitants also built the churchyard wall, administered the tithe, and even elected the priest.[32] A second wave of the phenomenon originated in late medieval Switzerland, where – partly by way of privileges attained at the foundation of their capital cities, but partly by sheer bullying and military power – local communities eroded seigneurial patronage and acquired not only presentation rights (backed up by papal bulls), but the administration of tithes and even a share of ecclesiastical jurisdiction.[33] Here, as in Tyrol or in certain French parishes, priests had to sign detailed contracts before they were entrusted with the cure of souls. Many of these agreements lasted for only a year or two, and in cases of failure to provide 'value for money' clergymen were sacked without much ado.[34]

But how common was the appointment of incumbents by the parishioners? It remained exceptional and depended on relatively weak lordship, but examples can be found among Italian *pievi* (where elections required a two-thirds majority), French parishes, churches in the Pyrenees and the Basque Provinces, as well as in German urban and rural communities such as Dithmarschen in Lower Saxony, the virtually lordship-free areas of Frisia, or in towns like Braunschweig and Cologne.[35] Dietrich Kurze has identified 107 cases in Central Europe, and a quota of up to 10 per cent of advowsons in certain regions. In addition, particularly in German Imperial Free Cities, town councils could exercise rights of patronage, occasionally over nearly a third of the churches.[36] The same, on a more modest scale, applied to London or Norwich, but elsewhere in England the feudal and ecclesiastical hierarchy managed to monopolise the privilege.[37]

32 H. E. Feine, 'Die genossenschaftliche Gemeindekirche im germanischen Recht', *Mitteilungen des Instituts für österreichische Geschichtsforschung*, 68 (1960), 171–96. Catalonia was another area with many communal foundations: H. Kamen, *The Phoenix and the Flame: Catalonia and the Counter Reformation* (New Haven, 1993), p. 158.

33 Feine, 'Gemeindekirche', 192ff; cf. Pfaff, 'Pfarreileben', *passim*, and H. C. Peyer, *Verfassungsgeschichte der alten Schweiz* (Zurich, 1978), pp. 62–4.

34 *Ibid.*; one agreement in Aubrun, *Paroisse*, document 38; see also P. Bierbrauer, *Die unterdrückte Reformation. Der Kampf der Tiroler um eine neue Kirche 1521–27* (Zurich, 1993), p. 29, and for another example of priests as mere 'functionaries' of the community: Kamen, *Catalonia*, p. 158.

35 Examples in Feine, 'Gemeindekirche', Genicot, *Rural Communities*, p. 100, Hay, *Church in Italy*, p. 24, R. Mousnier, *Les institutions de la France* (2 vols, Paris, 1974), i. 433, and R. Ganghofer, 'Les communautés rurales en Europe occidentale et centrale depuis le Moyen Age', in *Communautés rurales*, p. 54.

36 D. Kurze, *Pfarrerwahlen im Mittelalter* (Cologne, Graz, 1966), pp. 327–42, 435; Hergemöller, 'Parrocchia', p. 157.

37 Kümin, *Shaping of a Community*, pp. 44–6.

II

Many localities made no clear distinctions between secular and ecclesiastical activities. Weekly religious assemblies provided obvious opportunities to discuss everyday problems or to stage social events, while church and yard served as multi-purpose public buildings and – occasionally – as places of refuge.[38] The French *curé* would use Sunday mass for the proclamation of seigneurial or state regulations just like his English or Italian counterparts, and sometimes secular dignitaries were elected in church.[39] A comparative analysis reveals a great variety of relations between parishes and local government units. In areas such as Scandinavia, Tyrol, or Lower Saxony, the parochial network followed the outlines of older court districts, both in the case of the high medieval minsters (which coincided with whole counties, *Fylkes*, or *Gaue*), and the more localised later churches, whose areas corresponded to those of smaller subdivisions of the districts.[40] Elsewhere, however, parishes could antedate and shape the development of secular communities.[41] English congregations, for instance, soon expanded into estate management, public works, and a great range of cultural activities,[42] providing the rather amorphous secular unit of the vill with an institutional home and a focus for increased self-government.[43] A similar 'creative' role of ecclesiastical units can be found in Cologne, Rostock, Tuscany, or Iceland. In Portugal and Catalonia, the erection of a church was often the first collective activity and a crucial factor in the development of communal identity.[44] The parish formed the nucleus of early modern Swedish political organisation and the importance of religious cults for the institutionalisation of secular life is by no means just a European phenomenon.[45]

German cities provide an insight into the dynamics of the relationship. Some used their parishes throughout for administrative purposes, while others like Osnabrück or Lüneburg switched to secular quarters, wards, or neighbourhoods towards the close of the Middle

38 K. S. Bader, *Dorfgenossenschaft und Dorfgemeinde* (3 vols, Cologne, 1962), ii. 198; Ganghofer, 'Communautés rurales', p. 53; for towns see e.g. G. H. Cook, *The English Medieval Parish Church* (London, 1954), p. 35.

39 Aubrun, *Paroisse*, pp. 180–1; Cook, *English Parish Church*, p. 35.

40 Feine, 'Gemeindekirche', 180–1.

41 'The parish was an important, probably the most important, factor in the birth and maturation of the rural community': Genicot, *Rural Communities*, p. 105 (quote); similarly Bader, *Dorfgemeinde*, ii. 213, and Fossier, *Peasant Life*, ch. 5.

42 Kümin, *Shaping of a Community*, pp. 53–64, R. Hutton, *The Rise and Fall of Merry England* (Oxford, 1994), chs 1, 2, and see Chapter ten in this volume.

43 C. Dyer, 'The English medieval village community and its decline', *Journal of British Studies*, 33 (1994), 428–9.

44 Hergemöller, 'Parrocchia', p. 144; Violante, 'Sistemi organizzativi', p. 24; Feine, 'Gemeindekirche', 179; Genicot, *Rural Communities*, p. 105; Kamen, *Catalonia*, p. 159.

45 P. Aronsson, *Bönder gör politik* (Lund, 1992), p. 347; W. Davis, 'Parish guilds and political culture in village Japan', *Journal of Asian Studies*, 36 (1976), 25–36.

Ages.[46] Clearly, whatever the context, local government cannot be studied without reference to parishes, nor should religious history be written without due attention to its urban or rural setting. The formation of secular and ecclesiastical communities was an interrelated process, in which one strengthened the other.[47] Both relied on the same type of 'middling sort' personnel to fill their respective offices, be it in England, France, or Catalonia. The units are often hard to distinguish. Parish and village assemblies look interchangeable and in smaller places the church-wardens doubled up as *syndics* or *jurats*, who must have found it difficult to keep the two functions apart.[48]

III

While secular lords and Church authorities played an important part in the early development of the local ecclesiastical network, they had a much more limited share in the making of the self-governing parish community of the later Middle Ages.[49] Both saw it as a religious unit and a source of legal and financial benefits rather than as a springboard for lay emancipation. A number of responsibilities specified in canon law and synodal statutes, however, provided indirect encouragement.

The laity, for instance, was expected to participate in church build-ing and maintenance throughout Western and Central Europe from about the thirteenth century. Most German communities introduced special collection boxes, and patrons or tithe-owners paid only where this failed to happen. Quite often, there is evidence for the 'English' differentiation between chancel and nave.[50] In France, parishioners felt a similar need to 'bear certain charges, to store some money for this purpose, and to engage in various collective activities'.[51] Here, too, rectors normally

---

46 Hergemöller, 'Parrocchia', pp. 143–9.
47 H. E. Feine, 'Kirche und Gemeindebildung', in T. Mayer (ed.), *Die Anfänge der Landgemeinde und ihr Wesen* (Stuttgart, 1964), p. 54.
48 Mousnier, *Institutions*, pp. 431–3; Kamen, *Catalonia*, p. 159; Genicot, *Rural Com-munities*, p. 104. Regional varieties, however, must be taken into account: 'in the north and centre [of France], the institutions of the *communauté* corresponded to the village or *seigneurie*, while in the west, the formal institutions of local governance were largely indistinguishable from the parish': V. Magagna, *Com-munities of Grain* (Ithaca, London, 1991), p. 133.
49 Feine, 'Kirche und Gemeindebildung', pp. 55–6; Reynolds, *Kingdoms and Com-munities*, pp. 79ff; Bader, 'Universitas', p. 11.
50 W. Schöller, *Die rechtliche Organisation des Kirchenbaues im Mittelalter* (Vienna, Cologne, 1989), p. 358. F. X. Künstle, *Die deutsche Pfarrei und ihr Recht zu Ausgang des Mittelalters* (Stuttgart, 1905), p. 105, sees at least towers and part of the nave as communal responsibilities, while parsons were required to keep up the chancel.
51 B. Jacqueline, 'Les paroisses rurales en Normandie au Moyen Age', in *Commu-nautés rurales*, p. 423 (original quote in French), and G. Huard, 'Considérations sur l'histoire de la paroisse rurale', *Revue d'Histoire de l'Eglise de France*, 24 (1938), 15–16.

maintained the chancel and the laity the nave, even though other arrangements coexisted.[52] One exception were 'communally owned churches', where the entire building was kept up by the parish.[53] The canonical requirement to provide certain ornaments and liturgical books became another 'official' stimulation for lay involvement. A classic English list dates from 1305, but similar duties were shouldered elsewhere.[54]

These responsibilities for the laity, however, were intermittent, and no higher authority expected parishioners to develop a sophisticated administrative machinery. The emergence of permanent offices and communal funds is thus more plausibly explained as a result of initiatives by the lay people themselves. Particularly important was the ever increasing number of monetary and landed bequests which accrued to the parish and required constant attention.[55] The first evidence for such 'fabric' funds (distinct from those belonging to the incumbent's benefice) derives from twelfth-century France and Germany, and lay officeholders appear soon thereafter.[56]

The range of titles testifies to the proliferation of the position: churchwardens, *gardiani*, and *procuratores ecclesiae* in England, *Kirchmeier* (or *-pröbste*) and *Heiligenpfleger* in Germanic areas, *fabriciens*, *trésoriers*, and *marguilliers* in France, *kerkmeesters* in the Netherlands, *vitrici* or *operai* in Italy, *obrers* in Catalonia – and many other varieties.[57] The language of the sources is not always unambiguous, but on the whole parish representatives were elected – with more or less subtle pressure – by their communities. The phrase 'ar chosen by the hole assent of the paryssh for church wardens', documented at St Botolph Aldersgate in London in 1525–26, is typical and occurs throughout the Continent.[58] The main

52 The 'bâtiments du choeur' were normally maintained at the cost of the 'gros décimateurs': P. Goujard, 'Les fonds de fabriques paroissiales', *Revue d'Histoire de l'Eglise de France*, 68 (1982), 100. Aubrun, *Paroisse*, p. 153, argues a similar case, but quotes exceptions; seventeenth-century legislation formalised the chancel/nave division: G. Constant, 'Une source négligée de l'histoire ecclésiastique locale: les registres anciens de marguilliers', *Revue d'Histoire Ecclésiastique*, 34 (1938), 524.

53 Feine, 'Gemeindekirche', 178.

54 Moorman, *Church Life*, p. 142; statutes of the Council of Rouen 1335 (C. Drew, *Early Parochial Organisation in England* (London, 1954), p. 9); a Swiss example in Pfaff, 'Pfarreileben', p. 242.

55 See Drew, *Early Parochial Organisation*, Kümin, *Shaping of a Community*, ch. 2, S. Schröcker, *Die Kirchenpflegschaft* (Paderborn, 1934), R. Fuhrmann, *Kirche und Dorf* (Stuttgart, 1994), and M. Clément, 'Les paroisses et les fabriques au commencement du XIIIe siècle', *Mélanges d'Archéologie et d'Histoire* (1895), 387–418.

56 Genicot, *Rural Communities*, p. 101; Schröcker, *Kirchenpflegschaft*, pp. 70–9; Aubrun, *Paroisse*, p. 150; Feine, 'Gemeindekirche', 185; Drew, *Early Parochial Organisation*, p. 6.

57 Fuller references in Schröcker, *Kirchenpflegschaft*, pp. 172–203.

58 CWA of St Botolph Aldersgate: GL, MS 1454; similar the late fifteenth-century regulations of Bruneck in Tyrol ('wenn ain gemain ain kirchprabst setz': I. von Zingerle and J. Egger (eds), *Die Tirolischen Weisthümer* (1888), iv. 472), or the

responsibility of the wardens is emphasised equally widely. Once the officers had served their term, parishioners expected a detailed account of all income and expenditure, be it at Lambeth near London ('at the yeres ende they shall geve accomptes'), Goslar in Thuringia ('schal ... rekenschup don ... alle jarlikes'), or Kaltern in Tyrol ('wenn sein jar aus ist, so sol er varraiten').[59] The geographical distribution of extant records is very uneven, but the similarity of European parish finance is confirmed by a quick comparative survey.

English archives contain over 200 pre-Reformation sets of church-wardens' accounts, some Continental cities are also fairly well documented, but French and German survival looks rather more patchy.[60] Judging from the evidence there is, accounting took the form of single-entry bookkeeping, audits were carried out by the parishioners or a special committee, and the most important expenditure items (fabric and property maintenance, ornaments, ceremonies, candles, administrative costs, and – particularly in the sixteenth century – poor relief) were financed by a combination of collections, social events, landed revenue, and the occasional rate. An early glimpse at the accounts for the church of Our Lady at Alençon in northern France reveals that the two *thrésoriers* relied pre-dominantly on rents and household-based contributions, those of Dijon on voluntary donations, compulsory levies in times of extraordinary needs, and – a peculiarity – sponsorship by the town authorities, while later sixteenth-century Meudon benefited from vineyards and tenements given as pious benefactions, regular Sunday collections, a number of gifts, and sales of various materials.[61] At Goslar, a job profile rather than an account

practice in the Netherlands (A. Duke, 'The Reformation of the backwoods', in his *Reformation and Revolt in the Low Countries* (London, 1990), p. 258). D. Kurze, 'Hoch- und spätmittelalterliche Wahlen im Niederkirchenbereich', in R. Schneider and H. Zimmermann (eds), *Wahlen und Wählen im Mittelalter* (Sig-maringen, 1990), p. 205, supports the validity of comprehensive phrases such as 'universitas parochianorum'.

59 C. Drew (ed.), *Lambeth Churchwardens' Accounts 1504–1645* (London, 1941), p. 1 (1505); K. Frölich, 'Eine vorreformatorische Gotteshaus- und Kirchenpflegerord-nung für die Marktkirche in Goslar', *Zeitschrift für Kirchengeschichte*, 40 (1922), 145 (1472); Zingerle and Egger (eds), *Tirolische Weisthümer*, iv. 314 (1458). Summarising the election and duties of churchwardens: Aubrun, *Paroisse*, p. 150, Genicot, *Rural Communities*, pp. 101–2, Bader, *Dorfgenossenschaft*, p. 207.

60 Hutton, *Merry England*, pp. 263–93; B. Haggh, 'Music, Liturgy, and Ceremony in Brussels 1350–1500' (Ph.D., Illinois University, 1988), appendix, G. Constant, 'Une source trop négligée de l'histoire paroissiale: les registres de marguilliers', *Revue d'Histoire de l'Eglise de France*, 24 (1938), 172. Tyrol has a relatively broad survival (E. Egg, *Gotik in Tirol. Die Flügelaltäre* (Innsbruck, 1985), p. 35), and many archives, particularly in Imperial Free Cities such as Nuremberg, harbour considerable treasures, but the evidence from the *Kirchenrechnungsbuch* of Plön (H.-J. Freytag, 'Zur Geschichte der Reformation in Plön', *Jahrbuch Plön*, 20 (1990), 32–5), covering 1540–98, is described as 'very early'.

61 H. Legros, 'Le "Thrésor de l'Esglise parroichial Nostre-Dame d'Alenzon"',

survives from the late fifteenth century, but the *vormunde* were responsible for all building projects, the gathering of rents, the provision of candles, and – a nice illustration of lay confidence – the supervision of all parish clergy.[62] In 1542, the *vorstender der kercken* of St Nicholas, Kiel, recorded various capital and landed rents, plus revenues from bells and stocks of possessions in kind.[63] In addition there is much local colour: early expenses for communion wine and orphans at Alençon, Kiel seems to have enjoyed church music, and Plön offers an intriguing insight into the coexistence of Catholic and Lutheran religious practices well into the 1550s.[64]

Parish government was broadly based. Offices could be held by humble artisans and peasants, householders were expected to attend annual audits and important assemblies, and decisions were not simply 'imposed' by social elites. In practice, of course, wealth, experience, and local power made some parishioners 'more equal' than others, but church administration must have reinforced the horizontal ties in local society.[65] Everyday problems, such as the parish's lack of corporate status, were circumvented with some aplomb. The exploitation of legal loopholes such as the *Hauptgeldstiftung autonoma* in Germany and 'enfeoffment to use' in England allowed the community to accumulate property informally.[66] Two closely intertwined motives accelerated the process of institutionalisation. First, the preoccupation with the accessibility of sacraments and, second, the preparation for the after-life.

To start with the former, it is generally recognised that the parochial network fossilised at around 1200.[67] After that date the *status quo* was stoutly defended by rectors and patrons who feared for their existing privileges. As a result, the system became increasingly inadequate. Multi–

Revue des Questions Historiques, 125 (1936), 67–85 (income of 1444–46), and 126 (1936), 78–86 (expenditure); D. Viaux, *La vie paroissiale à Dijon à la fin du Moyen Age* (Dijon, 1988), pp. 150–1 (late fifteenth century); Constant, 'Source négligée', 511–24 (Meudon, 1564).

62 Frölich, 'Kirchenpflegerordnung', 145–7.
63 F. Grundlach (ed.), *Das Kieler Denkelbok* (Kiel, 1908), pp. 158–9 (one of the wardens was Hans Kolman, an alderman). I am grateful to Jürgen Beyer for his information on German CWA.
64 For another example of how parish funds and wardens supported the development of sophisticated musical provision see B. Hagg, 'Crispijne and Abertijne: two tenors at the church of St Niklaas, Brussels', *Music and Letters*, 76 (1995), 325–44.
65 On parish government see e.g. Kurze, 'Wahlen im Niederkirchenbereich', pp. 197–225; Kümin, *Shaping of a Community*, ch. 6.2; Viaux, *Vie paroissiale*, pp. 153–7; Genicot, *Rural Communities*, pp. 100–7; Bader, 'Universitas', p. 25.
66 Hergemöller, 'Parrocchia', p. 150; C. Burgess, 'Strategies for eternity', in C. Harper-Bill (ed.), *Religious Beliefs and Ecclesiastical Careers* (Woodbridge, 1991), p. 23. (Both devices established a form of trusteeship.)
67 J. Kloczowski, 'Communautés rurales et communautés paroissiales en Europe médiévale et moderne', in *Communautés rurales*, p. 96; J. Gaudemet, 'La vie paroissiale en occident au Moyen Age et dans les temps modernes', in *ibid.*, p. 73; Künstle, *Deutsche Pfarrei*, p. 7; Blair, 'Introduction', p. 14.

village parishes coexisted with those catering for just one nucleated settlement, newly established towns found themselves without a fully privileged church, while some rural communities – owing to shared lordship – played host to more than one parochial incumbent.[68] Local initiatives to amend the most blatant deficiencies, invariably emphasising the need for improved sacramental provision, thus became a *Leitmotiv* of medieval ecclesiastical history. Many succeeded against all the odds. The disintegration of the Ufenau parish in Switzerland provides a striking example. The mother church of SS Peter and Paul, an early medieval foundation in the gift of the monks of Einsiedeln, was built on an island, and for those living in the scattered communities on the north and south banks of Lake Zurich attendance at mass involved a long and delicate journey over a footbridge. In the space of 600 years, one chapel after another separated from the parish. Stäfa acquired independence in the tenth century, Altendorf in the eleventh, Wädenswil and Richterswil in the thirteenth, Freienbach and Hombrechtikon in the fourteenth, finally Ürikon and Schirmensee in the Reformation period. Another initiative in the Alpine canton of Uri offers a glimpse at the motives. The inhabitants of Spiringen petitioned the Bishop of Constance in 1290 for permission to build a fully privileged church at their own cost, arguing that it was well-nigh impossible to get to Bürglen 'in the wintertime', so that 'men risked dying without having communion and last rites administered to them'.[69]

Similar moves to obtain 'one's own' parish church can be traced all over Europe, but the success rate varied.[70] In northern Germany the network proved almost unalterable and most new foundations became at most chapels of ease, while conditions farther south and in coastal areas such as North Brabant remained more flexible. It has been calculated that in the Western Palatinate, no less than 15 per cent of dependent communities separated from their mother churches between 1400 and 1525.[71] Similarly in Italy, the break-up of the minster-style *pievi* system, which derived in part from late Antiquity and featured a great number

68 See e.g. P. Hughes, *The Reformation in England* (2 vols, London, 1950), i. 35, and Avril, 'Paroisse', 98.

69 P. Kläui, 'Zur Frühgeschichte der Ufenau', *Mitteilungen der Antiquarischen Gesellschaft in Zürich*, 43 (1965), 30ff; *Quellenwerk zur Entstehung der Schweizerischen Eidgenossenschaft*, Part 1 (Aarau, 1933), i. 739 (Spiringen; original quote in Latin).

70 Chapel foundations reflect the 'désir des villageois voulant une église à eux': Binz, *Vie religieuse*, p. 242; cf. Bader, *Dorfgemeinde*, p. 194.

71 Hergemöller, 'Parrocchia', pp. 137–8; Bijsterveld, 'North Brabant'; R. Fuhrmann, 'Kirche im Dorf', in P. Blickle (ed.), *Zugänge zur bäuerlichen Reformation* (Zurich, 1987), pp. 151–2, 169. The driving forces reflected local power structures, but often involved a concerted corporate effort: great numbers of – communally engineered – initiatives were undertaken in the Grisons and Tyrol between 1400 and 1520: over twenty separations crowned the former (I. Saulle, *Pfarrei und Gemeinde in Graubünden* (Chur, 1997)), but none attained independence in the latter (Bierbrauer, *Unterdrückte Reformation*, pp. 19–27).

of dependent chapels without full sacramental rights, was more successful
in the countryside north of Rome than in the cities.[72] Even in England,
where historians have spoken of the 'cold hand of canon law' paralysing
the network, separations occurred in many parts of the country, from
Lancashire to Somerset and even in the City of London.[73]

A related phenomenon is the 'boom' in construction work. In the canton of Zurich, half of all churches were reconstructed or enlarged between
1470 and 1525, a similar process was under way in many other German
regions, and in England the same period has been called 'the great age
of parish church rebuilding', marked by thousands of collaborative efforts
and contrasting sharply with the lull in the first post-Reformation decades.[74] Church houses were added to accommodate secular and cultural
activities, and parishioners on both sides of the Channel distinguished
themselves as patrons of the arts. Over 2,000 altar paintings were commissioned in late medieval Tyrol, most of them by rural and urban
communities with a particular liking for Our Lady, helper saints, and
other 'popular' motives.[75] After the devastations of the Hundred Years
War, French parishes, too, turned to the 'reconstruction of ruined buildings
and the extension and embellishment of those which had remained standing'. Italy, perhaps, lagged somewhat behind. Visitation records routinely
refer to the dilapidated state of churches, and Italian travellers were
astonished at the number of building projects north of the Alps.[76]

Closely connected with the desire for easier access to the sacraments
was a second factor which accelerated parochial development, the preoccupation with the after-life. Historians of 'popular religion' tend to insist
on the ubiquity of challenges to the official Church, but parochial sources
fail to confirm this impression. Some dissenters may have stayed clear of
religious activity altogether, others just kept their heads down, yet many
must have experienced contemporary Catholicism as a broad and accom-
modating umbrella.[77] The evidence for the popularity of orthodox

72 Hay, 'Contributo italiano', p. 49; Violante, 'Sistemi organizzativi', pp. 17, 36–8.
73 C. N. L. Brooke, 'Churches of medieval Cambridge', in D. Beales and G. Best
    (eds), *History, Society and the Churches* (Cambridge, 1985), p. 54 (quote); examples
    in Kümin, *Shaping of a Community*, pp. 175–8.
74 P. Jezler, *Der spätgotische Kirchenbau in der Zürcher Landschaft* (Wetzikon, 1988),
    p. 12; A. Knoepfli, *Die Kunstgeschichte des Bodenseeraums* (Sigmaringen, 1963), ii.
    156; Lander, *Government and Community*, p. 148.
75 P. Cowley, *The Church Houses* (London, 1970); Egg, *Gotik in Tirol*, pp. 21, 50,
    454 (contracts between artists and local communities/churchwardens: pp. 35–41);
    the beautification of East Anglian rood screens (see Chapter eight in this volume)
    is a striking English equivalent.
76 Rapp, 'Paroisse', p. 29 (original quote in French); Hay, *Church in Italy*, pp. 56–7;
    Johanek, 'Germania prima della Riforma', p. 25, quotes Antonio de Beatis's
    impressions from his German tour in 1517.
77 Some English Lollards served as churchwardens: R. G. Davies, 'Lollardy and
    locality', *TRHS*, 6th Series 1 (1991), 206; a critical assessment of conventional
    assumptions about 'popular religion' in Avril, 'Paroisse', 109.

practices is overwhelming. Wherever we look we see a feverish urge to secure masses and intercession, with incessant endeavours to 'increase divine service' and clerical manpower.[78] Traditional religious life in the Champagne provides one example of the great efforts 'made to cultivate reciprocal aid among Christians' and the rural parish of Frizet in present-day Belgium supplies another: half the resident families founded an anniversary for their ancestors at some point during the late Middle Ages, while those of Floreffe near Namur, numbering perhaps 180, donated 353 rents for the same purpose.[79] In Germany and France, obit endowments were equally common.[80] A comparative analysis of English churchwardens' accounts suggests that large-scale landed bequests were more prominent in metropolitan than in rural contexts, but the peasantry were no less concerned to provide masses, to obtain a place on the bederoll, or to join a humble fraternity.[81] The parish had established itself as the unrivalled centre of local religious life,[82] and the resulting flurry of activities demanded more sophisticated communal organisation. Priests, as indicated above, were acting under the watchful eye of a self-confident laity. As most recent studies agree, nothing could be more distorting than to speak of the 'decline' or the 'clerical dominance' of the late medieval Church.[83] Instead, the parish offered humbler members of society a platform not only for the expression of their religious sentiments, but also for the exercise of an unusual degree of responsibility and political power.

---

78 'Das volkstümliche Leben im Rahmen der Pfarrei war ... geprägt von Bussfröm-migkeit und Totensorge': Pfaff, 'Pfarreileben', p. 269; Avril, 'Paroisse', 107; C. Burgess, '"For the increase of divine service": chantries in the parish in late medieval Bristol', *JEH*, 36 (1985), 46–65.

79 A. Galpern, *The Religions of the People in Sixteenth-Century Champagne* (Cambridge, Mass., 1976), p. 28 (quote); Genicot, *Rural Communities*, pp. 106–7.

80 P.-J. Schuler, 'Das Anniversar', in his (ed.), *Die Familie als sozialer und historischer Verband* (Sigmaringen, 1987), p. 87; J. Avril, 'La paroisse médiévale et la prière pour les morts', in J. L. Lemaître (ed.), *L'Eglise et la mémoire des morts dans la France médiévale* (Paris, 1986), pp. 53–68.

81 C. Burgess and B. Kümin, 'Penitential bequests and parish regimes in late medieval England', *JEH*, 44 (1993), 610–30.

82 Confirmed e.g. by burial choices: 'L'étude des lieux de sépulture a confirmé que la structure paroissiale occupe une place centrale dans la vie religieuse des laïcs lausannois': V. Pasche, *"Pour le salut de mon âme": les Lausannois face à la mort (XIVe siècle)* (Lausanne, 1989), p. 117; similar R. Dinn, '"Monuments answerable to men's worth": burial patterns, social status and gender in late medieval Bury St Edmunds', *JEH*, 46 (1995), 243.

83 For the strength of traditional practices and local control see C. Haigh, *English Reformations* (Oxford, 1993), Part 1; M. Forster, *The Counter Reformation in the Villages: Religion and Reform in the Bishopric of Speyer 1560–1720* (Ithaca, 1992), pp. 19–20; Häusler, 'Stadtgründung', pp. 97–8; O. Grell, 'The Catholic Church and its leadership', in his (ed.), *The Scandinavian Reformation* (Cambridge, 1995), p. 100 (Sweden); Kamen, *Catalonia*, pp. 158–9.

IV

The complexity of the religious changes of the sixteenth century naturally defies any attempt to summarise it in a few sentences. Only two aspects will be touched upon here: the possible influence of late medieval parish developments on the conception of religious reform, and – in turn – the impact of the dogmatic upheavals on the local ecclesiastical community.[84]

In a number of recent approaches, the causality of the Reformation has been turned upside down. Just as anticlericalism, increasing individualism, and the Church's excessive powers used to be cited as reasons for the outbreak and success of the movement, explanations are now sought in diametrically opposed factors such as growing lay control and more widespread communal values. Lay access to and disposition over ecclesiastical property appears as a 'natural' springboard for broader ideas of secularisation and political dominance,[85] while the early ecclesiology of the 'great' reformers, particularly those with personal experience of Swiss constitutional models, is interpreted as a reflection and intellectual development of the 'communalisation' of late medieval Church and society.[86]

Parishioners, in other words, were setting a trend, but some may have lived to regret it. Protestant rulers stripped them of their art and 'superstitious' assets,[87] Tridentine Catholicism reasserted the powers of the clerical hierarchy,[88] local ceremonial life was severely disrupted,[89] and secular governments appropriated parochial institutions for local government purposes.[90] The dismantling of the doctrine of Purgatory and the rise of gathered churches posed a serious threat to communal religious life,[91] although the 'confessional age' applied enormous – and at least

---

84 For recent European surveys see E. Cameron, *The European Reformation* (Oxford, 1991), A. Pettegree (ed.), *The Early Reformation in Europe* (Cambridge, 1992), R. W. Scribner, R. Porter, and M. Teich (eds), *The Reformation in National Context* (Cambridge, 1994), and Kümin (ed.), *Reformations Old and New*.

85 Swanson, *Church and Society*, p. 250.

86 P. Blickle, 'Reformation und kommunaler Geist. Die Antwort der Theologen auf den Verfassungswandel im Spätmittelalter', *Historische Zeitschrift*, 261 (1995), 365–402. Crucial elements of early reformed ecclesiology were the election of priests and the determination of doctrine by the congregation.

87 Duffy, *Stripping of the Altars*, Part 2; H. Cohn, 'Church property in the German Protestant principalities', in E. Kouri and T. Scott (eds), *Politics and Society in Reformation Europe* (London, 1987), pp. 158–87.

88 A. Borromeo, 'Tridentine discipline: the Church of Rome', in L. Grane and K. Hørby (eds), *The Danish Reformation against its International Background* (Göttingen, 1990), pp. 241–63.

89 Hutton, *Merry England*, ch. 3; Peter Burke speaks of the 'triumph of Lent': *Popular Culture in Early Modern Europe* (Aldershot, reprint 1988), pp. 207–43.

90 For England see S. and B. Webb, *The Parish and the County* (London, 1906), *passim*; for France, J. Gaudemet, 'Vie paroissiale en occident au Moyen Age et dans les temps modernes', in *Communautés rurales*, p. 83.

91 See, for instance, the tensions between the established parish community and the reformed *gemeente* in the Netherlands: Duke, 'Reformation', p. 258.

superficially successful – pressure to ensure conformity.[92] The parish, to cut a long story short, survived the turmoil and did its best to adapt rather than simply absorb official directives. It was a new regime, but local priorities still mattered.[93]

In conclusion, the English parish displays a number of distinctive features. It is richly documented and allows an unusually detailed insight into local ecclesiastical life. Staffed on the whole by conscientious clergymen, it formed part of a comparatively centralised state and remained under the firm supervision of secular lords and Church institutions. Parishioners here never acquired the kind of communal sovereignty found in parts of the Continent. And yet they developed initiatives which transformed their community into the country's universal local government unit. On the other hand, similarities between English and Continental parishes are perhaps even more striking. Structural problems such as incorporations and inadequate ecclesiastical boundaries, sustained efforts to improve local pastoral provision, large-scale investment in ornaments and church buildings, widespread belief in the efficacy of intercession, the appointment of wardens with growing religious and social responsibilities, complex overlaps with the local secular community, and broadly based forms of parish government were equally prominent on both sides of the Channel. At the time, travelling to a foreign country must have been a daunting experience; parish life, however, would have looked reassuringly familiar.

---

92 Summarizing Schmidt, *Konfessionalisierung*.
93 Illustrated – for different confessional contexts – in Forster, *Counter Reformation*, and C. Scott Dixon, *The Reformation and Rural Society: The Parishes of Brandenburg-Ansbach-Kulmbach 1528–1603* (Cambridge, 1995).

PART II

Parochial sources: their variety, potential and limitations

3   *John Schofield*

Medieval parish churches in the City of London: the archaeological evidence

This chapter reviews the evidence for the physical development, architectural style, and internal furnishing and embellishment of the parish churches in the City of London in the medieval period to 1550. Most of the evidence is from the fifteenth and sixteenth centuries. The chapter highlights the contribution of antiquarian observation and archaeological excavations, but also draws on the renditions of churches in the eastern half of the city which are found on the surviving sheets of the copperplate map of the City *c.* 1559.

These various sources provide a fragmented but often detailed picture of religious observance and church building in the City of London. The evidence can help to advance our knowledge and to point to future research. In this chapter the following issues are addressed: section I looks briefly at origins; section II considers fifteenth- and sixteenth-century adjustments and whether London, as shown by the number of its churches, shared in the late medieval decline observed in other English towns; section III outlines the structural development of parish churches 1200–1550; section IV considers architectural style and patronage.

In their discussion of the contribution of archaeology to the study of Saxon and medieval London parish churches, the historians Christopher Brooke and Gillian Keir suspected, from work up to about 1970, that 'the spade has a great deal more to tell us still, but we cannot expect miracles'.[1] The overall conclusion of an archaeological survey twenty-five years later is that the parish churches of London, though damaged by time, fire, and bombing, do indeed have considerable potential for adding to our understanding of many aspects of medieval religious and urban life.[2]

---

1 C. Brooke and G. Keir, *London 800–1216: The Shaping of a City* (London, 1975), p. 91.

2 This chapter elaborates on a number of architectural and historical issues raised by a larger survey, with detailed supporting evidence and a gazetteer of fifty church sites in the City which have been observed or excavated by antiquaries and archaeologists since 1818: J. Schofield, 'Saxon and medieval parish churches in the City of London: a review', *Transactions of the London and Middlesex Archaeological Society*, 45 (1994), 23–146. Details of the individual churches may be found in the longer work.

I

Archaeological investigation makes a particular contribution to the study of the range of origins of parish churches and their chronology of foundation. A brief survey may therefore be appropriate.

London had over 100 parish churches by 1200. This exceptional number reflects the city's rise to wealth in the tenth to twelfth centuries, which is indicated in documents and by numismatic and other archaeological finds. It should be noted, however, that we know very little about ecclesiastical development before 1000. A recent consideration of all the archaeological evidence for Saxon London suggests that the tenth-century evidence (both structures and finds) is in fact quite slim, and that all of it could be compressed into the last third of the century.[3]

The majority of churches were presumably privately owned (*Eigenkirchen*), as were all other churches mentioned in Domesday Book and similar contemporary churches in France and Germany.[4] The most usual mode of origin for parish churches must have been as a private chapel on a prominent tenement, as an adjunct to a notable residence; a pattern found also in other pre-Conquest towns such as Lincoln, Winchester, York, and probably at Stamford.[5] In many cases the siting of a medieval church, set back from the street frontage, suggests such an antecedent. In contrast, other churches occupied prominent positions, for instance at street corners, or in the middle of streets. In 1244 the City reported that the churches of All Hallows Fenchurch, St Magnus the Martyr, St Audoen, St Michael le Querne, St Peter Paul's Wharf, and St Alphage were situated on the king's highway, and those of All Hallows London Wall and St Augustine Papey were on the City wall.[6] Such churches presumably served neighbourhoods or prominent points of public congregation rather than private households.

Two examples of a third kind of origin, that of a church associated with a particular social (often trading) group, are St Martin Vintry, called *baermannecyrce* (church of the porters) in the eleventh century, and All Hallows the Great, called *Semanes cyrce* in 1106, both on the waterfront. Here, however, the cognomen may have as much to do with use by a group as with the church's origin. All Hallows was one of four medieval churches to lie south of Thames Street, bordering the river. Because a church would attract to it traffic, access ways, and secular buildings, these

---

3 Brooke and Keir, *London 800–1216*, p. 128; A. Vince, *Saxon London: An Archaeological Investigation* (London, 1990); A. Vince (ed.), *Aspects of Saxo-Norman London*, iii: *The Finds and Environmental Evidence*, London and Middlesex Archaeological Society Special Paper 12 (London, 1991), pp. 27–8.

4 F. Barlow, *The English Church 1000–1066* (2nd edn, London, 1979), p. 152.

5 F. Hill, *Medieval Lincoln* (Cambridge, 1948, reprint Stamford 1990); M. Biddle (ed.), *Winchester in the Early Middle Ages*, Winchester Studies 1 (Oxford, 1976).

6 H. M. Chew and M. Weinbaum (eds), *The London Eyre of 1244*, London Record Society 6 (London, 1970), p. 276.

four churches probably signify centres of activity and reclamation into the river during the late tenth, the eleventh, and the twelfth centuries.

Twenty-seven of the fifty churches which have produced archaeological or antiquarian evidence were at least probably, and in some cases certainly, established by 1100. Their plans are similar, with a simple nave and square or apsidal chancel. Recent excavations at St Nicholas Shambles show that a church first mentioned in the twelfth century, like the majority of parish churches in the City as a whole, might well reveal origins up to a century older when investigated archaeologically.[7]

II

By 1300 there were 108 churches in the City of London and this number remained almost totally constant until 1540. During the fifteenth century, the numbers of churches in other larger towns declined, but there was comparatively little cutback in London. Though the parish of St Augustine Papey was submerged in the fifteenth century and three parish churches were made redundant at the Reformation (St Nicholas Shambles, St Audoen, St Mary Axe), there was no large-scale reduction in the number of churches, as there was for instance at Lincoln, where forty-six parishes with churches were reduced to a mere nine in 1549, or at York, where the number of parishes was rationalised from forty to twenty-five.[8] Indeed, the three redundant churches were replaced by four others, based on buildings in monastic precincts, namely the new parishes of Christ Church Greyfriars, which absorbed the nearby St Nicholas and St Audoen (1550), St Anne Blackfriars (1548), St Bartholomew Smithfield (1548), and St James Duke's Place (1622). Presumably the ecclesiastical rearrangement, rather than pruning, reflected London's spiritual needs. By 1550 the city's population was beginning to equal the early fourteenth-century figure and would soon eclipse it.[9] Future pressure from population numbers would be felt in the suburbs, resulting eventually in the Commission for Fifty Churches in the early eighteenth century, which built or subsidised nineteen churches in such places as Shadwell, Southwark, Spitalfields, Gravesend, and Deptford.[10]

---

7 For the report on St Nicholas Shambles, J. Schofield, 'Excavations at St Nicholas Shambles, City of London, 1975–9' (in preparation).

8 Hill, *Medieval Lincoln*, pp. 147–8; D. M. Palliser, *Tudor York* (Oxford, 1979), p. 240.

9 R. Finlay and B. Shearer, 'Population growth and suburban expansion', in A. L. Beier and R. Finlay (eds), *London 1500–1700: The Making of the Metropolis* (Harlow, 1986), pp. 37–59.

10 M. H. Port (ed.), *The Commission for Building Fifty New Churches*, London Record Society 23 (London, 1986).

III

Even though most of the buildings have long been destroyed, we can assemble the evidence of documents and archaeology to provide an architectural tour around a large number of London's medieval churches. This section looks at the development first of the church building, viewed mostly from the outside, and then reviews the internal characteristics.

To begin with the chancel, this could be originally rounded or square. Apsidal east ends, a feature of Romanesque churches, are found in the City at St Bride Fleet Street, St Martin Orgar, St Michael Bassishaw, and St Pancras. More of the pre-1100 churches in the City known from excavation, however, originally had square chancels, slightly narrower than the nave. This form came to replace the rounded apse in many cases elsewhere in England after about 1130.[11] In London, at both St Martin Orgar and St Michael Bassishaw, the apse was replaced by a square chancel probably in the thirteenth century.

A second thirteenth-century development was the extension of the chancel to the east. Two possible reasons for this were a wish to enhance the dignity of the altar by moving it eastwards, or to provide a space for prestigious burials, rather as the choirs of contemporary monastic and friary churches were becoming favoured places for tombs of secular patrons. In London there were examples at St Bride's (?twelfth-century), St Nicholas Shambles (1150–1250 or slightly later), and possibly All Hallows Barking (see Plate 3.1; there is no direct evidence on this plan, one of our best for a medieval parish church, but it may have been contemporary with the aisles of 1230–40, as shown by the arcades). The addition to the chancel of 'aisles' by the middle of the thirteenth century is considered under 'chapels' below.

The earliest documented extension of a parish church in the City by the addition of one or more aisles to the nave may be that of St Magnus, 'enlarged' in 1234.[12] References in 1244 confirm that this extension was into a street, probably Thames Street. All Hallows Barking had two aisles in the second quarter of the thirteenth century, as shown by the style of its north and south arcades (see Plate 3.1). During the thirteenth century, also, a north aisle was built at All Hallows Lombard Street, and a south and probably a north aisle at St Michael Bassishaw.

Aisles are increasingly mentioned in London documents in the fourteenth century. St Giles Cripplegate had a south aisle by 1339 and St Dunstan in the East was extended with a south aisle, designed by Henry Yevele, in 1381. St Ethelburga was rebuilt in a similar fashion at about this time, and St Botolph Aldersgate had a new south aisle in about 1400. The building of north aisles is not well documented, but they appear in

11 Details of parish churches outside London from N. Pevsner's *Buildings of England* series; there is a volume for each historic county.
12 *Calendar of Patent Rolls 1232–37*, p. 82.

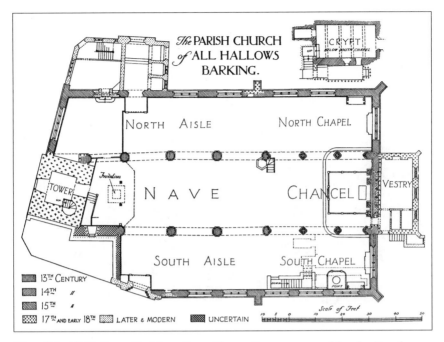

Plate 3.1 All Hallows, Barking, Great Tower Street, surveyed by the Royal Commission on Historical Monuments in 1929. In 1940 bomb damage revealed that the block of 'Uncertain' masonry at the south-west corner of the church was a Saxon arch, probably of eleventh-century date. The church has now been rebuilt, but incorporates much of its medieval fabric. [Royal Commission on Historical Monuments]

general to be later, for example that of St Olave Jewry in 1436. It is not clear, in some cases, whether the first known building was the first extension or a rebuilding of an aisle, as in the case of the north aisle of St Mary at Hill in 1487–1503. The central church of All Hallows Lombard Street showed in excavation that its pre-Fire north aisle had been rebuilt twice after the original extension.

As at York the aisles added to a church could be of differing dates or a comprehensive rebuilding of the site could result in a nave and two aisles of a single build and style. The former is suggested at St Botolph Aldersgate where the 'new aisle' of 1431 is demonstrably the south aisle,[13] and yet the church had a nave and two aisles by the time of the Great Fire in 1666. By 1400, a nave and two aisles was the norm. This is illustrated by the cumulative plans of churches and by those which were rebuilt afresh, as at All Hallows Barking, St Bride Fleet Street, St Michael

13 P. Basing (ed.), *Parish Fraternity Register: Fraternity of the Holy Trinity and SS Fabian and Sebastian in the Parish of St Botolph without Aldersgate*, London Record Society 18 (London, 1982), p. 67.

Plate 3.2 St Olave Hart Street, by J. LeKeux in 1837. This view shows the
three-aisled medieval church which had escaped the Great Fire in 1666,
though now with the addition of the seventeenth-century vestry and carved
gateway to the churchyard, both of which remain, and remodelled windows in
the tower. [Guildhall Library]

Bassishaw, St Olave Hart Street (see Plates 3.1 and 3.2), St Sepulchre,
and St Swithin, one of the earliest examples in its rebuilding of 1400–20.
From around 1500, further instances are supplied by All Hallows Lombard
Street in 1494–1516, St Botolph Aldgate in the early sixteenth century,
and St Andrew Undershaft in 1520–32. A nave and two aisles is also
suggested by the overall dimensions of St Stephen Walbrook on its new
site in 1428, and by 1451 at St James Garlickhithe, when the City allowed
the rector and parish to build four buttresses of stone against the east
end of their church, providing that the common way was not narrowed.[14]

Several London churches, however, only had one aisle. In the two
smaller and possibly less wealthy parishes, St Ethelburga and All Hallows
London Wall, only a south aisle was ever constructed, in the latter case
as late as 1528. In both these cases, constrictions of the site did not allow
a north aisle. At All Hallows, the City wall formed the north wall of
the nave. Similar considerations presumably applied at the corner site of
St Martin Outwich, where a north aisle would have encroached into

14 H. A. Harben, *A Topographical Dictionary of London* (London, 1918), p. 552; City
    of London Record Office, Card Calendar to Property References in the Journals
    and Repertories, under St James Garlickhithe.

Threadneedle Street. It is clear that there were many factors involved in which aisle, north or south, was built first, and the London churches do not display any clear patterns of choice in this matter.

The 'copperplate map', the surviving two plates of a much larger panorama of the Tudor city around 1559, shows the eastern half of the City of London (see Plate 3.3). Nearly all the naves of parish churches shown on the copperplate are battlemented. No doubt this was partly a convention of the artist to specify the body of the church without further elaboration, but battlements are also shown on many churches in Hollar's panoramic engraving of 1647. The earliest documented reference appears to be a bequest for the workmanship of the battlements at St Sepulchre in 1473, perhaps to finish off the recent rebuilding there. The reconstruction of St Dionis slightly earlier in 1466, however, may have included the battlements which are shown as a convention on the copperplate map. Battlements on the north side of St Michael Cornhill were mended in 1474, suggesting that they had been there for some years by that date, and further references now become common. In 1479 and 1485 St Mildred Poultry had money left to it for the making of battlements, St Mary at Hill had battlements added to its nave and south aisle in 1513–14, and about 1520 John Bridges, draper and mayor, repaired and embattled St Nicholas Acon.[15]

Evidence of roofs is scanty before the fifteenth century, when several churches had their roofs rebuilt, endowed by individual parishioners or churchwardens who often had their arms placed in the roof timbers; All Hallows Staining, St Mildred Poultry, St Peter Cornhill, and St Olave Hart Street (1455) are examples. The ceiling of the north aisle at St Andrew Undershaft, of 1532, has the arms of its builder Stephen Jennings in each of the squares of its panels. Several churches on the copperplate have the topsides of their roofs divided by lines into compartments, suggesting lead sheets.

The occurrence of crypts in churches is a rarity and governed by individual or special circumstances. Several churches stood above a vault or vaults let out to secular occupation: such as those at All Hallows Honey Lane, All Hallows the Less, Thames Street, and St Mary Colechurch. In the light of this practice, the two-bay crypt of *c.* 1270 which survives under the west end of the nave of St Olave Hart Street is of interest (see Plate 3.4). There are no parallels for an ecclesiastical crypt or undercroft in this position. The entrance, formerly directly to the open air, was later

15 W. H. Overall, *The Accounts of the Churchwardens of St Michael Cornhill 1456–1608* (London, 1869), p. 54; J. Harvey, *English Medieval Architects* (London, 1987), p. 316; C. L. Kingsford's notes to his edition of J. Stow, *Survey of London* (Oxford, 1971), ii. 397. The copperplate and 'Agas' maps have been published and discussed most recently by A. Prockter and R. Taylor (eds), *The A to Z of Elizabethan London* (London, 1979).

Plate 3.3 Some of the churches shown on the copperplate map of *c.* 1559, from the wider survey on which this chapter is based (Schofield, 'Parish Churches'). *Key*: 22 St Dunstan in the East; 23 St Edmund the King; 24 St Ethelburga Bishopsgate; 25 St Gabriel (or All Hallows) Fenchurch; 26 St George Botolph Lane; 27 St Helen Bishopsgate; 28 St James Garlickhithe; 29 St John the Baptist Cloak Lane (Walbrook); 30 St Katherine Cree; 31 St Lawrence Pountney; 32 St Lawrence Jewry; 34 St Magnus; 35 St Margaret Fish Street Hill (Bridge Street); 36 St Margaret Lothbury; 37 St Margaret Pattens; 38 St Martin Pomary; 39 St Martin Orgar; 40 St Martin Outwich; 41 St Martin Vintry.

Plate 3.4 St Olave Hart Street. The undercroft below the west end, of around 1270, perhaps part of a medieval house subsumed into the body of the church in the fifteenth century. [Royal Commission on Historical Monuments]

incorporated within the tower. The crypt may, therefore, have been part of a previous house on the site, later subsumed into the body of the church, or it may have been a further case of a church built over a separate vault intended for secular use. The date of construction of this undercroft, *c.* 1270, was near the beginning of the period when a good number of secular vaulted undercrofts were built in the City, including several near by in Fenchurch and Aldgate Streets. An even more complicated history of expansion of a church into an adjacent secular building is shown by St Botolph Billingsgate, excavated in 1982.[16]

A second group of crypts which were also inside or attached to churches were smaller structures, and probably relate to the fashion of having chapels at the east end of the church. Two churches had small crypts under an aisle or chapel at their east end in the fourteenth century: at the south-east corner of All Hallows Barking (see Plate 3.1) and beneath the north-east corner of St Bride's (both of which survive). The latter, running north–south, was entered from outside the church, and had a window in its east side. It probably supported a fourteenth-century Lady chapel, either wholly or in part. The crypt at All Hallows Barking also appears to have had an exterior entrance, this time to the east (see

16 The excavation will be published in J. Schofield and T. Dyson, *Medieval Waterfront Tenements: Excavations in Thames Street, London, 1974–1982* (in preparation).

Plate 3.1). A third probable example of this is the vaulted medieval undercroft which survives beneath the churchyard of Wren's St Mary Abchurch, about half-way along the south side of the church.

A mid-fifteenth-century crypt of one rectangular quadripartite bay, approached by a stair descending from the south aisle, was recorded beneath the chancel of the medieval St Dionis Backchurch during the demolition of its Wren successor.[17] While this may have been another example of a chapel which originally protruded south from the chancel, more probably it pertained to the contemporary and fairly new wish of prominent parishioners or patrons to be buried in vaults. From the early sixteenth century, some leaders of the community chose burial in vaults. Henry Keble (d. 1518), grocer and mayor, included a vault for himself on the north side of the choir in his rebuilding of St Mary Aldermary; the vault was later used for two other grocer-mayors in 1556 and 1565, reinforcing its significance. At the same time burial both outside and inside parish churches must have become a difficult and packed affair. Before his death in 1496 Sir Hugh Brice added a chapel called a charnel to St Mary Woolnoth.[18]

Pre-Reformation towers survive largely intact at All Hallows Staining, St Andrew Undershaft, the lower stages of the tower at St Giles Cripplegate, St Olave Hart Street, and St Sepulchre; parts of towers survive within later rebuildings at St Andrew Holborn, SS Anne and Agnes (including part of a fourteenth-century doorway at the second stage), and at St Katherine Cree (1504). They no doubt survive within the fabric of towers of other Wren churches.

As shown in the sixteenth-century panoramas, some churches perhaps still retained their Romanesque towers. There are no traces on the copperplate of round church towers, though the foundations of one were reportedly seen in 1914 antedating the late medieval tower at St Michael Paternoster Royal, and round towers have been noted in the surrounding countryside (for example, formerly at Tooting, now in south London, and surviving at South Ockenden, Essex). The other Romanesque style of square tower with paired windows or paired blind windows may be present at St Margaret Bridge and St Martin Orgar, as shown in the panoramas, but these may equally be later in date. The tower of the medieval St Bride's can be dated to the twelfth century from its architectural detail; it seems to have been demolished (apart from its vaulted lowest storey) during the fifteenth-century rebuilding, to be replaced by a more conventional tower at the west end of the nave, the position reused by Wren.[19] The earlier tower or belfry of St Bride's was separate from the body of

17 G. Street, *The Builder*, 16 (1858), 508.
18 Stow, *Survey*, i. 204.
19 W. F. Grimes, *The Excavation of Roman and Medieval London* (London, 1968), pp. 182–97.

Plate 3.5 All Saints Fulham, in south-west London. The tower is of 1440–41; the nave was rebuilt in medieval style in the nineteenth century. [Museum of London]

the church, but was not alone in this; clearly the use of heavy bells sometimes dictated that the tower should be only vestigially attached to the church, as at St Botolph Aldgate in its rebuilding of the early sixteenth century. Towers expressly to hang bells were apparently attached to some churches for the first time from the opening of the fifteenth century (1418–20 at St Swithin; 1429 at St Michael Wood Street, Huggin Lane).[20]

A large proportion of the towers seen in the sixteenth-century panoramas of the City seem to be Perpendicular in style, confirming that many had been rebuilt in the late fourteenth and fifteenth centuries. The largest group are of the type called Kentish, though the distribution is found in north Kent, Middlesex, north Surrey, and south Essex. The type was built from the late fourteenth century to the Reformation; two of the earliest seem to be that at St Mary, Lambeth, built in 1370, and the tower of Maidstone (Kent) collegiate church in 1395–98, attributed to Henry Yevele, who lived and sometimes did work in London. An example dated to 1440–41 survives at All Saints, Fulham (see Plate 3.5), which was built by Richard Garald, who lived in the London parish of St Sepulchre.[21]

20 Stow, *Survey*, ii. 223–4; P. Norman, 'On the destroyed church of St Michael Wood Street, in the City of London, with some notes on the church of St Michael Bassishaw', *Archaeologia*, 58 (1902), 196.
21 Harvey, *English Medieval Architects*, p. 114; J. Schofield, *The Building of London from the Conquest to the Great Fire* (2nd edn, London, 1993), Figure 92.

The latest dated example in the immediate London area is at St Mary, Hornsey, of *c.* 1500. The characteristics of these towers are a level embattled parapet, without angle pinnacles; an external stair turret, round or polygonal, at one corner, rising a little above the parapet; and buttresses stopping below the top stage at a well marked string course. They also often had prominent west windows. South views of variants of the type, mostly undated, can be seen on the copperplate at St Benet Gracechurch, St Clement Eastcheap, St Magnus, St Martin Ironmonger Lane (Pomary), St Mary Abchurch, St Mary Bothaw, possibly St Mary Woolnoth, St Stephen Walbrook (perhaps dating from the initial building of the new church in 1428), and St Swithin Cannon Street (*c.* 1420). A more elaborate tower appears on a small number of churches, not necessarily those of larger size. At All Hallows the Great, St Lawrence Jewry, and St Martin Vintry (tower possibly dating to shortly after 1397) the corner buttresses are carried up into a small spirelet at each corner. These parishes were in the central part of town, though individually they were not conspicuously wealthy.

There were also a small number of spires or broaches. The timber broach of St Ethelburga is shown in West and Toms' engraving of the church in 1736. St Edmund had a small spire, while St Dunstan in the East and St Lawrence Pountney were prominent in all the panoramas for their tall, possibly thirteenth-century, spires. It may have been intentional that these two churches, which had the tallest spires, were on the crest of the ground as it rose above the river, and they would have been visible for many miles from the south.

Whenever the ground-floor stage of the church tower can be seen on the copperplate, the main entrance to the church is very often in the tower's south side. This even occurs in the suburban church of St Botolph Aldgate, where any constrictions of space would have applied less. It seems, therefore, that the entrance through the south side of the tower is a London tradition or fashion. It is in contrast to the normal entrance in churches in other towns such as Norwich and York, which is into the nave. The entrance to the nave or the south aisle was not unknown in London (for instance, at All Hallows Barking – see Plate 3.1 – and St Nicholas Shambles), but it was rare. The factors influencing this repeated siting of the entrance may have stemmed from a common position for the original churches within their surrounding properties and access ways, or, in addition, the significance of using the ground storey of a tower as a porch. By the time of the Great Fire the entrance through the tower had become standard. The tower was usually the most substantial part of the ruin confronting Sir Christopher Wren in the years after the Great Fire in 1666, and he retained the pre-Fire tower in the majority of his rebuildings. In many cases, the entrance through the tower was also retained.

Examples of porches are known by 1339 and were built until at least 1505. A two-bay stone porch of the fifteenth century into the nave survives, rebuilt, at St Sepulchre. It originally incorporated a statue of the sponsor, Sir John Popham (d. 1463), but this had decayed or been defaced by the time of the chronicler John Stow in 1598. By 1559, according to the copperplate map, some external entrances into towers also had a porch (St Benet Sherehog, St Margaret Pattens), and in one case it is known that a stone porch, erected at All Hallows Lombard Street in 1544, came from a dissolved priory. The fifteenth-century doorway and panelled partition which stood on the inner side of the entrance at St Ethelburga Bishopsgate, perhaps a timber porch, is now preserved in the Museum of London (see Plate 3.6). A more modest alternative was a simple pentice over the main entrance, as at St Michael le Querne by 1585. But with the main entrance into the church so often being in the tower, there cannot have been many porches of any architectural note in London.

At this point various features of the exterior of the church may be noted. The drawing of St Michael le Querne in 1585 by Treswell shows that the church had two sundials, one at the east end and the other on the south side of the tower.[22] On the copperplate map St Magnus is shown with an external clock on brackets, hanging over the approach to the Bridge. Otherwise, the walls of churches were probably roughcast rubble in the majority of cases. Only two examples of ashlar facing on exterior walls are known, at comparatively wealthy churches around 1500. Towers were nearly always also of uncoursed rubble, though there was at least one exception: the blocks of Reigate stone used in the lower stages of the tower at St Giles Cripplegate of 1396 are of various sizes, carefully laid, and many of the blocks are larger than can be obtained from quarries today.

We can pass now to the inside of the medieval parish church. Chapels are mentioned infrequently in wills of the late thirteenth and early four-teenth centuries in London, as at St Michael Bassishaw in 1278 and at St Botolph Bishopsgate in 1303.[23] In the 658 wills surviving on the Husting Rolls, from the earliest example in 1259 to 1300, fifty-nine perpetual chantries are recorded as being founded in London parish churches. From 1300 to 1402, in the same series of wills, an average of twenty-eight permanent chantries were founded every ten years.[24] Often the endow-ment proved insufficient within fifty years, and the abundance both of underfunded chantries and of chantry priests led to the foundation of colleges for the priests.

22 J. Schofield (ed.), *The London Surveys of Ralph Treswell*, London Topographical Society Publication 135 (London, 1987), frontispiece.
23 R. R. Sharpe (ed.), *Calendar of Wills Enrolled in the Court of Hustings* (London, 1889–90), i. 36, 158.
24 W. Page (ed.), *VCH London* (London, 1909), i. 192, 205–6.

Chapels took a range of forms, from special buildings attached to the body of the church (most often the chancel), to simple modifications of space by the use of timber partitions. Records of many London parish chapels are, however, too vague to specify what kind of construction was involved. Some chapels were described by Stow as 'built' within the church, implying substantial structures, such as the chapel of William Hariot, draper and mayor, in 1481 at St Dunstan in the East, or that of Sir James Yarford, mercer and mayor, who built a chapel on the north side of the choir at St Michael Bassishaw before his death in 1527. Similarly William Cantelow built a chapel at St Mary Magdalen Milk Street and was buried

Plate 3.6 St Ethelburga Bishopsgate. Part of the inner porch, now in the Museum of London (removed from the church in the 1930s); the largest piece of interior woodwork surviving from a medieval London parish church. [Museum of London]

there in 1495, and Henry Coote, goldsmith, founded one dedicated to St Dunstan's in St Vedast Foster Lane before his death in 1509; but the form of these chapels is unknown.[25] Presumably they had screens of timber or sometimes of stone, but were otherwise not integral to the structure of the church itself, and as such were removed at the Reformation.

A small number of churches had chapels built against the church so that they protruded from the fabric, and these were no doubt more substantial structures. Examples are recorded at All Hallows Bread Street in 1350, St Sepulchre in the fifteenth century, and St Bartholomew Exchange, where the substantial chapel on its own basement erected by Sir William Cappell, mayor, in 1509 can be seen in the copperplate map of *c.* 1559.[26] John Darby, a warden of the Drapers' Company, added a south chapel or aisle to St Dionis before his burial there in 1466; in this case the distinction between aisle and chapel was unclear to Stow, and the copperplate shows no special addition.[27]

While it may be commonplace for chapels to have been erected towards the east end of the parish church, some London churches show that the chancel area may have been embellished with chapels added to the north and south before the body of the nave was given aisles, to produce a T shape in plan. The clearest case is St Alban Wood Street, where the undated but medieval development of the Saxon church resulted in chapels to north and south of the chancel. At St Bride Fleet Street, probably in the fourteenth century, the north chancel aisle included a chapel on a north-south vaulted undercroft. It therefore seems likely that during the fourteenth century, at several churches in London, specially built chapels were added to chancels. Some were on undercrofts with external entrances. At present there is no hard evidence for the use of the vaulted substructures, though some parishes may have used them later as a charnel house. That three of the undercrofts had external entrances to the churchyard seems significant, and would militate against the room being a sacristy for the chapel above.

The interior of a London parish church, as in its counterparts elsewhere, contained fixtures such as the rood, font, pulpit, and pews; glazing and images (either paintings or statues); and floor tiles and monuments. Very few of these items have survived or (apart from the finding of floor tiles on several church sites) have been recorded by archaeologists, but documentary evidence provides a brief overview.

The rood screen is mentioned at St Benet Gracechurch Street and at St Dionis in 1342, at St Martin Vintry in 1350, and at St Christopher le Stocks in 1352. At All Hallows London Wall in 1455, the rood loft had

25 Stow, *Survey*, i. 135, 289, 295, 314.
26 *Ibid.*, 185.
27 *Ibid.*, 201.

a representation of Judas on it.[28] The normal external turret for the rood stair is known from either present plans or engravings at All Hallows Barking, St Andrew Undershaft, St Bartholomew Exchange, St Dionis, and St Magnus. No medieval fonts survive intact from a City parish church, though they are mentioned occasionally in records and a fragment has recently been recognised among excavated material at St Bride's. The pulpit of St Margaret Bridge is mentioned in 1400 and that of St Botolph Aldersgate in the rules of the Fraternity of Holy Trinity, written probably around 1398.[29]

Thirteenth-century pews survive at St Mary and All Saints, Dunsfold, Surrey, and seating for prominent persons in the chancel was accepted by thirteenth-century church statutes, but the earliest London references to seats for the congregation are of the second half of the fourteenth century. In 1364 a testator wished to be buried in St Martin Ludgate, in the place where he used to sit during service, and in 1386 Stephen Dawbeny, skinner, wished to be buried in front of his accustomed seat in the chapel of St Katherine in St Michael Cornhill.[30] Thereafter there are references to seating in an aisle (1431), a chapel adjoining the choir (1436), and even in the chancel at St John Walbrook (1461).[31]

Donors were commemorated by their arms in windows from at least 1299, when the executors of Mathew Columbars, a Bordeaux wine merchant, celebrated his major contribution to the rebuilding of St Martin Vintry by placing his arms in the new east window; other examples are recorded in 1376–77 at St Nicholas Cole Abbey and frequently throughout the fifteenth century.[32] There is, however, virtually no medieval glass surviving in churches in the City of London; the fragments formerly at St Helen Bishopsgate have survived the recent IRA bombs, and are incorporated in the upper tracery of a new north aisle window. Thirty-six shields of contributors to the rebuilding at St Andrew Undershaft of about 1532, which survive largely intact at the church, are, therefore, a precious remnant.

From at least the twelfth century parish churches generally had painted decoration of one sort or another. Traces of paint have been found on moulded stones (arches and capitals) from St Nicholas Shambles and most recently on medieval features uncovered during the rebuilding of St Helen Bishopsgate. There are several medieval records of 'images', but it is often not clear whether they were paintings or statues. An image of St Botolph, for instance, stood on the south side of the high altar at

---

28 J. P. Malcolm, *London Redivivum: or, An Ancient History and Modern Description of London* (London, 1803–07), ii. 66.
29 Basing (ed.), *Parish Fraternity*.
30 Sharpe (ed.), *Calendar of Wills*, ii. 84, 261.
31 Basing (ed.), *Parish Fraternity*, p. 67; Sharpe (ed.), *Calendar of Wills*, ii. 505, 546.
32 Harben, *Topographical Dictionary*, p. 387 (Columbars); Stow, *Survey*, ii. 3.

St Botolph Billingsgate in 1361; one of St Christopher at St Andrew Baynard Castle in 1410. At St Christopher le Stocks in 1483 were twelve 'tables', including portraits of SS Anne, Christopher (three images), Crasynus, Gregory, James, and Sebastian.[33] Evidence for statues is also rare, but a fourteenth- or fifteenth-century stone statue of St Christopher holding the infant Christ, probably from a church, was recovered from a wall on the site of Newgate Prison in 1903 and is now in the Museum of London. Documentary evidence records a bequest of 1348 to place a crown on the head of an image of the Blessed Virgin at St Mary le Bow. In 1414 St Margaret Bridge had an image of St Christopher in its churchyard.[34]

There are no securely documented examples of paintings which hung or stood in medieval London parish churches, but there is the enigma of the Tate Panel now at All Hallows Barking. It comprises four panels from a winged triptych, possibly by a Flemish artist, and dating to around 1500. The present arrangement of the panels was made by Horace Walpole of Strawberry Hill, who had them in his collection. They were presented to the parish after the Second World War. The central scene would have been the Adoration of the Magi, and incorporated what are now arranged as the outer panels, which show the donor and saints, including St Joseph; the present inner panels, which show two other saints, would have been originally on the outer sides of the folding leaves. The painting bears arms of Tate, though these have been added to the original painting at a later date. Robert Tate, mayor in 1488, was buried in Barking Chapel which stood on the north side of the church or in the north churchyard and it is this possible association which brought the painting to the church.

Glazed floor tiles have been excavated or recovered from several parish church sites, and in three cases some relaid examples are still in place. They are a mixture of 'Westminster' types of the thirteenth century, tiles from Penn in Buckinghamshire of the period 1330–80, and fifteenth-century Flemish types. The Flemish tiles underline the point that decorative items for religious as well as secular buildings were commonly imported from across the North Sea in the fifteenth and sixteenth centuries.

Stow recounts how the City's churches contained many monuments. Up to the twelfth century it was usual only for priests to be buried inside parish churches. Noble and civic dignitaries joined royalty by being buried in London's monasteries from the later part of that century. By the middle of the thirteenth century effigies of knights are known in parish churches

33 Sharpe (ed.), *Calendar of Wills*, ii. 22, 392; *VCH London*, i. 241, where images in other churches are also noted.
34 A. G. Dyson, 'A calendar of the cartulary of St Margaret, Bridge Street', *Guildhall Studies in London History*, 1 (1974), 163–91.

outside London, for instance in Essex and Surrey, and monumental brasses survive from the 1270s; latten images let into stone are recorded from 1208.[35] Thus it may be expected that burials of prominent citizens inside parish churches date from some time in the early thirteenth century. Brasses of figures other than nobility (such as tradesmen or merchants) survive elsewhere from the middle of the fourteenth century, and two major firms of makers of brasses were probably working in London by this time. In 1352, a London hosier asked that a brass be set in his tomb.[36] A plan of St Martin Outwich in 1790 shows what are probably the original medieval positions of two brasses, in this case of priests, within the small chancel area. In 1892 a total of forty-one medieval monumental brasses could be counted from City churches.[37] The largest collection today is at All Hallows Barking, where there are seventeen brasses or fragments, the earliest being a roundel of the arms of William Tonge (d. 1389). A second group of eleven brasses, including four from St Martin Outwich, are at St Helen Bishopsgate.

Alabaster seems to have come into use during the second quarter of the fourteenth century and its frequency increased in the decades after 1350. It was carved into small reliefs, sometimes grouped in wooden frames to form reredoses or retables and effigies. Images of alabaster, probably life-size effigies, are recorded in several London churches. John Lovekyn, stockfishmonger, rebuilt St Michael Crooked Lane in four stages between 1348 and 1366, and was buried in the choir in 1368 under a tomb with images of himself and his wife in alabaster.[38] The late fourteenth-century alabaster effigies of John de Oteswich and his wife, formerly in St Martin Outwich, are now in St Helen Bishopsgate and have survived the recent bomb blasts. From towards the end of the fifteenth century survive two more complete examples of marble tombs with traceried canopies: the tomb of John Croke (d. 1477) at All Hallows Barking and that of Hugh Pemberton (d. 1500) from St Martin Outwich, now at St Helen Bishopsgate. In each case small brasses of the dedicatee and his family were originally set into the rear panel of the canopy. On these tombs, perhaps because of the difficulty of carving Purbeck marble, there were no weepers or other statuary.

Bridget Cherry has drawn attention to the group of late fifteenth- and early sixteenth-century tomb chests in and around London, which

35 On brasses see J. F. A. Bertram, 'Gleanings from the City churchyards', *Monumental Brass Society Transactions*, 14/2 (1987), 143–50; J. Coales (ed.), *The Earliest English Brasses: Patronage, Style and Workshops 1270–1350*, Monumental Brass Society (London, 1987).
36 J. Evans, *English Art 1307–1461* (Oxford, 1949), p. 142; Sharpe (ed.), *Calendar of Wills*, i. 656–8.
37 A. Oliver, 'Monumental brasses in the City of London', in W. P. W. Phillimore (ed.), *The London and Middlesex Notebook* (London, 1892), pp. 79–81.
38 Stow, *Survey*, i. 219; Sharpe (ed.), *Calendar of Wills*, ii. 117.

include those mentioned and the tomb of Johane Alfrey (d. 1525) at St Helen's. She suggests that 'the small canopied altar tomb can be seen as an abbreviated version of the canopied tomb-chest with life-size effigies, crossed with the older tradition of the founder's tomb set in a low wall niche'.[39] The tomb of Johane Alfrey was intended to be used also as an Easter sepulchre, where the crucifix and sacrament were deposited between Good Friday and Easter Sunday. No special architectural feature except the table-top of the tomb chest would be required for this. Cherry suggests that this dual function may have been common for table tombs on the north side of the chancel – the place also of Croke's tomb at All Hallows. She further suggests that the popularity of this form may have reflected a change in religious attitudes, a rejection of the private chantry chapel in favour of a commemorative monument in a prominent position, which would at the same time have formed part of the ritual at the most important ceremonies of the year.

The liturgical space may also have had, as another religious focus, a collection of relics. Some parish churches assembled collections of relics, perhaps in part as souvenirs of parishioners' pilgrimages, and these may have influenced the internal arrangements in London churches. A special space may have been arranged around them or access created to them. A relatively poor church such as All Hallows London Wall reported in 1500–01 that it only possessed one relic, a bone of St David, but a remarkable list of over thirty relics survives for St Margaret Bridge Street in 1472.[40] Unfortunately, archaeologists have not yet been able to study the liturgical use of the interior space in a parish church, because the medieval floor levels have never been found intact over more than miniscule areas. But it remains a possibility for future excavations.

Outside, the churchyard could have several notable features and not only monuments or graves. The cloistered churchyard of St Michael Cornhill had a preaching cross, erected by Sir John Rudstone, mayor in 1528. He died in 1531 and was buried in a vault beneath it. Churchyard crosses, used as one of the focal points of the Palm Sunday procession, are also shown on the copperplate map in eight churchyards. Several others had a well, such as those at St Antholin (built or endowed 1348), St Giles Cripplegate, and St Helen Bishopsgate. They must have formed a secular meeting-point for local people, since only some private properties had their own wells. Churchyards were used more actively than they are today, being often the sites of open-air meetings.

39 B. Cherry, 'An early sixteenth-century London tomb design', in J. Newman (ed.), *Design and Practice in British Architecture: Studies in Architectural History Presented to Howard Colvin*, Architectural History, 27 (1984), p. 89.
40 Dyson, 'St Margaret Bridge Street'.

IV

Architectural embellishment of the church was a matter of patronage, whether private or corporate. The character of private sponsorship in the form of monuments, glass, and occasionally whole building additions has been explored in the previous sections. In addition many trade gilds or fraternities were associated with a parish church, often the one in whose parish their hall lay. The gild stored banners and other equipment in the church and went there on their saint's day. In London there seems to be little evidence of the building or embellishment of churches by the crafts as corporate bodies, or by parish fraternities, as opposed to some of their individual distinguished and rich members. The rebuilding of St Andrew Undershaft in 1520–32, with its commemorative glass, is a rare case where corporate sponsorship can be seen at work. Otherwise little is known of the historical circumstances of individual church rebuildings.[41]

Named medieval masons and carpenters who worked on pre-Fire parish churches in London are mentioned only rarely in documentary sources. Henry Yevele designed the south aisle of St Dunstan in the East in 1381, Walter Walton worked on St John Walbrook in 1412, the carpenter William Serle made the rood loft of St Mary at Hill in 1427, Thomas Mapilton built St Stephen Walbrook on a new site in 1429, and John Warner made the battlements on the nave and south aisle at St Mary at Hill in 1513–14.[42] Masons such as Yevele and Mapilton were figures of national importance. Certain new ideas were given their first trial in the capital, such as the innovations which became the hallmark of Perpendicular architecture in the period 1290–1335, and the widespread adoption of belfry towers from 1370 may have spread a London fashion to the surrounding area. As far as we can tell, embellishment of parish churches was a continuous process throughout the fourteenth and fifteenth centuries, and up to 1540, with no perceptible peaks and troughs. There are more known rebuildings in the fifteenth century than in the fourteenth, but this is no doubt at least partly a result of our better documentary sources for the later period.

This chapter has considered four aspects of the history of the London parish church: the variety of origins, the adjustment to the number of churches in the city in the fifteenth and sixteenth centuries, the structural development of churches and their component parts in the medieval period, and what these churches can tell us about developments, some of them national, in architectural style and patronage.

Archaeological work on church sites continues to elucidate the flowering of church building in the tenth and eleventh centuries. The

41 Stow, *Survey*, i. 543.
42 These references are collected by Harvey, *English Medieval Architects*, who gives what is known of their careers.

subsequent changes in church design, especially the addition of aisles and chapels, in the twelfth and thirteenth centuries is so far imperfectly understood but presumably reflects the rise in London's population to its peak in 1340. More is known of the churches after 1370. Many had new belfries built, and the nave with two aisles is a standard form by 1400. In the fifteenth century, as shown by the churches, London was different from other towns, both large and small. In other major towns, such as York, decline set in after about 1470,[43] but in London, churches continued to be rebuilt or embellished until at least 1520. There was virtually no late medieval decline in church numbers in the City, only rearrangement at the Reformation. There were, it is true, fewer notable chapels in London churches after 1450, and at the same time a new form of table tomb, which doubled as an Easter sepulchre, became common.

Few architectural fragments of the period such as tombs survive, but what does can still be appreciated in something like the original setting. The combined nunnery and parish church of St Helen Bishopsgate has recently been rebuilt after bomb damage. The floor has been raised back up to approximately its level in 1475, counteracting a nineteenth-century reduction in floor level when burials were removed *en masse*. To the south-east is the chapel built by Adam Fraunceys in 1372. It contains the tomb of Sir John Crosby (d. 1475), the eminent grocer, and the transposed effigies of John de Oteswich and his wife from St Martin Outwich. It is perhaps significant that Crosby, whose executors rebuilt the church, lies not in a special chapel of the late fifteenth century, but among the work of his fourteenth-century predecessors from the merchant community of London. By 1475 the fashion for building chapels had almost totally died out; but that for erecting prominent tombs remained strong.

There is still much to be learned about the external and internal character of the parish churches in medieval London. This survey has at least shown that study of the physical remains, whether a church site devastated by a bomb or pieces of fabric now in a museum store, is beginning to present a coherent picture of religious life at the parish level; and as investigations continue in the present City of London, new insights are bound to be forthcoming.

43 D. M. Palliser, 'Urban decay revisited', in J. A. F. Thomson (ed.), *Towns and Townspeople in the Fifteenth Century* (Gloucester, 1988), pp. 1–21.

Northern light? Parochial life in a 'dark corner' of Tudor England

Any study of sixteenth-century parochial life in Cumbria is bedevilled, first, by the area's geography and, second, by the fragmentary documentation. Together they present the historian with formidable obstacles: empirical evidence is at a premium and the topographical variety renders generalisations elusive. This chapter cannot hope to produce an exhaustive analysis of the county, but it attempts to collect and juxtapose the surviving pieces of information on local religious life. The result, it will be argued, produces a picture rather different from that in the nucleated 'communal' south, both in terms of the tenacity of the 'old ways' and the towering role of individual leadership. The two major methodological problems, however, must first be sketched in some more detail.

I

As if being at the extreme north of England were not daunting enough, the sheer size of a parish was often exceptional. The Midland norm of 1,000 acre parishes was regularly exceeded, with only 5 per cent of parishes being of that size or smaller. Nine per cent were between 1,000 and 2,000 acres; a further 19 per cent between 2,000 and 3,000. The remaining two-thirds were often greatly over 3,000 acres, and 10 per cent in excess of 20,000 acres. The three great parishes of St Bees, Greystoke, and Crosthwaite, sweeping across the centre of the region, contained the grand total of 188,026 acres between them. Of the four poorest border parishes, where ignorance was a byword among Protestant clergy and where reiving was endemic,[1] the smallest was over 11,000 acres and the largest nearly 27,000 — localities of which Bishop Barnes wrote in 1570 that they knew 'neither fear faith virtue nor knowledge of god nor regard of any religion at all'.[2]

Size was a by-product of the history of settlement. The smallest west coast parishes under single lordship were in the oldest areas of settled civilisation; later, huge baronies, like those of Greystoke or Kendal, gave rise to equally huge parishes. The border communities quoted above were the greater part of the land of Lord Dacre of Gilsland. Seigneurial power,

---

1 Cross-border plundering and pillaging, usually involving the theft of cattle and often accompanied by arson. It was regarded as the normal occupation of the members of the border clans. For a detailed discussion see G. M. Fraser, *The Steel Bonnets* (London, 1971), ch. 12.
2 PRO, SP 15/20/84.

however, cannot be measured simply in terms of territorial possessions.[3] Much of Greystoke's acreage was occupied by the northern range of mountains, called fells in the local Norse dialect, around Blencathra. Even in a modest parish like Croglin, of about 3,000 acres, half was accounted fell. The population was therefore concentrated in the lower-lying cultivable areas. Some parishes centred on the nuclear village of their title, but in upland areas congregations were scattered in non-nucleated hamlets and farmsteads with little connection with the parish church. Westward or Arthuret, for example, had no village centre at all; the church provided such focus as there was. Crosthwaite and Greystoke included so many hamlets in addition to the titular church village that they needed four and five chapelries respectively to serve their populations. The huge number of twenty-four priests listed at Kendal in 1525–26 or 1554, and the still considerable twelve clergymen recorded in 1562, were obviously vital to serve a parish that covered nearly half of Westmorland.[4] Leland was not exaggerating when he thought that 'there longith about a 30 chapells and hamlets to the hedd church of Kendale'.[5]

There were of course urban settlements, but few like Kendal, a prosperous woollen marketing town. Carlisle was the border fortress, while Appleby, the county town of Westmorland, had decayed since the fourteenth century to the point where it could hardly support parliamentary burgesses.[6] The modern west coast communities were hardly more than fishing villages, Workington a 'litel prety fischer towne' in Leland's estimation. Attempts at founding seigneurial boroughs at Egremont or Kirkoswald had not been a commercial success, although Cockermouth fared better. Kirkby Stephen, Kirkby Lonsdale, even Penrith, were of limited importance.[7]

Size of parish and size of population bore little relation to each other. In 1563 Greystoke's great acreage accounted for only 200 households. West coastal Bromfield, with half the acreage of nearby Holm, had two-thirds as many households. Burgh by Sands extended over less than one-third the acreage of Holm, but both served 100 households. The parishes of Carlisle diocese had an average of 459, if we apply Haigh's multiplier; more than York (412) and far greater than Ely (298) or Canterbury (294), but still only a quarter the size of the Lancashire ones.[8] If large but widely scattered parishes were prevalent, such isolated

3 For a full discussion see A. J. L. Winchester, *Landscape and Society in Mediaeval Cumbria* (Edinburgh, 1987), pp. 23–7.

4 PRO, E 36/61, 21–2; Chester RO, EDV 1/1, 2/5.

5 J. Leland, *Itinerary*, ed. L. Toulmin Smith (London, 1907–10), iv. 47.

6 *LP*, iii. 236.

7 Winchester, *Mediaeval Cumbria*, pp. 122–8; M. W. Beresford and H. P. R. Finsberg, *Handbook of English Mediaeval Boroughs* (Newton Abbot, 1973), *sub nomine*.

8 BL, Harleian MS 594, fos 85, 86; C. Haigh, *Reformation and Resistance in Tudor Lancashire* (Cambridge, 1975), p. 223.

existence had been the norm of the Norse ancestors of the people of the central fells, and their descendants had experienced little change of lifestyle. In outlook they remained akin; their experience of reformation shows similarities too.[9]

Logistically, even the most pastorally minded of Cumbrian parsons would face great problems, and the value of his parish might be insufficient to outweigh its disadvantages. Great parishes like Kendal brought a proportionate reward: £92 in the *Valor*, making it a valuable addition to the income of a Crown servant, Thomas Magnus. The border parish of Bewcastle, however, was worth at best 40s., and in time of war, nothing. The nearby parish of Kirkland, about the same size, was better – £8 10s. – but still only one-fifth of the value of Caldbeck, whose acreage was similar.[10] Had Bewcastle and Kirkland not been staffed by canons of Carlisle, who did not depend on their parochial income, it might have been impossible to get a priest at all. In 1599, Bishop Robinson complained that the border parishes would have no ministration, but for certain 'beggarly runners' who came out of Scotland.[11]

Because of the fragmentary nature of Cumbrian records, one is grateful for such snapshots of the parish clergy as are provided by the *Valor*, even if the only priest named is the incumbent, not the curate, for whom one is often reliant on the 1526 subsidy returns or the 1559 visitation.[12] Call books, listing clergy present at episcopal visitations, do exist for Chester diocese, which covered the southern part of the county, after 1541,[13] but a massive lacuna in Carlisle's records, from 1392 to 1562, is frustrating for the Reformation historian. If little is known of the clergy, information on their parishioners, from diocesan sources, is even scarcer. There is no record of the turnover of clergy; the churchwardens' accounts, used to such good effect for the path of the Reformation in the south-west, are virtually non-existent.[14] The wills, that overworked source for religious change, are few and survive only in family muniments or prerogative courts before the 1560s.[15] In the old archdeaconry of Richmond much of the documentation is known to have been lost in the seventeenth century, though some Kendal wills survive from the 1520s

---

9 For the progress of reform in Norway see O. P. Grell (ed.), *The Scandinavian Reformation* (Cambridge, 1995), chs 2 and 5.

10 J. Caley and J. Hunter (eds), *Valor Ecclesiasticus* (6 vols, London, 1810–34), v. 278, 290, 286.

11 PRO, SP 12/273/56.

12 PRO, E 36/61; SP 12/10/44–end.

13 Chester RO, EDV 1/1, 2/5 in particular.

14 For Carlisle diocese only those of Great Salkeld 1548–49 and 1584 survive: C. M. L. Bouch (ed.), 'The Churchwardens' accounts of the parish of Great Salkeld', *TCWAAS*, NS 49 (1949), 134–41. For Chester, the earliest are Askham 1580 (WPR/11/W1), Morland 1588–89 and 1600 (WPR/76/W1), and Cartmel 1597 (WPR/89/W1), all in the Kendal RO.

15 E.g. Carlisle RO, Dean and Chapter Machell MSS, v. 393, 413; PRO, Prob 11/32.

and 1530s. Chester's diocesan registers are unhelpful on Cumbria.[16] One is heavily reliant, therefore, on the occasional snippet: wills preserved in family papers, chatty parsons maintaining their registers, cases in Chancery involving clergy or wardens. Provincial papers occasionally amplify the record: a Carlisle diocesan interregnum of 1508–09 is covered by York records, and Wolsey conducted a *sede vacante* visitation after the death of Bishop Penny in 1520.[17] Rather late in the century, the Institution Act Books at York begin to record some detail of Cumbria, just as archiepiscopal visitations of the 1570s give some idea of provincial standards.[18] Light is thus only really shed on Cumbria when it is caught up in some wider sphere of action. Suddenly the Pilgrimage of Grace, in 1536–37, the chantry commissions of 1547–48, or the returns submitted to the Marian Cardinal Pole can turn the spotlight on Cumbria and amplify the picture of parochial life which flickers intermittently, for want of full record, on its own.[19]

II

What impression of parochial life can thus be obtained? One would expect, in an area so remote from the reforming ferment of the south, to find conservatism, and so one does. If plague, murrain, and the proximity of the Scots had created numerous worldly preoccupations, traditional religious practices were apparently still cherished. There is a protective element in the Pilgrimage of Grace, in the resistance to chantry closures, in the reports of the church goods commissioners and their aftermath, which suggests that the church, as Cumbrians knew it, was valued. The apparent economic grievances of the Westmorland men in 1536 included demands which may be called Catholic reformist: for taxes to be paid by beneficed men and absentees, their negligent and non-contributing clergy. Such men should be ejected and replaced by 'oder that wald be glad to

16 See J. Addy, 'The archives of the archdeaconry of Richmond', *Archives*, 33 (1965), 25–33; J. Raine (ed.), *Richmondshire Wills*, Surtees Society 26 (Durham, 1853), pp. xx–xxv.

17 Borthwick Institute, Reg. 5a, fos 528v–533r, 580v–612v; 622v–641v, 670r–671r; Reg 27, fos 134r–136v.

18 Borthwick Institute, V. 1578–9: CB2, fos 67–79; CB3, fos 56–89; HCAB 1, fos 16v, 29v, 98, 130; HCAB 2, fos 65v, 71v, 73, 77; HCAB 4, f. 17v; HCAB 5, f. 231v; HCAB 6, fos 13v, 19v, 26, 63v, 67v, 68–9, 104–5, 120, 126–7, 148, 155, 181.

19 For the Pilgrimage see M. S. Harrison, *The Pilgrimage of Grace in the Lake Counties* (London, 1981), and M. A. Clark, 'The Reformation in the Lake Counties 1500–1571' (Ph.D., Trinity College, Bristol, 1990). Chantry surveys are edited by R. L. Storey, 'The chantries of Cumberland and Westmorland Part I', *TCWAAS*, NS 60 (1960), 66–96 (for Cumberland), and 'The chantries of Cumberland and Westmorland Part II', *ibid.*, NS 62 (1962), 145–70 (for Westmorland). Cardinal Pole's returns: J. Wilson (ed.), 'The victims of the Tudor disestablishment in Cumberland and Westmorland during the reigns of Edward VI and Mary', *ibid.*, OS 13 (1894–95), 364–88.

kepe hospytallyte', to fulfil what was seen as one of the traditional roles of the clergy.[20] For, said they, some were no priests, and others were Lord Cromwell's chaplains. The Westmorland men knew what they were talking about. The incumbent of Kirkby Stephen was Peter Vannes, the king's Latin secretary, only in minor orders, and that of Great Musgrave another absentee, being indeed one of Cromwell's chaplains.[21] It was a genuine complaint from the Eden Valley about the clergy they had to sustain; the role of the priest in society seems to have been taken more seriously by the laity than by the institutional Church. These religious grievances do not appear in the Pontefract Articles drawn up by the rebels' council. Their omission has obscured the fact that it was the editors, not the men of Westmorland, whose grievances were chiefly economic.[22]

The dissolution of the chantries touched one of the many aspects of parish pride, in the church, its chapels, saints, fabric, and ornaments. If interest in the monasteries and friaries was waning – although it was far from eclipsed – there was no question of such decline in concern for the parish church, where chantries, lights, and, for Lord Dacre, the uncrowned king of the West March, even colleges, provided an attractive means to express religious devotion. Even in Cumbria, some parishes were centres of pilgrimage. 'Our lady of Brough' had her well, of which the seventeenth-century local historian could sketch a Tudor cover, and a well provided-for chantry with a priest/schoolmaster, responsible for the site, as a result. Leland referred to it as a 'great pilgremage'.[23] The chapel at the well was founded in 1506 by John Brunskill, who also gave money for bells. Another family, the Blenkinsops, built a new steeple for the parish church in 1513 and a new choir next to the Lady chapel in 1522. There seems to have been some rivalry between the parish incumbent, and his supporters, and the chantry priest, who was benefiting from the tourist trade.[24] The fact that the priest of 1535 continued to act as schoolmaster until 1574 saved some of the books, but he was unable to protect the goods and Latin service manuals which the chantry surveys had listed.[25]

But for the will of a York merchant of 1518, who sent his wife to both Carlisle and Brough for the health of his soul, we would not be

20 *LP*, xi. 1080, printed in A. Fletcher, *Tudor Rebellions* (3rd edn, London, 1983), p. 108.
21 *Valor*, v. 294, 297; D. S. Chambers (ed.), *Faculty Office Registers* (Oxford, 1966), p. 189.
22 Compare *LP*, xi. 1080, with *ibid.*, 1246, para. 9.
23 Leland, *Itinerary*, v. 47.
24 J. Nicolson and R. Burn, *History of Westmorland and Cumberland* (2 vols, London, 1777; reprint East Ardesley 1976), i. 569–76.
25 *Valor*, v. 297; Carlisle RO, P. 1574 J. Beck; A. F. Leach, *English Schools at the Reformation* (London, 1896), pp. 252–3; Storey, 'Chantries of Westmorland II', 146–7.

aware that 'Our Lady of Carlisle' might equally merit a pilgrimage.[26] The city apparently had a new, bejewelled statue to encourage the devotion of the visiting faithful. There is no mention of it by the time of the visits of chantry or church goods commissioners, and what happened to all her ornaments and the other gifts of the faithful cannot be proved. However, the canons, later the prebends, of the cathedral, who bankrupted their institution in 1564 by their misappropriation of revenues, may well have embezzled some church goods, too.[27]

Chantries and colleges were still being founded in sixteenth-century Cumbria. If some fell into disuse, others replaced them. The college at Kirkoswald was unfinished at the time of the dissolution and its closure was strenuously resisted. There was also, as will be illustrated below, a general lack of interest in acquiring confiscated chantry property, all of which reinforces the impression that this expression of piety was by no means dying out when legislation condemned it. Apart from the will of Thomas Magnus (d. 1550), who although vicar of Kendal hardly counts as a Cumbrian parson, the latest request for a chantry has been found in the will of Sir Thomas Curwen in 1542.[28] The upkeep of another is at issue in a Chancery case of the 1520s where the parson of Great Salkeld sued the parson of All Hallows, Honey Lane, over a rent in Eastcheap which was supposed to be funding a chantry priest in the Cumbrian church.[29] All Hallows, however, as one of the centres of reform, was highly unlikely to favour the support of a priest to pray for the souls of the departed, and probably allocated the resources within its own borders. The parson of Salkeld may have resented paying someone else's dues, but held no doctrinal qualms about the validity of chantries. Lord Dacre, whose ancestors had established a priory by his castle of Naworth and a college next to that of Greystoke, founded in the 1520s another college to complement Kirkoswald castle. Despite a clean bill of health at the visitation of 1535 – hardly surprising in a house barely a dozen years old – it was doomed to closure. The resentment of the lord of the manor and the master of the college can be inferred from their refusal to obey a letter from the Privy Council in April 1547, demanding that the master and fellows 'conforme them selves for thalteracion of that College to another use'.[30] Thomas Lord Wharton and his fellow commissioners had to retire ignominiously. Wharton might be the West March Warden, but he counted for nothing in a Dacre parish. That rising star of Tudor Cumbria maintained an apparent enthusiasm for change which deceived

---

26 R. B. Dobson, 'Fifteenth century cathedral chapters', *Northern History*, 19 (1983), 41.
27 Discussed in detail in Clark, 'Lake Counties', pp. 163–84. See PRO, SP 12/40/100, for an abstract of the investigation into the cathedral's finances.
28 Leeds RO, RD/RP6 25; also printed in Raine (ed.), *Richmondshire Wills*, p. 44.
29 PRO, C 1/567/14.
30 J. R. Dasent (ed.), *Acts of the Privy Council* (32 vols, London, 1890–1907), ii. 484.

his masters until the reign of Elizabeth; his compatriots were less easily duped.[31] By June he and his fellow commissioners were assured that the master and fellows of the college had appeared before the council for their contumacy and disobedience, but had now professed repentance; in consideration whereof, 'and other suche causes of staye as they alleged', the lords thought their trouble and expense in making the journey punishment enough. The commission was to meet again and take the surrender of the house in writing, but then to allow the inmates to remain in occupation until further arrangements had been made for their pensions.[32] The other cause of stay was probably Dacre. When possession was finally taken, it was with the remarkable rider that 'as for any Jewels plaite Anowermentes or Implementes, gooddes or cattalles pertening to the said colledge of Kirkoswalde, ther is none ... by cause the house was unfynished'.[33] The house known as the College still stands opposite Kirkoswald church, manifestly containing sixteenth-century work on the basis of an earlier pele tower, having been in continuous occupation by the same family since 1595.[34] In 1584 it was said to have been unoccupied for twenty years – since, that is, the death of the master of the college, who had continued in residence after the dissolution.[35] If there were no jewels and plate, they must have been across the road, either in the church or in the castle, both out of the commissioners' reach.

The Provost of Greystoke College, backed again by Lord Dacre, was equally prepared to resist closure of his institution. He put his legal training to good use, arguing that Greystoke was a parsonage, not a college, and, having been made collegiate by papal authority, not royal assent, was not a legal corporation within the scope of the Act.[36] Judgement was given in his favour, curiously, in view of the foundation charters of Edward III and Richard II. Greystoke's omission from Pole's list of 1556 may suggest its survival in collegiate form into Mary's reign, but, if so, the staff had been reduced by 1563 to a rector and two curates. A similar campaign had to be fought by the parson's staunch Protestant successor in 1575, as if the parish's exact status were still ill-defined.[37]

If baronial pride, rather than that of the parish at large, was behind

---

31 Discussed in M. James, 'Change and continuity in the Tudor north: Thomas first Lord Wharton', reprinted in James, *Society, Politics and Culture* (Cambridge, 1986), ch. 3.

32 Dasent (ed.), *Acts of the Privy Council*, ii. 504.

33 Quoted in Leach, *Schools*, pp. 43–4.

34 A defensive tower, common in the Border areas. See Fraser, *Steel Bonnets*, pp. 36–7.

35 PRO, E 178/582.

36 Discussed in detail in J. Wilson (ed.), *VCH Cumberland* (2 vols, London, 1901–05), ii. 207–8; Nicolson and Burn, *History*, ii. 363.

37 BL, Harleian MS 594, f. 86; PRO, E 123/5/130, E 123/6/46, 47, 54.

these attempts to resist college closure, there can be no doubt of the general reluctance to take dissolved chantry lands, which Wharton, as Marcher Warden, found to his surprise among the Borderers:

And as to the chauntres, I humble beseche your grace to pardon me of my former letters, myndding noo commoditie thereof to my self, but I thought the notable Bordrers on the Kinges majesties service wold receve comfort with the preferment of them; whoo laitlie hathe maide no Sute to me therefore.[38]

True, the estates were small, a few pounds at most in value, but chantries were also foundations closely connected with the health of one's soul and with the familiar parish church; their priests were part of the local community. The chantries may have been much closer to men's consciences than were the abbeys. There was certainly none of the lay pressure for secularisation which can be found at York. The only example of a secularised Cumbrian chantry can be found at Brigham, commandeered by an absentee priest whose Protestantism, revealed in his will formula of 1549, appears to have been learned in London.[39]

Below the endowment of college and chantry, at the bottom of the scale of adornment of the parish church, came the parish lights, of which little evidence survives. Four messuages in the Appleby area, given for lights, were sold in 1548, along with chantry land.[40] Further traces of this devotional option for the humbler parishioner emerge in the Elizabethan quest for concealed land, which revealed the pitiful little parcels, worth pence at most, which had funded the lights in churches up and down the county. Many seem to have been in the west coast parishes. The apprisings of Henry Curwen in April, June, and October 1572 only found a few shillings' worth, barely justifying the expense of identifying and selling them.[41] They suggest there was plenty of giving to the church, but do not answer the question of whether the gifts were corporate (from the whole parish or the fraternities identified by Professor Scarisbrick) or individual. A rural gild is the less likely explanation, for unlike farther south, or even unlike the county of Durham, the scattered settlements of Cumbria did not often combine in religious fraternities.[42] The only one noted in the chantry surveys was the Trinity gild at Kendal, of which the priest of 1546 was dead by the time of the second survey, when the gild had been amalgamated with St Christopher's chantry, whose incumbent

38 PRO, SP 15/2/11.
39 A. G. Dickens, *Lollards and Protestants in the Diocese of York* (2nd edn, London, 1982), p. 207; M. A. Clark, 'Richard Robinson, chantry priest of Brigham', *TCWAAS*, NS 88 (1988), 97–105.
40 *Calendar of Patent Rolls Edward VI* (6 vols, London, 1924), i. 17.
41 PRO, E 302/1/30, 33, 36.
42 J. J. Scarisbrick, *The Reformation and the English People* (Oxford, 1984), ch. 2; W. Page (ed.), *VCH Durham* (3 vols, London, 1905–28), iii. 26–30.

in turn died in 1548.[43] A clergy will of 1486 included a bequest to the Trinity gild at Penrith, as well as St Mary's altar there.[44] If these were the only two religious gilds in Cumbria, and the bequest was a personal one, fraternities cannot have been popular. The whole nature of Cumbrian society, upland and independent, would have run counter to the idea of such corporate action.

Concerted attempts, often led by the gentry, were at least made in defence of ecclesiastical goods. Hence the delay in selling church plate, reported from Kendal and Copeland deaneries by the Bishop of Chester in 1548; hence too the evident concealment of church goods from the Edwardian commissioners.[45] The meagre lists returned sound as if Cumbrian churches were desperately poor. The goods admitted to at both the Border parishes of Stapleton and Arthuret, 'Item one chales of tyn one vestment', may well be true. Kirkoswald, however, owning to two silver chalices, three vestments, ten altar cloths, two latten candlesticks, a Sanctus bell, six little bells, and a brass holy water stoup was, despite the greater quantity, almost certainly lying. Compared with Stapleton, it was rich; compared with what Crosthwaite, apparently much poorer in goods, turned out to have in 1571, its equipment for a master and college was scanty. The convenient proximity of Dacre's castle may have concealed much, and the same may well be true of Greystoke, also poorly equipped for a provost and college.[46]

The commissioners themselves probably colluded with concealment. Reporting in 1556, those of Cumberland knew that part of the total amassed was still in the hands of Sir Richard Musgrave's executors; those of Westmorland, that the sum total of what they had collected was £9, and that plate had been redelivered to the churches, 'having no particular bills for preve of delivery of the same, but wilbe Alwayes redye to make prefe therof'- a blithe assurance suggesting that the plate had never left the churches in the first place.[47] Nine pounds for the whole of Westmorland? Kendal alone, or Brough, should have been worth far more. Reluctance to take chantry land had developed into resistance to the despoiling of the parish church, and was no less valid for finding its expression through the leading gentlemen.[48] True, the surviving record is largely of gentry activity, whether as lords of the manor or ecclesiastical

43 Storey, 'The chantries of Westmorland II', 157, 160–1.

44 Printed by W. G. Collingwood, 'Gleanings from Rydal muniments', *TCWAAS*, NS 31 (1931), 4–6.

45 PRO, SP 10/3/4.

46 Church goods returns printed in full by R. Whitehead (ed.), 'Church goods in Cumberland in 1552', *TCWAAS*, OS 8 (1885–86), 186–204. For Crosthwaite see below.

47 PRO, E 117/13/24, 26; C. Kitching, 'The quest for concealed lands in the reign of Elizabeth I', *TRHS*, 5th Series 24 (1974), 63–78.

48 Cf. Chapter twelve below.

commissioners; an area on permanent stand-by for hostilities with the neighbouring Scots expected this kind of leadership, and the attitude of the commons, when they are exceptionally seen in action, as in the Pilgrimage, suggests no great taste for corporate action without such direction.

Of the parish itself operating as a unit there are only a couple of examples, sufficiently interesting to make one wish they were amplified by more mid-century churchwardens' records than the surviving fragments from Great Salkeld. For parishes moving in opposite directions in the Reformation era, one can usefully contrast Crosthwaite, containing the now better-known Keswick, and Kendal. Until the reign of Elizabeth there is nothing to indicate any strength of religious feeling in Crosthwaite. One of the largest Cumbrian parishes, it covered a wide scattering of hamlets and chapelries, represented in parochial administration by 'jurymen', eighteen sworn men from these outlying areas. Its *Valor* rector was the far-away Dean of Arches, its absentee incumbent at the 1559 visitation a scion of the local family who owned the rectory; the first one hears of the dependent chapelries being staffed is in 1573.[49] The death of the vicar in 1567 gave the reforming Bishop Best of Carlisle a chance to bring in John McBray, a Scot who had learned German during his Marian exile, and a noted preacher; both necessary skills, for the Keswick copper deposits were being developed by Daniel Hechstetter, and there was a degree of ethnic friction which called for a bilingual preacher.[50] McBray was also a Carlisle prebendary and in 1568 appointed to St Nicholas Newcastle, which curtailed his influence at Crosthwaite, where he had provided the first taste of reform.[51] When in the 1570s Bishop Barnes turned his ultra-reforming eyes on the parish, things started to change. In 1571 he summoned the churchwardens, William Mason, Hugh Tickhill, and John Willson, to appear before the consistory court; the wardens were in trouble, and were summoned back repeatedly over the next two years.[52] It was as well that this huge parish had also its sworn men to help in its administration,[53] as Barnes produced a formidable list of 'such popish reliques and monuments of superstition and idolatrye as presently remain in the said parish', and was not satisfied until all pre-Reformation

49 *Valor*, v. 284; PRO, SP 12/10/163; Carlisle RO, DRC/3/2, unpaginated.

50 C. H. Garrett, *The Marian Exiles* (Cambridge, 1938), pp. 223–4; PRO, SP 12/46/80; for a general history of the copper mines: M. B. Donald, *Elizabethan Copper* (Ulverston, 1994).

51 Carlisle RO, DRC/3/2, unpaginated; Nicolson and Burn, *History*, ii. 388; Newcastle appointment in the Durham diocesan registers printed in G. Hinde (ed.), *The Registers of Cuthbert Tunstall, Bishop of Durham 1530–59, and James Pilkington, Bishop of Durham 1561–76*, Surtees Society 161 (Durham, 1952), p. 168.

52 Carlisle RO, DRC/3/1, unpaginated.

53 For the role of the sworn men in Cumbrian society see C. M. L. Bouch and G. P. Jones, *A Short Economic and Social History of the Lake Counties 1500–1830* (2nd edn, Manchester, 1968), pp. 150–5.

furnishings had been sold or defaced, and replaced by communion cups and flagons. Four vestments, three tunicles, and five chasubles were to be defaced, sold, or made into cushions; thrice-yearly communion in the Protestant fashion was enjoined, with the setting up of a lectern for morning and evening prayer, properly furnished with prayer book, psalter, homilies, and paraphrases. Forbidden saints' days were not to be kept, nor superstitious prayers, nor requiem masses said.[54] In other words, Barnes had found Crosthwaite in full pre-Reformation vigour and in need of a powerful iconoclastic drive to curb it. In the absence of strong clerical guidance, one must here suppose a positive lay interest in the church, supported perhaps by the more traditional curates; one of those in 1559 was a former chantrist of Greystoke.[55]

The quantity of church goods is interesting. The Edwardian commissioners of 1552 had recorded three silver chalices, two more in the chapels, three velvet and four silk vestments, three altar cloths, great and little bells, four candlesticks and four old copes. The vestments roughly tally with the 1571 list of goods Barnes found, but not the other furnishings. It is most unlikely that a place as poor in church goods as Crosthwaite claimed to be in 1552 had managed within the five years of Mary's reign to purchase so much, and far more probable that most had simply been concealed in Edward's day, brought back into use, and never discovered until Barnes intervened. Barnes complained of a wealth of Popish goods:

namely, two pixes of silver, one silver paxe, one cross of gold which was on a vestment, one copper crosse, two chalices of silver, two corporase cases, three hand bells, the scon whereon the Paschall stood, one pair of censures, one shippe, one head of a paire of censures, xxix brasen or latyne candlesticks of six quarters longe, one holy watter tankard of brasse, the canopies which hanged and that which was carried over the Sacrament, two brasen or latyne chrismatories, the vaile cloth, the sepulcher clothes, the painted clothes with pictures of Peter and Paul and the Trinity; and all other monuments of poperye, superstition and idolatrye.[56]

Relying on its situation in the heart of the fells and on the borders of Carlisle and Chester dioceses, the parish of Crosthwaite continued to run in the old way, until a particularly keen Bishop of Carlisle, visiting Chester parishes during the inhibition of authority of the lazy and ineffectual Downham, chanced to find them out. Even Barnes was unable to change everything, and Crosthwaite still has some medieval candlesticks. Its rare evidence of the wealth of church furnishings gives only a hint of

---

54 Printed in F. Eeles, *The Parish Church of St Kentigern Crosthwaite* (Carlisle, 1953), appendix III, p. 59.
55 PRO, SP 12/10/163; Storey, 'The chantries of Cumberland I', 94.
56 Eeles, *Crosthwaite*, p. 59.

what many of the better-endowed parishes must once have had; this 'dark corner' was rich enough in goods and devotion to beautify its churches.

If parochial co-operation in Crosthwaite was intended to thwart reformation, in Kendal it was designed, after the death of Thomas Magnus in 1550, to promote it. In this it is the one, urban, exception to the rule of Cumbrian conservatism, as was Manchester in Lancashire, or Lewes in Sussex. It was clearly under the influence of the reformed preaching of James Pilkington, Marian exile and later Bishop of Durham, the vicar in 1551, and of Nicholas Assheton until 1562.[57] Almost at once the difference in religious outlook can be seen, most especially in the wills of the Wilson family. With Thomas Wilson of Stricklandgate in 1553 we are on familiar Protestant ground: a will preamble that contains a statement of solifidian belief, followed by a request for a funeral sermon:

Item that a sermon funerall be made at my buriall if it may possibley be had at that time, or elles as sone after as may be conveniently, to put men in remembraunce bothe of the frailte and misery that is in this wretched world, and also of the joy and bliss that remaineth after this mortall life, and how to frame our lyves to be partakers of the same, and the preacher to be recompensed for his paynes honestly taken in that behalfe.[58]

In Marian England such statements were defiant. Another Thomas Wilson, later the Elizabethan Dean of Worcester, found exile the safest option in the 1550s. A student at St John's, Cambridge, and a protégé of Grindal's, he had equally firmly adopted the new doctrine.[59] By 1559 yet another Thomas Wilson was free to make a will as radical as he chose, and the preamble is a sermon in itself.[60] At the end of the century, one Alderman Wilson was the great encouragement of the vicar, Ralph Tyrer, who delighted in his parishioners' freedom from both papistry and extreme dissent, and their faithful support of their parson.[61] That this family was but the tip of the Protestant iceberg among the respectable bourgeoisie becomes obvious whenever the voice of the churchwardens is heard. They had little time for Ambrose Hetherington, the unenthusiastic Trinity man who succeeded Assheton, and by the 1570s had reported him to Grindal at York. Hetherington had to answer to Barnes on the bishop's visitation of Chester diocese, receiving an official reprimand; he was to 'preache sound doctrine and conformablie behave himselfe in doctrine and behaviour ... to be a zealous fartherer of the gospell'.[62] That apparently was what the Kendal laity were used to and required of their clergy. They reported him again in 1578: 'the vycar doth not vysyte sycke being

57 Chester RO, EDA/1/1/ f. 38v, February and December.
58 Raine (ed.), *Richmondshire Wills*, p. 77.
59 Garrett, *Marian Exiles*, p. 338.
60 Raine (ed.), *Richmondshire Wills*, p. 138.
61 E. M. Wilson, 'Ralph Tyrer', *TCWAAS*, NS 78 (1978), 71–84.
62 Borthwick Institute, HCAB 5, f. 231v; HCAB 6, fos 13v, 19v, 26, 69v.

thereunto requyred',[63] and detailed arrangements are included for the provision of a weekly sermon, as well as a rearrangement of the seating plan in church. The presentations of the Kendal churchwardens of this period are noticeable for their keenness on lay morality. Four folios of the York Visitation Court Book of 1578–79 are taken up with their presentments of shopkeepers serving customers during service time, fornicators and adulterers, outlying chapelries whose altars remained standing, which lacked proper communion vessels, and whose parishioners were lax and immoral. The comparison with the brief reports from other parishes in the deanery, many of whom have nothing to report except the lack of sermons which bishops wanted more than did clergy or people, speaks volumes for the Protestant zeal of the middling sort in Kendal.[64] Parochial co-operation to defend its Protestant character could be just as strong as the defence of traditional leanings elsewhere.

The obstinately unreformed outlying chapelries show, however, the limitations of the power of the Kendal laity to enforce reform in the whole parish. In the chapelries reform came up against the local recusant gentry. It was hardly surprising that the altars were still in use at Skelsmergh or Selside when the Leyburns had their seat at one, and the Thornboroughs theirs at the other. Greyrigg, another chapel lacking proper furnishings, was home to the Ducketts, among whom ranked a Catholic martyr. In such company, the ordinary fell farmer was hardly to be touched by reformation. His parish, almost coterminous with Kendal barony, was too vast to attract allegiance, and the mother church too distant for regular attendance. His local chapel was staffed, in all likelihood, by one of the quantity of Marian and earlier priests with whom Kendal abounded, continuing to serve with the support of the local gentry, in the time-honoured manner. If this was the case in a barony headed in name at least by a Protestant, William Parr, Marquis of Northampton, and run by a Protestant elite, what chance was there of change where both these elements were lacking?

Precisely this situation occurred in the north of Cumbria, under the authority of Lord Dacre of Greystoke and Gilsland. The likelihood of reform in Cumbria may be summarised as 'not if Lord Dacre could help it', and until the mid-1560s the family successfully supported a rearguard action against Protestant progress. Bishop Best was only too aware of it. His report to Cecil in July 1561 on the state of his new diocese and its reaction to his visitation was gloomy. Of the three non-subscribing clergy, two served in parishes of the barony of Gilsland and had fled; 'about xii or xiii churches in gylsland all under my lord Dacre do not appeare ... At Stapleton sundry of the other yet have masse openly, at whom my

63 Borthwick Institute, CVB (Y) 1578, quoted in C. M. L. Bouch, *Prelates and People of the Lake Counties* (Kendal, 1948), p. 210.
64 Borthwick Institute, V. 1578–9 CB2, 76–9; CB3, 78–80.

lorde and his officers wynk', although they stood excommunicate. Without the firm backing of the President of the Council of the North Best dared not intervene, for fear of trouble; Dacre was 'something to myghtie in this countrey as it were a prynce'.[65] Most of the first two pages of Bishop Best's brand new diocesan register book are taken up with the problem of effecting the deprivation of Hugh Hodgson, sometime Provost of Queen's College, Oxford, and vicar of Skelton, a Dacre parish of his Greystoke barony.[66] It was achieved only with difficulty. Dacre's defiant reaction was to replace him with a Marian priest of his own family who lived until 1597 and to shelter Hodgson at Kirkoswald castle, from which the commissioners of the President of the North tried in vain, and in fear of incurring Dacre's wrath, to extract him.[67] Best's letter to Cecil of the following January was even more despairing. Every day men looked for a change back to the old ways; those desirous of the same openly said and did as they willed, while the rulers and JPs 'wynke at alle thynges and loke throughe the fyngers'. Those of evil religion were encouraged to be stubborn, and any receivers of true doctrine were discouraged and dared not show their feelings for fear of retribution. On paper Best dared go into no detail, but referred Cecil for such to the bearer; veiled references to 'great men' showed why.[68]

Yet how the mighty were to fall. Lord William Dacre died in 1563, and his eldest son three years later, leaving a minor as heir. The Howards took over Dacre lands by the Duke of Norfolk's marrying the widow, and in due course marrying off the daughters to his offspring. Lord George Dacre died as a child in 1568 and suddenly the greatest power in Cumbria was annihilated. John Dacre, parson of Greystoke, died in 1567 and, after a year's insignificant ministry by a priest of whom nothing is known, was replaced by the royal presentee, Mr Edward Hansby. John Dacre's will had been noncommittal, but a codicil discussed arrangements for purchasing some vestments which, at the height of the Vestiarian Controversy, he was arranging to bring from London, provided the churchwardens paid the bill; one wishes their accounts survived to show whether or not they did.[69] Hansby was a complete contrast. He noted against his induction in 1568 that he was 'of St John's College, and a preacher'. Two years later he recorded of a parishioner he buried, 'a true Protestant and professor of the gospell'.[70] Much could happen, even at conservative heartlands like Greystoke, in two years. Hansby was succeeded by another MA who consistently styled himself 'preacher of the word of God, and

65 PRO, SP 12/21/13.
66 Carlisle RO, DRC/1/3, pp. 1–3.
67 Carlisle RO, DRC/1/3, p. 4; *ibid.*, P. 1597: H. Dacre; Kendal RO, WRO/WD/Ry/HMC/11a, 12.
68 PRO, SP 12/21/13.
69 Carlisle RO, P. 1567: J. Dacre.
70 Carlisle RO, DRC/1/3, pp. 22, 25; parish register, *sub anno*.

parson of Greystoke'. Finally, at the turn of the century, the energetic
Bishop Robinson held the living *in commendam*, preaching regularly and
holding evangelistic missions. There was no chance of Elizabethan Greystoke's relapsing into reactionary control, now the power of the barons
was broken.[71]

Newly Protestant Greystoke, like newly Protestant Kendal, still faced
considerable challenge from its chapelries. The curate of Mungrisdale
appointed in 1577 was found two years later baptising his own bastard
daughter; hardly the example of Protestant zeal to set before the inhabitants of that remote hamlet.[72] One wonders whether disenchantment with
the established Church may explain the enthusiasm with which, in the
following century, the people of this chapelry became Quakers.[73]

Parochial life thus depended very largely on the influence of individuals, in particular the local lord or gentleman, and the parson. That
there was corporate parish life, particularly in larger places like Crosthwaite or Kendal, is plain; in remote rural areas, where corporate action
was impossible and local interests limited, it is less certain. Cumbria is
not the ideal place to find causes of reformation in concerted anticlericalism or tithe litigation, or to search for sources of communal friction. One
usually needs a larger community than an agricultural hamlet, its farms
strung out along the beck side or the fell bottom, where individuals help
their immediate neighbour or starve, to indulge in such luxuries. There
were few nucleated villages and few real urban centres: Carlisle a border
fortress, Appleby decayed, Kendal alone a market town approaching the
southern norm. The instances of friction that are noted usually come
from the settlements of the west coastal plain. Even so they are individual
instances, and one can scarcely generalise about a trend.

Anticlericalism probably, and tithe litigation certainly, appear to be
effects, not causes, of the Reformation, and results rather of changes in
the law than changes of belief. There is nothing to be found in the records
of Star Chamber, Chancery, or the Court of Requests before the 1530s;
when tithe disputes do occur in Chancery in the mid-1530s, it is as suits
between laymen, arguing over former clerical property. Robert Hudson,
farmer of the parsonage of Brigham, sued Oliver Hawkings, yeoman, for
the tithe corn of Cockermouth, one Lancaster sued another over the tithe
corn of some land at Kendal, and two husbandmen of Allonby sued a
third over the tithes and other profits of the parish.[74] At about the same
time one possible anticlerical suit occurs. Gabriel Heightmoor informed

71 Greystoke parish register, *passim*; Bouch, *Prelates and People*, p. 246.
72 Greystoke parish register, *sub anno*.
73 M. Grubb, *The Quakers of Mosedale* (London, 1976), pp. 1–6; J. Besse (ed.), *A
    Collection of the Sufferings of the People called Quakers* (2 vols, London, 1753), ii.
    127–30, 132–3.
74 PRO, C 1/822/8, 845/16–17, 910/28.

against John Ireby, vicar of Aspatria, that he 'did accursse' for non-pay-
ment of mortuaries and refused such persons the sacrament.[75] A few
isolated tithe cases of the 1540s precede a moderate burst of activity in
the next decade, of which some at least are an aspect of a personal
quarrel. Others relate to leases of tithe: Thomas Blenkinsop of Helbeck
and Stephen Nevinson of Canterbury, wanting their tithe corn of King's
Meaburn, leased from St Mary's York, or Robert Barwyke arguing with
Thomas Denton over the tithes at Aspatria, leased from Carlisle. The
unfortunate Hugh Hodgson, vicar of Skelton, had enough trouble without
a layman forcibly helping himself to the vicar's tithe.[76] Similar cases can
be found in the 1560s, at about the same frequency. Nothing at all occurs
among the ecclesiastical cause papers in York until the 1580s.

None of this suggests parochial friction as such over matters ecclesiastical, but rather personal disputes over property which had once
happened to have ecclesiastical overtones. Similarly the Pilgrimage of
Grace had provoked attacks on tithe barns, directed not at the church
but at lay impropriators. Thomas Lamplugh's letter of January 1537
makes it plain that the tithe barns looted at Broughton and Tallentire
were regarded by gentry and commons alike as being Sir Thomas Wharton's and Peter Middleton's respectively, and that they were attacked as
part of the general hostility to unpopular landlords, hoarding in a period
of bad harvests. Sir Thomas Curwen thought the commons had gone on
to despoil all barns west of the Derwent – where he, as a member of the
same kinship nexus, could expect to bear his share of opprobrium.[77] In
Kendal barony Sir James Leyburn, farmer of the tithe corn of St Mary's
in various townships, was an equally unpopular collector.[78] Tithe was thus
a source neither of anticlerical complaint nor of parochial friction with
the clergy in pre-Reformation Cumbria.

What one can safely infer from the time of the Pilgrimage onwards
is a lessening respect for the priest as part of the community. Before the
1530s clergy are mentioned in lawsuits as lending weight to the case of
one party, while their absence thereafter, except as the party complained
of, suggests a diminution of status.[79] Surviving records suggest no significant decline in numbers, another possible explanation, before the
epidemic of 1558–59. Percy Simpson's complaint, made as the Pilgrims
approached Carlisle, that the heads of the clergy who would but betray
them should be cut off, has earned almost unparalleled notoriety.[80] The
remark, however, appears to have been made in a fit of exasperation that

75 PRO, C 1/819/19.
76 PRO, C 1/1404/50–6, 1493/13, 1441/60.
77 *LP*, xii/1.18, 185.
78 *LP*, xii/1.914.
79 PRO, C 1 *passim*, e.g. 397/42, 541/96, 576/56; 746/38, 1054/30–1, 1172/16.
80 *LP*, xiii/1. 687.

the monks and secular clergy on whose behalf the commons had risen
were proving so lukewarm about the affair. The curate of Kirkby Stephen
who failed to bid bedes on St Luke's day 1536 was certainly threatened
by his congregation, and a few weeks later the curate of Kendal prayed
for the Pope and bid the bedes under threat of a ducking by 'sundry
persons of no substance'.[81] That the incident should have been reported
in such terms indicates a rather greater chasm between the respectable
and the rest than between clerk and layman. Such lay attitudes to the
clergy are perhaps an aspect of urban, rather than of parochial, existence;
any Londoner complaining about lawless apprentices would have sym-
pathised with the Westmorland experience of a disruptive underclass.
Rebellion in defence of the traditional and familiar, rather than the novel
and radical, was neither unusual nor necessarily anticlerical. An exceptional clerk might indeed cause friction in his parish not merely by trying
to carry out orders to reform, but through positively advocating it. William
Rede at Dalton and his accomplice Robert Henshaw at Hawkshead,
reading heretical literature and experimenting with iconoclasm, incurred
the wrath of vicar-general and parish alike.[82] When nobody in south
Lakeland was prepared for reform, attempts to introduce it could only
provoke dissent.

III

Cumbrians were, and remain, stubborn individualists, their outlook
formed by centuries of independence from, and contentment at their lack
of contact with, London. A Celto-Norse people, they had more in common
with the Irish resistance to the Tudors or with their distant Norwegian
kinsmen, leading a similarly isolated existence in their pastoral fiords and
resenting the Reformation imposed on them by Christian of Denmark,[83]
than with the English south of the Humber. Concerned with continued
survival on upland terrain, under constant pressure from the Scots, they
took a certain pride in their own Border clans, their own barony and
lord, their own parish church, or, as might be the same thing at Holm
Cultram, their neighbouring abbey. Not an urbanised population, not
even normally dwelling in nucleated villages, often scraping a living in
conditions which would strike the outsider as direst poverty, communal
action was familiar to them only in terms of banding together under the
direction of the local lord to resist the Scot, who as late as 1593 could
penetrate to Caldbeck in the heart of Cumberland.[84] Leadership was
expected from the gentry or clergy, and, where Dacre or his protégés
gave it, resistance to reform was obstinate. Kendal was most noticeable

81 *LP*, xii/1. 384.
82 *LP*, vi. 287; xii/1. 842.
83 See Grell (ed.), *The Scandinavian Reformation*, ch. 2.
84 Fraser, *Steel Bonnets*, p. 100.

in its degree of reformation, perhaps because of its degree of urbanisation; most nearly approaching the model of an English town, it displayed a more sympathetic reaction to reformed teaching. Elsewhere traditional medieval Catholicism was the norm amongst parishes whose population was most concerned with physical survival against the odds of both terrain and neighbours. Untouched by a demand for reform, reluctantly acceding to its imposition, their reaction was similar to that of populations in other parts of the Celto-Norse fringe where reform came late. In Cumbria Reformation began in the 1570s, not the 1530s. 'Dacre's Raid' in January 1570, the final attempt by the heir-general to regain control of the North, marked the end of that family's conservative dominance.[85] It was swiftly followed by the appointment of Bishop Barnes, whose energetic Protestantism in Carlisle (1570–77) and then Durham (1577–87) transformed them. Similarly, Sweden gained its reformed church ordinances and Norway its first evangelical Protestant bishop only in 1571.[86] Scotland followed yet later, mass being said on the Borders as late as 1601, and Ireland never at all.[87] It was not until the end of the sixteenth century that Cumbria could be thought of as part of the Protestant nation, as the vicar of Kendal was proud to boast.[88] Its indigenous reformation was a hundred years later than that in the south of England, and its protagonists were called Quakers.

85 *Ibid.*, pp. 261–3.
86 Grell (ed.), *Scandinavian Reformation*, pp. 125, 147.
87 I. B. Cowan, *The Scottish Reformation* (London, 1982), p. 179.
88 Wilson, 'Ralph Tyrer', 77.

Churchwardens' accounts of early modern England and Wales: some problems to note, but much to be gained

The scattered churchwardens' accounts which have survived for the early modern period have generated great interest amongst historians in recent years.[1] Long treasured by local historians, they are now seen to hold the keys to numerous academic debates spanning quite disparate fields. For some, they provide a means of looking at popular culture and customs. Much may be deduced, for instance, from patterns in bell-ringing, the festivities associated with saints' days, or perambulations of parish boundaries.[2] It has been suggested that these humble accounts may reveal distinct cultural regions within the country, the analysis of which could have a bearing on the debate about the origins of the British Civil War.[3] For other historians, churchwardens' accounts yield details about specific policies relating to the restoration of churches or the reintroduction of particular pieces of church furniture such as altars, screens, and rails. This has great relevance to current debates about the nature of church policies enforced in the 1630s.[4] For social historians, these records reveal much about how a community functioned, who was trusted to hold office

1 I would like to thank Kenneth Fincham, Conrad Russell, David Ormrod, Andrew Butcher, Julia Merritt, Jackie and Richard Eales, and all who attended seminars I led at the University of Kent at Canterbury and at the Institute of Historical Research for helpful advice when first I unveiled some of the fruits of this research. Beat Kümin has kindly encouraged me since, as have other members of the parish studies group led by Clive Burgess in London. The editors of this volume have provided helpful, positive criticism, while Katherine French also kindly allowed me to read as yet unpublished material. I am very grateful to J. S. Johnston for translating my material into such excellent maps. The article is dedicated to Liz's memory.

2 See David Underdown, *Revel, Riot and Rebellion: Popular Politics and Culture in England 1603–1660* (London, 1987); David Cressy, *Bonfires and Bells: National Memory and the Protestant Calendar in Elizabethan and Stuart England* (London, 1989); Ronald Hutton, *The Rise and Fall of Merry England: The Ritual Year 1400–1700* (Oxford, 1994).

3 Underdown, *Revel, Riot and Rebellion, passim*.

4 Nicholas Tyacke, *Anti-Calvinists: The Rise of English Arminianism c. 1590–1640* (London, 1987); Julian Davies, *The Caroline Captivity of the Church: Charles I and the Remoulding of Anglicanism* (London, 1992); Peter White, *Predestination, Policy and Polemic* (London, 1992); Kevin Sharpe, *The Personal Rule of Charles I* (New Haven, 1992); Andrew Foster, 'Church policies of the 1630s', in R. Cust and A. Hughes (eds), *Conflict in Early Stuart England* (London, New York, 1989), pp. 193–223.

in the church, and how money was collected for major projects or in response to 'briefs' which circulated periodically amongst parishes canvassing support for charitable causes.[5] Yet systematic use of these sources may also help us when dealing with larger questions concerning the pace and success of the Protestant Reformation, or put another way, the survival of ancient customs from the medieval Western Church.[6] Historians of the Interregnum have already quarried such material for evidence of the success of 'Anglicanism' when faced with its most severe test.[7] Together with surviving churchwardens' presentments and material from the whole panoply of church courts, these records provide valuable insights into the history of parish communities – looked at to some extent from below – always bearing in mind that they were created by authorities for particular purposes, including the rarely popular custom of revenue collection.

This chapter represents a summary report on various interrelated projects. My original interest in churchwardens' accounts grew out of enquiries into the implementation of Church policies at parish level in the 1630s, looking particularly at church restoration programmes. This soon broadened to the wider debate about ways of gauging the speed and effectiveness of the English Reformation. The more I became immersed in these matters, the more I became interested in the nature of the sources themselves and the methodological problems associated with their use. This interest has been sharpened in recent years by a steady stream of excellent parish community studies published in both England and America.[8] It thus seems an opportune moment, particularly in a volume of this nature, to share some thoughts on the projects noted above with a wider audience. The chapter falls fairly naturally into two parts, the first of which seeks to expose and discuss some of the methodological problems associated with systematic use of churchwardens' accounts. The period under close scrutiny spans 1558–1660, but the methodological

5 D. Hey, *An English Rural Community: Myddle under the Tudors and Stuarts* (Leicester, 1974); J. S. Craig, 'Co-operation and initiatives: Elizabethan churchwardens and the parish accounts of Mildenhall', *Social History*, 18 (1993), 357–80; Eric Carlson, 'The origins, function, and status of the office of churchwarden, with particular reference to the diocese of Ely', in Margaret Spufford (ed.), *The World of Rural Dissenters 1520–1725* (Cambridge, 1995), pp. 164–207; Julia Merritt, 'The social context of the parish church in early modern Westminster', *Urban History Yearbook* (1991), pp. 20–31; Beat Kümin, *The Shaping of a Community: The Rise and Reformation of the English Parish c. 1400–1560*, St Andrews Studies in Reformation History (Aldershot, 1996).

6 Christopher Haigh, *English Reformations* (Oxford, 1993); Eamon Duffy, *The Stripping of the Altars* (New Haven, 1992); Patrick Collinson, *The Religion of Protestants* (London, 1982) and his *The Birthpangs of Protestant England* (London, 1988).

7 John Morrill, 'The Church in England 1642–1649', in his (ed.), *Reactions to the English Civil War* (London, 1982), pp. 89–114.

8 See the discussion of the recent historiography of the parish in section II of Chapter one above.

issues raised will no doubt be of concern to all historians who work on these sources. The second part offers some thoughts on the particular debates highlighted above and draws on a sample of 100 sets of accounts, dealing chiefly with the period 1600–40. This therefore also serves as a case study which should illustrate both strengths and limitations entailed when using churchwardens' accounts.

I

Those historians who have made large-scale use of churchwardens' accounts in the past have traditionally used samples. It has been customary to regard between 100 and 200 sets of accounts as providing a reasonable basis for generalisations.[9] The pioneering J. Charles Cox provided a list of material in 1913, a total of some 140 sets of accounts surviving for the sixteenth and seventeenth centuries.[10] In a recent work on *The Rise and Fall of Merry England*, Ronald Hutton has done the historical community the service of providing an invaluable appendix with a full list of churchwardens' accounts which he consulted for the entire country. This includes all sets of sources with evidence from before 1690, listed by counties, and the total number which he has discovered for the period 1558–1660 (inclusive) comes to 662.[11] At last we have a reasonably accurate idea of the nature and rate of survival for the country at large, and this opens the door to a host of interesting questions.

The door may have been opened, but it is important to remember that we are still dealing with rough figures at this stage. Ronald Hutton has carefully acknowledged that even his magnificent list by counties is not complete. At least 100 sets of churchwardens' accounts have survived in such poor condition that they are now unfit for production in record offices; some may still remain unlisted in parish churches. It is unlikely that any one historian – however meticulous and hard-working – is going to be able to see all the surviving accounts for this period. Indeed, some years ago, it looked as if a group of scholars was going to emerge to tackle this very task, and that may yet provide the best way to take research forward in this area.[12] Yet it seems fair, at this stage, to move to some of the issues which will eventually need to be addressed when more accurate figures for the survival rate of churchwardens' accounts do emerge.

At the heart of matters lie questions relating to the very number of churchwardens' accounts which have survived. Estimates based on earlier

9 This seems to be a feature common to much of the work noted above by Christopher Haigh, John Morrill, and David Cressy.

10 J. C. Cox, *Churchwardens' Accounts from the Fourteenth Century to the Close of the Seventeenth Century* (London, 1913), pp. 44–52.

11 Hutton, *Merry England*, pp. 263–93.

12 Late medievalists and early modernists need to collaborate in this project and to some extent this book contributes to these labours.

research suggested that we could expect around 750 for England and Wales, with survival rates differing from diocese to diocese between 4 and 10 per cent.[13] Ronald Hutton's list, together with his caveats over the number of accounts not consulted for his book, suggests that we may eventually expect some 800 accounts to survive for England and Wales for the period 1558–1660, about 8 per cent of the parishes and chapelries of the country.[14] But is the survival random or can we detect certain trends or abnormalities which we ought now to bear in mind when drawing conclusions based on this material? We need to look carefully at the pattern of geographical survival and to consider how far the surviving accounts possibly over-represent certain types of parishes, whether by wealth or patronage. It is important to pursue such apparently basic questions, for the answers may have some bearing on the debates noted above.

The ecclesiastical network in England and Wales was very uneven. If we rely on the figures collated for Archbishop Whitgift in 1603, there were 9,244 parishes, but the density of provision varied significantly from region to region.[15] Looking at Table 5.1 and Fig. 5.1, we can see that Lincoln and Norwich dioceses contained 2,376 parishes (25 per cent of the total), and together with London, Exeter, York, and Coventry and Lichfield, no fewer than 4,735 (just over half the country's overall figure). Ideally, churchwardens' accounts should survive for every community and contain neat runs of full receipts and details of expenditure. In reality, this is rarely the case. Beautifully illuminated records like those of Wimborne Minster in Dorset or the parchment rolls which exist for Sherborne Abbey are the exception rather than the rule.[16] As has already been noted, churchwardens' accounts often survive in poor condition, so poor that even the work of dedicated archivists cannot render them fit for production for researchers. They were probably neglected records when first created – for who does not find the storing of old accounts burdensome

13 Conrad Russell kindly invited me to give a paper for his seminar on seventeenth-century history at the Institute of Historical Research in June 1991, where I hazarded this guess, which I now revise only slightly upwards to take account of Ronald Hutton's work and the appearance of records for chapelries as well as parishes.

14 The matter of chapels may yet prove crucial in determining the number and percentage of accounts which survive, for while we have maybe 800 accounts to consider if chapels are taken into account, the figure of 9,244 parishes so often quoted as our base figure should perhaps be raised to around 10,000, hence my rough approximation of 8 per cent (see Table 5.1).

15 BL, Harleian MS 280, f. 157; figures printed in R. G. Usher, *The Reconstruction of the English Church* (2 vols, [London], 1969), i. 241. There is reason to believe that the figures produced for Whitgift underestimated the number of livings in the country as part of the establishment's effort to defuse Puritan complaints about the lack of a learned ministry: see A. Foster, 'Chichester diocese in the early seventeenth century', *Sussex Archaeological Collections*, 123 (1985), 188–9.

16 Dorset RO, PE/WM/CW1/41 (1581–1636), PE/SH/CW1/73–111 (1600–40).

Table 5.1 *Total number of parishes and surviving churchwardens' accounts for English and Welsh dioceses c. 1558–1660*

Dioceses (in size order)	No. of parishes	No. of surviving accounts	Survival rate in % of parishes in diocese
Lincoln	1,255	52	4
Norwich	1,121	83	7
London	613	99	16
Exeter	604	54	9
York	581	25	4
Coventry and Lichfield	561	41	7
Bath and Wells	412	46	11
Winchester	362	32	9
Hereford	313	8	3
Canterbury (inc. pecs)	306	32	10
Peterborough	293	12	4
Gloucester	267	19	7
Chester	256	22	9
Chichester	250	17	7
Salisbury	248	36	15
Worcester	241	12	5
Bristol	236	23	10
Oxford	194	16	8
Ely	141	8	6
Durham	135	8	6
Rochester	98	8	8
Carlisle	93	3	3
[Sodor and Man]	17	0	—
St David's	305	2	1
Llandaff	177	0	—
St Asaph	121	4	3
Bangor	61	0	—
Totals	9,244 [+17]	662	7
Adjusted	10,000a	800b	8

Notes
a To take account of chapels.
b Including an allowance for CWA either unfit for inspection or yet to be found.

Sources BL Harleian MS 280, f. 157; Hutton, *Merry England*, appendix pp. 263–93.

and tedious? – and they have not been at the top of any list when conservation tasks have been allocated. With honourable exceptions, it is only comparatively recently that economic historians, joined later by social, ecclesiastical, and local historians, have come to appreciate fully the value of this kind of material. Very rarely do full sets of accounts survive for a long run of years, and many are very patchy indeed.

It is important to stress that the documentation we possess is very scrappy, difficult to read, and open to conflicting interpretations – not to put people off using the source but to urge sophisticated use by historians aware of the dangers. The number of surviving sets for the country is low, but it is also rather variable in unsuspected as well as more obvious ways. As one might predict, the situation is much better for the south than for the north. The province of Canterbury yields just over 91 per cent of the surviving accounts, but then it did contain over 88 per cent of the parishes according to the 1603 survey.[17] But matters become more complicated when one looks in more detail at the figures. Wales, perhaps not surprisingly, is severely under-represented with less than 1 per cent of the total when it accounted for over 7 per cent of the parishes. Indeed, if Hutton is correct, we possess only six sets of accounts for the whole of the principality, none at all for the dioceses of Llandaff and Bangor. On the other hand, the top six sees in terms of absolute numbers of extant churchwardens' accounts, all in the province of Canterbury, contain no less than 57 per cent of the available evidence: London has ninety-nine sets, Norwich eighty-three, Exeter fifty-four, Lincoln fifty-two, Bath and Wells forty-six, and Coventry and Lichfield forty-one. Lincoln and Norwich, with a quarter of the parishes between them, yield a more or less appropriate quota of 20 per cent of the surviving records, but representation gets progressively worse the farther one moves north. York and Chester dioceses yield only forty-seven sets of accounts; Carlisle and Durham, admittedly much smaller sees – a mere eleven.

More intriguing still are the differences that emerge when one looks at survival rates by dioceses (cf. Figs 5.1 and 5.2). London, which accounted for under 7 per cent of the country's parishes in 1603, has provided historians with records for 16 per cent of its livings. This marks a serious skew distribution in our material to urban livings. It appears that church-wardens' accounts are over twice as likely to survive for the diocese of London as for most other dioceses.[18] Perhaps more surprising, though,

17 I transposed the figures into dioceses to make comparisons easier, for we know more about parishes in relation to dioceses than we do in relation to counties. It is still useful to think of counties, because this may make comparisons easier when estimating the wealth of regions, so often based on local government boundaries.

18 This happily accords with Beat Kümin's work on the period 1400–1560 (*Shaping of a Community*, ch. 3.1), and with Julia Merritt's research findings on the splendid material which survives for Westminster parishes.

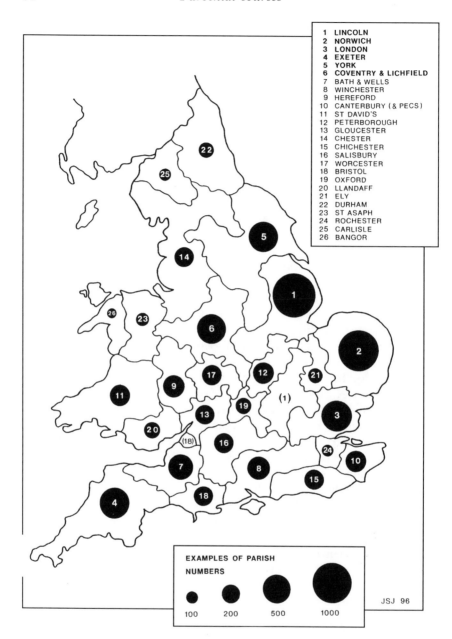

Figure 5.1 Number and distribution of parishes in English and Welsh dioceses *c*. 1603.

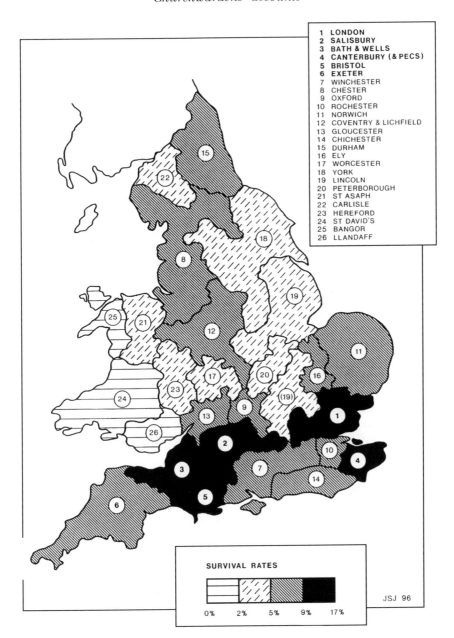

1 LONDON
2 SALISBURY
3 BATH & WELLS
4 CANTERBURY (& PECS)
5 BRISTOL
6 EXETER
7 WINCHESTER
8 CHESTER
9 OXFORD
10 ROCHESTER
11 NORWICH
12 COVENTRY & LICHFIELD
13 GLOUCESTER
14 CHICHESTER
15 DURHAM
16 ELY
17 WORCESTER
18 YORK
19 LINCOLN
20 PETERBOROUGH
21 ST ASAPH
22 CARLISLE
23 HEREFORD
24 ST DAVID'S
25 BANGOR
26 LLANDAFF

SURVIVAL RATES

0%   2%   5%   9%   17%

JSJ 96

Figure 5.2 Survival rates of churchwardens' accounts in English and Welsh dioceses 1558–1660 (%).

is the fact that we possess over five times the number of accounts for Salisbury that might be expected if survival simply represented size of dioceses. The average survival rate across the country is about 8 per cent, but only London (16), Salisbury (15), Bath and Wells (11), Canterbury (10), Bristol (10), and Exeter (9) provide historians with more than this figure. While the corresponding rate for Norwich is just over 7 per cent, representing 12 per cent of the total number of surviving accounts, roughly in proportion to its size, it is Lincoln that appears to be badly under-represented. Lincoln has a survival rate of 4 per cent, contributing under 8 per cent of all 662 sets, when it might have been expected to yield almost double that figure. Further research may iron out some of these differences, for it may be that the large diocese of Lincoln, which spans many counties, is as yet ill served by comprehensive, linked catalogues. The other discrepancies are more difficult to explain.[19]

More research is necessary to investigate the full significance of the geographical distribution of surviving accounts, but dioceses of the south and south-west in particular are certainly over-represented in our evidence as it now stands. And, given the conservative nature of the south-west, this may have some significance for those historians who like to argue about the survival of Catholic traditions nationally. Yet, even within dioceses, local historians may detect regional imbalances. Cultural divisions alluded to above may be further clouded by calculations based on different proportions of accounts drawn from, say, upland or lowland regions, pasture or arable. Other historians may wish to comment on what we should deduce about the representation of urban livings in our surviving accounts, for, even leaving the good showing of London apart, the number is well over double what one might have expected in proportion to rural benefices.

If one takes the work of Peter Clark and Paul Slack as a benchmark, we may assume the existence of between 600 and 700 towns in early modern England.[20] Taking a figure of approximately 120 parishes for London and calculating an average of twenty for six major regional centres like York, Newcastle, and Norwich, we arrive at a figure of 240 parishes for major urban centres.[21] To this we should add a further average of say eight parishes for each of 100 county towns like Gloucester, Chichester, Canterbury, and Oxford. Assuming, finally, one parish for each of the remaining 500–600 small market towns, one arrives at a total of between

19 Care should be exercised with these figures, for they are based strictly on what Hutton has been able to use; when other accounts come to light, or are restored for use, the picture may change slightly.

20 Peter Clark and Paul Slack, *English Towns in Transition 1500–1700* (London, 1976).

21 S. Brigden, *London and the Reformation* (Oxford, 1989), pp. 23–5, suggests a figure of 106 city parishes in the sixteenth century; I have raised this slightly to allow for urban sprawl.

1,540 and 1,640 parishes which may be crudely termed 'urban'. This would represent something in the order of 17 per cent of all parishes in the country, yet our surviving sample contains 37 per cent of such 'urban' churchwardens' accounts. The imbalance may be partly explained simply by the fact that there were more towns in the south than in the north, and this coincides with the geographical distribution noted above. It may also be the case that urban churchwardens may have been of a slightly better social standing, wealthier, more businesslike than the average churchwarden and, of course, handled larger sums of money than their rural counterparts, hence taking better care of the records.[22] Before we place too much stress on the survival of urban records, however, it is useful to remember that the very fact that over 60 per cent of our records represent rural – and often poor – parishes is a matter of delight to many who point to the scarcity of such records on the Continent.[23] Nor is it my point here to enter complex debates concerning why records have survived; I simply wish to draw attention to the situation, leaving others more expert than I to deduce significance for different regions and periods. The imbalances which I have detected for the period 1558–1660 may alter sharply for medievalists or for those studying the eighteenth century.

A bias of a different kind may be detected when one analyses the surviving records according to wealth. Whitgift concluded gloomily that less than 10 per cent of all parishes of England and Wales were worth more than £26 *per annum*.[24] Yet a rough analysis of Hutton's list suggests that over 30 per cent of our 662 sets of accounts may come from parishes worth over this figure. In other words, we are three times more likely to have wealthier parishes represented in this survey. Again, this may not be surprising, for they had more reason to keep good records which would survive, but it is a factor which should perhaps be borne in mind when looking at expenditure patterns in different periods. Efforts may need to be made to offset findings from certain parishes against sets from much poorer and more typical communities, bearing in mind that approximately 35 per cent of all parishes were worth less than £5 *per annum* in the late sixteenth century.[25] This is an occasion when it is useful to look at Hutton's original list compiled by counties, for that permits comparisons to be drawn with Roger Schofield's important study of the geographical distribution of wealth between 1334 and 1649. The south, in the shape of London/Middlesex, Somerset, Gloucestershire, Huntingdonshire, and

22 Craig, 'Co-operation and initiatives', 363–5.
23 I am grateful to Beat Kümin for this observation.
24 Usher, *Reconstruction*, i. 219; for a more recent discussion of the problem see R. O'Day, *The English Clergy* (Leicester, 1979), pp. 172–3.
25 *Ibid.*; for the classic interpretation of some implications of this situation: C. Hill, *Economic Problems of the Church* (London, 1956).

Wiltshire captured the top five places in Schofield's list of the wealthiest counties in the early sixteenth century. Of those, London/Middlesex and Somerset also appear in the top five counties for surviving churchwardens' accounts.[26]

Further problems may arise when one considers the pattern of survival according to patronage of livings. Of those extant accounts for parishes with identifiable patrons, about 40 per cent of the livings were in the hands of ecclesiastical institutions or university colleges, over 11 per cent in the gift of the Crown, and nearly 42 per cent under lay control. It is important to ask whether this represents the balance of the time, or whether once again we shall find some peculiarities. Interesting consequences may follow from this line of investigation, for we might reasonably expect livings in the control of ecclesiastical authorities to reveal greater obedience to the dictates of Church policy in any given period than those in the hands of laymen. This may have some bearing for those historians who seek to use this kind of material for answers to vexed questions on the nature of Church policy in the 1630s. Writing in 1910, R. G. Usher speculated that roughly 27 per cent of all livings were under Crown control, 19 per cent in ecclesiastical hands, and the remaining 54 per cent under lay patronage.[27] If these figures are correct, this would suggest over-representation of ecclesiastical livings in our surviving accounts. Further research into the precise distribution of livings in lay hands would of course be useful, for it might reveal the activities of Catholic laymen in some regions, as well as the machinations of better-known Puritan Feoffees for Impropriations.[28]

The surviving material not only poses dilemmas of a geographical kind, which will clearly render the drawing of comparative conclusions from diocese to diocese difficult, but we are also faced with time-scale problems. For systematic research we really require good runs of material over several decades for the same parish. Yet although it initially looks as if we have such good material for roughly 60 per cent of the accounts in Hutton's list – by which I mean details spanning more than twenty years – this figure frequently hides problems posed by covering dates on volumes with large gaps. Moreover, even where we do possess such a run, it is necessary to be cautious over what factor we should build into our thinking to take account of inflation. How much of the increased expenditure of the 1630s, for example, may be simply laid at the door of rising prices? If we accept the view that the rate of inflation between 1600 and 1640 was approximately 40 per cent, this would suggest that every £10 spent

26 R. S. Schofield, 'The geographical distribution of wealth in England 1334–1649', *Economic History Review*, 2nd Series 18 (1965), 483–510.
27 Usher, *Reconstruction*, i. 111.
28 I owe this idea to one of my students, Joan Barham, who is making a close study of the restoration of churches in the diocese of Chichester 1550–1640.

in 1600, quite a large figure for most parishes, would come out as £14 in 1640.[29] The construction of a specialist price index from sets of accounts would provide one way of clarifying the extent of this difficulty, but that too would be subject to regional variations and might also fall foul of 'custom and practice' relating to what churchwardens chose to record.

We may all cherish certain assumptions about what churchwardens were supposed to record in their accounts, but recent research has exposed just how careful we have to be concerning who became churchwardens, how they were selected, the required literacy levels, let alone how they later came to operate within particular parish traditions.[30] We have to remember that these officers may have exercised discretion over what they recorded – and of course over what they omitted. Wardens were expected to account for all church goods and annual expenditure in what we now appreciate may have been quite a ritualised, theatrical 'annual general meeting' for the parish, carefully mingling oral and written testimony. Yet it is often difficult to compare sets of accounts because, while some itemised extensively, others chose to record payments by kind in lump sums. While some recorded every drink given to a bell-ringer on every occasion, others simply noted a block allowance. Anyone who has looked at more than a few sets of accounts may wonder whether it is wise to think of a system at all, so many local variations occur. On many occasions it is difficult to suppress the suspicion that the recording of monetary transactions represents only a fragment of the 'real' financial arrangements which underpinned parish life. Skilled craftsmen may have become churchwardens at precisely the times when the parish had need of their skills. We shall never know how many obligations were rendered to the parish 'in kind'. Useful research is now being carried out into yet another layer of apparently basic questions concerning the nature of record-keeping in medieval and early modern England, the intermingling of oral and written traditions, and the ways in which parish communities often subverted the intentions of those who imposed record-keeping upon them. It is through this kind of research that we shall eventually answer some of the questions posed above.[31]

II

It is one thing to draw attention to problems entailed in these sources; it is quite another matter to show that, in spite of everything, they may still provide us with fascinating and reliable insights into current debates.

29 For the classic work on this topic: E. H. Phelps Brown and S. V. Hopkins, 'Seven centuries of the prices of consumables compared with builders' wage rates', *Economica*, 23 (1956), 296–314; for a more recent view: R. B. Outhwaite, *Inflation in Tudor and Early Stuart England*, Studies in Economic History (London, 1969).

30 See the articles of Carlson, Merritt, and Craig already cited.

31 Here I am grateful to Katherine French for allowing me to read as yet unpublished research along these lines.

Of central concern at the moment is the matter of how one can date the settled establishment of the Church of England, or, in other words, the success of the Protestant Reformation.[32] Can the evidence of churchwardens' accounts be of any use here? Would it help if we could discern some patterns in expenditure levels over the period? It has generally been assumed that the period between 1558 and certainly the late 1620s was a very bleak one for church maintenance, hence the need for Archbishop Whitgift's survey of churches commissioned in 1602 and the later proclamation appealing for a restoration campaign in 1629.[33] Due attention has been paid in recent years to the efforts made by Archbishops Neile and Laud to improve matters in the 1630s, but this has served only to reinforce the impression of limited activity in the period before then.[34]

This prevailing orthodoxy is perhaps best summed up in the words of Patrick Collinson, who remarked that 'whereas it is proper to measure the strength of pre-Reformation religious sentiment by its material remains, it would be a mistake to gauge the quality of post-Reformation religion by the same criterion'.[35] This assessment relies heavily on the gloomy view of English churches taken by Stubbes in 1593, which has influenced most modern writing on the subject.[36] Architectural historians have also contributed to the gloom, for it is rare to find favourable mention of late sixteenth and early seventeenth-century church features in the works inspired by the late Sir Nikolaus Pevsner.[37]

Only comparatively recently have doubts been expressed about this grim picture. In a stimulating article suitably entitled 'The myth of the English Reformation' Diarmaid MacCulloch drew attention to the task before architectural historians in coming to a realistic appreciation of what did happen between the 1550s and the 1660s.[38] The key thing has to be to shed myths and prejudices about the wonderful things that apparently happened before and after this period. The difficulties to be surmounted may be great, but lack of records and the activities of Victorian

32 The Neale Colloquium held at University College, London, in January 1996 was dedicated to the theme of the 'Long Reformation'.

33 A. Foster, 'The function of a bishop: the career of Richard Neile 1562–1640' in R. O'Day and F. Heal (eds), *Continuity and Change: Personnel and Administration of the Church of England 1500–1642* (Leicester, 1976), pp. 33–54.

34 *Ibid.*; see also A. Foster, 'Church policies of the 1630s', in R. Cust and A. Hughes (eds), *Conflict in Early Stuart England* (London, 1989), pp. 193–223; Tyacke, *Anti-Calvinists*, pp. 181–244; Davies, *Caroline Captivity*.

35 'The Elizabethan Church and the new religion', in C. Haigh (ed.), *The Reign of Elizabeth I* (London, 1984), p. 171.

36 D. M. Palliser, 'Introduction: the parish in perspective', in Susan Wright (ed.), *Parish Church and People: Local Studies in Lay Religion* (London, 1988), pp. 5–28.

37 See the *Buildings of England* series produced for each county; Malcolm Airs, *The Buildings of Britain, Tudor and Jacobean: A Guide and Gazetteer* (London, 1982), pp. 111–18; Richard Morrice, *The Buildings of Britain, Stuart and Baroque: A Guide and Gazetteer* (London, 1982), pp. 75–98.

38 'The myth of the English Reformation', *Journal of British Studies*, 30 (1991).

rebuilders should not blind us to achievements and deter research. Mac-Culloch was quite clear about the prize:

I would hazard that what such investigation will reveal will be a minor 'building revolution' in churches that gathered momentum from the last years of the sixteenth century: an heroic effort to reequip Catholic worship spaces for Protestant use. This revolution may have been signaled by Archbishop Whitgift's energetic sponsorship of a national survey of church fabrics in 1602; it significantly predated the Laudian campaign for church restoration from the late 1620s, and it had different priorities from the Laudian programme.[39]

It is in the context of this kind of research that our study of churchwardens' accounts can contribute so much, and all findings to date thoroughly endorse MacCulloch's claims. In other words, it looks as if we may use the very criterion which Patrick Collinson rejected to register the consolidation and success of the Church of England. For surely, if we can show that people were starting to spend again on their churches in the late sixteenth and early seventeenth centuries, this is a good measure of commitment?

Church repairs and extensions, dutifully carried out as and when the need arose in different parishes, do seem to have been achieved fairly willingly, as far as one can judge from surviving churchwardens' accounts. Assessment for major repairs needed the consent of parishioners and large sums appear to have been raised without difficulty after the 1590s. The matter of 'how willingly' money was paid and indeed the tricky question of 'initiative' for projects will be discussed later, but now it is time to furnish examples from yet another 'sample'. My survey covers 100 parishes culled from the dioceses of York, Durham, Chichester, Bath and Wells, Bristol, and Winchester: an area spanning roughly ten counties. It therefore represents parts of the country where you would expect to find approximately a quarter of English parishes, but, as has already been noted, the southern dioceses are better represented than those in the north. The survival rate for Durham is very poor, with only one set of accounts coming from the archdeaconry of Northumberland. This is particularly irritating, since we know of a church restoration campaign carried out in that archdeaconry under the orders of Bishop Neile between 1619 and 1621, when roughly 40 per cent of all the churches were ordered to carry out repairs.[40] Indeed, there is also some evidence of work carried out earlier under Bishop James.[41]

---

39 *Ibid.*, 13.
40 Analysis of the surviving visitation records for the archdeaconry of Northumberland: Department of Palaeography and Diplomatics, University of Durham, DDR VIII/2, (1619–21) DDR VKIII/3 (1619–23).
41 I owe this reminder to Kenneth Fincham; see his *Early Stuart Church 1603–42* (London, 1993), p. 259, n. 9.

In keeping with earlier words of caution about our sources, I should acknowledge at the outset that, of the 100 churches in my sample, fewer than sixty offer real scope for comparative analysis, for only that number provide full details and cover a reasonable span of time between 1600 and 1640, let alone before and after those dates. In other respects, too, the sample conforms to the patterns already described concerning over-representation of wealthy parishes and also those in the hands of ecclesiastical authorities. The significance of this will be appreciated later. On the basis of this material, however, it looks as if a parish median expenditure could be put at about £12 *per annum*, rising sharply in the 1630s. With this figure in mind, it takes little imagination to consider the wrench it must have been in the community of Kingston upon Thames when £153 was spent on major interior work between 1607 and 1609, and a further £100 between 1625 and 1628. This yielded a high average expenditure of roughly £28–£33 over the period 1600 to 1640.[42] The community of Holy Cross, Ryton, in County Durham raised £124 in 1627, when its average expenditure was roughly £10 *per annum*.[43] The parish church of Corfe Castle in Dorset was more or less entirely rebuilt for £124 between 1617 and 1618.[44]

My survey indicates quite an impressive degree of restoration work of a major structural kind – involving very large sums of money for the time being spent on galleries, new seating, towers, and bells. Forty-three out of the 100 churches can be included in this category, and that is based on a strict definition of 'major repairs' which should be counted out of the ordinary. The statistic becomes all the more impressive when one considers the loss of evidence for many of the 100 churches in the survey. A large number of those churches experienced further major campaigns in the 1630s, but what is really new and important here is the evidence of activity *before* 1625, a testimony perhaps to the Jacobean consensus which many feel marked the true establishment of the Church of England.[45] Moreover, the evidence for general repairs seems sufficient to take account of all the in-built problems already noted concerning our surviving accounts.

It is too early to be definite about findings and it is still true to say that few entirely new churches or chapels were built during this period, even though George Yule continues the useful quest to find some.[46]

---

42 Surrey County RO, KG2/2/3 (1567–1650).
43 Durham County RO, (EP/Ryt/4/1 (1597–1638).
44 Dorset County RO, PE/CoC/CW1 (1563–1633).
45 For a comprehensive rendering of this thesis see Fincham (ed.), *Early Stuart Church*, particularly the introduction and the article by R. Fincham and P. Lake on 'The Ecclesiastical Policies of James I and Charles I', pp. 23–49.
46 'James VI and I: furnishing the churches in his two kingdoms', in A. Fletcher and P. Roberts (eds), *Religion, Culture and Society in Early Modern Britain: Essays in Honour of Patrick Collinson* (Cambridge, 1994), pp. 182–208.

Nevertheless, we do have one possible explanation ready to hand for much of the new repair work. This comes from the architectural historian Andrew Woodger, who claims that new developments relating to the casting of bells entailed measures to strengthen and improve hanging arrangements in church towers.[47] This breakthrough accounts in turn for the revival of bell-founding in the seventeenth century. Certainly, this argument would fit thirty-three out of forty-three churches which underwent large-scale repairs. Other causes of expenditure in the Jacobean period can be located with new pews, galleries, and the well loved 'Jacobean pulpits'.

Woodger's theory is based on rather technical architectural evidence and has been vigorously challenged, but work on bells was a significant and undeniable factor throughout this period.[48] The following figures based on the production of Sussex bellfounders yield some idea of what was happening nationally. During the 1590s ten bells were cast in the county; this figure jumped to thirty-one in the next decade, thirty-four in the 1610s, twenty-two in the 1620s, and forty-two in the 1630s.[49] The Eldridge family of Horsham and Chertsey account for ninety bells which survive today from this period in Sussex.[50] It looks as if more bells were cast in the first four decades of the seventeenth century than in the next sixty years. Another way of gauging the significance of this work is to note its effect on a single parish. At Horsham in Sussex considerable work was carried out in providing new bells and making adjustments to the tower in 1616 and again in 1633; on both occasions the costs involved accounted for more than two-thirds of the expenditure for those years.[51]

Diarmaid MacCulloch put forward another interesting hypothesis which relates to the better-known campaigns of the 1630s, claiming 'It is likely that Archbishops Laud and Neile aroused such hostility in their campaigns for church restoration not because they were stirring up previously inactive church officers to save tottering and neglected fabrics but precisely because they often interfered with recently completed schemes for refurnishing and restoration'.[52] I think the picture is a little more complicated. It is perhaps no coincidence that general source problems mentioned earlier may also have a greater bearing on the more specific debates concerning the implementation of Church policies in the 1630s.

47 'Post-Reformation mixed Gothic in Huntingdonshire church towers and the campanological associations', *Archaeological Journal*, 141 (1984), 269–308.
48 George Bernard, 'The dating of church towers: Huntingdonshire re-examined', *Archaeological Journal*, 149 (1992), 344–50.
49 A. Daniel-Tyssen, 'The church bells of Sussex', *Sussex Archaeological Collections*, 16 (1864), 158.
50 A. Daniel-Tyssen, 'More on Sussex bells', *Sussex Archaeological Collections*, 57 (1915), 87–93.
51 West Sussex County RO, Par 106/9/1 (1610–1770).
52 MacCulloch, 'Myth', 14.

Certainly it looks as if churchwardens had been far from inactive before
Laud and Neile applied themselves in the 1630s. It also seems clear that
much of what the latter strove to achieve may have run counter to previous
restoration schemes and caused offence out of all proportion to the real
costs involved. Heavy-handed interference from outsiders is never popular
in the parishes! Yet it looks as if the policies pursued in the 1630s caused
local irritation for quite varying reasons. For many it may have been the
horror of turning their communion table into an 'altar' and providing a
rail – relatively insignificant though these were in financial terms. But,
for others, the 1630s did mark a peak of activity concerning church
repairs in general. Arminian notions of the 'beauty of holiness' added a
nasty spice to routine maintenance programmes to which people were
again asked to commit large sums of money.[53]

In confirmation of earlier research on the northern province, expenditure levels rose sharply in the 1630s.[54] Bearing in mind earlier
caveats relating to how we need to think of inflation during this period,
of thirty-nine parishes offering reasonably comparable material on expenditure levels over two or more decades, all bar five reveal increased
expenditure levels in the 1630s sufficient to take account of inflation.
Five parishes actually spent over £100 in an individual year in the 1630s.[55]
Within this expenditure we find the new and more divisive costs of church
fittings – raised altars, altar rails, reorganised seating, font covers, shifted
pulpits, new organs, and major schemes for artistic 'beautification'. Thirty-
two of the 100 churches contain references to communion table rails and
often new communion tables as well. The average cost of a good walnut
table was £3, and £5–£6 for those with fitted rails. Such expenses were
negligible in comparison with the sums already noted for new bells,
seating, and strengthening of towers, but they may have provoked more
anger amongst a theologically minded minority.

This sort of work on churchwardens' accounts has already made
quite a contribution to our understanding of events in Bath and Wells in
the 1630s. The diocese also provides a useful case study of the importance
of considering the source problems already alluded to in the earlier part
of this chapter when interpreting material. In her study entitled *Laud's
Laboratory*, Margaret Stieg concluded that 'such success as the Laudians
enjoyed was superficial'.[56] Initially, this remark seemed perfectly sound,
for she made the obvious comment that 'the Laudians were too dependent upon others, the churchwardens, to execute orders and to initiate

53 Tyacke, *Anti-Calvinists*, and Foster, 'Church policies'.
54 A. Foster, 'A Biography of Archbishop Richard Neile 1562–1640' (D. Phil., Oxford University, 1978), pp. 246–8, 257–8, 265–7, 306–7; for a summary of this
   work see my 'The function of a bishop', pp. 48–9.
55 Howden, Worksop, Mortlake, St Mary's, Scarborough, Puddletown.
56 *Laud's Laboratory: The Diocese of Bath and Wells in the Early Seventeenth Century*
   (Lewisburg, 1982), p. 306.

corrective measures'.[57] All who have worked on diocesan records would appreciate this kind of caution. The zealous Archbishop Neile had required the help of roving commissioners operating under orders from his Chancery Court in order to compensate for the shortcomings of his visitation courts and to supplement the efforts of his archdeacons in respect of church surveys and repairs. Sadly, however, Margaret Stieg did not consult any churchwardens' accounts in order to cross-check visitation material. The overwhelming majority of those that do survive – two-thirds, to be exact – testify to a pretty successful campaign to get Somerset churches equipped with altar rails between 1633 and 1635. And this is evidence from a diocese which we know to possess one of the best sets of surviving accounts in the country.[58] Yet here too we have to exercise caution, for cross-checking with other court records and the testimony of Bishop Piers reveals that the churchwardens' accounts which we possess may be creating a rosy picture, possibly because of the skew distributions already noted towards wealth and ecclesiastical patronage.[59] Here is definitely a case where we have to tread carefully, bearing in mind the general problems detected in our sources.

Somerset churches provide some useful examples of what was generally involved in the Arminian campaigns of the 1630s, when work around the communion table frequently went hand in hand with general programmes of 'beautification'. One such example is the small chapel of Williton in west Somerset. In 1634 the congregation of this chapel spent £17 6s. 1d., compared with an annual average expenditure of £1 in the 1600s, £2 in the 1620s, and £3 for the rest of the 1630s.[60] So 1634 was clearly a big year for this congregation! Of the £17, a new Bible, book of Homilies, a book for 5 November, and a table showing degrees of marriage came to £3 2s. 8d. A cover for the chalice cost 3s., a new communion table and rail £4 8s. 8d., and a carpet to go with it £2 10s. This left the remainder of the £17 to be spent on minor practical matters like new thatch for the minister's cottage! Here is a good example where Arminian concerns could lead to what might be considered locally as major expenditure, yet, on the other hand, it could still be just an irritant swallowed up in the detection of the need for more general repairs.

Another classic example is to be found at Puddletown in Dorset, where with reference to royal orders, probably the proclamation of 1629, and under episcopal scrutiny later backed by commissioners working for

57 *Ibid.*
58 CWA survive for approximately 11 per cent of the parishes of Bath and Wells diocese (see Table 5.1 and Fig. 5.2).
59 Bishop Piers noted in January 1636 that 140 churches out of 469 had followed instructions over altars and rails, but that others needed pressure to act – hardly a comment on a successful campaign: Stieg, *Laud's Laboratory*, p. 306; William Prynne, *Canterbures Doom* (1646), pp. 98–9; Davies, *Caroline Captivity*, pp. 226–7.
60 Williton chapel: Somerset RO, DD/WY 1 C/306 Box 37/1 (1590–1713).

the Archbishop of Canterbury, parishioners carried out a set of instructions the results of which may still be viewed today. They were commanded to remodel the interior to divide the nave from the chancel, to adjust the position of the pulpit and reading place, to establish a new communion table with 'a frame about it', to erect a gallery at the west end, to provide a new font cover, and establish uniform seating throughout the church. All this was costed at £130, to be raised by 5s. pew rates and general assessments, five rates to be carried out between 1634 and 1637. The highest amount any one person paid was £11 10s.[61] Where it has been possible to trace accounts into the 1640s, it is noticeable just how dramatically expenditure levels dropped in that decade, as one might expect. Hence expenditure levels fell from an average of £30 *per annum* to £12 at Axbridge in Somerset in the 1640s.[62]

It is important to consider the matter of the initiative for changes. One important difference between work before the 1630s and that after is that churchwardens' accounts reveal less evidence that work came as a result of surveys, presentments, or campaigns led by bishops before the 1630s. This is why we talk of the campaigns of the 1630s as representing the 'ideological' take-over of the Church by Arminians. Churchwardens were under constant pressure to carry out their work diligently, pressure which came – in various mixtures – from within their own community, from their local archdeacon charged with close supervision of their work, their bishop, and indeed the dictates of higher authorities. We get glimpses of the work of roving commissioners in various places in the 1630s. Thus at Axbridge 1s. 6d. was spent on filling 'commissioners that viewed the church' in 1634 with wine, something which failed to save them from subsequent major expenditure on railing the communion table, reorganisation of seats, and general painting and beautification.[63] Beer for only 6d. was likewise unsuccessful at Crewkerne in 1633, where a year later they had to spend £54 on church organs and a new carriage of bells.[64]

It is pressure from above and from Archbishops Laud and Neile that we detect so clearly in the 1630s. Yet this should not blind us to earlier, less publicised campaigns of the Jacobean era. Archbishop George Abbot (1611–33), for example, was as interested as was Laud later in the economic problems of the Church and organised a thorough review of glebe terriers through his metropolitan visitation.[65] Bishop Lancelot Andrewes was concerned about communion tables and fittings at

---

61 Memoranda and rate list, 1634: Dorset RO, PE/PUD/CW 5/1.
62 Somerset RO, D/P/Ax 4/1/1 (*c.* 1570–1770).
63 *Ibid.*
64 Somerset RO, D/P/ Crew 4/1/1 (1625–1700).
65 Somerset RO: analysis of surviving glebe terriers reveals best figures for production in 1606, 1613, 1634, and 1638.

Winchester between 1619 and 1624;[66] Bishop Samuel Harsnett was likewise worried about the general fabric of Sussex churches in the years 1610–11.[67] Tantalising scraps of information already noted reveal action under Neile at Durham long before his more celebrated campaigns of the 1630s. Yet these earlier campaigns were more localised, more dependent upon particular individuals, than those sanctioned by royal and archiepiscopal authority in the 1630s. We need to know more about the pattern of church restoration and expenditure in each diocese, set against a full appreciation of the sources which have survived, before we can pronounce finally on these matters.[68]

These examples of research into church buildings, both generally during the period in relation to the debate on the 'Long Reformation' and on specific policies associated with the 1630s, bring us full circle in noting what may come out of more systematic research into churchwardens' accounts. Thanks to Ronald Hutton and a growing host of other scholars on both sides of the Atlantic we are now a little closer to realising the scale of the task in front of us, appreciating more the peculiarities of what has survived, and hence moving towards more sophisticated use. Even the late Professor Elton, who was notoriously pessimistic about the survival of churchwardens' accounts for the period before 1640, still noted that they 'have important things to say about the very base of society and still await systematic exploitation'.[69] We are now happily closer to that goal.

---

66 K. Fincham, *Prelate as Pastor: The Episcopate of James I* (London, 1990), p. 140.
67 *Ibid.*, pp. 138–9.
68 This is the kind of work being carried out by Joan Barham for the diocese of Chichester; Valerie Hitchman produced an M.A. thesis on 'Aspects of Parochial Religion in Seventeenth-century Kent' for the University of Kent at Canterbury in 1994. She usefully drew attention to a variety of parochial initiatives in Kent parishes (pp. 56–62) and also noted Cressy's heavy reliance on London parishes for evidence on bells (p. 89).
69 G. R. Elton, *England 1200–1640: The Sources of History* (London, 1969), p. 114.

Popular religion and the parish register 1538–1603

On 1 March 1575, Agnes Littlewood, of the West Riding parish of Almondbury, gave birth to a boy. Four days later he was christened Thomas, but any rejoicing in the Littlewood household all too quickly came to an end. Ten days after the ceremony (almost exactly half-way through the mother's period of lying-in), around midnight, Agnes quietly arose from her child-bed, left the house and in the darkness went to a nearby well. Although it held less than two feet of water, there she drowned herself.[1] Today we might interpret this as an instance of postnatal depression, but the vicar of Almondbury, Robert Staynton, offered the obvious rationalisation for a world that saw itself as the battleground between the spiritual forces of good and evil – clearly such an act could only have been 'by the instigation of the devil'.[2] It is to Staynton, not a coroner's report, a local history, a letter, or a diary, that we owe this small insight into early modern understanding of ill fortune, the human mind, and the influence of the supernatural. Staynton, the incumbent of the parish from 1557 until his death in 1598, made a habit of recording such occurrences, and much else besides. He did so in the pages of what should have been simply a list of names and dates, of baptisms, marriages, and burials, the register of his parish.

This chapter will examine (I) the historiography of this source over the last two centuries, (II) the legal and ecclesiastical framework that brought the parish register into existence, (III) the pattern of survival in a regional case study, and (IV) the light the register can shed on the social and religious history of post-Reformation England.

I

Staynton, although he may have been unusual in the detail of information he noted about his community, was not at all unique in his habits of recording. Anecdotes, like the sad end of Agnes Littlewood, caught the attention and interest of antiquarians in the nineteenth and early twentieth centuries. This led to a number of works that used such records as a means of observing social and religious life in the past. The first of these, J. S. Burn's *History of Parish Registers in England*, was originally published

---

1 H. Taylor (ed.), *The Parish Registers of Almondbury*, 1: *1557–1598*, YPRS 139 (privately printed, 1974), p. 112.
2 *Ibid.*

in 1829.[3] It demonstrated many of the glaring flaws of the antiquarian approach to the past, being, as a later antiquarian, J. Charles Cox observed, 'ill digested throughout and confusedly arranged'.[4] In 1882 R. Chester Waters published a more concise guide to the contents of parish registers, but it was Cox himself who in 1910 produced the largest and most comprehensive work in this genre.[5] Although his companion volume on churchwardens' accounts has been much used by recent historians, Cox's work on parish registers remains largely neglected.[6] It is far less rambling (and contains rather fewer errors of fact) than the works of his predecessors. Cox demonstrated a thorough understanding of and extensive familiarity with his topic, but his work remains unapologetically antiquarian in nature. Like many of his predecessors and contemporaries he failed to assess the typicality of what he had found or its wider significance.[7] It was for these reasons that historians from Carlyle onwards have tended to condemn the work of antiquarians and with them the subject of their interest.[8]

In these circumstances English parish registers did not receive serious scholarly attention until the middle decades of the twentieth century. The pioneers of English social history, whether they opted for a literary approach (like Trevelyan) or an economic emphasis (exemplified by Tawney), fought a difficult battle for academic respectability and were at pains to distance themselves from accusations of antiquarianism.[9] The success of proponents of the socio-economic approach in the development of scientific and statistical methodologies means that sources previously used only by antiquarians have enjoyed something of a renaissance. This trend is most closely associated with members of the Cambridge Group for the History of Population and Social Structure, who (although undoubtedly influenced by French historians of the *Annales* school) were pioneers in the recovery of the demographic record of the

3 J. S. Burn, *The History of Parish Registers in England* (London, [1829] 1862).
4 J. C. Cox, *The Parish Registers of England* (London, 1910), p. vii.
5 R. E. Chester Waters, *Parish Registers in England: Their History and Contents with Suggestions for Securing their Better Custody and Preservation* (London, 1882) and Cox, *Parish Registers*. See also T. F. Thiselton-Dyer, *English Social Life, as Told by the Parish Registers* (London, 1893). The most important link with modern local and social history is W. E. Tate, *The Parish Chest: A Study of the Records of the Parochial Administration in England* (Cambridge, 1946).
6 J. C. Cox, *Churchwardens' Accounts from the Fourteenth Century to the Close of the Seventeenth Century* (London, 1913).
7 For a useful (and very hostile) definition of antiquarianism see G. R. Elton, *The Practice of History* (London, 1967), pp. 151–3. An interesting and more positive examination is J. D. Marshall, 'The antiquarian heresy', *Journal of Regional and Local Studies*, 15/2 (1995), 49–54.
8 G. M. Trevelyan, *English Social History: A Survey of Six Centuries, Chaucer to Queen Victoria* (London, 1944), p. viii.
9 J. Kenyon, *The History Men: The Historical Profession in England since the Renaissance* (London, 1983), pp. 234–50.

past.[10] Among the records they have employed the parish register, approximating as it does to a record of births, marriages and deaths, played a crucial role.

Demographic historians have, however, benefited greatly, if indirectly, from the work of the antiquarians. Men like Cox played a significant part in preserving parish registers and contributed to their collection and collation inside county record offices. Their work also played a part in inspiring interest among amateur historians, particularly those who had a curiosity about the history of their locality or families. The tangible results of their efforts are visible in the hundreds of parish registers transcribed and published by county societies.[11] Today the registers are without doubt one of England's most accessible historical sources.

II

The growing interest in social history forced a transformation of the study of almost every other branch of historical study. There is now widespread agreement about the need to consider social factors in the study of any area of the past.[12] Here I am largely concerned with the expanding common ground between social and religious history in sixteenth-century England, or what is usually referred to as popular religion.[13] In this area the sources which antiquarians employed can provide important new insights: for example, historians have begun to give a 'second look' to the (in many ways parallel) records of churchwardens' accounts.[14] In a similar way parish registers can throw considerable and perhaps unique light on popular religion in the English Reformation.

The parish register, like any other historical source, cannot be understood without reference to its legal and administrative context. Firstly, it presents us with perhaps the best evidence of a Tudor revolution

10 M. Anderson, *Approaches to the History of the Western Family 1500–1914* (London, 1980), pp. 17–18.
11 The Parish Register Society was formed in 1877. There have been over twenty county parish register societies and numerous other associations that have also printed large numbers of parish registers. See Tate, *Parish Chest*, p. 54.
12 J. E. Sharpe, 'History from below', in P. Burke (ed.), *New Perspectives on Historical Writing* (Cambridge, 1991), pp. 24–45.
13 B. Reay, 'Popular religion', in B. Reay (ed.), *Popular Culture in Seventeenth Century England* (London, 1985), p. 91.
14 See J. S. Craig, 'Co-operation and initiatives: Elizabethan churchwardens and the parish accounts of Mildenhall', *Social History*, 18 (1993), 357–9. I am grateful to Dr Craig for some interesting discussions of the relationship between CWA and parish registers. The major recent works using this source include C. Haigh, *Reformation and Resistance in Tudor Lancashire* (Cambridge, 1975), J. J. Scarisbrick, *The Reformation and the English People* (Oxford, 1984), E. Duffy, *The Stripping of the Altars: Traditional Religion in England 1400–1580* (New Haven, 1992), R. Hutton, *The Rise and Fall of Merry England: The Ritual Year 1400–1700* (Oxford, 1994), and B. A. Kümin, *The Shaping of a Community: The Rise and Reformation of the English Parish c. 1400–1560* (Aldershot, 1996).

in government. Its creation was in many ways more significant for the inhabitants of early modern England than changes in the central administration of the state. Thomas Cromwell is usually credited with the creation of the registers, since, as vicar-general, he issued an injunction on 4 September 1538 requiring parish clergy to keep 'one book or register' in which they were to put 'the day, and year of every wedding, christening and burying in their parish and the name of the persons wedded, christened or buried'.[15] Cromwell was probably copying practices that he had encountered while in the Netherlands, but which had originated in Spain at the close of the fifteenth century.[16] It is, however, also notable that a number of surviving registers antedate Cromwell's injunction, some by several years.[17] It is possible to suggest that he was enforcing nationally what had already become customary in some localities. Nevertheless, it was his action that began the process of standardising the form of the records. Just as important, the government now punished poor maintenance of the registers with fines of 3s. 4d.[18]

Cromwell's injunction was reissued under Edward VI in 1547.[19] However, those produced by Cardinal Pole for the Province of Canterbury in 1556 and 1557 instructed enquires to be made of parochial clergy as to 'whether they so keep the book or register of christenings, buryings, and marriages, with the names of the godfathers and godmothers?'.[20] There are no extant Marian injunctions for the northern province, but it seems logical to assume that they contained a similar instruction, as a number of such entries for this period survive in local registers. Injunctions in the reign of Elizabeth, starting with those from 1559, dropped the requirement of recording the identities of godparents, reiterating the formulas of previous reigns to state 'the day and year of each wedding, christening, and burial made within their parish ... and also therein [they] shall write every person's name that be so wedded, christened, and buried ...'.[21]

The significant innovation of Elizabeth's reign lay not in the form of the records but in the way in which they were to be kept. A 1597 constitution issued by the convocation of Canterbury 'for the better maintenance of parish registers' contained four important items.[22] First, all

15 *LP*, xiii/2.114 (no. 281).
16 Cox, *Parish Registers*, p. 1.
17 Cox lists eighteen sets, but a number of these actually started after 1538. The earliest known English register is Alfriston, Sussex, which begins in 1506: *ibid.*, pp. 239, 237, and D. J. Steel (ed.), *National Index of Parish Registers: Sources of Births, Marriages and Deaths before 1837* (London, 1968), i. 24.
18 *LP*, xiii/2. 114.
19 W. H. Frere and W. M. Kennedy (eds), *Visitation Articles and Injunctions of the Reformation Period* (3 vols, London, 1910), ii. 40.
20 *Ibid.*, pp. 389, 422.
21 *Ibid.*, iii. 12.
22 Tate, *The Parish Chest*, pp. 44–5.

entries from the preceding week were to be read out on Sunday after either matins or evensong. Second, each completed page had to be signed by the minister and churchwardens. Next, a copy of the entries for the preceding year (the so-called Bishop's Transcripts) was to be sent to the diocesan registrar in the month after each Easter. Finally, future registers were to be written on (and previous entries copied on to) parchment, rather than cheaper and less durable paper.

These instructions may have had a profound impact on the surviving records. The public reading of registers (although only in force till 1603) and the signing by ministers and churchwardens (even if rarely evident) arguably made the registers a more public document. Potentially this facilitated a process of transformation from what had been an official, but essentially private, record of the minister to one belonging to the parish community as a whole. Moreover, Bishop's Transcripts, which necessitated extra expense or time and only required the minimum of information, may well have made the recording of other details and events less likely.[23]

The move away from paper may have had a similar impact on the records. The costs of buying a parchment volume and copying hundreds of entries were not insignificant expenses for a parish. In some areas it was a major event, as at Pitchford in Shropshire, where the opening page of the parchment register has the following description:

The Register Booke of all weddings, Christenings and Burialls of the forsaid parishe from the beginning of the Queenes Ma ties Reigne unto the 17 th day of November Anno D'ni 1598 was made and written in parchment agreeing with the old paper books at the cost of the parishners of the forsaid parish:– according to an Ecclessiastical Constitution in that case provided.[24]

As in a few other parishes considerable local pride was literally bound up in the expensive covers and occasional illustrations of these parchment books. It would not be surprising if as a result of the change much superfluous information, not required by the regulations, was omitted. This may in itself explain why registers containing a rich variety of incidental evidence now appear so rare. It is possible that surviving parchment registers are mere skeletons of their paper predecessors.[25] Even more significantly, when similar instructions were issued at the beginning of the reign of James I, they ordered the copying of registers 'so far as the ancient books thereof can be procured, but especially since

---

23 For some interesting insights into Bishop's Transcripts see D. Ashurst, 'St Mary's Church, Worsborough, South Yorkshire: a review of the accuracy of a parish register', *Local Population Studies*, 55 (1995), 46–58.

24 T. R. Horton (ed.), *The Registers of Pitchford, Shropshire*, Parish Register Society Publications 31 (privately printed, 1900), p. 1.

25 The suggestion can be found in Cox, *Parish Registers*, p. 49. See also Tate, *Parish Chest*, pp. 45–6.

the beginning of the reign of the late Queen'.[26] It is thus not difficult to understand why so many registers apparently begin in 1558 or 1559 and quite impossible to judge exactly how many registers were kept in the early sixteenth century. In addition we must account for the losses of the last 400 years. Finally, the lack of uniform development of the parish register makes an assessment of its exact nature very difficult.

Historians must approach the register fully cognisant of the forces that produced it and with the understanding that the information it contains was never recorded to provide answers to the questions which modern historians are likely to ask. The initial entries of the 1530s were made amidst rumours that the government would use the information for tax purposes. However, Cromwell justified the keeping of registers to 'avoid disputes touching ages, titles or lineal descents'.[27] Parish registers have been an invaluable source of this type of information. The recording of illegitimate births in the registers, which made Peter Laslett's pioneering studies of bastardy possible, was a logical extension of this role.[28] Given their costly and time-consuming compilation, parish registers provide a good indication of the preoccupation with legitimacy and inheritance in early modern England.[29] However, the registers were not primarily what they have become now, a long-term genealogical record. The interest in legitimacy and the recording of kinship extended only to the recent past. This is exemplified by the canons of 1603, which ordered the copying of records only for the preceding reign – a period approximating to two generations. There was perhaps also a wish to bolster the rites of passage of the Church and a very 'modern' concern with recording the people. The strength of these considerations is symbolised by the double locked parish coffers in which the records were kept.[30]

III

To illuminate the changes in form and content in the sixteenth century it is necessary to undertake a systematic examination of the surviving registers. This chapter attempts to do so on a regional basis, focusing on evidence drawn from Yorkshire and Lancashire for the period 1538–1603.[31]

---

26 *The Constitutions and Canons Ecclesiastical (Made in the Year 1603 and Amended in the Year 1865): To which are Added the Thirty Nine Articles of the Church of England* (London and Bungay, 1908), p. 39 (no. 70).

27 *LP*, xiii/2. 43 (no. 1010).

28 P. Laslett, *Family Life and Illicit Love in Earlier Generations: Essays in Historical Sociology* (Cambridge, 1977).

29 K. V. Thomas, 'Puritans and adultery: the Act of 1650 reconsidered', in K. V. Thomas and D. Pennington (eds), *Puritans and Revolutionaries: Essays in Seventeenth Century History Presented to Christopher Hill* (Oxford, 1978), pp. 257–82.

30 *Constitutions and Canons*, p. 39 (no. 70).

31 The sample includes registers from the Borthwick Institute, LDA, MDCLW, and NYCRO; registers printed by the Yorkshire and Lancashire Parish Register Societies and twenty-six privately printed registers.

As can be seen from Table 6.1, sixteenth-century registers are now extant for only 392 out of 1,152, or around a third, of all the parishes in the two counties. This may reflect the general problems of record survival, and in part (particularly before 1558) the problems already outlined of the loss of original registers. However, anecdotal evidence suggests that many registers were never kept. For example, the parishioners of St Sampson in York were presented in 1575 because they not only lacked 'a coffer with two lockes and keyes for kepinge the register booke ...', but also 'theye lacke a register booke for christenninges and weddings etc.'[32]

Table 6.1 *The dates from which registers or transcripts are extant for Yorkshire and Lancashire parishes*

Region	Approx. total No. of parishes	1538		1553		1558		1603	
		No.	%	No.	%	No.	%	No.	%
East Riding (including York)	256	6	2.3	20	7.8	39	15.2	111	43.4
North Riding	242	5	2.1	9	3.7	18	7.4	101	41.7
West Riding	356	14	3.9	26	7.3	37	10.4	119	33.4
Lancashire	298	4	1.3	11	3.7	15	5.0	61	20.5
All areas	1,152	29	2.5	66	5.7	109	9.5	392	34.0

Source C. R. Humphery-Smith (ed.), *Phillimore Atlas and Index of Parish Registers* (Chichester, 1984).

The apparent correlation between the proportions of surviving registers evident from the three ridings of Yorkshire and all of Lancashire, and the relative prevalence of recusancy in these areas is striking. It is generally accepted that recusancy was least evident in the East Riding of Yorkshire, but it was more prevalent in the North and far more so in the West Ridings.[33] However, the key area of English recusancy in the sixteenth century was Lancashire.[34] This ranking appears to reflect the relative absence of parish registers in the Elizabethan period. Survival is best in the East Riding (with over 43 per cent) and worst in Lancashire (with just over 20 per cent). It is therefore tempting to conclude that the

32 W. J. Sheils, *Archbishop Grindal's Visitation 1575: Comperta et Detecta Book*, Borthwick Texts and Calendars: Records of the Northern Province 4 (York, 1977), p. 3.
33 J. C. H. Aveling, *Post-Reformation Catholicism in East Yorkshire 1558–1790* (privately printed, 1960), his *Northern Catholics: The Catholic Recusants of the North Riding of Yorkshire* (London, 1966) and his *The Catholic Recusants of the West Riding of Yorkshire 1558–1790* (privately printed, 1963).
34 Haigh, *Reformation and Resistance*, p. 264.

survival rate of registers can act as a rule of thumb for the progress of the English Reformation in the north. While such a conclusion would be highly tenuous it can be argued that these figures reflect the ability of the authorities to penetrate and regulate the recording of religious rites of passage in Yorkshire and Lancashire. The evidence suggests that not until towards the end of Elizabeth's reign did the systematic recording of these events become in any way generally operative in this part of England. Even by then, only around a third of parishes can be seen to have co-operated.

IV

Evidently the authorities failed to ensure that registers were kept in all local communities. This raises the issue of how successful they were in dictating the form of the records. In a survey of 368 Yorkshire and ninety-five Lancashire registers in the period 1538 to 1700 all the sets examined appear to contain the minimal information required by injunctions – the names of infants, at least one (usually male) parent, marriage partners, and the dead. There is also some evidence that these requirements were adhered to when the records underwent their only significant (and temporary) alteration to include also the names of godparents. As can be seen from Table 6.2, of sixty-six registers in the sample examined which are extant for this period, seven recorded the identities of baptismal sponsors systematically for the reign. One (South Cave) was in the East Riding of Yorkshire, but the remainder (Horton in Ribblesdale, Halifax, Kirkburton, Rotherham, Ledsham, and Robert Staynton's parish of Almondbury) were all in the West Riding.[35] However, this small number of cases is hardly evidence that the new injunctions were universally enforced, with none being evident from the North Riding or Lancashire. The absence of godparents in registers from these areas, and in particular from Lancashire, implies that godparenthood was not necessarily associated with religious conservatism. It is possible that such habits of recording had more to do with effective administration or record survival.

---

35 Borthwick Institute, Parish Register of Rotherham (facsimile); NYCRO, Parish Registers of Horton in Ribblesdale, ref. 494; S. J. Chadwick (ed.), *The Parish Registers of South Cave, Co. York (1898)*; J. W. Clay (ed.), *The Parish Registers of Ledsham in the County of York*, YPRS 26 (privately printed, 1906); F. A. Collins (ed.), *The Parish Register of Kirkburton, Co. York* (2 vols, Exeter, 1887), i; E. W. Crossley (ed.), *The Parish Registers of Halifax, Co. Yorkshire* 1: *1538–1593*, YPRS 37 (privately printed, 1910); G. Guest (ed.), *The Parish Registers of Rotherham 1556–1563* (privately printed, 1879) and Taylor (ed.), *Parish Registers of Almondbury*, 1.

Table 6.2 *The recording of godparents in Yorkshire and Lancashire parish registers extant for the period 1553–58*

Region	No. of extant registers	Godparents not recorded		Godparents recorded	
		No.	%	No.	%
East Riding (including York)	20	19	95	1	5
North Riding	9	9	100	0	0
West Riding	26	20	77	6	23
Lancashire	11	11	100	0	0
All areas	66	59	89	7	11

Sources Parish registers from Borthwick Institute; LDA; MDCLW; NYCRO; registers printed by the Yorkshire and Lancashire Parish Register Societies and six privately printed registers.

Several registers continued to record the names of godparents long after the government ceased to require that information to be kept. Three registers (Almondbury, South Cave, and Ledsham) did so for a number of years after it had become legally unnecessary. More surprisingly eleven appear to have begun keeping such records during the reign of Elizabeth. Again Ledsham, having abandoned the practice in 1568, resumed it from 1590 until 1606. In this category of register there is some evidence of loss of data from the records. Unusually, the register of the parish of St Margaret in York survives in two versions.[36] One was written on paper and, although it does not begin until 1590, is probably one volume of the original register, giving the names of godparents until 1614. The second is a neater version on parchment starting in 1558, but with no mention of god-parents. Given the dates and material used in this second version, it almost certainly reflects the influence of the later injunctions on the copying of registers. The chance survival of the St Margaret's paper register implies that the injunctions ordering the copying of registers on to parchment may well have resulted in the loss of a considerable amount of such information, and yet, contrary to the assumptions of some modern historians, significant records of godparenthood in early modern England do survive.[37]

The existence of lengthy and detailed records of the identities of godparents provide a window of empirical evidence on relationships

36 York, Borthwick Institute, Parish Registers of St Margaret's, York, Y/Marg 1 and 2. Chester Waters, *Parish Registers*, p. 10, cites a similar survival for Staplehurst, Kent.

37 D. Cressy, 'Kinship and kin interaction in early modern England', *PaP*, 113 (1986), 66.

created through baptism in sixteenth-century England. Until 1534 such spiritual ties carried similar incest prohibitions to those associated with kinship though blood or marriage and thus the bonds of godparenthood have often been described as a form of 'fictive' or 'spiritual' kinship.[38] Parish registers can illuminate popular religious practice as theology shifted throughout the English Reformation. Changes were reflected in the choices of baptismal sponsors and the naming of children. As a record, registers allow a unique insight into the interplay between religion and social life in the parishes of sixteenth-century England.[39]

The case of godparenthood indicates that parish registers did not, and do not, contain only the information specified by the authorities of Church and state. This can be seen in the other rites of passage of the English Church. No sixteenth-century register in the sample recorded details of confirmations.[40] Because the ceremony was an irregular occurrence dependent on the presence of a bishop, it was arguably less likely to be noted in the registers than events and circumstances associated with baptism, marriage, and burial. However, there are a handful of references to 'communicants', such as the list of gentry for 1574–78 given in the register of St Michael Le Belfry in York.[41]

Another case in point is the rite of the purification or thanksgiving of a woman after childbirth, popularly known as the 'churching of women'.[42] One register in the sample, Preston in Lancashire, did contain such records for the period 1611 to 1619.[43] Less systematic references can be found in the sixteenth-century register of Kirkburton in the West Riding of Yorkshire.[44] Entries of this kind are perhaps more likely to survive from the latter years of Elizabeth's reign and into the early seventeenth century. In this period there was a growing debate between Puritans and conservatives over the validity of the ceremony and its maintenance, which became part of the wider divisions evident under Archbishop Laud.[45]

38 S. Wolfram, *In-laws and Outlaws: Kinship and Marriage in England* (London, 1988), p. 23, and J. Goody, *The Character of Kinship* (Cambridge, 1974), pp. 168–71.
39 W. Coster, 'Kinship and Community in Yorkshire 1500–1700' (D. Phil., University of York, 1992), pp. 181–217.
40 Cox, *Parish Registers*, p. 42, cites a few instances.
41 F. Collins (ed.), *The Parish Register of St Michael Le Belfry, York*, 1: *1565–1653*, YPRS (privately printed, 1899), pp. 102–3.
42 W. Coster, 'Purity, profanity and Puritanism: the churching of women 1500–1700', in D. Wood (ed.), *Women in the Church*, SCH 27 (Oxford, 1990), pp. 377–87; D. Cressy, 'Purification, thanksgiving and the churching of women in post-Reformation England', *PaP*, 141 (1993), 106–46; A. Wilson, 'The ceremony of childbirth and its interpretation', in V. Fildes (ed.), *Women as Mothers in Pre-industrial England: Essays in Memory of Dorothy McLaren* (London, 1990), pp. 88–97.
43 A. H. Hodder and M. B. Stafford (eds), *The Register of Preston, Lancashire, 1611–1635*, Lancashire Parish Register Society 48 (privately printed, 1913), pp. 1–80.
44 Collins (ed.), *Parish Register of Kirkburton*.
45 Coster, 'Purity, profanity and Puritanism', pp. 383–4, and Cressy, 'Churching of women', 107.

Parish registers can be used to assess the effectiveness of attempts to make the ceremony part of the communal Sunday service and to move it away from the ritual gap of one month after childbirth, which may have been the norm in the pre-Reformation period.[46]

Another interesting feature of the baptismal records of Kirkburton is the references to the burial of 'chrisom children', between 1568 and 1710, on what appears to be a regular basis.[47] Historians have tended to disagree over what a chrisom child was.[48] Clearly such children took their name from the white 'chrisom cloth' in which they were wrapped during the ceremony, and ultimately from the chrism oil used to anoint them. What is unclear is whether they were infants dying before baptism, or between baptism and their mother's churching, when the cloth was returned to the church. Understanding the exact meaning of the term is important for an analysis of infant mortality, but it also has implications for the study of popular religion. The evidence of Kirkburton suggests that the definition changed during the sixteenth century. This can be seen from a comparison of the baptisms and burials of such children, which indicate a shift of definition from meaning baptised infants to the unbaptised.[49] The significance of this change lies in the symbolism of the white chrisom cloth in which a very young child was buried, implying a state of innocence at death. This phenomenon may be connected with the Church's attempt to delay baptism until the first Sunday after birth – making it, like churching, a communal event.[50] This must have meant that a greater number of children died before baptism, undermining the role of the rite in salvation. In a similar way contemporary Protestant theologians denied the necessity of baptism for salvation.[51] In these circumstances what may be evident here is an important psychological shift for bereaved parents. In redefining innocence they removed their unbaptised children from the state of original sin, or even demonic

---

46 Coster, 'Purity, profanity and Puritanism', p. 385.
47 Collins (ed.), Parish Register of Kirkburton.
48 E.g. M. Drake, 'Introduction', *Population Studies from Parish Registers: A Selection of Readings from Local Population Studies* (Matlock, 1982), p. xxii; E. Morrison, 'Comment', *Local Population Studies*, 32 (1984), 61–2; and J. J. Greenwood, 'Letter', *Local Population Studies*, 33 (1984), 71.
49 Collins (ed.), *Parish Register of Kirkburton*. During the 1580s chrisom children noted in the burial register ceased to be named and were described by the use of their parents' names, implying that they were unnamed and thus unbaptised. In addition a falling proportion of 'chrisom children' buried can be traced to a preceding baptism. Over 25 per cent can be so traced in the period 1569 to 1591, but under 4 per cent between 1638 and 1660. These data suggest that this is the tail end of a change of definition, but such a hypothesis can be tested only if similar registers for an earlier period are found.
50 D. M. Berry and R. S. Schofield, 'Age at baptism in pre-industrial England', *Local Population Studies*, 25 (1971), 453–66.
51 G. W. Bromiley, *Baptism and the Anglican Reformers* (London, 1953), pp. 122–7.

possession, which implied an after-life in limbo and even hell.[52] The new understanding, in contrast, meant that they were already fit for heaven.

Additional information of this kind is clearly more likely to have been recorded where it was simply an expansion of the basic framework of baptisms, marriages, and burials. For example, the register of St Michael Le Belfry in York identified several of the children christened as foundlings.[53] Abandonment of children in this way has been seen as an indication of the impact on social life of poverty and concepts of illegitimacy.[54] The number of children left on the doorstep of the church may in part be taken as an indication of the high status of members of a parish, which in this case included many eminent clerics. In this respect St Michael's appears to have fulfilled something of the role undertaken by Dionis Backchurch and the Middle Temple in London.[55] Children in the respective London parishes were most likely to be named Dennis Backchurch or given the surname Temple; in York the name Michael Belfry was relatively common. In a similar way the early seventeenth-century register of All Saints Pavement in York recorded the locations of burials within the church between 1643 and 1792.[56] These indicate how, in this prosperous urban parish, hierarchy and family were reflected not only in the seating arrangements of the living but also in death. Other early seventeenth-century registers include similar additional information. One example is Dewsbury in the West Riding, where the records list details, not only of the rites of passage that took place, but also the times at which the ceremonies were held.[57] Together these registers suggest that the process of standardisation of the record was not complete by the end of the sixteenth century.

More anecdotal information can also be found, and this is perhaps in many ways the most revealing material for understanding the concerns, ideas, and priorities of sixteenth-century people. Eamon Duffy has recently drawn attention to the way in which churchwardens' accounts may be used as an indicator of religious conviction in the turbulent central

52 K. V. Thomas, *Religion and the Decline of Magic: Studies in Popular Beliefs in Sixteenth- and Seventeenth-Century England* (London, 1971), p. 40.

53 Collins (ed.), *Parish Register of St Michael Le Belfry*.

54 V. Fildes, 'Maternal feelings reassessed: child abandonment and neglect in London and Westminster 1550–1800', in Fildes (ed.), *Women as Mothers in Pre-industrial England*, pp. 139–78.

55 J. L. Chester (ed.), *The Parish Register Booke of Saynte De'nis Backchurch (City of London) 1538–1754*, Harleian Society 3 (London, 1878), pp. 80, 99, 101; and G. D. Squib, *The Register of the Temple Church, London*, Harleian Society (London, 1979).

56 T. M. Fisher (ed.), *The Parish Registers of All Saints Church Pavement, in the City of York, 1554–1690*, YPRS 100 (privately printed, 1934), and his *The Parish Registers of All Saints Church Pavement, in the City of York, 1690–1738*, YPRS 102 (privately printed, 1936).

57 S. J. Chadwick (ed.), *The Parish Registers of Dewsbury* (privately printed, 1898).

decades of the sixteenth century.[58] In a more limited way parish registers contain similar statements of religious sentiment. Perhaps the most detailed in the country is from the parish of Much Wenlock in Shropshire. Unfortunately the original register has been lost and only printed extracts now survive.[59] They do, however, give something of an indication of the impact of the Reformation and reactions to it in one sixteenth-century parish. The vicar, Sir Thomas Butler (or Boteler), began his paper register with an entry for 26 November 1538, presumably in response to Cromwell's first injunction. It ends in 1562, having continued throughout the oscillations of religious practice in between. There is little doubt that he regarded the progress of reform with a less than welcoming gaze. Butler's attitudes must also be understood in light of the fact that his living, when he first obtained it, belonged to the neighbouring monastery of St Milburga at Wenlock. The first entry of his register suggests something of the ties between parish and monastery. For 21 January 1538/39 Butler noted that he acted as a godparent in baptism and that among his 'gossibs' (or co-godparents) was one of the monks of the monastery.[60] In the same year he mentions the baptism of children of both the brewer to the monastery and the servant of the Prior. This close relationship between parish community and monastic institution was, however, soon to be ended. One of the first entries of 1539 observed without comment, 'The Monastery of Wenlock surrendered on the morrow of the feast of the Conversion of St Paul.'[61] Thus Butler's community was among those most directly affected by the progress of the Henrician Reformation in England.

Over the next eight years the registers suggest that Butler carried out his parochial duties, at least as far as baptism, marriages, burials, and the mass were concerned. He also noted some extraordinary events such as the deaths of several octogenarians and the execution of numerous felons. Clearly he protected the role of his 'mother church of the Holy Trinity of Much Wenlock' as the centre of local religion, over and against the claims of the chapels of the area.[62] But one has a sense of the grinding effect of time and mortality on the old religion in his many references to the burials of former clerics from the dissolved monastery. In late 1547 he noted cataclysmic burning of numerous images from local churches and the relics of St Milburga.[63] But one also gets a retrospective view of

58 Duffy, *Stripping of the Altars*, pp. 497–503.
59 C. H. Hartshorne, 'Extracts from the register of Sir Thomas Butler, vicar of Much Wenlock in Shropshire', *Cambrian Journal*, 4 (1861), 81–98, and W. A. Leighton, 'The register of Sir Thomas Butler, vicar of Much Wenlock', *Transactions of the Shropshire Archaeological and Natural History Society*, 6 (1883), 93–132.
60 Hartshorne, 'Extracts from the register of Sir Thomas Butler', 83.
61 *Ibid.*, 83.
62 *Ibid.*, 85.
63 *Ibid.*, 91.

religious life in the period before the Reformation. Butler refers intriguingly to John Chistoke or Seltocke, who had died of the pestilence on 1 September 1532, 'an honest server of the Churrch and taught scolars playne song & prick song full well so that the churche was well served in his time', and 'who gaf unto this Churche with the consent of Julanne his wif in their lyf tyme a crosse of Copor gilt and a Banner with a ymage of the trnite of Silke'.[64]

The clearest indications of attitudes to religious change, however, derive from the contrasting records Butler made on hearing of the deaths of the three monarchs that occurred in the period. On 5 February 1546/47 he noted that 'word and knowledge came hither to this borough of Much Wenlock that our Sovereign Lord King Henry the 8th was departed out of this transitory life, whose soul God almighty pardon'.[65] It may be an error to take the implication of a need for forgiveness as a criticism. However, the brevity of the obituary contrasts sharply with the 384 words Butler lavished on Sir William Covehill, priest, who died the following May.[66] Covehill is described as an expert in the liberal arts, in masonry, organ and clock making, carving, weaving silk, painting, the mending of musical instruments, and even bell-founding. He goes on, 'and many good gifts the man had, and a very paciant man, and full honeste in his conversation and lyving ...'.[67] It is perhaps no surprise to find that Covehill had formerly been a monk at Much Wenlock Priory.

Butler's mention of the death of Edward VI was even briefer than that of Henry VIII. Far more significant for him was the subsequent accession of Mary I. His joy was undisguised, and he makes it clear that others shared this attitude:

at Bridgenorth in the fair, there was proclaimed Lady Mary Queen of England, &c., after which proclamation finished the people made great joy, casting up their caps and hats, lauding, thanking and praising God Almighty with ringing of bells and making Bonfires in every street.[68]

Butler's pleasure at the change of regime appears to have been largely religious in nature. Just as he had noted the gradual erosion of the Catholic faith under Henry VIII and Edward VI, he now observed the gradual return of the old religion. On 7 October 1553 he recorded that the first child had been christened 'in the Latyne tongue by the booke called the Manuale', and on the last day of the same month he noted the use of the Latin service after the Sarum rite for the first burial of a child since Mary's coronation.[69]

---

64 *Ibid.*, 87.
65 *Ibid.*, 89.
66 *Ibid.*, 89–90.
67 *Ibid.*, 90.
68 *Ibid.*, 93.
69 *Ibid.*, 93.

So the process continued until St Catherine's Day 1558, when, ironically, on his way to conduct mass, Butler was stopped by the Sheriff of Salop.[70] The later had just come from London with news of the death of Mary and the accession of Elizabeth. The sheriff instructed Butler to come down after the offertory to the body of the Church,

and to the people here being should say these words in open audience and loud voice. Friends you should pray for the prosperous estate of our most noble Queen Elizabeth, by the Grace of God queen of England France and Ireland, defender of the faith, and for this I desire you every man and women to say that Pater Noster with ave maria.[71]

After mass had been said the sheriff went out with the congregation and in the market place had the crier proclaim Elizabeth as queen. Butler continues to give details of how the accession of Elizabeth was secured in Wenlock. The Sunday after next a deputation of local notables approached Butler and 'willed' him to repeat the same declaration with a few additions.[72] He then announced an afternoon bonfire and the distribution of bread, cheese, and drink to the poor. After this detailed narrative the register continues, as before, to note rites of passage, but one more entry illuminates the swing of the religious pendulum. On 25 June 1559 he noted that 'it is to be had in remembrence that the celebration of the devine Service in the English Tongue was begun this day in crastino Nativiat S^{ti} Joh^{is} bapt.'[73] Butler's register ends in 1562, and it is difficult not to feel he died a disappointed man.

The Much Wenlock register is a quite exceptional document. It contains not only a great deal of additional information, but long passages describing what the incumbent saw as significant events. Both these elements go towards creating a picture of attitudes to changing religious practice in the 'crisis' years of the mid-sixteenth century. But although the detail in Butler's register is perhaps unparalleled, the act of recording (systematically and anecdotally) additional information in parish registers appears to have been relatively frequent. Like Butler, Robert Staynton of Almondbury had the same interest in the fate of his parishioners. Beside the tragic death of Agnes Littlewood, Staynton recorded another suicide, three murders, six accidental deaths, the names of schoolboys, three irregular baptisms, and five burials at night.[74] Like Butler he notes the first celebration of holy communion in 1559.[75] Other registers contain even more idiosyncratic information. The register of Bilton in Ainsty notes unusual events, scrawled on the inside of the front cover, such as

70 *Ibid.*, 95–6.
71 *Ibid.*, 96.
72 *Ibid.*, 96.
73 *Ibid.*, 98.
74 H. Taylor (ed.), *Parish Registers of Almondbury*.
75 *Ibid.*, p. 8.

the fall of the bells from the tower in the seventeenth century, while that of St Margaret, York, contains two pages of poetry on the history of the city and details of legal disputes between local burgesses.[76]

Some of this information appears trivial, but other elements are highly revealing of the nature of sixteenth-century parish life. The existence of both types of information raises the issue of why it was included in what should have been a formal record of three rites of passage. These registers suggest that, for many incumbents, the line between an official and an informal record, and between a communal chronicle and a personal one, was blurred. Many diaries of the period originated as the financial accounts of an individual or an estate, but once the record had been established the habit of noting other information transformed the document. It appears that, at one extreme, parish registers could turn into personal chronicles. Other registers, in contrast, even when containing much superfluous information, remained records of the life of a community, with little evidence of personal input or bias.

An additional factor that should not be overlooked is confusion amongst the parochial clergy concerning what exactly they were expected to record. Even allowing for the loss of original paper registers, it appears unlikely from the sample of Yorkshire and Lancashire parishes that anything resembling a majority recorded the identities of godparents in the period when it was required. On the other hand, a number did so when it was no longer necessary. This gap between theory and practice may well simply reveal ignorance about what exactly a parish register was meant to be. The most common point of orientation must have been previous practice. In the Yorkshire registers examined, the period in which there were references to godparents often coincided with the incumbency of a particular clergyman. This was the case with George Thompson at St Margaret's, York, between 1590 and 1614.[77] However, after the death of Robert Staynton at Almondbury in 1598 the register continued to record godparents and make other observations for another three years.[78] The most revealing example is that of Bilton in Ainsty, where references began in 1571 with the arrival of Sir William Lambert as vicar.[79] Lambert's register is written in a good hand and carefully divided into three parts, with a page for baptisms that also gives the names of godparents and one page for both marriages and burials. Thus (since entries of baptisms took up roughly twice the space needed for marriages and burials) the three parts of the register stay roughly parallel in chronology. After his death his successor Thomas Belwood continued

76 Borthwick Institute, Parish Registers of Bilton in Ainsty, Bil. 1 and Parish Registers of St Margaret's, York.
77 Borthwick Institute, Parish Registers of St Margaret's, York, fos 1–30.
78 Taylor (ed.), *Parish Registers of Almondbury*, 2: *1598–1601*, pp. 1–27.
79 Borthwick Institute, Parish Registers of Bilton in Ainsty, Bil. 1, f. 1.

the practice until the end of the page, but then divided each single page into three with far from straight vertical lines. As a result, baptisms raced ahead of marriages and burials and the register became extremely untidy and unbalanced. It was probably for this reason that Belwood stopped recording the identities of godparents in 1607. In both these cases it appears that the model of what should be in a register was the existing register and if no model existed clergy may well have simply recorded what they felt appropriate.

Despite the injunctions that they should be read publicly, it is not certain that the congregation at large knew the content of the registers. Additionally, unlike churchwardens' accounts, they were not audited or checked by representatives of the community, and as a result much of the additional information may not be comprehensive. Furthermore, comparisons with the pre-Reformation period are limited by the fact that so few registers survive from before 1538. Nevertheless, as this chapter attempts to indicate, like churchwardens' accounts they are an important source of information on popular religion. Particularly, perhaps, if they are used in conjunction with churchwardens' accounts and if all the additional information is compiled on a nation-wide basis.

It is also possible to suggest that the nature of the registers themselves was undergoing considerable change throughout the early modern period. Additional information, for instance, appears to be increasingly rare in the registers. Of the twenty-four Yorkshire sets systematically recording godparents in the sixteenth and seventeenth centuries, sixteen were doing so in the second half of the sixteenth century, fourteen in the first half of the seventeenth, but only four between the Interregnum and the end of the century and only three in the late seventeenth century. The registers of the later seventeenth century appear more regular, perhaps in some ways more reliable, but containing less information than those of the sixteenth. As a source for popular religious feeling and practice, it appears that the parish register enjoyed its heyday between about 1550 and 1650.

Their period, of course, was also marked by a major transformation of the English parish. The Cromwellian injunctions of the 1530s greatly influenced the duties of the parish as a centre of civil and religious administration. Over the next seven decades, as a by-product of the Reformation, the parish elite gained responsibility for the administration of charity, for taxation, and for recording the comings and goings of people, while retaining its position as the religious heart of the community. During and after the first Civil War this dual role was disrupted in many areas. Nonconformity created alternative religious centres, which, although they may not have been significant in numerical terms, were important in removing a virtual religious monopoly. Just as this affected the unity of religion, so too the parish register began to lose its role as the authoritative record of the life cycle of the community.

In many ways, for a brief period when religious change was at its most furious, the parish register can provide a window into popular religious practice and belief. But the same process of change, coupled with the increasing standardisation of the records, means that this window is a small one and later registers cannot be put to the same uses. Thus the development of the parish register was linked with the rise and fall of the post-Reformation parish, and the development of a unified system of local record-keeping reflects the fortunes of the English parish in the turbulent years after the separation from Rome.

PART III

Community action and expectation

Parochial fund-raising in late medieval Somerset

Maintaining the parish church – its nave, churchyard, and liturgical items – was the laity's responsibility. To meet these needs parishioners developed different fund-raising strategies. Comparing these strategies exposes some of the differences between communities, showing that financial obligations were not just another burden imposed on the laity by a remote clergy, but an expression of local, communal, and spiritual expectations. Membership was not simply coercive and burdensome; the parish was a meaningful forum for collective action dependent upon and informed by local resources and needs. The financial demands of maintaining a parish were too large and too important to depend solely on parishioners' occasional generosity. Altars needed candles, sacred images required repainting, and priests – for the often numerous side altars – demanded salaries and vestments. The community thus needed more permanent and reliable ways of providing a steady flow of income.[2] The specific methods of fund-raising growing out of these demands were largely at the community's discretion. They used shrewd advertising and peer pressure and exploited popular activities and community concerns.[3] A parish could thus use its financial strategies to situate itself within the larger experiences of the English Church. Fund-raising became a means of integrating individuals into the community of the parish and commenting on official religious policy.

The sociology of fund-raising allows us to expand our notion of religious culture. Parish participation involved much more than receiving the sacraments or attending the liturgy. Never far from any parish project was the idea that it was for God and the Church. A pious bequest could

1 A previous version of this chapter was given at the First International Medieval Congress at Leeds. I want to thank the archivists at the Somerset Record Office for their help during my research, and Barbara Hanawalt and Edmund Kern for their advice during various stages of this project. Financial support was provided by the Department of History at the University of Minnesota, the London School of Economics, and a Charlotte W. Newcombe Doctoral Dissertation Fellowship.
2 Charles Drew, *Early Parochial Organisation in England: The Origin of the Office of Churchwarden*, St Anthony Hall Publications 7 (York, 1954), pp. 10–11.
3 Edmund Hobhouse (ed.), *Churchwardens' Accounts for the Parishes of Croscombe, Pilton, Yatton, Tintinhull, Morebath and St Michael's Bath*, Somerset Record Society 4 (Taunton, 1890), pp. xii–xiii.

help ease a soul out of purgatory.[4] The parish's financial needs, thus, become a field of expression for religion understood as local practice, rather than simply an expression of Church doctrine or polity.

One way of assessing the range of fund-raising practices and the implications of such variation is to look at one diocese. For the diocese of Bath and Wells, roughly contiguous with the medieval county of Somerset, there are pre-Reformation churchwardens' accounts still surviving from twenty parishes. They are of varying quality and come from a variety of parishes throughout the diocese – large and small, urban and rural. The accounts show that in these parishes financial support came from a combination of individual donations and larger planned strategies. There were essentially five categories of fund-raising: gifts, rents, sales, collections, and entertainment, with each one employing its own set of administrative concerns. On its own, this taxonomy oversimplifies any understanding of parochial fund-raising; the categories are not always distinct, and they do not account for any unusual circumstances that both required or brought in money.[5] By considering the geographical, social, or economic context of these strategies, we can add to this taxonomy and explore how fulfilling episcopal requirements to maintain the parish church also created a unique local religious culture that drew upon the local setting. Most pronounced are the differences between urban and rural parishes.[6] These differences allow us to see how each local economy created, and was created by, the particular social and religious expectations of the parishioners. How parishes raised money helped define the roles that they played in the community.

The type of expense also influenced a community's annual fund-raising. Each year brought a variety of regular and irregular financial demands. Parishioners needed to supply the numerous candles and oil for the many altars, along with ensuring that someone did the cleaning, decorating, and repairing. The laity sought not only to repair their churches but to embellish and expand them, and an unexpected disaster, such as a tree falling on the church roof, could strain even the largest budget. Any given year combined both the usual fund-raising methods and attempts to meet unforeseen expenses. Contextualising the five

4 Clive Burgess, 'The benefactions of mortality: the lay response in the late medieval urban parish', in D. Smith (ed.), *Studies in Clergy and Ministry in Medieval England*, Borthwick Studies in History 1 (York, 1991), pp. 65–86.

5 Warren O. Ault, 'Manor court and parish church in fifteenth-century England: a study of village by-laws', *Speculum*, 42 (1967), 53–67. Ault discusses manorial regulations that turned over to the parish church part of the fines collected by the manorial court. There are a few examples in Somerset, but they are infrequent and do not appear to be a regular part of parish income. See CWA Tintinhull: Somerset RO, D/P/tin 4/1/1, f. 2.

6 Andrew Brown, *Popular Piety in Late Medieval England: The Diocese of Salisbury 1250–1550* (Oxford, 1995), pp. 83–91.

categories of fund-raising methods shows that parish communities had a sense of financial planning and were often able to accommodate the changes in needs that confronted them.

Variations between parish fund-raising strategies not only help characterise the socio-economic nature of the community, but they frequently distinguished one parish from another in the eyes of contemporaries. Fund-raising brought the laity together in different ways for a common goal. Many activities specifically planned as fund-raisers also fostered neighbourliness, shared experiences, and spiritual well-being that added to a sense of community membership and local identity.

Individual donations, given at death or as an act of piety, are the most ubiquitous, but erratic of the fund-raising categories. All Somerset parishes depended on them to some degree, but the corporate strategies of fund-raising provide the clearest examples of local expectations for parishes. Corporate strategies determined the duties of the parish's churchwardens, many of the community's activities, and the relationship between members and the institution of the parish. Some strategies involved the whole community, others were left in the hands of the wardens. In this chapter I will look at the four main categories of corporate fund-raising in more detail: (I) the sale of church goods, (II) leases of parish property, (III) collections, and (IV) communal entertainments.[7]

I

Focusing on the differences between urban and rural parishes of Bath and Wells shows that the latter employed a greater number of fund-raising strategies and did so in ways that not only aided the parish but benefited the parishioners. Rural parishes had fewer resources and relied on a greater variety of activities to raise money that directly involved the parishioners in parish affairs. Conversely, town parishes, such as those in Bath, Glastonbury, Bridgwater, and suburban Bristol, had greater resources and relied less on direct parishioner participation as a means of raising money.[8]

Selling goods was not a constant feature of any parish's annual receipts; it depended largely on what the wardens or parishioners had available for sale, which in turn usually depended on the donations and bequests accumulated throughout the year. However, the large town parishes did not sell things on the same scale as their rural counterparts. The reasons seem related, in part, to the ways that individuals remembered their parishes in their testamentary bequests. With the greater availability of cash in the towns, urban parishioners left money to their

---

7 Katherine L. French, 'Local Identity and the Late Medieval Parish: the Communities of Bath and Wells' (Ph.D., University of Minnesota, 1993), pp. 80–142.
8 Clive Burgess and Beat Kümin, 'Penitential bequests and parish regimes in late medieval England', *Journal of Ecclesiastical History*, 44 (1993), 622–5.

churches, whereas rural ones tended to receive goods such as clothing, jewellery, livestock, and tools.[9] Unless the items received were immediately appropriate to the church, the churchwardens were obliged to sell them, making the parish a clearing house for goods that other members might find useful. The accounts for Tintinhull, Yatton, and Croscombe regularly report money received from selling donated goods. In 1479 the wardens of Tintinhull sold a gown left as a bequest for 5s.[10] The same year, the Yatton wardens sold for 12d. a sheep left to them by the will of one Margaret Knight.[11] Holding on to unnecessary goods and livestock cost money, since gift items had to be stored and animals had to be fed.

Churchwardens also sold off old furnishings. This not only made some money for the church but solved the problem of disposing of old materials. When Tintinhull built its new pews, it sold the old ones for 5s. 4d.[12] In Yatton, where fifty years of accounts are concerned with expanding the nave, the wardens regularly sold limestone, lead, old boards, nails, and even the old church doors and gate.[13]

What parishes sold generally reflected the local economy. The churchwardens of Trull supplemented their income by selling apples and grass gathered in the churchyard, while Pilton and Tintinhull parishes owned some milk cows.[14] Sales of cattle appear regularly at the beginning of the Tintinhull accounts but gradually become less important, disappearing altogether after 1453. During a good year, such as 1441–42, the livestock brought them 8s. 8d. (but the possibility of sterility and death apparently made animals an uncertain investment).[15] Although clearly not an important revenue source, even the city parish of St Michael's in Bath had a flock of sheep. In 1504 the wardens sold 2 lb of wool for 8d.[16]

While town parishes did not generally market goods, they often sold seats or pews. Most parish churches had no permanent seats until the fifteenth or sixteenth centuries, but even with the introduction of pews, they still do not figure in all accounts.[17] The country parishes of Tintinhull, Yatton, Banwell, and Trull had seats installed, but the accounts never

---

9 Christopher Dyer, *Standards of Living in the Later Middle Ages: Social Change in England* c. *1200–1520* (Cambridge, 1989), pp. 178–87.

10 CWA Tintinhull: Somerset RO, D/P/tin 4/1/1, f. 57.

11 CWA Yatton: *ibid.*, D/P/yat 4/1/1, f. 143.

12 CWA Tintinhull: *ibid.*, D/P/tin 4/1/1, f. 96.

13 CWA Yatton: *ibid.*, D/P/yat 4/1/1, fos 52, 61, 69, 80, 88.

14 CWA Trull: *ibid.*, DD/CT 77, fos 20, 56; CWA Pilton: *ibid.*, D/P/pilt 4/1/1, f. 24, *passim*; CWA Tintinhull: *ibid.*, D/P/tin 4/1/1, fos 1, 2, *passim*.

15 *Ibid.*, D/P/tin 4/1/1, fos 23–5, 8–16.

16 CWA Bath: *ibid.*, D/P/mi. ba 4/1/1, no. 50.

17 Margaret Aston, 'Segregation in church', in W. J. Sheils and Diana Wood (eds), *Women and the Church*, SCH 27 (Oxford, 1990), pp. 264–6; J. Charles Cox, *Churchwardens' Accounts from the Fourteenth Century to the Close of the Seventeenth Century* (London, 1913), pp. 186–7.

record them as earning the parish any income.[18] Of the twenty parishes for which there are records, only the larger, relatively urbanised communities of Bath, Bridgwater, Glastonbury, Ilminster, Yeovil, and St Thomas in Bristol sold seats.[19] They never constituted a major source of income, appearing more as a convenience offered to those who could pay than as a serious attempt to increase revenue.[20]

Care for the goods to be sold required extra work on the wardens' part. Either they had to collect the items for sale, or they had to find someone else to do it. If the parish was in a position to own livestock or farm land, the same concerns prevailed. Either the wardens had to tend the land or animals or they had to hire another individual to do so.

II

Leasing property, services, or goods was a more common way of raising money. As with selling goods, the items a parish leased helped to determine the churchwardens' duties and the parish's position within the community. Property ownership turned churchwardens into *de facto* landlords. They spent time negotiating leases, collecting rents, fixing houses, and dealing with the problems associated with being a landlord. Those parishes with only a few fields or tenements used rents as just one of many income sources, thus diversifying the wardens' duties.[21] Comparatively few parishes in Bath and Wells owned enough property to make rental income the major source of revenue. Those that did were the city or large town parishes of St Michael's, Bath; St Mary's, Bridgwater; St John's, Glastonbury; and the suburban Bristol parishes of St Mary Redcliffe and St Thomas. Burgage tenure, practised only in boroughs, made it much easier for the parish to own property which the wardens then rented out on behalf of the community.[22] St Michael's, Bath, began acquiring property before the extant records and it continued to do so throughout the late medieval period. In the first account of 1349 the

18 The medieval seats still survive in Trull. They were built in 1527 (CWA Trull: Somerset RO, DD/CT 77, f. 11). In Yatton the wardens had seats installed in 1454 (CWA Yatton: *ibid.*, D/P/yat 4/4/1, f. 38) and in Tintinhull they were built between 1511 and 1513 (CWA Tintinhull: *ibid.*, D/P/tin 4/1/1, fos 95–6). For further examples see Peter Poyntz Wright, *The Rural Benchends of Somerset* (Amersham, 1983).

19 Anecdotal evidence, however, suggests that selling seats was not exclusively limited to town parishes. There is a pew dispute from the coastal parish of Minehead tried in the Star Chamber Court. The petition states that it was the custom for residents to buy their pews. PRO, STAC 2/12/224–6.

20 This is not the case for all parishes. The accounts for St Edmund in Wiltshire show that seats became an important way for the parish to raise money. In 1484–85 the wardens received 10s. 6d. Cox, *Churchwardens' Accounts*, p. 67.

21 Ault, 'The village church', 211–12.

22 Susan Reynolds, *An Introduction to the History of English Medieval Towns* (Oxford, 1977), p. 93.

parish earned 5s. 9½d. in old rents and 10s. 9d. in new ones. The acquisition of new properties meant that by 1400 the annual income from rents had increased to £6 6s. 8d. and by 1503 to £11 19s. 8d. After 1380 the parish earned between 60 per cent and 100 per cent of its income from rents.[23]

St Mary's in the borough of Bridgwater also increased its reliance on rents, but not to the same extent as St Michael's. As the parishioners lost interest in contributing to their annual collection, the wardens began acquiring rental property. From 1428 rents are a regular feature of the accounts, though their significance to the overall income is never more than about 50 per cent.[24] St John's, Glastonbury, seems to have earned upwards of 80 per cent of its income from its rents as early as the fourteenth century.[25] Similarly, the suburban parishes outside Bristol, St Thomas and St Mary Redcliffe, supported themselves largely through rents.

The smaller borough parishes of Stogursey and Yeovil also owned land, but on a much more limited scale. Some time between 1457 and 1516 Yeovil parish acquired two houses that the wardens continued to rent out well into the reign of Edward VI. This money never amounted to more than 6 per cent of the parish's total income.[26] In Stogursey rents constituted only about one-tenth of the receipts and they declined in value. In 1507 the accounts record income from two tenements, two workshops, and two acres of land. By 1521 there were only five properties, of unspecified type.[27] The real drop, however, was not in the number of leases but in the amount of money they earned the parish. Rental income had stabilised in 1524 to between 10s. and 12s., but this was a decrease from the first years of the sixteenth century, when they had earned over £1.

Rural parishes generally did not rely on property rents or on a policy of acquiring land; they were, at best, a minor source of income.[28] Nettlecombe owned one tenement in nearby Taunton, which first declined in value and then disappeared from the accounts altogether.[29] Banwell, a large parish in northern Somerset, owned eight fields which contributed roughly 10 per cent of the annual income. The property disappears from

---

23 CWA Bath: Somerset RO, D/P/ba. mi 4/1/1 no. 1, 4/1/2 no. 13, 4/1/4 no. 49.
24 CWA Bridgwater: *ibid.*, D/P/bw nos 22, 14.
25 CWA Glastonbury: *ibid.*, D/P/gla. j 4/1/1–3.
26 CWA Yeovil: *ibid.*, D/P/yeo. j 4/1/6, fos 5, 28.
27 CWA Stogursey: *ibid.*, D/P/stogs 4/1/1, fos 4, 25.
28 Ault, 'The village church', 211–12. Ault finds that rural churchwardens regularly appear in the manorial courts and assumes that this means that the parish owned a great deal of property. This is not a good assumption, because one acre of meadow could still bring the churchwardens into court on a regular basis and yet not provide much monetary support.
29 CWA Nettlecombe: Somerset RO, DD/WO 49/1, fos 1, 3, 17.

the accounts in 1521, but the parishioners made up for it by building a church house which they then leased for private ale brewing.[30]

Some time between 1490 and 1496 the rural parish of Tintinhull acquired some pasture which earned 9*d.* a year. The rent rose to 12*d.* in 1528 and to 15*d.* three years later, suggesting that to some extent it was keeping pace with inflation. By 1536 the parish added a cottage to its properties, increasing income by another 15*d.* Although the parish occasionally added to it possessions, it does not appear to have been particularly interested in pursuing a deliberate policy of land acquisition. In 1547 William Smith left the church a field, which the wardens immediately sold for 6*s.* 8*d.*[31]

Parishes had varying success with rental property. The big boroughs continued to acquire rents which made up an ever-increasing part of their total income. The reversal of fortunes which many English towns suffered in the sixteenth century, however, affected property values and brought about a decline in some parishes' income. Starting in 1427 St Michael's, Bath, regularly reported lost revenue from defaulted rents. Initially it was only 4*s.*, but the sum increased continually throughout the rest of the period. In 1459 the parish could not collect £2 0*s.* 9*d.*, and in 1547 it was £2 5*s.* 6*d.* short.[32] It may be that these properties were not leased or the tenants were poor and the wardens did not rigorously demand payment.[33] As farm land was not affected by rent declines in the same way, rural parishes were perhaps in a better economic position.[34] Although burgage tenure made it easier to own property within a borough, urban land was not necessarily as profitable as rural possessions. In general, it seems that the smaller boroughs, such as Stogursey, were in the most difficult position. They needed their rents, but could not acquire enough property to offset the effects of the stagnating late medieval economy.

Those parishes without tenements or gardens to lease earned some money by renting out the church house for baking, brewing, or other activities. An inventory of goods for the Nettlecombe church house lists a variety of vats and caldrons probably used for brewing ale.[35] A church house and its contents enabled small householders to expand their income by means of small-scale brewing without having to purchase the necessary

30 CWA Banwell: *ibid.*, D/P/ban 4/1/1, fos 27, 69, *passim.*
31 CWA Tintinhull: *ibid.*, D/P/tin 4/1/1, fos 70, 116, 120, 127, 147.
32 CWA Bath: *ibid.*, D/P/ba. mi 4/1/2 nos 21, 28, 4/1/6 no. 68.
33 C. B. Pearson (ed.), 'The Churchwardens' accounts of the church and parish of St Michael without the north gate, Bath, 1349–1575', *Somerset Archaeological and Natural History Society*, 23 (1877), ii.
34 Reynolds, *English Medieval Towns*, pp. 154–9; Charles Phythian-Adams, *Desolation of a City* (Cambridge, 1979), pp. 31–67.
35 CWA Nettlecombe: Somerset RO, DD/WO 49/1, f. 82.

equipment.[36] Yeovil offered the same service.[37] With the loss of its property Banwell also lost about a tenth of its annual income. The parish made up the deficit by building a church house that the wardens leased to individual parishioners. Rents from this property were not as consistent as leases of land, but the parish recovered most of the lost income.

The rural parishes of Nettlecombe, Croscombe, Trull, Yatton, and Tintinhull also leased their church houses, but only Tintinhull's earned a significant and regular amount of money. Tintinhull's church house, which the parish itself leased for 13*d.* from the priory of Montacute, first appears in the warden's records in 1436, three years after the first surviving account. One individual generally leased the house for the entire year, using it for baking. With a fixed rent, it was a stable and dependable source of revenue, contributing anywhere from 20 per cent to 60 per cent of the receipts. Some years it provided the only income. The parishioners came to depend on it less as they developed other ways of raising money. In 1497 they built their own church house, which allowed the parish to expand its activities. The wardens began renting it out for private brewing. They still maintained and rented the old house, now referred to as 'la olde bakehouse', although after 1459–60 the parish no longer seems to have paid rent for it.[38]

Even communities without extensive property could add to their annual income by letting miscellaneous items to individuals who could otherwise not afford them. Periodically Tintinhull and Stogursey leased the church oven, located in their church house.[39] The accounts for Yeovil provide the best example of the variety of services and items that parishes could offer for hire.[40] In addition to funeral items the parish rented out space in the churchyard on market days, weights and measures, an anvil, and loaned their vestments, linens, and liturgical items to a nearby but poorer parish. In 1457 these rentals provided a quarter of the parish's income. By 1516, the date of the next surviving account, the parish had ceased renting the churchyard and weights, but loaned instead various vessels and other large pots and pans, as they continued to do up to Edward VI's reign.[41]

36 Judith Bennett, 'The village ale-wife: women and brewing in fourteenth-century England', in Barbara A. Hanawalt (ed.), *Women and Work in Preindustrial Europe* (Bloomington, 1986), pp. 20–36.

37 CWA Yeovil: Somerset RO, D/P/yeo. j 4/1/6, fos 9, 13, 17, 20, 23, 25, 28–9.

38 CWA Tintinhull: *ibid.*, D/P/tin 4/1/1, fos 3, 33, 41, 47, 74–5.

39 It was not a significant source of income, bringing in at the most 22*d.* It does not appear before 1521 and it is not a regular feature of the accounts. CWA Stogursey: *ibid.*, D/P/stogs 4/1/1, fos 25, 26, 28v, 36v, *passim.*

40 John G. Nichols (ed.), 'Accounts of the proctors of the church of Yeovil, Co. Somerset, 36 Henry VI–1457/8', *Collectanea Topographica et Genealogica*, 3 (1834), 161–70 (original lost).

41 CWA Yeovil: Somerset RO, D/P/yeo. j 4/1/6; bishops had never approved of business being conducted in the church or churchyard. In 1334 the Bishop of Bath and Wells republished the diocesan statues which forbade these kinds of activities. Register of Ralph of Shrewsbury: Somerset RO, D/D/B reg. 2, f. 132.

Different parishes placed different emphases on rents as a source of revenue. For the larger town parishes dependence on leases grew to the exclusion of other income sources, providing wardens with a much more consistent idea of their parish's annual income. Unlike their rural colleagues they did not have to depend on potentially unreliable sources such as ales and revels or selling and leasing goods. An era of rising inflation, however, could threaten this stability.

Rent-collecting also concentrated financial responsibility in the hands of the churchwardens, separating the rest of the parishioners from the business of supporting the parish. Parish property was not always within the parish boundaries or leased to members. The wardens, as representatives of the community, negotiated the contracts, and parishioners, who were neither in the office of churchwarden nor actually renting the property, were uninvolved in the transaction. This meant that non-officeholders had fewer financial exchanges with the parish than their rural counterparts.

The rural or poorer parishes, with only a few leases, used them to create a different kind of atmosphere. The parishes' corporate wealth was used to benefit their members. Here we see a greater number of parishes letting church houses for baking and brewing. These communities also provided ovens, anvils, and other tools that parishioners occasionally needed but might not be able to afford.[42] Leasing out brewing or baking tools allowed parishioners to supplement not only the church's income, but their own as well. The rural parish was not just a landlord, but a co-ordinator of goods and services.

III

Community-wide collections – or gatherings, as they were often called – were a more prominent and widespread fund-raising strategy. Parishes used them to meet a variety of regular and special expenses. Collections paid for *ad hoc* needs such as new vestments or building projects, or they contributed to the general fund or supported specific endowments within the church.[43] Social and legal pressures meant that contributions to these collections were probably not voluntary, although how exactly the wardens could enforce payment depended on whether defaulters could be distrained or prosecuted at law.[44] Frequently there were several collections

---

42 James E. Thorold Rogers, *A History of Agriculture and Prices in England*, 3 (Oxford, 1881; reprint London, 1963). Rogers's price index shows just how much of an investment these items could be. Brewing equipment could range from 1s. to 40s. a pan (pp. 555 iv; 559 iv; 561 ii). A set of weights sold for 9s. (p. 549 i) and anvils ranged from 16s. 8d. to 33s. 4d. (pp. 558 ii; 577 ii).

43 F. A. Gasquet, *Parish Life in Mediaeval England* (London, 1906), p. 128.

44 Gasquet, *Parish Life*, p. 125; Drew, *Early Parochial Organisation*, pp. 13–14. There is some suggestion by Gasquet and Drew that the collections for wax were voluntary and those for the whole fabric were not. These distinctions are not

in a year, the most common ones being for the candles at Easter, Christmas, and to stand by the font. Some parishes did pay for wax out of the general fund, but most had wax collections. These guaranteed a certain level of income; a new tower or wall could be postponed, but the liturgy required candles. In Glastonbury the wardens collected between 10s. and 12s. annually for the Easter taper, while in Banwell it was somewhat less, between 6s. and 8s. Throughout the late medieval period the amount remains relatively stable, implying a continued commitment to the liturgy.

Collections were also a way of providing large sums of money for rebuilding a church or buying new ornaments. In 1325 the hamlet of Wembdon, in the parish of Bridgwater, levied a church rate to rebuild its ruined chapel.[45] Bridgwater also used this method to raise sufficient funds for a new bell in 1319 and a new spire in 1367.[46] The spire required so much money that the collectors had to go out twice. In 1437 the parishioners of Tintinhull collected £1 16s. 10d. in order to buy a new cross and chalice and three years later £1 18s. 1d. for four processional torch holders. When the parishioners wanted to rebuild the church house in 1530 the wardens again solicited money in this manner, and from 1539 to 1541 they paid for the new bell tower with yet another collection.[47]

While most parishes had small collections, a few also relied on them for a large portion of their annual income. Until the mid-fifteenth century Bridgwater used an annual parish-wide collection as the source of most of its income.[48] As enthusiasm for the collection declined, the wardens increasingly relied on their rental property and individual gifts. Whereas in 1415 money from the collection constituted 97 per cent of the total income, by 1445 it had dropped to only 23 per cent. At this point the parish was levying it only as a means of financing specific projects, and the parishioners and burgesses had to agree to its assessment. Antipathy towards the collection appears to have increased and after 1455 the parish stopped it altogether, despite having paid £1 10s. 0½d. for the collectors' new vestments.[49] The

---

clear in the accounts, but generally wax collections did not bring in enough money to make chasing defaulters into court financially worth while. Collections for the whole fabric were a different matter, as offenders violated canon law.

45 Register of John Drokensford: Somerset RO, D/D/B reg. 1, f. 240a.

46 CWA Bridgwater: *ibid.*, D/P/bw nos 3, 23.

47 CWA Tintinhull: *ibid.*, D/P/tin 4/1/1, fos 3, 7, 119, 135.

48 Cox, *Churchwardens' Accounts*, p. 2. See Drew, *Early Parochial Organisation*, pp. 12–13, for some earlier examples and Gasquet, *Parish Life*, pp. 125–9, for later ones. Hobhouse (ed.), *Churchwardens' Accounts for Croscombe*, pp. 230–1, comments on how unusual Bridgwater's fund-raising was.

49 CWA Bridgwater: Somerset RO, D/P/bw no. 2 (1394): 'Et de 108s. 6d. receptis de quandam collectione assessa super parochianos ville pro reparatione fabrice ecclesie.' D/P/bw no. 41 (1415): 'Et de £20 receptis de quandam collectione assessata super parochianos tam infra villam quam extra pro diversis defectibus in ecclesia …'.

switch in fund-raising strategy again reminds us of the different expectations parishioners had of their communities. The amount a Bridgwater parishioner contributed to the collection depended on his or her wealth. It was, therefore, a more egalitarian way of supporting the parish. The community, however, rejected this method in favour of individual gifts and rental property, methods that limited the number of people directly supporting the church.

Banwell, Nettlecombe, and Croscombe also used parish-wide collections, but they did not obviously garner the same resentment found in Bridgwater. These gatherings were tied to parish entertainments and they relied on different kinds of community dynamics.[50] Although they played different roles in each parish's annual budget, the annual collections show a sustained level of income for the duration of the accounts. For Banwell the collection was the primary source of income, making up anywhere from 47 per cent of the annual receipts at its lowest point in 1542 to 87 per cent in 1544 at its highest. Nettlecombe's collection was much less important. Before it disappeared from the accounts after 1541, proceeds ranged between 3 per cent and 19 per cent of the annual receipts in 1514 and 1528 respectively. Nettlecombe probably used its collection as a way of making up for other losses or for financing a new project. During difficult times it could be dropped. Using entertainment as an enticement to contribute also increased the laity's involvement in the process.

Croscombe's accounts show this link with entertainments particularly well. The parish gilds, rather than the wardens, were in charge; each conducted its own collection and turned part of the proceeds over to the parish's common fund. Some groups provided entertainment to accompany the fund-raising exercises and all represented diverse interests. Two gilds, the weavers and the tokers, were specifically related to trades, while two others were dedicated to saints – the gild of St Michael and the gild of St Nicholas (although the latter disappeared from the accounts in 1477). The remaining four gilds (the maidens, the young men, the hoglers, and Robin Hood and his company) supported the church by sponsoring revels or dances. Once a year, at the audit, the respective gildwardens turned their proceeds over to the churchwardens. Part of the proceeds went to the gild's light, 4*d.* was returned to finance the next year's activities, and the rest went on the church fabric. The biggest fund-raiser was the Robin Hood collection, but it was held only when there was a major building project or other significant expenditure. The youth gilds, particularly the maidens, ran very successful collections during Hocktide. Together they usually contributed between 20 and

---

50 CWA Banwell: *ibid.*, D/P/ban 4/1/1; CWA Nettlecombe: *ibid.*, DD/WO 49/1.

30 per cent of the total income, although the maidens alone raised that much in 1493.[51]

The differences between the Bridgwater parish collections and those of Banwell, Croscombe, and Nettlecombe underlie larger issues of how parishioners integrated fund-raising into community activities. There is regular evidence that Bridgwater resisted the collection. For example, in 1415 the parishioners living in the outlying hamlet of Horsey protested against the assessment by withholding 6s. 8d. They claimed that, because they maintained their own chapel, they should not have to pay the same amount as other hamlets. Specifically they were referring to the hamlet of Bower, which had no chapel and was assessed at the same rate of 26s. 8d.[52] The Bridgwater churchwardens started legal proceedings in the archdeacon's court, but apparently failed to carry them to a conclusion. By adding entertainment Nettlecombe, Banwell, and Croscombe changed the nature of the collections and perhaps minimised local resistance. While individuals may have stayed away from the games or refused to contribute when the collectors came around, the accounts do not show the same widespread lack of interest as was found in Bridgwater.

IV

Entertainments include a variety of activities, such as revels, ales, and plays, which are historically associated with the pre-Reformation parish.[53] Although they are found in some form in all Somerset accounts, their use as fund-raising activities is generally found in rural communities. The forms of entertainment staged by parishioners also express some of their attitudes towards ecclesiastical duties. Although the sums earned suggest a continuing confidence and interest in the Church at the local level, the specific themes and figures invoked at parish gatherings provide a critique of parish involvement.

Robin Hood, a figure that accompanies some parish collections, is the most obvious example of social commentary.[54] There is a certain irony in linking Robin Hood with parish collections. As an outlaw known for using his criminal activities to help those in need, who could be more appropriate in persuading the parishioners to support their church, even if it did feel like a shake-down? Giving the role of Robin Hood to the

---

51 Hobhouse (ed.), *Churchwardens' Accounts for Croscombe*, p. 20; for more on Hocktide see my article 'To free them from binding: women in the late medieval English parish', *Journal of Interdisciplinary History*, 27 (1997), 387–412.

52 CWA Bridgwater: Somerset RO, D/P/bw no. 41.

53 Cox, *Churchwardens' Accounts*, p. 288; Alexandra F. Johnston, 'Parish entertainments in Berkshire', in J. A. Raftis (ed.), *Pathways to Medieval Peasants*, Medieval Studies 2 (Toronto, 1981), pp. 335–8; Ronald Hutton, *The Rise and Fall of Merry England: The Ritual Year 1400–1700* (Oxford, 1994), pp. 5–68.

54 R. B. Dobson and J. Taylor (eds), *The Rymes of Robyn Hood: An Introduction to the English Outlaw* (Gloucester, 1989), p. 37.

warden or other prominent local figures added further bite to the revel by calling up themes of inversion. The role-playing transformed the warden from an upstanding member of the parish into a bandit.

The frequency of Robin Hood revels also provides a good example of how parishes used similar practices for different purposes. In some places the character of Robin Hood was a regular feature of fund-raising and entertainment, while other parishes used him only to raise money for a major project. Robin Hood appears in the records of five Somerset parishes, all located in the south-eastern portion of the county between the rivers Parrett and Axe. Yeovil introduced this revel as part of a springtime collection at some point between 1458 and 1515. The account for 1519 describes the activities: 'Received of Richard Hacker that year being Robin Hood, by his good provision & diligent labors and by the good devotion of the town and country he presented to God & holy church £6 8s. 0½d.'[55] In 1516 the 'good devotion of the town and country' that Robin Hood tapped brought in nearly 50 per cent of the total receipts, and the profit never dropped below 20 per cent for each subsequent appearance. The parish of St Cuthbert in Wells also held an annual Robin Hood ale, complete with dancing girls. In 1498 the festivities ran into trouble and the town council authorised an investigation into what had happened to the money.[56] The burgesses, in their capacity as parish overseers, apparently had subsidised the event and lost track of the proceeds.

Robin Hood was also a frequent, but not annual, figure in Croscombe. The parish in fact provides the earliest known 'impersonation' of the character.[57] Here his May Day activities alone contributed anywhere from 12 per cent to 47 per cent of the parish's income. His success, however, came at the expense of the proceeds of the youth gilds' Hocktide collections. With Hocktide falling on the second Monday and Tuesday after Easter Robin Hood's May Day revel created competition for the parishioners' money. Limited resources meant that people had to choose which activity to support, the youth games or the costumed revel.

Only two other parishes staged Robin Hood activities and in both

---

55 CWA Yeovil: Somerset RO, D/P/yeo. j 4/1/6, f. 5, T/PH/bm 31 s/1800; the Robin Hood figure in Yeovil was usually a former churchwarden. His duties involved organising the Whitsun ale and its accompanying entertainment as well as collecting the money which he presented to the churchwarden. James Stokes points out that '[t]hose integrated duties required a person who could be trusted, who could organize ... who knew the traditional entertainments ... and who could persuade parishioners to give him their hard-earned money': 'Robin Hood and the churchwardens of Yeovil', in Leeds Barrol (ed.), *Medieval and Renaissance Drama in England* (New York, 1986), iii. 7.

56 'Wells Convocation Book', *First Report of the Royal Commission on Historical Manuscripts* (London, 1874), p. 107; E. K. Chambers, *The Mediaeval Stage* (Oxford, 1903), i. 176; Dobson and Taylor (eds), *Rymes of Robyn Hood*, p. 39.

57 Dobson and Taylor (eds), *Rymes of Robyn Hood*, p. 39.

cases it was a single event that helped to raise money for a major renovation project. In 1512 the rural parish of Tintinhull received 11*s.* from 'Robyne Hoods All' that helped pay for new pews.[58] St John's in Glastonbury held a Robin Hood revel in 1500 that earned the parish £8 7*s.* 8*d.*, a handsome profit considering the 14*s.* paid for costumes.[59] The parishioners were also raising money for new seats and paying for extensive restoration of their St George image.

The use of the Robin Hood figure to finance such a statue is an interesting decision on the parish's part. Like Robin Hood, St George was a popular figure in spring festivals.[60] By juxtaposing these two characters the Glastonbury parishioners comment on their relationship to the Church. Both figures serve as metaphors for parish activities and blend the seemingly secular world of the churchyard with the sacred space of the nave. Croscombe also positions Robin Hood and St George in opposition to each other; as the former disappeared from the fund-raising schedule the churchwardens replaced him with their own successful ale held in honour of St George. Switching springtime figures symbolically represents the parish's direct appropriation of fund-raising obligations. As a non-religious event, Robin Hood's revel was outside the direct control of the wardens and the parish, but St George's was not.

Another popular revel was a Christmas-time celebration called hogling. What exactly hogling entailed is something of a mystery. Scholars long thought that it was unique to south-western England, but more systematic study of churchwardens' accounts reveals that it was a popular form of celebration throughout England.[61] The lack of explanation or description in the churchwardens' accounts makes it difficult to know exactly what form these celebrations took, but they were apparently part of Christmas or New Year's entertainments, carried out by the men.[62] According to a witness deposition in 1630 from Keynsham parish, during 'theire hogling they have used to singe songes & be very merrie & have good entertaynement att such howses thay went to …'.[63] Another witness

---

58 CWA Tintinhull: Somerset RO, D/P/tin 4/1/1, f. 96.
59 F. W. Weaver (ed.), 'Churchwardens' accounts, St John's Glastonbury', *Somerset and Dorset Notes and Queries*, 4 (1895), 332–6.
60 Dobson and Taylor (eds), *Rymes of Robyn Hood*, p. 38; Chambers, *Mediaeval Stage*, i. 160–81, 205–27. In one of the Paston letters John Paston complains that the servant he kept 'thys iij yer to pleye Seynt Jorge and Robyn Hood and the Sheriff of Nottingham …' has left him upon acquiring a good horse. J. Gardiner (ed.), *Paston Letters* (reprint Gloucester, 1983), v. 185.
61 James Stokes, 'The Hoglers: evidences of an entertainment tradition in eleven Somerset parishes', *Notes and Queries for Somerset and Dorset*, 32 (1990), 807–17; Hobhouse (ed.), *Churchwardens' Accounts for Croscombe*, p. 251; Hutton, *Merry England*, p. 50.
62 Hutton, *Merry England*, pp. 50–1.
63 Somerset RO, D/D/Cd 17, f. 42. See also Stokes, 'The Hoglers', 808.

declared that he was hospitable 'to those of Kainsham that came a hoglinge to him, & afforeded them good cheere & beere'.[64]

Nettlecombe, Croscombe, and Banwell all held hogling activities. In Nettlecombe the annual collection of money revolved around something called 'hogling bread', which may have been the bread or cake of the hogmanay, a New Year's celebration more usually associated with seventeenth-century Scotland. The Banwell accounts describe their collection process as hogling and the men who collected the money as hoglers. Here the entertainment was part of the winter observances. In 1588 the churchwardens of Banwell wrote in their accounts: 'the hoglers shall paye theire monye all wais the Sondaye beffore Sayntt nycholas dayes (6 December) accordynge to the ould order.'[65] Croscombe also received money from the hoglers along with the other gilds, prompting one historian to speculate that they may have been another parish fraternity.[66] Pilton, Glastonbury, and Tintinhull parishes all had hogling lights in the church, which particular individuals or groups supported.[67]

Collections, incorporated into the annual cycle of festivals, involved the parishioners in the community in a different way from just levying a parish rate. Revels were more than bribes to coerce payment; the surrounding festivities immediately assembled the community and bound them together, expressing active involvement as both a religious and a social experience.[68]

The most common combination of entertainment and fund-raising, however, were church ales. Not only were they financially successful, they further demonstrated the close tie of sociability and religious experience on the local level. People who worshipped together drank together.[69] In general, those parishes that relied on rental property for their income did not hold ales, making them more a rural rather than a town occurrence.[70] For those parishes holding ales entertainment was their major source of income, so the success or failure of the festivities was crucial to

---

64 Somerset RO, D/D/Cd 17, f. 42v. See also Stokes, 'The Hoglers', 808.

65 CWA Banwell: Somerset RO, D/P/ban 4/1/1, f. 164.

66 Hobhouse (ed.), *Churchwardens' Accounts for Croscombe*, pp. 251–2; Hobhouse thought they were labourers or other low-status parishioners who organised themselves into their own gild.

67 Hobhouse (ed.), *Churchwardens' Accounts for Croscombe*, pp. 1–48; CWA Tintinhull: Somerset RO, D/P/tin 4/1/1, fos 40, 74; CWA Glastonbury: *ibid.*, D/P/gla. j 4/1/7, 8; CWA Pilton: *ibid.*, D/P/pilt 4/1/1, fos 27, 12, 17.

68 Gail McMurray Gibson discusses local drama as not only drawing upon local events and circumstances but further defining and identifying the community: *Theater of Devotion* (Chicago, 1989), pp. 19–46.

69 Lawrence Blair, *English Church Ales* (Ann Arbor, 1940), pp. 1–2.

70 There are the occasional exceptions, such as the 1428 ale held by the parishioners of St John's in Glastonbury or the periodic ones held at St Michael's in Bath. CWA Glastonbury: Somerset RO, D/P/gla. j 4/1/7; CWA Bath: *ibid.*, D/P/ba. mi 4/1/5 no. 53, 54, 56. Conversely, the rural parish of Banwell did not hold ales.

the support and maintenance of various parish activities and projects. One ale a year was usually not enough to earn adequate funds, consequently many parishes held multiple ales. The permanent or occasional addition of an extra ale demonstrates a sense of economic rationality on the part of parochial administrators.

The churchwardens' accounts for Yatton record the most extensive and successful use of ales. Usually there were three ales a year – at Whitsun, midsummer, and Hocktide – each sponsored by one of the three parts of the parish: Yatton, Claverham, and Cleve.[71] In 1499 Yatton had to hold two extra ales because one Davy Gibbs had stolen the church plate the year before.[72] The parishioners not only had legal expenses, but they had to replace the missing items. Income from Yatton's ales grew throughout the whole period, as did the parish's dependence on them for its income. In 1530 the wardens added a minstrel to the festivities to enhance their attraction.[73] There are no records of resistance to supporting the parish in this fashion, and indeed the sums earned by the ales were substantial enough to pay for the construction of a large and elaborate nave, complete with a stone rood screen rather than a wooden one.[74] The ales provided a way for the whole parish to support the church in a more convivial and active way that was anticipated and appreciated, unlike the 'tax' imposed by Bridgwater.

Tintinhull began with only one ale, on the feast of St Margaret. In 1447, after two years of low receipts, the parish held an additional ale on the feast of SS Philip and James (May Day). This became an annual event in 1481, eventually outstripping the St Margaret ale in profits. For undisclosed reasons the parish had held no St Margaret's day celebrations for the previous three years (1445–47) and the parish cow, which previously had earned the parish upwards of 8s., became sterile.[75] The drop in income made these lean years for the parish.[76] The financial straits were not completely alleviated by a once-only extra ale, but the permanent staging of a second ale returned the parish to its earlier income levels.

Nettlecombe, which already had a successful Pentecost ale, introduced a second one in 1536 which they held on one of the feasts of the Virgin.[77] The date of the new ale is probably not a coincidence. Scheduling the new ale on a feast of the Virgin Mary was a way of commenting on,

---

71 Cox, *Churchwardens' Accounts*, p. 289.
72 CWA Yatton: Somerset RO, D/P/yat 4/1/1, fos 229–331.
73 CWA Yatton: *ibid.*, D/P/yat 4/1/1 f. 78.
74 C. Platt, *Parish Churches of Medieval England* (London, 1981), p. 97.
75 CWA Tintinhull: Somerset RO, D/P/tin 4/1/1, fos 12–16, 25, 28, 61, *passim*.
76 Income had dropped to only 16s. 8d. and £1 2s. 11d. in 1445 and 1447 respectively, whereas the previous five years had brought in an annual income ranging from £1 6s. 8d. to £3 8s. 8d.
77 CWA Nettlecombe: Somerset RO, DD/WO 49/1, f. 63. It is not clear which feast day the parishioners were celebrating.

or protesting against, Henry VIII's religious policies, which had rearranged the liturgical calendar and would abolish the saintly images from the churches. Similarly, Tintinhull also used its ales as a way of protesting against religious reforms. By the 1490s the Margaret ale was earning less than £1, compared with the £2–£3 pounds earned by that held for SS Philip and James. In 1536, when the feast of St Margaret was deleted from the ecclesiastical calendar, the St Margaret ale began earning more revenue, and by 1547 the parish was collecting £3.[78] The ale allowed the parish to continue honouring its patron saint even though she was no longer officially sanctioned and her image had been removed from the church.

The experience of St Margaret's in Tintinhull, like that of other parishes in this chapter, demonstrates the local nature of social and religious life in the fifteenth and sixteenth centuries. This study of fundraising is an easy way to see the uniqueness of each parish and how it adapted to its setting. Geographical, legal, and economic differences played a major role in determining the parish's economic structure, which in turn informed the social and religious experience of its members. Fund-raising helped create social bonds between the laity and their church that had underlying religious goals. Through the economic options available to each community, the parishioners themselves created a particular kind of parish life. Raising money at an ale was a substantially different experience from paying a tax or letting houses to people who may not have been members of the parish. For rural parishioners the parish was one of the primary forms of association. It served not only as a religious and liturgical centre, but also as a social and economic one. The diverse forms of fund-raising reflect this central position. The town offered urban parishioners far more diversions. The parish did not constitute the only form of social life and activity, nor was it the only venue for religious expression; the fund-raising practices reflect this situation. Borough parishes raised money in such a way as to draw upon the likely experiences of the wardens and to raise the maximum sum with the minimum amount of effort.

A parish's economy determined the size of parish projects and community spending. Wealthy parishes had bigger churches, more decorations, and more elaborate celebrations than poorer ones. In Somerset the division between modest and wealthy does not run exclusively along urban/rural lines, but these differences, to a certain extent, do inform how a parish raised and spent its income. In town parishes entertainment and diversions such as processions, plays, and other spectacles appear on the expense side of the accounts, not on the receipts side as they do in

---

78 CWA Tintinhull: *ibid.*, D/P/tin 4/1/1 fos 121, 125, 147; Eamon Duffy, *Stripping of the Altars: Traditional Religion in England c. 1400–1580* (New Haven, 1992), pp. 394–5.

rural parishes. The stability and size of the rents collected by the parishes of Glastonbury, Bridgwater, and Bath allowed larger and more permanent celebrations, churches, and endowments, but they were only part of the laity's parochial experience. The process by which the community achieved its goals says as much about its shared religious life as the liturgical splendour it could ultimately afford.

The parish, piety, and patronage in late medieval East Anglia: the evidence of rood screens

The fifteenth century was marked by unprecedented lay investment in the parish, and it has been rightly said that in England 'there is no period at which money was lavished so freely on parish churches'.[1] The wills of the late medieval laity are filled with religious bequests for the adornment and equipping of their local churches, and the huge number of buildings erected, extended, or altered in the Perpendicular style remain as monuments to the energy and scale of the great rebuilding which those parishioners undertook and paid for.

The nature, social location, and motivation of this pious investment have increasingly interested historians. Who gave to the church and why, and what was the balance in pious giving between devotion, conspicuous consumption, and the desire for influence or prestige in the community? The answers to many of these questions can only ever be conjectural, but in this chapter I want to throw light on some of them at least by examining benefactions for one specific purpose – the erection and adornment of the rood screen, the partition between chancel and nave which divided the high altar and choir from the people and supported the great crucifix flanked by statues of Mary and John (see Plate 8.1). These screens, the largest and most complex single piece of furniture in the late medieval parish church, were a feature of every parish in the land until the Reformation.[2] Though the crucifixes they existed to support and honour

1 A. H. Thompson, quoted in Beat Kümin, *The Shaping of a Community: The Rise and Reformation of the English Parish c. 1400–1560* (Aldershot, 1996), p. 186.

2 The standard works on screens are F. B. Bond, *Screens and Galleries in English Churches* (London, 1908), F. B. Bond and Dom Bede Camm, *Roodscreens and Roodlofts* (London, 1909), and Aymer Vallance, *English Church Screens* (London, 1936). There is a good brief account in G. H. Cook, *The English Medieval Parish Church* (London, 1961), pp. 150–62. On the iconography of the screens: Bond and Camm, *Roodscreens*, 2 (for Devon), and Bede Camm, 'Some Norfolk rood screens' in Christopher Hussey (ed.), *A Supplement to Blomefield's Norfolk* (London, 1929), pp. 239–95; W. W. Williamson, 'Saints on Norfolk roodscreens and pulpits', *Norfolk Archaeology*, 31 (1955–57), 299–346; M. R. James, *Suffolk and Norfolk* (London, 1930), *passim*; W. W. Lillie, 'Screenwork in the county of Suffolk', *Proceedings of the Suffolk Institute of Archaeology*, 20 (1930), 214–26, 255–64; 21 (1931–33), 179–201; 22 (1934–36), 120–6. All these are essentially listings and, unless otherwise stated, identification of saints on the rood screens discussed are taken from these sources. Something more ambitious is attempted in

were destroyed in Edward's reign and again under Elizabeth, hundreds of the screens themselves did in fact survive the Reformation and, in two regions especially, mid-Devon and East Anglia, many retain the supporting images of the saints with which their lower sections or dados were decorated. In Norfolk eighty of the surviving screens retain some or all of their paintings, in Suffolk thirty-nine, and in Devon forty-two. Some Devon churchwardens' accounts, such as those for the market town of Ashburton and the Exmoor village of Morebath, preserve details of the

Plate 8.1
Attleburgh. The rare survival of the medieval loft makes the Attleburgh screen ensemble one of the most complete in East Anglia and conveys the effect of screens in medieval churches. Over the loft can be seen the remains of a painting, either a doom or the adoration of the cross. The decoration for the cross-bar of the rood itself can be seen between the upper and lower Romanesque windows (inserted during Victorian 'restoration').

W. G. Constable, 'Some East Anglian rood screen paintings', *The Connoisseur*, 84 (1929), 141–7, 211–20, 290–3, 358–63; see also E. Duffy, 'Holy maydens, holy wyfes: the cult of women saints in fifteenth- and sixteenth-century England', in D. Webb (ed.), *Women in the Church*, SCH 27 (Oxford, 1990), pp. 175–96, and *The Stripping of the Altars* (London and New Haven, 1992), pp. 110–13, 157–60.

Plate 8.2 (*left*) Ranworth, the north altar, with surrounding screenwork. To the left of the altar is the door to the rood stairs, and the upper door can be seen above the loft, only the floor of which remains.

Plate 8.3 (*right*) Ranworth, north altar, detail. The incomplete figure on the right, with scroll, is John the Baptist. Over his head the underdrawing of a demi-angel is visible, but it has been covered up with an ornamental diaper pattern. The figure to the left was originally a seated archbishop, and the rim and central rib of the mitre can still be seen in the hair of the figure. When the adjacent painting of John the Baptist was abandoned, this figure was repainted to replace it (indicating a special link between the altar and the Baptist), with leaping lamb and flag, a bushy forked beard (now almost invisible) and a camel-hair robe.

erection of new screens and lofts, but the bulk of the testamentary evidence which would enable us to date the Devon screens and to identify the donors went up in flames in the World War II bombing of the Exeter Probate Office.[3] For Norfolk and Suffolk, however, wills containing bequests for the making or decoration of these screens survive in their hundreds, and so it is possible to establish an approximate chronology of the screens and their paintings, to say something about the character of the piety represented by them, and to establish a crude social profile

3 A. Hanham (ed.), *Churchwardens' Accounts of Ashburton 1479–1580* (Torquay, 1970), pp. 70ff; J. Erskine Binney (ed.), *The Accounts of the Wardens of the Parish of Morebath, Devon, 1520–1573* (Exeter, 1904), pp. 70ff.

of the donors.[4] These rood screens have a special value for historians of the English parish, since they were overwhelmingly the most important single focus of imagery in the people's part of the Church. The screens supported the main parochial image of Christ, itself a centre of cult which was expressed in the rows of lamps which burned before it on the 'candilbeme'. They were also covered with at least one and often two rows of smaller images of the saints, on the dado (or lower pannelling, from ground to waist height) and the loft front. The screens, moreover, often formed the backdrop to nave altars maintained by the parish, gilds, or individual families, at which the daily votive and requiem masses were celebrated (see Plate 8.2). The rood screen, therefore, was a crucial focus of ritual activity and piety, of direct interest to every parishioner. Like so much else in the medieval parish church it was the product of quite complex patterns of benefaction. Though, as we shall see, screens were sometimes paid for by a single individual, on the whole their cost ruled out one-off benefactions. Most were parish efforts managed by the war-dens, and documentation survives for a number of such projects for parishes throughout England.[5] In Norfolk and Suffolk many, perhaps most, screens were paid for by multiple gifts, varying hugely in size and often spread out over an extended period. The East Anglian screens are the most copious surviving source of medieval popular devotional imagery for which we have anything approaching adequate supporting document-ation. Attention to these benefactions, and to the images, altars, and other ritual arrangements associated with them, gives us a unique insight into late medieval devotional preferences and the relation between individual pious motivation, choice, and initiative, as well as into the corporate activity and consciousness of the parish.

We need first to register the character and complexity of the rood screen and the extent to which it dominated the parish church. The role of the screen as a divider had very practical as well as symbolic implica-tions. The area to the east of the screen was, in most cases, the responsibility of the rector or patron of the church and the parish had no obligations for its upkeep or adornment. The whole area to the west of the screen, including the screen itself, was the responsibility – and the property – of the parish. This meant that it was the western face of the

---

4 The fundamental work on dating, based largely on wills from the NCC in the Norfolk RO, has been done by Simon Cotton, for Norfolk in 'Medieval rood-screens in Norfolk – their construction and painting dates', *Norfolk Archaeology*, 40 (1987), 44–54 (references for 150 parishes), and for Suffolk in an unpublished hand-list kindly made available to me by Dr Cotton (references for just under 100 parishes). In the course of other research using NCC wills I have been able to add just over two dozen further parishes, mostly in Suffolk – these are cited individually as they arise.

5 A range of examples printed in J. Charles Cox, *Churchwardens' Accounts* (London, 1913), pp. 175–80.

screen, the side the people saw, which became the exclusive focus of lay concern and benefaction; it was on the west face of the screens that there developed an elaborate and often revealing iconography.

The rood screen was normally a stone or wooden partition, solid to waist height, and then pierced with openings to allow sight of the high altar, and a doorway to permit access to the officiating ministers. A great crucifix was usually supported by a heavy beam stretching along the top of the screen. In the West of England the screen opening was invariably fitted with lockable doors; in East Anglia doors were sometimes omitted. By the later Middle Ages this basic structure had been elaborated. The creation of large east windows and of high arches between chancel and nave left the crucifix starkly silhouetted against the light, rendering its detail invisible to the people in the church.[6] To remedy this, it became customary to fill the arch behind the crucifix with a solid boarded or plastered tympanum, more or less continuous with the east wall of the nave. The solid expanse of wall thus provided behind the rood cried out for decoration, and the subject chosen almost everywhere was the doom (or last judgement). It was believed that when Christ came again to judge the living and the dead he would display his wounds – as signs of condemnation to those whose sins had caused them, as signs of mercy to all who were truly penitent. The angels who attended Christ would carry the instruments of his passion, and the association of the doom with the crucifixion was thus theologically very compelling.[7]

As the cult of images grew more elaborate it became a customary act of parochial or individual piety to endow candles or lamps to burn, sometimes in their dozens, before the great crucifix. In the course of the Lenten liturgy the crucifix had a veil suspended before it, which was ritually drawn aside during the liturgy of Palm Sunday. To facilitate the maintenance of these lamps and the other ritual activities surrounding the rood, a walkway or loft above the screen and below the crucifix became a universal feature of the screens. These lofts acquired a variety of other functions. In all but the smallest churches they served as a musicians' gallery: organs were placed there, and they became choir lofts for the singers accompanying the liturgy. At Louth in Lincolnshire, Long Melford in Suffolk, and many other great churches, the singing of the Passion during the Solemn Liturgy on Good Friday was done, appropriately, from the rood loft at the foot of the great crucifix. More practically the lofts were useful store-places for parish chests containing the church records and valuables (see Plates 8.1 and 2).[8]

6 Cook, *English Parish Church*, p. 151.
7 Duffy, *Stripping of the Altars*, pp. 246–8.
8 Surviving examples of musicians' 'squints', both in Wales, illustrated in Vallance, *Screens*, plates 32–3; Charles Kerry, *A History of the Municipal Church of St Laurence, Reading* (Reading, 1883), pp. 55–9; David Dymond and Clive Paine (eds), *The*

By the early fifteenth century almost every parish church in England would already have had a rood screen and loft, but the replacement or enhancement of the screens as a whole or of some of their component parts was to continue right up to the Reformation. The testamentary evidence from 280 parishes in Norfolk and Suffolk used in this study suggests a steady increase of devotional investment in rood screens and their images from the 1450s to the end of the decade 1500–09, with significant further activity up to the late 1520s, halted only by the religious disturbances of the 1530s and the general nervousness then about the implications of royal religious policy for parochial devotional expenditure (see Table 8.1).[9]

Table 8.1 *Norfolk and Suffolk parishes undertaking work on their rood screens 1450–1539 (sample of 280 parishes)*

Decade	Parishes
1450–59	12
1460–69	24
1470–79	27
1480–89	21
1490–99	33
1500–09	52
1510–19	38
1520–29	29
1530–39	14

Sources See note 9.

One of the commonest reasons for the replacement or refurbishing of the screen was the extensive rebuilding of churches which was such a feature of fifteenth-century England. Since it divided chancel from nave, any major restructuring of either part of the church was liable to involve alterations to or total replacement of the screen.[10] The magnificent new screen erected at Mattishall in the 1450s was a consequence of the rebuilding of the nave in the 1440s and 1450s.[11] In 1508 Robert Gardener of the Norwich parish of St Andrew directed that 'the perke [screen] in

Spoil of Melford Church (Ipswich, 1992), p. 3; R. C. Dudding (ed.), *The First Church-wardens' Book of Louth 1500–1524* (Oxford, 1941), p. 214; Cook, *English Parish Church*, pp. 155–7.

9 The sources for this table, which simply codifies the information from 280 parishes in which bequests for work on the rood screen have been found, are cited in note 4 above (the scattered pre-1450 references are not included).

10 Cotton, 'Roodscreens', 52; Paul Cattermole and Simon Cotton, 'Medieval parish church building in Norfolk', *Norfolk Archaeology*, 38 (1981), 271.

11 Cattermole and Cotton, 'Church building', 255; NCC: Aleyn, 153.

the same chirche be made at my cost in the myddes of the same accordyng to the olde werke made on both sydis'.[12] The rood screen at St Andrew's had been attracting bequests for painting only a generation before, but the church had recently been entirely rebuilt, the work having been completed in 1506. In the course of it the chancel had been enlarged and extended, and the central part of the screen evidently no longer fitted, though the parish retained the old parclose screens at the sides.

Such new screens were often an integral part of a projected rebuilding, because access to the lofts was normally by a staircase, either built into the masonry of the chancel walls or housed in specially constructed turrets. Large-scale work on structural features of that sort would have needed careful planning and the consent of the parish.[13] Testators leaving money for the rood screen, therefore, were frequently joining in parish projects by providing funding for particular aspects, often before the work actually began. Gregory Galion of Besthorpe in Norfolk left 30s. in 1507 towards the carving and gilding of the rood loft in his parish church, provided that 'it be in makynge by the space of iii yerres after thys day', otherwise the money was to be given to a priest to say mass for his soul.[14] Richard Clemens, a Norwich tanner, left the huge sum of £10 in 1534 for the gilding of the perke, 'at suche tymys as the Perysshennes of the same p[ar]isshe ... go forward' with the work, and the Norwich mason Robert Mayour left 3s. 4d. to his parish of All Saints, Ber Street, to gild the rood there 'when yt ys p[er]formed'.[15] Thomas Drake of Bunwell left 3s. 4d. in 1533 towards the rood screen, 'on this condicon if the parisshonors of Bunwell goo forwarde wt it and sett ytt up', and Robert Clerke of Thorndon left 6s. in 1526 to the making of the new rood loft, 'to be paid in the iij yers that the kerver is in makynge thereof'.[16]

In all these cases private donations, great or small, were contributions to a parish project which had clearly been planned and in many cases launched before all the funding was in. Parishes could routinely count on raising funding as work progressed, since the project might take years. The contract for the elaborate screen commissioned from the carvers John Daw and John Pares for the Cornish parish of Stratton in 1531 spread the work over seven years.[17] The Kentish parish of Hackington

---

12 Cattermole and Cotton, 'Church building', 257; NCC: Spyltymber, 93; N. Pevsner, *North East Norfolk and Norwich* (Harmondsworth, 1962), p. 235. Gardener was just one of a number of benefactors paying for furnishings and decoration in the wake of the rebuilding.

13 Roodstairs survive in literally hundreds of churches. Representative examples can be seen in Edingthorpe and Castle Acre in Norfolk or Hessett in Suffolk. For a turret housing the rood stairs see St John's, Needham Market, or the 'Clopton turret' at Long Melford.

14 NCC: Spyltymber, 124.

15 NCC: Godsalve, 20; Alpe, 216.

16 NCC: Platfoote, 23; Spyltymber, 85; Briggs, 227.

17 Vallance, *Screens*, p. 65.

commissioned a screen in October 1519 from the carver Michael Bonversall of Hythe, the work to be completed by 1523. He was to be paid 20*s*. a foot for the work, £7 in hand, and the rest on completion.[18]

The indenture between Bonversall and the parish was signed by the vicar, but in most cases such parish projects will have been managed by the wardens. As part of a general refurbishment of the church which involved extensive reglazing and pewing, the parish of Great St Mary's in Cambridge commissioned a new rood loft in 1518. Specially appointed parish officers took collections 'of mennys goode wyll every sunday by a certeyn Roll' for a whole year, averaging 6*s*. 8*d*. a week. The wardens sold some rings from the church 'jewels' to augment funds, and as the work advanced prominent parishioners left legacies towards its cost. In 1521 Robert Goodhale, who had been churchwarden in the year the project was launched, left £10 towards its cost, while 'lorkeyn', servant to William Abington, another former churchwarden, left 36*s*. 8*d*. The Cambridge rood loft, which cost the immense sum of £92 6*s*. 8*d*., was funded, therefore, by a mixture of organised parochial fund-raising and individual pious benefaction.[19]

At Morebath on Exmoor in September 1534 the parish completed an extensive programme of renovation and pious decoration of their church. They commissioned the carver William Popyll to make a new crucifix, with statues of Mary and John, together with a carved and gilded celure or ceiling of honour. Popyll was to receive £7 in all for the work, 40*s*. in hand, a further 40*s*. at Lady Day (25 March) 1535, and the remainder when the work was complete, which was to be in time for the parish's patronal festival on St George's day, 23 April 1535. Popyll was to find and erect all the materials except the great beam on which the rood group would rest and the wall plates to support it, which the parish provided and set up. The parish also made separate arrangements for the painting and gilding of the carved work, involving two other craftsmen and their assistants.[20] The new rood at Morebath was emphatically a parish project, but in fact its funding was not handled straightforwardly by the churchwardens. The initial payment of 40*s*. was provided by the Young Men's or Grooming Store, and the gilding of the completed carvings was paid for by the Maydens' Store. The logic of this arrangement no doubt sprang from the fact that both the Young Men's Store and the Maydens' Store maintained tapers before the 'high cross', and the Young Men regularly presented their accounts to the parish on the Sunday nearest Holy Rood Day. Hence the contract with Popyll and the first

18 Indenture printed in *Archaeologia Cantiana*, 44 (1932), 267–8.
19 J. E. Foster (ed.), *Churchwardens' Accounts of St Mary the Great, Cambridge, from 1504 to 1635* (Cambridge, 1905), pp. 15, 36, 41, 43, 46, 48; Cook, *English Parish Church*, p. 161.
20 Binney (ed.), *Morebath*, p. 70.

payment were made, appropriately enough, on Holy Rood Day 1534. This was a characteristic early Tudor mix of piety and practicalities, the spreading of financial burden within the parish, together with a symbolically appropriate devotional gesture. For all that, the parish kept tight control of the management of the project. The workman employed to paint the figures evidently ran short of cash before the work was complete and the vicar unwisely advanced him 20s. from his own purse, without clearing the payment with the wardens, an act which, despite the generally good relations between priest and people at Morebath, was resented by his parishioners because it was done 'agaynst the p[a]rysse wyll'. The vicar was eventually reimbursed from the funds of the Maiden Store, but in view of the tension caused by his unilateral action he donated the money to another parish project.[21] Financial sponsorship of a parochial initiative by a gild, store, or other sub-group within the parish was of course commonplace. The early sixteenth-century screen in the parish church of Thorpe le Soken, Essex, for example, had a painted inscription informing the reader that 'This loft is the bachelers, made by Alles' (i.e. funded by ales), exactly as at Morebath.[22]

If gilds and stores might initiate, adopt, or partially fund parish projects, so too might individuals, and there are many examples of rood screens being bestowed upon parishes by wealthy clergy or laity. In 1505 Robert Reydon, a gentleman and lavish benefactor of the parish of Creeting St Peter in Suffolk, left money for the carving and gilding of a new rood, Mary, and John.[23] Robert Northern, vicar of Buxton in Norfolk, left £20 to his church in 1508 'toward the makyng of a new perke after the newe perke in the chapell of the ffelde in Norwyche', and the Norwich rood screen he here prescribed as the model to be followed at Buxton was itself the result of the lavish gift of £40 by Henry Bachcroft of Little Melton in 1502.[24] The benefactor bestowing this sort of benefit on a parish must always have had the principal say in the character and decoration of the screen he or she paid for, but such bequests needed the consent and acceptance of the parish, and benefactors had to consult and carry the parish with them. In 1483 Alice Chester, a wealthy widow of the Bristol parish of All Saints, 'considering the rood loft of this church was but single and no thing beauty', decided to replace it 'at her own proper cost' with something much more splendid. She proceeded with care, however:

according to the parish entente, she, taking to her counsel the worshipful of this parish with other having best understanding and sights in carving, to the honour and worship of almighty God and his saints, and of her special

21 *Ibid.*, pp. 94, 112.
22 Vallance, *Screens*, p. 65.
23 NCC: Rix, 243.
24 NCC: Popy, 20; Spyltymber, 79.

devotion to this church, has let to be made a new rood loft in carved work filled with twenty-two images.[25]

Consultation with the 'worshipful' of the parish must have been a necessary part of every such endowment, particularly when, as often happened, other parishioners wished to add their contributions to the main bene-faction. A number of screens attributed by inscriptions to a single donor are known to have been in fact the object of many smaller supplementary donations by other parishioners. The screen at Ludham has a carved scroll on the dado with the date 1493, requesting prayers for John Salmon and his wife Cecily 'that gave forten pounds', but it also commemorates 'alle other benefactors' and there is surviving testamentary evidence between 1491 and 1508 of a host of smaller but still substantial donations of a mark or a pound towards its gilding and painting (see Plate 8.4).[26] At East Harling the magnificently carved early sixteenth-century screen is covered with the armorial bearings of the dominant local gentry family, yet once again we know there was a stream of smaller benefactions from parishioners between 1499 and 1513.

Screens were expensive projects, which often attracted very substantial donations from the well-to-do. Surviving will evidence from Norfolk and Suffolk suggests that screens were rarely the focus of giving by the poorest testators, though gifts of 6s. 8d. or even 3s. 4d. are not uncommon. But even substantial donors might not get the credit of a specific ascription. At Marsham the screen was inscribed in memory of John de Norton and his wife Margaret, yet between 1503 and 1509 several other parishioners contributed significant sums of between £1 and £3 towards its gilding and painting; at Garboldisham a screen which attracted many benefactions is similarly inscribed for William and Katherine Bole.[27] The precise dynamics of such corporate efforts under the umbrella of a single donor are mostly concealed from us, but may reflect the standing of the donors or their families in the community, their initiative in beginning the project, or their long-term and lifetime benefactions to the parish, rather than the amount donated in wills towards the screen itself. At Foxley in Norfolk the screen has portraits of two donors, John Baymonde and his wife, kneeling before the saints on the screen doors.[28] Baymonde left just five marks towards the painting of the screen in his will in 1485. It is thus very much iconographically 'their' screen, yet £3 8s. 4d. does

25 Clive Burgess (ed.), *The Pre-Reformation Records of All Saints', Bristol*, Bristol Record Society Publications 46 (Bristol, 1995), i. 16.

26 Cotton, 'Roodscreens', 49. According to his gravestone near the screen Salmon died in 1486, so in all probability his widow initiated the screen as their joint memorial.

27 F. Blomefield and C. Parkin, *An Essay towards a Topographical History of the County of Norfolk* (London, 1805–10), i. 316–33: Cotton, 'Roodscreens', 48–9; NCC: Popy, 27; Johnson, 87.

28 Illustrated in Duffy, *Stripping of the Altars*, plate 124.

Plate 8.4
Ludham, south
screen (1493). On
the rail is part of
the carved
inscription asking
prayers for John
and Cecily Salmon
*'and for all other
benefactors'* of this
screen. Below are
two of the Latin
Doctors: St
Gregory's papal
tiara and St
Jerome's cardinal's
hat have been cut
out of the panels
during Henry VIII's
reign, a gesture of
hostility to the Pope
but not the saints.

not seem an overwhelming benefaction, and we know there were other donors. Five marks will certainly not have covered the whole cost of even the small screen at Foxley, but it may be that Baymonde's bequest for painting the screen was merely a deathbed addition to earlier and larger benefactions; perhaps he initiated the project, thereby establishing his claim to the central place on the screen itself. Certainly the family were and remained major benefactors of the parish. Two generations later, in 1543, a Joan Baymonde, widow, left a range of gifts to the parish, including a surplice, altar cloths, and £6 for a new cope.[29]

Many screens, then, were the result of joint benefactions by a large number of donors. At Trunch in Norfolk the screen, which is dated 1502, attracted many bequests and donations between 1496 and 1505, and has a carved inscription in Latin along the dado, enjoining the onlooker to

29 Cotton, 'Roodscreens', 48; NCC: Attmere, 373.

'Pray for the souls of all the benefactors of this work, which was made in the year of the lord 1502, to whose souls may God be favourable. To him be glory, praise, honour, virtue, and power, and to him be jubilation, thanksgiving, and love unfailing, through endless ages. Amen.' The Latin inscription may well be the composition of the late fifteenth-century rector of Trunch, Richard Mytton, who appears as witness to the will of the principal benefactor of the screen, John Gogyll, and who may have encouraged ailing parishioners to make bequests towards the work.[30]

The benefactors of the screen at Trunch are unnamed in the commemorative inscription, an indication perhaps that there were too many of them for this to be practicable, as there were for most rood screens erected in the late Middle Ages. Nevertheless, the injunction to pray for them pinpoints the principal motivation for their giving. Late medieval testators liked value for money in this matter and they preferred their benefactions to be attributed, like their tombstones and brasses, 'for a remembrance that some such of my Evencristianes as shall see and loke upon it wull of ther charite pray for or soulys'.[31] They might spell out the terms of the bargain they were striking with the community, as John Mottes of Thorpe by Haddiscoe in Norfolk did in 1534, when he gave a new perke 'upon condicon the towneship yerely every yere aftre my decease do kepe an obite in Thorpe to the value of vid.'.[32] With no close relatives, a parish benefaction was Mottes's best hope of remembrance and intercession after death, but his impulse was shared by many who left loving relatives behind.[33] Some donors even had themselves portrayed on the screen they had donated, like the Baymondes at Foxley, the Bacon family at Fritton, William and Joan Groom at Burnham Norton, or the donor praying to St Sylvester at Houghton St Giles (see Plate 8.5).[34] The nine men and seven women crowded into a single panel at Ipswich St Matthew are probably the brethren and sisters of the Erasmus gild there.[35] Portraits of donors, however, were never common, and group portraits are rarer still. But many screens with multiple donors

30 *Trunch Miscellany* (cyclostyled pamphlet available at Trunch, no place or date), pp. 6–7, though I have modified the translation of the inscription given there. The Latin runs 'Orate pro animabus omnium benefactorum istius operis quod factum fuit anno domini millesimo quingentesimo secundo quorum animabus propitietur Deus. Cui sit gloria, laus, honor, virtus et potestas atque jubilatio, gratiamin actio, amor indeficiens per infinita saeculorum saecula. Amen dicant omnia'; Cotton, 'Roodscreens', 52.
31 NCC: Brigges, 152.
32 NCC: Platfoote, 115.
33 On this whole subject Clive Burgess, 'The benefactions of mortality: the lay response in the late medieval urban parish', in D. M. Smith (ed.), *Studies in Clergy and Ministry in Medieval England* (York, 1991), pp. 65–86.
34 The Fritton screen is illustrated in Duffy, *Stripping of the Altars*, plate 125.
35 Lillie, 'Screenwork in Suffolk', 21 (1930–31), 189.

Plate 8.5 Burnham Norton. Lay eagerness for devotional investment provoked competition. In 1450 John and Kate Goldall commissioned a painted pulpit, with portraits of themselves venerating the Four Latin Doctors. John Goldall is visible here, kneeling with a scroll, on the right of the pulpit. Eight years later another wealthy parishioner, William Groom, had the screen painted with similar donor portraits of himself and his wife, kneeling before saints who included St Gregory. The screen paintings have been almost totally obliterated, but fragments of the donor inscription remain visible on the screen panelling.

nevertheless at least listed their names or at any rate the names of those whose gifts rose above a certain level. The screen at Westhall in Suffolk had an inscription naming at least five donors, including one still living when the inscription was made.[36] Similar inscriptions are or were once visible in Norfolk, at Attleburgh (where a former parish priest, several married couples, and the gild of All Saints are named), North Burlingham, Aylsham, Wellingham, Weasenham All Saints, Wiggenhall St Mary, and elsewhere. Part-donors of screens might have their particular contribution specified, as at Cawston, where donors made themselves responsible for painting single panels or 'panes' of the screen and where William Atereth and his wife Alice in 1502 had an inscription placed asking for prayers for them 'the wheche dede these iiij panys peynte be

36 Judith Middleton-Stewart, 'Patronage, personal commemoration and progress: St Andrew's Church, Westhall, *c.* 1140–1548', *Proceedings of the Suffolk Institute of Archaeology*, 3 (1986), 312–13.

the executors lyff'.[37] In the same way at Aylsham in 1507 one of the principal donors of the screen, the worsted weaver Thomas Wymer, had an inscription placed under the pictures he had paid for, informing the reader that he had 'caused this part ... of this work to be gilded'. The panels he paid for included the Apostle Thomas, his name-saint, and Wymer's Christian name appears directly under the image of the Apostle (see Plate 8.6).[38] Such specificity sought to personalise an otherwise rather anonymous absorption into a parish project. So John Funber of Martham made his will on Holy Cross Day 1507, requesting burial in the church there 'before the Image of the Crucyfyx and by my seete in the sayde churche' and bequeathing five marks 'to the payntyng of one payne of the perke before my grave'.[39] At Eye in Suffolk in 1504 the widow Joan Busby 'adopted' one part of what was clearly an already fixed programme for the new rood screen there, stipulating that the 'Medylpane of the Newe candilbeme in which xall stan an ymage of our Lord be payntid if it may be born'.[40]

Such prescriptions for the painting of particular portions of the screens raise the whole question of responsibility for the iconographic schemes of the screens as a whole. To some extent this was fixed by convention. The upper part of the screen invariably carried the crucifix with the doom behind it, but the loft front and the dado left more room for personal devotional preference. Some screens, especially in poorer parishes, were decorated only with formal geometric or floral patterns and perhaps the names of donors, as on the screen at South Walsham, but by the fifteenth century the overwhelming majority had elaborate sequences of saints painted on the dado and painted or carved in niches on the loft front. The choice of these figures was influenced by a range of factors – visual and religious convention, specific theological concerns, workshop styles, pattern books, and individual devotional preference. Parish and individual commissions were often inspired by encounter with a particularly striking screen elsewhere. A parishioner in St Swithun's parish, Norwich, left money in 1520 to gild the rood and directed that 'the same Rode have a scene after the Rode of Seint Laurence'.[41] The parishioners of Hackington in Kent specified that their new screen should be 'made Carven & wrought in every forme of woorkemanship or better as nowe is wrought & made after the newe Roodloft nowe sett and being

37 Cotton, 'Roodscreens', 47; Blomefield and Parkin, *Norfolk*, vi. 266; NCC: Ryxe, 131 – Richard Brown of Cawston, four marks 'to the peynting of a pane of the Rode lofte'; for the Attleburgh inscriptions: Camm, 'Some Norfolk roodscreens', 249. Atereth's 'iiij panys' make up the whole north side of the screen.
38 Blomefield and Parkin, *Norfolk*, vi. 278.
39 NCC: Spyltymber, 150.
40 NCC: Garnon, 16. She also left money for the gilding of an image of St Saviour, before which she asked to be buried.
41 NCC: Robynson, 93.

Plate 8.6 Aylsham. The first four figures on the north screen commemorate the donor, Thomas Wymer, and his wives, Joan and Margaret. The donor's Latin inscription is clearly visible under the saints, with Wymer's Christian name appearing under the painting of his name saint, the Apostle Thomas. Wymer's paintings are on vellum, cut around the figures and glued to the screen, and of markedly better quality than those next to them (here, extreme right). Note the gesso moulding on the upright between panels 2 and 3; the same moulding occurs at Cawston and Westhall. At the Reformation iconoclasts gouged out the saints' eyes.

in the parishe Churche of the Holie Crosse of Westgate at the Citee of Canterburie'.[42] Rivalry as well as imitation played a part here, for individuals and parishes were anxious that the furnishing of their churches should reflect the community's pride and be 'aftyr the best faschone off anny her abowth'.[43] The parishioners of Morebath instructed their carver that their new rood should be 'accordyng to the patent of Brussorde *or better*', Brushford being a village two miles away across the Somerset border. The churchwardens of Yatton in Somerset in 1446–47 rode to Easton in Gordano to inspect a model rood loft with a gallery and to

42 *Archaeologia Cantiana*, 44, 267–8.
43 NCC: Garnon, 23.

enquire about costs before commissioning their own work. The wardens
of Stratton similarly travelled round a number of churches in the region
before commissioning a new screen for their own church; in such cases,
where a satisfactory pattern was found, no doubt the same workshop was
often employed.[44] We know next to nothing about these workshops,
however, though often more than one will have been involved in any
particular project, presenting wardens and executors with considerable
problems of co-ordination and organisation. The screens in East Anglia
were probably prefabricated in the workshop and assembled locally, but
once erected would be painted and gilded *in situ*. In many cases elaborate
gesso work (moulded plaster designs; see Plate 8.6) were also applied. At
Aylsham the figures paid for by William Atereth were painted on vellum
and glued on to the screen. They were markedly better than the cruder
paintings next to them: it looks as if a wealthier man sent farther afield
to get better-quality work. There is a similar discrepancy on the south
screen. Any one commission, therefore, involved a range of crafts and
personnel. Morebath's new rood involved three separate craftsmen: William Popyll the carver, John Creche the gilder, and John Painter. It is
sometimes possible to identify the same workshop in different commissions – the same gesso mouldings of the saints can be found on the
font at Westhall in Suffolk and on the screens at Aylsham, Cawston, and
Marsham in Norfolk, for example.[45] Stylistic similarities are trickier to
handle, though the paintings of St Barbara on the Norfolk screens at
Ranworth (see Plate 8.2), North Walsham, Filby, and North Elmham are
clearly related to each other in some way, as are the Apostles at Ranworth,
Hunstanton in Norfolk, and Southwold in Suffolk. The demi-angels in
the arches above the saints on the Ranworth screen occur again at
Attleburgh and at Gooderstone, but we have no certain way of deciding
whether the similarities stem from a common pictorial source, the same
painter or workshop, another firm using second-hand patterns, or simple
imitation. Of these screens only Attleburgh can be dated approximately
from commemorative inscriptions for donors who died in 1446 and 1458:
stylistically it looks just as early as the paintings on the Ranworth screen,
which some experts date as early as the 1430s.[46]

   The conventions governing the choice of images on a screen were
determined partly by theology, partly by decorative requirements. Theologically, the screen and tympanum as a whole was a complex
eschatological image. Its theme was mercy and judgement. The saints

44 Cox, *Churchwardens' Accounts*, pp. 175–6; Cotton, 'Roodscreens', 44; Binney (ed.),
    Morebath, p. 70.
45 Ann Eljenholm Nichols, *Seeable Signs: The Iconography of the Seven Sacraments
    1350–1544* (Bury St Edmunds, 1994), p. 351.
46 Discussion in P. Lasko and N. Morgan, *Medieval Art in East Anglia 1300–1524*
    (Norwich, 1973), pp. 39–40, 49, 60; Pauline Plummer, 'The Ranworth rood-
    screen', *Archaeological Journal*, 137 (1980), 291–5.

and angels on it would accompany Christ when he came to judge the living and the dead and could now be recruited as 'advows' or intercessors. Spatially the loft front and dado of the screen divided most naturally into a series of niches or panels, in which sequences of saints might stand, and there were a number of ready-made groupings to hand in late medieval iconography – Apostles, Prophets, virgin martyrs, the orders of angels.[47] Of these the most obvious and appropriate group were the Apostles, for Christ had said that they would sit on twelve thrones and judge Israel when he came again: they sometimes occur in the doom painting itself, as they do at the feet of Christ in the doom at St Thomas's, Salisbury, and they were an obvious choice to range along the panels of the dado. They appear on some of the earliest and best of the surviving screens in East Anglia, from the early or mid-fifteenth century (six only at Edingthorpe, the full set at Castle Acre, Ranworth, all in Norfolk, and Southwold in Suffolk), and they are by far the most frequently represented saints on the surviving screens in Norfolk as a whole – twenty-four sets out of eighty surviving screens – and Devon – twenty-seven sets out of forty-two (see Plates 8.6 and 8.10). Interestingly, they are less common in the admittedly much smaller group of surviving Suffolk screens (occurring on seven out of thirty-nine screens), where other sequences, for example Prophets, occur as frequently.

There being only twelve Apostles, and screens often having more than a dozen 'panes' or segments, the Apostles regularly occur in association with other sequences, alternating with or alongside Prophets or the Four Latin Doctors (St Gregory, St Jerome, St Ambrose, and St Augustine). These latter associations of Apostles and Prophets or Doctors were immensely popular all over Europe in the fifteenth century and had a 'learned' feel to them. In many medieval representations, though only rarely on the surviving screens of East Anglia, both Apostles and Prophets have Latin texts; in the case of the Apostles the articles of the Apostle's Creed, in the case of the Prophets messianic texts from their prophecies.[48] Apostles with Creed texts survive on the Norfolk screens of Mattishall, Gooderstone, Ringland, Weston Longville, and Salle, and the Doctors on the pulpit at Castle Acre have texts from their own writings.[49] The Doctors occur again on the pulpit at Burnham Norton (see Plate 8.5) and, as their association with pulpits suggests, even without texts their occurrence alongside the Apostles probably reflects the fifteenth-century Church's

---

47 For an exploration of the religious significance of the sequences of virgin martyrs which occur on many screens see Duffy, 'Holy maydens', *passim*.

48 The conventional texts are given in James, *Norfolk and Suffolk*, pp. 218–19; for fifteenth-century representations of Apostles, Prophets, and related sequences: Emile Mâle, *Religious Art in France: The Late Middle Ages* (Princeton, 1986), pp. 211ff.

49 For illustrations of these screens: Duffy, *Stripping of the Altars*, plates 17, 29, 31–2, 141, and Constable, 'Some East Anglian rood screen paintings', 146–7.

preoccupation with orthodoxy and catechesis.[50] At Poringland the screen was a gift to the parish by the rector, Robert Draper, in 1473, and the Apostles with the articles of the Creed on labels were part of an elaborate theological programme. This included not only prophets with messianic texts but the Fall and the expulsion of Adam and Eve from Eden.[51] This sort of learned scheme is hardly surprising on a screen commissioned by a wealthy and well educated priest, but the replication of similar schemes, at Salthouse, Gooderstone, and elsewhere, may have been a matter of convention and the contents of workshop pattern books. Yet there are some indications of a degree of theological self-consciousness even among lay donors. It is a curious fact that most of the surviving examples of donors portrayed on the screens they commisioned show them kneeling before or beside representations of the four Latin Doctors – at Houghton St Giles, Burnham Norton (pulpit; see Plate 8.5), Fritton, Foxley, and formerly on the reading desk at Cawston.[52] Given the range of saints found on East Anglian screens, this is a striking fact and can hardly be a coincidence. In Norfolk as elsewhere Lollards seem to have made a point of reviling the Four Latin Doctors, who represented the teaching of the Catholic Church, as 'heretikes, and here doctrine ... bey opin heresies'; although there is no evidence of a continuing threat from Lollardy in the Tudor period, overt devotion to the Latin Doctors may have been a recognised shorthand for a deliberate Catholic orthodoxy.[53]

Even where a single donor or group of donors funded the screen, the choice of images must generally have been a matter of negotiation. Dame Alice Chester agreed her choice of twenty-two images for the new screen at Bristol All Saints with the 'worshipful' of the parish, no doubt including the priest. In the same way Katherine Harston left five marks for a new banner for the church of St Mary Coslany in Norwich in 1534 and directed that it should be painted 'with suche stories of our blessed Ladie as shalbe devysed by myne executors with thassente of the most honest of the said parishe'.[54] Parochial projects funded by private bene-factions must always have involved this sort of negotiation. At Leverton in Lincolnshire in 1526 the parish accepted a legacy from William Franc-kysshe to fill the niches of the rood loft with alabaster images, but his money ran to only seventeen images, not enough to complete the work. The parish paid for the remainder and the wardens raised a levy of cheese from parishioners for the alabaster man while he was working in the church. Frankysshe's widow Janet oversaw the payment of his legacy and

---

50 For which see Duffy, *Stripping of the Altars*, pp. 53–87.
51 Blomefield and Parkin, *Norfolk*, v. 440.
52 Illustrated in Duffy, *Stripping of the Altars*, plates 124 (Foxley) and 125 (Fritton).
53 Norman Tanner, *Heresy Trials in the Diocese of Norwich 1428–31*, Camden Society, 4th Series 20 (London, 1977), p. 148; Nichols, *Seeable Signs*, pp. 72–3.
54 NCC: Attmere, 222.

doubtless had a say in the choice of images, but the parish was clearly also fully involved in the implementation of the project.[55]

In many cases parishes will have been content with conventional sequences, which may have been workshop standards – prophets or angels in Suffolk, virgin martyrs everywhere, or more random selections of saints arranged into a more or less symmetrical scheme. At Somerleyton in Lothingland the apparently unstructured assortment of saints on the screen proves on closer examination to consist of a series of matched 'pairs', working towards the chancel opening from the outer panels of the screen – St Michael and St George, each with their dragons, St Edmund and St Edward, both royal saints, St Apollonia and St Dorothy, 'helper' saints and virgin martyrs, the two deacons St Laurence and St Stephen, and so on. In symmetrical schemes of this sort, where every saint has to match another of the same type, it is hard to believe that the ensemble represents anyone's strong preference. Such screens present a representative selection of the most popular saints of the period and they were probably selected from a pattern book or left to the painter of the screen. But even a conventional layout of this sort might be adapted to locality. The magnificent screen at Ludham seems equally and utterly conventional, with paired helper and royal saints arranged on either side of the central group of the four Latin Doctors.[56] Mary Magdalene matches Apollonia, Stephen matches Laurence, Henry VI matches St Edward the Confessor. The one local touch is the pairing of the Norfolk saint Walstan, who had a popular local shrine at Bawburgh, with St Edmund, a pairing possible because Walstan, although the patron saint of agricultural labourers, is always portrayed crowned and wearing an ermine robe. Since Edmund, too, was the focus of an even more important East Anglian pilgrimage, the Ludham screen fits a specifically local piety neatly into a scheme which might otherwise have come straight from a workshop pattern book. The fact that eight surviving Norfolk screens had or have images of St Walstan, all of them within a seventeen-mile radius of the shrine at Bawburgh, indicates that this adaptation to local devotional preference was a regular feature of such commissions.[57]

Certainly, the range of imagery on screens in late medieval England shows ample evidence of consumer choice at work and of self-conscious didactic and devotional motivation on the part of the donors, sometimes resulting in what can appear idiosyncratic and even eccentric

55 Edward Peacock (ed.), 'Churchwardens' accounts of the parish of Leverton in the county of Lincoln', *Archaeologia*, 41 (1867), 349.

56 Illustrated in *Stripping of the Altars*, plates 73, 81, and in Constable, 'Some East Anglian rood screen paintings', 214.

57 At Barnham Broom, Burlingham St Andrew, Denton, Norwich (St James), Litcham, Ludham, and Sparham; the savagely defaced screen at Beeston next Mileham once had an image of Walstan, whose scythe and ermine hem are still visible. For the cult of St Walstan see Duffy, *Stripping of the Altars*, pp. 200–5.

representations. In 1514, shortly after the completion of the new rood screen at Bungay in Suffolk, Thomas Fynch left money for the making of a new altar on the north side of the church and commissioned three images to be placed behind it – All Saints in the centre, flanked by St Ursula and St Cornelius. Ursula was a popular figure in late medieval England, but Cornelius is a saint of such obscurity that Fynch's choice of him as advow is hard to account for, unless perhaps he had been born or baptised on his feast day.[58] On the screens, too, one often encounters clear signs of devotional preference by a donor. It interrupts, for example, an otherwise conventional iconographic pattern on the screen at Potter Heigham in the Norfolk Broads. The screen, painted about 1501, was a small one, with room for just eight painted saints, the Evangelists and Doctors, an obvious enough choice. But the set is incomplete. There are only three Evangelists, Matthew being replaced by St Loy, brandishing a hammer, an asymmetry impossible to account for unless one or more of the donors had a particular devotion to St Loy, patron saint of smiths and farriers.

At Cawston, too, the screen represents a mixture of convention and personal or local choice. The core of the scheme is a set of Apostles, flanking the four Latin Doctors on the doors (as at Gooderstone and Salle).[59] But the wide screen at Cawston had more than the sixteen panes necessary for the scheme, and the individual testators responsible for financing clusters of images on this screen seem to have dictated the choice of additional saints portrayed. Among those painted at the cost of William and Alice Atereth are six of the twelve Apostles, but also St Agnes and St Helena. Both these holy women were popular saints on East Anglian screens, but St Agnes was the patron saint of the parish, and the portrayal of the parish patron on screens is almost unheard of, since every parish had a carved image of its patron to the north of the high altar. But there was a gild of St Agnes at Cawston and maybe the Atereths were members.[60] Devotional gestures towards the patron of gilds to which testators happen to belong are a common feature of East Anglian wills, and this perhaps accounts for the presence of the gild patron on the screen at Cawston. In the same way the badly damaged carving of angels adoring the eucharistic host on the ruined screen at Gressenhall in Norfolk is probably a sign of the involvement of the local gild of Corpus Christi, or of one or more of its members, in the financing of the screen (see Plate 8.7). Similar

---

58 NCC: Multon, 135. All Saints was normally a Trinitarian image, in which the crowned figure of God the Father held the crucifix between his knees, hovered over by the Spirit in the shape of a dove. The 'All Saints' dimension was represented by the souls of the just, held by the Father in a napkin at his breast. For a representation: Francis Cheetham, *English Medieval Alabasters* (Oxford, 1984), colour plate 6.

59 Illustrated in Duffy, *Stripping of the Altars*, plate 33, and in Constable, 'Some East Anglian rood screen paintings', 292–3.

60 Duffy, 'Holy maydens', pp. 178–80.

Plate 8.7 Gressenhall. The screen has been savagely defaced. It is undocu-
mented, but the stylistic evidence suggests a sixteenth-century commission.
Over two of the painted saints (who included the Latin Doctors and St Michael
Archangel) was an elaborate carving of two angels adoring the elevated host,
the rim of which remains clearly visible here in the apex of the arch. The
corresponding section of the other surviving panel has only blank arcading.
The choice of theme for the carving almost certainly indicates the patronage
of the local Corpus Christi gild.

patronage by members of the local gild of the Head of St John the Baptist
may account for the carving of St John's head and of the *Agnus Dei* in the
spandrels on either side of the doorway of the screen at Trimingham in
Norfolk.[61]

One screen which certainly does depict a parochial dedication is the
magnificent and relatively early screen at Barton Turf on the edge of the
Broads. The church is dedicated to St Michael and All Angels, and the
bulk of the screen is taken up with a glittering representation of the Nine
Orders of Angels. These are stylistically so close to the angel of the
Annunciation in the early fifteenth-century altarpiece from St Michael at
Plea in Norwich that the same artist or workshop must have been involved

61 Blomefield and Parkin, *Norfolk*, vi. 264–7. (I owe information about the gilds at
Gressenhall, Trimingham, and Cawston to my research student, Ken Farnhill,
who has provided a checklist of Norfolk and Suffolk gilds in his forthcoming
Cambridge Ph.D. thesis on the relationship of gild and parish in late medieval
East Anglia.)

Plate 8.8 Barton Turf. Though no documentation survives, this screen was probably a parochial project, for it depicts the Nine Orders of Angels, reflecting the parish dedication of St Michael and All Angels. The remaining panels were filled with female helper saints – here, on the left, St Apollonia and St Zita of Lucca.

(see Plate 8.8).[62] To make up the twelve panes of the screen three female 'helper' saints have been added – St Zita (or Sitha) of Lucca, who had a flourishing cult in East Anglia and who recovered lost property for her mostly female clients, St Apollonia, patroness of sufferers from toothache, which was almost everyone, and St Barbara, protectress from sudden death and from thunder, fire, and explosions.[63] These 'helpers' were universally popular, all of them occurring time and again in glass and painting, including *naif* and 'folk' commissions like the screen at Westhall.

---

62 The Annunciation scene from St Michael at Plea is illustrated in Lasko and Morgan, *Medieval Art*, plate 56; the Barton Turf angels are reproduced in Edward G. Tasker, *Encyclopedia of Medieval Church Art* (London, 1993), plates 6.3–6.11; St Apollonia and St Zita from the same screen in *Stripping of the Altars*, plate 60.

63 Sebastian Sutcliffe, 'The cult of St Sitha in England: an introduction', *Nottingham Medieval Studies*, 37 (1993), 83–9.

But the Barton Turf angels carefully reproduce the standard lore about the qualities and activities of the Orders as found in the Golden Legend and that fact, combined with the magnificent quality and unity of the paintings as a whole, makes it clear that this is no folk commission, nor a piecemeal project funded over a long stretch of time.[64] Serious money and a good deal of sophistication and planning went into the screen, and, if its subject matter suggests that it was a self-consciously parochial project, its quality and execution suggest close supervision by a cleric or wealthy patron.

In many commissions, however, donors may have chosen some images and left others to the painter's discretion. When the Ludlow Palmers' Gild commissioned elaborately carved imagery for their chapel in 1524 they made detailed stipulations about the main scenes to be depicted, and their location within the finished scheme as a whole, demanding from the carver 'on the north side ... one substantial story according to his paper that is to be known St John Evangelist standing beneath in a godly story and the Palmers receiving the ring of him, and over him St Edward in a goodly story receiving the ring of the Palmers ... and the four Doctors of the Church with other divers Saints such as he thinketh best with two or three miracles of St John Evangelist'.[65] Here the specific and detailed requirements of the clients were sketched out by the craftsman for the gild to approve – hence the reference to 'his paper'. However, elements of the scheme clearly remained fluid. The carver was permitted to add his own selection of appropriate saints and vaguely required to portray 'two or three' miracles of St John. Such flexibility was likely to have been a feature of parish commissions, where funding for the paintings often took years to dribble in and where the work may well have been intermittent.

The late screen at Wellingham in Norfolk, dated 1532 and inscribed for Robert Dorant and his two wives Isabell and Beatrice, for John Neell, and for other donors 'who had it painted', was clearly a project attracting a range of benefactors, by no means all of whom were named on the screen inscription.[66] The iconography of the screen is correspondingly miscellaneous. To the north and south of the door are elaborate if naively painted scenes depicting St George and the dragon and the 'psychostasis' or weighing of souls by the Archangel Michael. These pictures are characteristic products of the sixteenth century, when donors seem to have developed a liking for narrative, probably under the influence of prints and book illustration. Painted scenes which are certainly based on prints, as opposed to single figures ultimately derived from niched sculpture,

64 Jacobus de Voragine, *The Golden Legend*, ed. and trans. W. G. Ryan (Princeton, 1993), ii. 203–4.

65 *Transactions of the Shropshire Archaeological Society*, 3rd Series 3 (1903), i–ii.

66 Cotton, 'Roodscreens', 52.

appear on other sixteenth-century screens in the region, such as Tacol-neston, Horsham St Faith, and Loddon, while several Suffolk screens had carved narrative panels of Gospel scenes, remains of which survive at Wyverstone and Gislingham.[67] At Tacolneston the source print for the panel of the temptation of St Anthony is known, an engraving by Lucas Van Leyden published in 1509.[68] But the remaining panels at Wellingham, one of them now illegible, included 'an image of pity' filling only the upper part of a panel and clearly meant to form the reredos of an altar, and some helper saints awkwardly crammed into the rectangular 'panes' and not quite filling the available space. The surviving pair on the north screen include a figure of St Sebastian, much invoked against plague in Tudor England, and a now unidentifiable crowned military saint with a chained king at his or her feet. The screen thus displays, in a variety of styles and with no apparent attempt to harmonise diverse elements, imagery adapted to the function of the screen as the location of a nave altar, paired and single figures of traditional helper saints, and story panels reflecting a liking for narrative scenes which was new on Tudor screens. It is difficult to believe that this hotchpotch does not in some way reflect the pattern of funding for the screen. A similar if less pro-nounced diversity of choice can be seen on another group project, the stylistically more coherent screen at Gately, with its images of the Latin Doctors, a two-panel visitation scene, and a handful of pilgrimage saints popular in rural Norfolk, three out of four of them uncanonised – St Etheldreda, Master John Schorne, Henry VI, and the mysterious 'Puella Ridibowne', who appears to have had a late fifteenth-century cult in East Anglia.[69]

By contrast some parochial projects, though funded by a stream of donations from the 'worshipful' of the parish, were clearly planned as an iconographic whole. An example is the magnificent screen at Southwold,

---

67 For Horsham St Faith, where the images of St Brigid of Sweden and St Catherine of Siena are borrowed from woodcuts in the Brigittine treatise *The Dyetary of Ghostly Helthe*, produced by Wynkyn de Worde in 1520, see *Stripping of the Altars*, plates 61–2 and p. 86; for Wyverstone, *ibid.*, plate 139; for the Loddon panels, Constable, 'Some East Anglian rood screen paintings', 359. Some sixteenth-cen-tury screens, such as those at Wiggenhall St Mary in the Norfolk Marshland and Belstead in Suffolk, retain single figures in each panel, but move away from the sculptured niche prototype and towards narrative by placing a continuous background, such as a landscape or wall, behind the figures.

68 Constable, 'Some East Anglian rood screen paintings', 294.

69 Only Gregory and Augustine appear at Gateley, but the other two doctors may have been on the doors, now gone. 'Puella Redibowne' has not been identified convincingly, but she had a shrine chapel at Cromer, and Alice Man, a widow of the parish of Lound, left money in 1502 both for the gilding of the rood beam and for the gilding of 'maid redybone', evidently a statue in the church there. NCC: Popy, 144; Williamson, 'Saints on Norfolk roodscreens', 308. Two of the saints from Gateley, including Master John Shorne, reproduced in Duffy, *Stripping of the Altars*, plate 72.

which was being worked on throughout the 1460s and 1470s and displays the Orders of Angels, the Apostles, and a series of Prophets.[70] But even unitary schemes might display puzzling inconsistencies. The complex screenwork at Ranworth is the most magnificent in Norfolk and the most complete for any English church.[71] Though a good many Ranworth wills survive, containing a steady stream of devotional giving, none record gifts to the screen, which cannot therefore be dated with any confidence; the testamentary silence about it suggests that it was in all probability the gift of a living single donor. The likeliest candidates are the Holditch family, who dominated Ranworth in the mid-fifteenth century and donated a now demolished double hammerbeam roof to the church some time before the later 1470s.[72] The screen, designed not only to support the rood but to enclose side altars to the north and south of the chancel arch, has a fine sequence of Apostles along the dado. At right angles to this dado are parcloses with paired groups of saints – bishops, deacons, and the warrior saints Michael and George, each with a dragon. Above each of the altars enclosed by the parcloses is a row of four saints: to the north a mixed series of Etheldreda, an archbishop(?), John the Baptist, and Barbara, to the south the 'holy kindred' or three Maries with their children (Jesus and six Apostles) plus St Margaret. As I have shown elsewhere this south altar was the Lady altar and, with its troupe of mothers, children, and Margaret, patron saint of women in labour, is a votive altar concerned with childbearing and safe delivery. Its choice as the theme of this part of the screen, and the source of its distinctive iconography, is a fascinating problem in itself.[73]

There were several painters involved in the Ranworth screen, but the ensemble as a whole in colour and arrangement is unmistakably a single scheme. Yet the north altar has several oddities which suggest the presence of an element of improvisation and adaptation (see Plates 8.2 and 8.3). The figure of John the Baptist is unfinished, abandoned while the underdrawing was still visible, the demi-angel in the arch above painted out and replaced with a diapered background. Pauline Plummer, the expert who conserved the Ranworth screen in the late 1960s, has drawn attention to the fact that the beardless and apparently female figure with a leaping lamb on its knee to the left of this unfinished image of the Baptist was originally drawn wearing a mitre, traces of which can be seen in the halo. The figure also wore a pallium (the circular stole made of white wool and

---

70 Some of the Southwold donations listed in Cotton, 'Roodscreens', 53; D. P. Mortlock, *The Popular Guide to Suffolk Churches*, vol. 3: *East Suffolk* (Bury St Edmunds, 1992), p. 185; the Southwold screen is illustrated in Constable, 'Some East Anglian rood screen paintings', 363–4.

71 *Ibid.*, 142–3, and Duffy, *Stripping of the Altars*, plates 56, 74, 108–9.

72 Ranworth wills and benefactions surveyed in A. W. Morant and J. L'Estrange, 'Notices of the Church at Randworth [*sic*]', *Norfolk Archaeology*, 7 (1872), 178–211.

73 Duffy, 'Holy maydens', pp. 194–6.

sent by the Pope to all new archbishops) just visible now under the blue overpainting of the cloak on the left shoulder. The figure is generally identified as St Agnes and the pallium is consistent with that, since the wool for making the pallia was blessed in Rome each year on her feast day.[74] But the saint is wearing an under-robe which has clearly been painted to represent St John's camel-skin, and round the face are the traces of a large curled beard, painted over the originally clean-shaven archiepiscopal saint. So it looks as if the original figure of an archbishop was altered at the same time as the drawing of John the Baptist next to it was abandoned. The most likely explanation for these changes is that, while the screen was still being painted and after all the saints on it had been drawn, another donor gave a tabernacled figure of Christ, Mary, or another saint to stand on the altar before these panels. The altar was certainly narrower than the present arrangement, occupying only the space under the three panels nearest the chancel arch, for the present altar, which extends the full width of the four panels, blocks access to the rood-loft stairway, which would have been in daily use. The tabernacled statue would thus have been the central and principal image above this altar. Yet it was clearly felt to be important to retain a figure of St John the Baptist above the altar, perhaps because this was the location of the St John's light which we know burned somewhere in the church. So the figure of a seated archbishop next to the statue was adapted to represent St John. It looks, therefore, as if a carefully planned scheme, funded by the wealthiest family in Ranworth, was adapted with some difficulty, while work was still in progress on it, to take account of pious giving by another donor.

The endowment of rood screens went on in parishes all over England into the early years of the Henrician Reformation. We know little about the pattern of endowment in the West Country, but the presence on many Devon screens of narrative scenes or elements of what Emile Mâle called the 'New Symbolism', such as sequences of pagan Sybils to match Apostles or Prophets, suggests vigorous activity well into the sixteenth century.[75] In East Anglia, so far as we can judge without an exhaustive search of all the surviving wills, donations tail off in the uncertain religious climate of the 1530s, but some of the most interesting surviving screens date from the years of the Reformation Parliament. Of these probably the latest is that at Burlingham St Andrew or North Burlingham in Norfolk.

Work began on the North Burlingham screen with a flurry of bequests in 1525 and 1526.[76] It continued for a decade, for an inscription,

74 Plummer, 'Ranworth rood screen', 292–5; D. H. Farmer (ed.), *The Oxford Dictionary of Saints* (Oxford, 1978), pp. 5–6.
75 Tasker, *Encyclopedia of Medieval Church Art*, plates 5.230–5.247.
76 NCC: Heyward, 74, 76, 78. The screen is illustrated in Constable, 'Some East Anglian rood screen paintings', 144–5, and Duffy, *Stripping of the Altars*, plates 58, 59, 79, 131.

now gone, recorded the completion of the screen and commemorated the main donors in 1536. Even then donations continued until February 1538, when William Goodwin, of the neighbouring village of Buckenham Ferry, left 20s. to the 'gyldyng of the Perke' at Burlingham St Andrews.[77] The donors manifestly exercised close control over the imagery on the screen. The north side was paid for by members of the Benet family, two of whom, Thomas and Margaret Benet, were alive when the screen was inscribed in 1536. Accordingly, their family patron, St Benet, appears on this screen and Thomas Benet's personal name saint, St Thomas of Canterbury, occupies the prominent panel by the chancel opening. The south screen was funded by bequests from John and Cecily Blake, whose names were commemorated under images of St John the Baptist and St Cecilia, while under the figure of St Katherine, Katherine and Robert Frennys were commemorated. Apart from name saints the 'theme' of the imagery on the screen seems to have been local shrines, with images of St Withburga, carrying a model of the church of East Dereham where she is buried, St Walstan of Bawburgh, and St Edmund of Bury St Edmunds.

With the last bequest for gilding being paid some time after June 1538, when William Goodwin's will was proved, the paint on the screen at Burlingham must virtually have been still wet when the Henrician attacks on imagery began. In November 1538 Henry VIII ordered the destruction of all images of Thomas Becket and the Burlingham parishioners dutifully scraped out his image to the knees, leaving the other saints untouched, though they were later defaced, more conservatively, probably in Edward's reign.[78] The destruction of St Thomas's image can hardly have been welcome to Thomas Benet, nor did it represent any widespread parochial hostility to imagery – a parishioner was to leave money to gild the image of Our Lady of Pity in 1540.[79]

The same selective defacement of images on parish screens is evident at Ludham, where, in Henry's reign, only the papal tiara of St Gregory and the cardinal's hat of St Jerome were damaged on the screen (see Plate 8.4). But, however unpopular it may have been, such activity by the Henrician authorities certainly put a rapid stop to this particular sort of parochial investment. And in Edward's reign the screens were to become the particular target of reforming zeal – above all their upper portions, including the great crucifix. The roods were pulled down, the tympanum and lofts either removed altogether or painted over or covered with canvas

---

77 NCC: Hyll, 42; details of some of the bequests for the screen, and about the inscription, are to be found in Simon Cotton and Roy Tricker, *Saint Andrew, Burlingham* (cyclostyled pamphlet available at the church, no place or date), pp. 4–5.

78 For the Henrician campaign against St Thomas: Duffy, *Stripping of the Altars*, p. 412.

79 NCC: Thyrkyll, 12.

and redecorated with the royal arms and with scripture texts condemning idolatry or enjoining obedience to the magistrate. Reworked tympanum boards of this sort survive at Wenhaston and at Ludham, while at Binham the dado remains, with texts from Cranmer's Great Bible painted over the rows of helper saints (see Plate 8.9).[80] Edwardian churchwardens' accounts are full of records of payments 'for the Wrytyng on the candelbeme', 'for the Colouryng of the panes ... before part of the rode lofte', 'for makyng of the frame over the Rood lofte for the [painter]', or for 'takyng downe of the thyngys in the Roodloft'.[81] The Marian authorities made the replacement of the rood group itself a major priority, but given the burdens in cash and effort which the Marian restoration imposed on parishes, in most places there can have been little energy or resources to spare for the brutalised images on the rest of the screen.[82] Yet given that so many of the screens were the result of widescale community

Plate 8.9 Binham. The saints on the dado were whitewashed in Edward's reign and texts from the Great Bible were painted over them. The saints are now 'ghosting' through again, and the remains of a Latin donors' inscription can be seen on the upper rail.

80 For Wenhaston and Ludham: Duffy, *Stripping of the Altars*, plates 55, 137–8.
81 P. Northeast (ed.), *Boxford Churchwardens' Accounts 1530–1561*, Suffolk Record Society 23 (Woodbridge, 1982), p. 58; A. G. Legge (ed.), *Ancient Churchwardens' Accounts of the Parish of North Elmham 1539–1577* (Norwich, 1891), pp. 43–4; J. L. Glasscock (ed.), *The Records of St Michael's Parish Church, Bishops Stortford* (London, 1882), pp. 47–50; W. H. Overall (ed.), *The Accounts of the Churchwardens of the Parish of St Michael Cornhill 1456–1608* (London, 1883), p. 65; Cox, *Churchwardens' Accounts*, pp. 180–4.
82 Duffy, *Stripping of the Altars*, pp. 545–8.

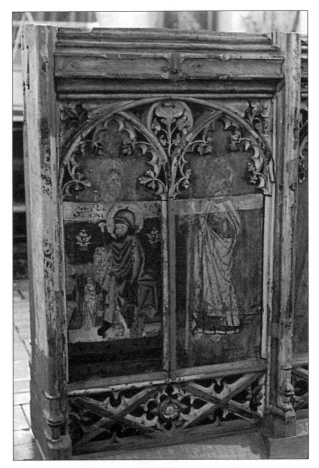

Plate 8.10
Lessingham. Now in the museum at St Peter Hungate, Norwich, this early sixteenth-century screen originally had standing figures of the twelve Apostles. Defaced during Edward's reign, it was partially repainted under Mary with the Four Latin Doctors and (here, seated and with diminutive attendant angel) St Roche, a favourite 'plague' saint. Plague swept Norfolk in 1555.

endowment and benefaction, the havoc of the Edwardian period can hardly have been popular. In a well-known passage the vicar of Morebath recorded in 1555 the return by his parishioners of items salvaged from the wreck of the rood loft they had commissioned in 1534: 'here was resceyvyd pagynntis and bokis and diversse wother thyngis concernyng our rowde lowfth lyke tru and fayzthefull crystyn pepyll this was restoryd to this churche by the wyche doyngis hyt schowyth thay they dyd lyke good catholyke men'.[83] One screen formerly at Lessingham, but now in the museum at St Peter Hungate in Norwich, provides the sole surviving trace in East Anglia of a Marian iconographic scheme to replace images on the dado defaced in Edward's reign (see Plate 8.10). The screen, originally painted with the twelve Apostles in the last years of Henry VII's reign, was defaced under Edward. Under Mary the parishioners appear

83 Binney (ed.), *Morebath*, p. 185.

to have commissioned some decidedly clumsy pictures on parchment of the Four Latin Doctors and of St Roche, and had them glued over some of the defaced Apostles. The choice of new images is a revealing one. The Doctors were emblematic of a restored Catholic orthodoxy and Roche was a plague saint much invoked in the 1550s; the small selection of masses usually included for a travelling priest's convenience in the printed breviaries of Mary's reign invariably include a mass of St Roche and often other plague masses as well. The restoration of only five out of the twelve panels of the screen suggests that once again the Marian project was funded by individual parishioners, a process interrupted by the death of Mary and the return of an iconoclastic Protestant regime.[84] For such attempts at restoration were short-lived. The hatchets, saws, and whitewash of the iconoclasts returned in Elizabeth's reign, and, though many parishes struggled to retain their lofts, the Elizabethan authorities, while ordering the retention of screens as a divider between chancel and nave, were adamant that the lofts and their crucifixes must go.[85] Along with the abandonment and destruction of stained glass the defacement which followed marked the end of an era in English religious and cultural life. It meant the effective end of the craft of the painter in regional centres like Norwich and, in the parishes, the disappearance of the most important single focus there had ever been for corporate artistic patronage and devotional investment in the local communities of England.

84 The point about plague masses is derived from an examination of the Marian Breviaries, listed in A. W. Pollard and G. R. Redgrave, *A Short-Title Catalogue of Books Printed in England, Scotland, and Ireland and of English Books Printed Abroad 1475–1640* (2nd edn, 1976), nos 15836–47.

85 F. Bailey (ed.), *Prescot Churchwardens' Accounts*, Lancashire and Cheshire Record Society 104 (Preston, 1953), p. 53. For discussion of the Elizabethan attack on images see Duffy, *Stripping of the Altars*, pp. 568–77.

New duties for the parish community in Tudor London

An adequate understanding of urban life in sixteenth-century London must include an assessment of parish functions, the ways in which the parish influenced and channelled human actions in the City.[2] The local ecclesiastical unit had assumed a wide range of ecclesiastical, social, economic, and political responsibilities. When Londoners organised responses to the many formidable problems which beset their city, it was usually at the parish level. Even if such attempts varied in their degree of success, few individuals questioned the crucial role of the parish. Both rulers and ruled accepted it as a fundamental institution, seeking to strengthen its cohesion, and to adapt the institution to changing times and circumstances. As a result parish operations were transformed over the course of the Tudor period. Consequently, Jacobean parish masters concerned themselves with matters far different from their Yorkist or even their early Tudor predecessors.

Specific patterns of change in parish concerns can be assessed by the evidence of purchases and charitable donations listed in churchwardens' accounts. Spending priorities reflect the social function of the parish and a strategy for dealing with a confusing array of urban problems. Furthermore, churchwardens' accounts contain a wealth of information regarding local religious and social activities. Looking at them from a long-term, comparative perspective, the change in functions is obvious (see Table 9.1). Three different periods – 1470–79 (or the earliest extant records), 1550–59, and 1600–09 – were analysed, and specific entries encoded and grouped according to their purpose, establishing ratios of

1 An early version of this chapter was presented at the Carolinas Symposium on British Studies 1993 conference, West Virginia University, Mountainlair, 31 October 1993, and a revised version at the First International Medieval Congress, University of Leeds, 6 July 1994. I am grateful for all of the suggestions I received at those conferences. I would also like to thank Martin J. Havran, H. C. Erik Midelfort, Duane Osheim, and Carlos Eire from the Corcoran Department of History at the University of Virginia for their help and advice during the initial stages of research.
2 Some recent research into parish life includes Clive Burgess and Beat Kümin, 'Penitential bequests and parish regimes in late medieval England', *JEH*, 44 (1993), 610–30, Beat Kümin, *The Shaping of a Community: The Rise and Reformation of the English Parish c. 1400–1560* (Aldershot, 1996), Katherine French, 'Local Identity and the Late Medieval Parish' (Ph.D., University of Minnesota, 1993), and Susan Wright (ed.), *Parish, Church and People* (London, 1988).

Table 9.1 *Average share of expenditure categories in a sample of London parishes* (%)

Category	Fifteenth century	1550–59	1600–09
Operations	48.43	39.11	37.38
Maintenance	32.65	31.08	20.89
Legal and financial	17.11	26.68	17.75
Royal, civic and Church hierarchies	0.17	1.5	4.69
Social relief	1.66	1.68	19.27
Totals	100.02	100.05	99.98

Sources (see footnotes for full bibliographic information). Fifteenth century: All Hallows London Wall 1470s, All Hallows Staining 1495–1505, St Andrew Hubbard 1470s, St Mary at Hill 1470s, St Michael Cornhill 1470s, St Stephen Coleman Street 1490s. 1550–59: All Hallows Staining, St Andrew Hubbard, St Benet Gracechurch, St Mary Magdalen Milk Street, St Michael Cornhill, St Peter Westcheap. 1600–09: All Hallows Staining, St Bartholomew Exchange, St Benet Gracechurch, St Christopher le Stocks, St Mary Magdalen Milk Street, St Stephen Coleman Street.

particular categories to the overall annual budget of a parish. Sometimes this was a straightforward task; for example, the purchase of nails being assigned to the category of 'maintenance'. Other times, however, the decision was not so clear. Does a sermon by a 'poor preacher' denote philanthropic or religious concerns? I counted it as the latter, but an argument could be made for the former. Similar interpretations had to be made on many other occasions, but consistency helped to create clear patterns which will form the subject of this chapter. In a final step I averaged the ratios from six parishes for each of the three decades being studied in order to establish an aggregate pattern. While the numbers cited below are the overall averages, the general pattern can be found in most parishes with extant records. Let us now take a close look at the individual categories.[3]

In the late fifteenth century almost half of parish revenues went toward the support of 'ecclesiastical operations'. Included in this category are liturgical items (such as bread, wine, and candles), staff salaries (clerks, priests,[4] scavengers, sextons), devotional and musical books, singers, sermons, chantries, festivals, and so on.[5] In the 1530s the churchwardens

---

3   Unfortunately the record survival does not allow the use of the same parishes for all three time periods.
4   Usually a special payment to the parish priest, whose salary was not covered by the churchwardens, or for the hire of an outside clergyman for special purposes.
5   I also included organ repairs under music. While such an expenditure may seem

at St Stephen Walbrook bought bread, ale, and wine for the singers who performed in the church on St Stephen's Day.[6] Two decades later, in 1557, their colleagues at St Benet Gracechurch ended St Benet's day by inviting their 'singingmen' to drinks at the Ram's Head tavern.[7] Officials at St Margaret Pattens scattered 'herbs' about the church on the occasion of an episcopal sermon in 1573.[8] Liturgical feast days in the late Middle Ages typically found the church decked with garlands of flowers or birch branches or even flags and pennants, as at All Hallows Staining on the feast of Corpus Christi and Midsummer in 1492.[9] In fact the pre-Reformation accounts reflect the importance of the Church calendar in both receipts and expenditures. In the mid-fifteenth century at St Margaret Southwark, church collections took place on St Lucy Day, Christmas, Candlemas, Easter, the feast of the Ascension, Whitsunday, St Margaret Day, the feast of the Assumption, and All Hallows Day.[10] Spending was also recorded on those days and included such concerns as the maintenance of the rood light, washing of the altar cloths, the purchase of ivy, and flags and garlands for festivals, especially the feast of Corpus Christi.[11]

These types of expenditures continued to be the largest single obligation of most parishes, but an obligation which did lessen over time. In the 1470s about half the money spent by the churchwardens concerned the operations of the church, but by 1600 it amounted to less than 40 per cent. Certain parish concerns remained surprisingly resilient, such as the support of liturgical music (in 1550 St Benet Gracechurch paid Thomas Osward 1s. 8d. 'for helping out in the choir at diverse times') or the expenditure on special devotional books (in 1579–80, the churchwardens at St Christopher le Stocks spent 12d. 'for bookes of prayers after the tyme of the Earthquake').[12] Still, the simplified liturgical needs of the reformed churches and the abolition of chantries brought about a general decline in expenditure on ecclesiastical operations. Furthermore, the nature of the purchases changed as well. The old liturgical year had been clearly influencing purchases in the fifteenth century, but the accounts

more appropriately assigned to the general upkeep of the church fabric, some entries did not delineate clearly between 'organ blowers', musicians, and general repairs. I thought it best to keep them all to one category. For a more detailed discussion of my methodology see my 'Parish Finance and the Urban Community in London 1450–1620' (Ph.D., University of Virginia, 1990).

6 CWA of St Stephen Walbrook: GL, MS 593/1, 1471–1683.
7 CWA of St Benet Gracechurch: GL, MS 1568, 1548–1620.
8 CWA of St Margaret Pattens: GL, MS 4570/2, 1558–1653.
9 CWA of All Hallows Staining: GL, MS 4956/1, 1491–1554.
10 J. P. Collier (ed.), 'Original papers: St Margaret Southwark', *The British Magazine*, 32 (November 1847), 481–96.
11 *Ibid.*
12 GL, MS 1568; Edwin Freshfield (ed.), *The Accomptes of the Churchwardens of the Paryshe of St Christofer's, in London, 1575 to 1662* (London, 1895), p. 9.

from St Christopher le Stocks for 1606 alluded to only one holiday: 'Itm for ryngers on the K:day ... 4s.'.[13] The devotional practices of the old faith had also disappeared. No candles are mentioned in 1606, nor any liturgical item other than 'bread & wine'. Jacobean churchwardens paid for items such as wages for clerk and sexton, the washing of linens, poor relief, and bell repairs. There were now clearly different tasks and priorities.

How did the living standards of parish employees fare during the Tudor era? There is no direct information concerning the parish priest or minister since their stipends and emoluments came largely from tithes and fees for ecclesiastical services – the church rates which were collected by the cleric at the time of his services and therefore not a part of the churchwardens' concern for accounting purposes.[14] However, the salaries of lesser officials were paid by the churchwardens and they can be traced throughout the period. In general, the salaries rose over time, but far below the rate of inflation. Economic historians have determined that living standards for the population in general probably fell by about 20–30 per cent in the sixteenth century.[15] Parish officials fared even worse.

A parish clerk in fifteenth-century London could expect an annual salary ranging from a shilling to several pounds, depending on the parish and time period. An undated assessment (*c.* 1545) for the clerk's wage at St Martin Outwich generated £1 16s. 10d. annually.[16] During the 1550s St Andrew Hubbard's clerk earned between £6 and £8 a year.[17] At St Stephen Coleman Street the parish clerk received a salary of £1 *per annum* in the 1470s.[18] A century and a half later, in the early seventeenth century, his successor earned £1 7s.[19] His counterpart at All Hallows Staining fared better at keeping pace with the cost of living, his salary rising from £2 13s. 4d. in the 1550s to £5 5s. at the beginning of the seventeenth century.[20] A salary of about £5 a year seems to have been typical pay for a parish clerk in the first decade of the seventeenth century.[21]

13 *Ibid.*, p. 42. For an interesting account of the transition of holy days into holidays see C. John Sommerville, *The Secularization of Early Modern England* (Oxford, 1992), ch. 3, and Ronald Hutton, *The Rise and Fall of Merry England: The Ritual Year 1400–1700* (Oxford, 1994), ch. 1.

14 Exceptions, of course, were the hiring of additional priests or ministers on special occasions.

15 Steve Rappaport, *World within Worlds: Structures of Life in Sixteenth-Century London* (Cambridge, 1989), p. 160.

16 CWA of St Martin Outwich: GL, MS 6482, 1508–46.

17 CWA of St Andrew Hubbard: GL, MS 1279/2, 1525–1621.

18 CWA of St Stephen Coleman Street: GL, MS 4457/1, 1468–1507.

19 GL, MS 4457/2, 1586–1640.

20 GL, MS 4956/1, 2.

21 The clerk at St Christopher le Stocks received about £4 in 1600 (although the parish was collecting more than £8 for his wage), while the clerk at St Peter Westcheap earned £5 6s. 8d. in the 1550s. See CWA of St Peter Westcheap: GL, MS 645, 1441–1601, and Freshfield (ed.), *St Christofer's*, pp. 35–6.

The reasons for the vast differences in wages for contemporary parish clerks were probably related to local economic realities, but also to the specific duties and obligations connected with the various positions. In addition, clerks could often augment their income by performing extra duties, such as cleaning vestments, keeping the clock, or doing chores around the church. The overall pattern demonstrates an effort to alleviate the worsening economic conditions of the clerk. Furthermore, some clerks may have received additional payments from general collections that were not recorded by the wardens.

Chantry priests and 'morrow-mass' priests usually earned a minimum of about £6 a year in the late fifteenth century. Furthermore, priests could earn some additional money by celebrating an occasional mass at other times or by performing some different service for a parish, as evidenced by the following quotations from the records at All Hallows Staining in the year 1492–93.

Paid for hallowing of the chalice . . . . 4*d.*
Paid to an old priest for a reward to sing in the church at diverse
   times . . . . 10*d.*
Paid to a priest for serving mass on mid-Lent Sunday and Passion
   Sunday . . . . 4*d.*
Item paid to the priest that sang masses in Easter week . . . . 12*d.*
To priest for mass on Our Lady Day . . . . 4*d.*[22]

It is not inconceivable that an industrious priest could earn £10 a year or more.

Priests, in the traditional sense, disappeared from the English Church in the sixteenth century. But comparisons can still be made with their Protestant successors. In 1601 and 1602 the vicar at St Stephen Coleman Street earned an annual salary of £11.[23] How insufficient that amount was in the London economy can be gauged by the fact that the parish voted him an additional £19 each year in 'augmentation of his pension and for his pains'.[24] An annual salary of £30 would have allowed the vicar a degree of comfort and security – if not prestige – in the Coleman Street area.[25] However, the overall picture for most parish officials was not so bright, since most experienced a steady decline in earnings. It has been argued that the lower living standards also lowered the quality of ecclesiastical officials in the Elizabethan era.[26] For the earlier part, at least, that is undoubtedly correct, yet the generalisation should be qualified to the

22 GL, MS 4956/1.
23 GL, MS 4457/2.
24 *Ibid.*
25 This is the same parish where the poorer tenements rented for 4*s.* and 5*s.* annually: *ibid.*
26 Christopher Hill, *Economic Problems of the Church from Archbishop Whitgift to the Long Parliament* (Oxford, 1968), pp. 200–23.

extent that parishioners could show much appreciation in tangible ways to a cleric or parish official they respected, as at St Stephen's.

As for the second main category, the responsibilities associated with maintenance of the church edifice and its precincts remained major concerns of parishioners throughout the period. Once again, however, their relative importance gradually diminished in the sixteenth century. In the 1470s maintenance comprised over 30 per cent of all parish expenditures, while in 1600–09 the figure was down to about 20 per cent. The costs of maintaining the local church had decreased. The liturgical changes of the Reformation had resulted in simplified interiors which required less upkeep than did the formerly more ornate furnishings and decorations. The pre-Reformation churches were filled with statues, paintings, tapestries, fine silks and linens of various colours and designs, altars, and relics and reliquaries, all illuminated by candles. In 1460 the churchwardens at St Andrew Hubbard paid for 'the painting of the George and the Christopher'.[27] A few years later 'Richard Bafford's wife' donated 1s. 8d. 'for painting of St Andrew'.[28] The 1480s saw the parish hiring 'the carver at London Wall for making of our Lady', paying a carpenter 'for St James and St John', and a workman 'for scrolling of the red cloth before the high altar'.[29] There were statues of the Blessed Virgin and St Anne in the Lady Chapel and images of St Katherine, St Andrew, St James, St John, St Nicholas, St George, St Christopher, and 'the Resurrection' at various points within the church of St Andrew Hubbard.[30] The parish even acquired a relic in 1495, the finger of St Andrew.[31] All Hallows London Wall painted, gilded, and purchased two alabaster images to decorate the high altar in 1477.[32] The parish churches in the late fifteenth and early sixteenth centuries produced a sense of the holy and an image of heaven. A parish church was a house of God, and all who had a modicum of theological understanding knew that He was present in the consecrated host housed in the ornate tabernacle. Incense and herbs sweetened the air in his honour, while the liturgical music probably struck the worshippers as ethereal. Many possessed organs and the hiring of extra singers on special feasts, such as St Stephen's Day at St Stephen Walbrook, probably allowed the parish to hear some of the more complicated polyphonic compositions.[33] The Latin liturgy added a mysterious

27 GL, MS 1279/1, 1454–1524.
28 *Ibid.*
29 *Ibid.*
30 *Ibid.*
31 For the bargain price of 1d. (see *ibid.*).
32 Charles Welch (ed.), *The Churchwardens' Accounts of the Parish of Allhallows London Wall, in the City of London, 33 Henry VI to 27 Henry VIII (A.D. 1455–A.D. 1536)* (London, 1912), p. 61.
33 For a survey of Tudor church music in the Reformation period see Peter Le Huray, *Music and the Reformation in England 1549–1660* (Oxford, New York,

element to the ceremonies and the religious culture imbued these items and actions with such meaning that they filled the individual with a sense of awe. Few would have doubted in the early Tudor period that God and the saints were present in the City's churches and that grace could be conveyed there through the sacraments.[34]

All this had changed by the mid-Elizabethan period. People donated and bequeathed much less for church beautification.[35] Theological and liturgical needs were different, emphasising the educational role of the church. Walls were whitewashed or left plain stone, as at St Margaret Pattens, where churchwardens hired a workman 'for whiting and plaistering the church walls' in 1548.[36] Other actions also followed. Images were destroyed as idolatrous, stained glass was replaced with plain glass (except for the occasional coat of arms), and altars were replaced with communion tables.[37]

Protestant churches were places where God's word was preached and where revelation and education were the primary focus of both liturgy and setting. Pulpits came to dominate the Elizabethan churches. They were more prominent than in the pre-Reformation churches, placed higher up in relation to the congregation, and farther removed from the chancel – all to facilitate the hearing of the Word. Decorations were largely limited to memorials, the royal arms, and the Decalogue. Many London churches, such as St Christopher le Stocks, displayed the 'tenne Commaundements' by the late Elizabethan era.[38] This transformation of church interiors to suit changing theologies could be quite costly for the parish. Churchwardens at St Mary Colechurch spent about £15 for that very purpose in 1549, to remove old images and place the king's arms above the high altar.[39] Windows which contained stained glass depictions of religious themes such as the Trinity or saints were systematically dismantled during the reigns of Edward VI and Elizabeth I.[40] Plain or glazed glass was often put in their place, but often secular images simply

1967); he named the following London parishes as celebrating choral services 1547–1603: All Hallows (no further identification), Guildhall Chapel, St Botolph Aldersgate, St Dunstan in the West, St Giles in the Field, St Lawrence, St Martin le Grand, St Mary at Hill, St Mary Woolnoth, St Michael (no further identification), St Stephen Walbrook: *ibid.*, pp. 13–17.

34 Susan Brigden, *London and the Reformation* (Oxford, 1989), ch. 1, and Eamon Duffy, *The Stripping of the Altars* (New Haven, London, 1992), Part I.

35 J. J. Scarisbrick, *The Reformation and the English People* (Oxford, 1984), pp. 85–108.

36 GL, MS 4570/1, 1506–57.

37 See the detailed discussions in, for instance, Brigden, *London and the Reformation*, Duffy, *The Stripping of the Altars*, Part II, and Christopher Haigh, *English Reformations* (Oxford, 1993), Part II.

38 Freshfield (ed.), *St Christofer's*, p. 10.

39 Thomas Milbourne, *The History of the City Church of St Mildred the Virgin, Poultry, in the City of London, with Some Particulars of the Church of St Mary Colechurch (Destroyed in the Great Fire, A. D. 1666)* (London, 1872), p. 40.

40 J. Charles Cox, *Churchwardens' Accounts* (London, 1913), pp. 86–9.

replaced the older religious ones. By the 1570s St Matthew Friday Street had the royal arms, the arms of the Goldsmiths' Company, and those of the Salters' Company in its choir windows.[41] Once the changes had been effected the cost of maintenance was smaller for the simpler settings. Besides, Elizabethan propaganda concerning pre-Reformation ecclesiastical wealth and corruption did not make people eager to adorn their churches once again. Memories of government confiscation also had a negative influence on giving.[42] And the Thirty-nine Articles forbade excess.[43]

Changing government legislation also had an impact on the third main category of parish expenditure. 'Legal and financial affairs' proved a greater burden in the mid-Tudor era, but accounted for only about 17 per cent of expenditures at the beginning and end of this study. This category includes the recording of wills, the keeping of records (including register books), the upkeep of tenements, dealings with the courts, scrivener fees, legal expenses, and payments connected with leases, contracts, annuities, and so on. Typical of these costs were the following transactions.

St Mary at Hill:

1479–81: Item paid to a sergeant for the arrest of our tenant that did us wrong . . . . 8*d*.[44]

All Hallows London Wall:

[Undated, reign of Henry VIII]: Item paid to the sergeant to get the house rent of Thomas Adams . . . . 2*d*.[45]

St Christopher le Stocks:

1603: Paid to Robert Cudner the 22nd of May 1602 for half a years [*sic*] annuity due unto him at Our Lady Day last past out of our rents in Fleet street . . . . £1.[46]

St Bartholomew Exchange:

1602: Paid for warning Bayneham before my Lord Mayor, he refusing to take upon him the constableship being thereunto chosen . . . . 1*s*.[47]

41 *Ibid.*, p. 88.
42 Scarisbrick, *Reformation*, pp. 85–108.
43 Many churches suffered decay in the reign of James I (see Cox, *Churchwardens' Accounts*, p. 12), but cf. Chapter five in this volume.
44 Henry Littlehales (ed.), *The Medieval Records of a London City Church (St Mary-at-Hill)*, Early English Text Society, OS 125 and 128 (London, 1904–05), i. 111.
45 Welch (ed.), *Allhallows London Wall* (London, 1912), p. 56.
46 Freshfield (ed.), *St Christofer's*, p. 37.
47 Edwin Freshfield (ed.), *The Account Books of the Parish of St Bartholomew Exchange in the City of London 1596–1698* (London, 1895), p. 23.

St Stephen Coleman Street:

1608–09: Paid for making a book of all the householders names which have lands within this ward the better to levy aid and paid by parishioners with land towards the same aid . . . . £1 14s.[48]

Much of the increase in the 1550s reflected the demands of government, especially in regards to church property. In 1556 the masters at St Benet Gracechurch paid 8d. to one William Braywood for gathering records concerned with the sale of church goods during the reign of Edward VI and 2s. more for the writing out of the information for the Queen's commissioners.

Item paid to Alexander Rutherford for making quittance for the money that rested in John Soda his hands and for writing out of the particulars of such church goods as were sold in the time of King Edward VI . . 2s.

Item paid to William Braywood for that he searched out certain accounts which were missing and that commissioners would see how the church goods were sold in the time of King Edward VI . . . . 8d.[49]

Proving the legal ownership of property and accumulating evidence of that ownership for royal commissioners was also an obvious concern for parish masters. For example, in 1547, St Andrew Hubbard hired a 'counsel' to prove ownership of parish property before the king's commissioners.[50] In 1553 the parish of St Mary Magdalen Milk Street paid 7s. to a clerk of the commissioners for his care in transporting a deed and other documents from the parish to the commission.[51] In 1562 the parish of St Michael Cornhill paid a scrivener 4d. to write 'an answer to the Queen's Commissioners for certain articles concerning concealed lands'.[52] When government confiscation of chantry lands and church plate ceased, legal concerns lessened once again.

One notable change in churchwardens' expenditures came in dealings with 'royal, civic, and ecclesiastical hierarchies'. This cost the parishes less than 1 per cent of their annual budgets in the 1470s, but had grown to 5 per cent under James I. The increase reflects greater integration of the parish into the government, which meant more frequent dealings between government officials and parish masters. Not only did the ecclesiastical

---

48 GL, MS 4457/2.
49 GL, MS 1568.
50 GL, MS 1279/2.
51 CWA of St Mary Magdalen Milk Street: GL, MS 2596/1, 1518–1606.
52 W. H. Overall and A. J. Waterlow (eds), *The Accounts of the Churchwardens of the Parish of St Michael, Cornhill, in the City of London, from 1456 to 1608* (London, n.d.), p. 155. For the confiscation and concealment of parish lands see also C. Kitching, 'The quest for concealed lands in the reign of Elizabeth I', *TRHS*, 5th Series 24 (1974), 63–78, Kümin, *Shaping of a Community*, pp. 204–11, and Chapter twelve in this volume.

hierarchy monitor religious life more assiduously, but both the civic and the royal government allocated new responsibilities and duties to parish officials, even as they oversaw local compliance. As a result the authorities were increasingly concerned with parochial affairs and operations. Government dealings cost All Hallows Staining more than £13 in 1553.

Item, paid and delivered unto the king and commissioners the 5th day of May Anno 1553 in ready money . . . . £13 17s. 4d.[53]

Episcopal initiatives cost St Benet Gracechurch 1s. in 1559.

Paid to the scrivener for writing of a bill which was delivered unto the archdeacon which was to certify then whether there were any anabaptist or erroneous opinions (within the parish) [crossed-out] . . . . 1s.[54]

In 1557 the parish of St Peter Westcheap paid 6d. to a commissioner 'for viewing the church', undoubtedly to establish that it conformed to the needs of the Marian Restoration.[55] And a visit from the archdeacon cost St Margaret Pattens £1 11s. in 1595.[56]

The records of the 1590s often make mention of Edward Stanhope (1546?–1608), the bishop's chancellor. He came to his office in 1591 and was frequently appointed to diocesan commissions and other tasks which brought him into dealings with London parishes.[57] In 1600 All Hallows Staining paid Dr Stanhope 1s. 8d. because of trouble resulting from the decay of their churchyard walls and another 1s. 8d. 'touching the boys playing dice in the church'. The following year the wardens were still communicating with an episcopal representative regarding 'youths' in the church, though it is not clear if these were the same youths or some new incident. That same year another payment was made 'for setting down an order by Dr. Stanhope's commandment touching our table for vestry men'. In 1604 the wardens recorded a payment of 2s. 'to Mr. Edward Stanhope at Great Allhallows in Thames Street being warned before him for what cause we know not'.[58]

After the break with Rome tenths and first fruits were collected for payment to the king and – although they were formally paid by clerical incumbents – parishes often shared in the burden.[59] Before the dissolution most payments of quit rent were made to monastic foundations; afterwards many were paid to the Crown. After 1548 parishes were required to equip

---

53 GL, MS 4956/2.
54 GL, MS 1568.
55 GL, MS 645.
56 'It[em] p[ai]d for our dinner at the archdeacon's visitation 31s.': GL, MS 4570/2.
57 Leslie Stephen and Sidney Lee (eds), *DNB* (22 vols, London, 1921–22), xviii. 894–5.
58 GL, MS 4956/2, 1600, 1601, 1604.
59 P. Carter, 'The fiscal Reformation: clerical taxation and opposition in Henrician England', in B. Kümin (ed.), *Reformations Old and New* (Aldershot, 1996).

two soldiers for the use of the king.[60] St Stephen Coleman Street raised money in 1601 for the government's use in putting down Essex's revolt and one year later about 10s. 'for setting forth soldiers at diverse times unto Ireland'.[61] It was also a parochial duty to care for the wounded and maimed soldiers of national wars, and such expenses can be found throughout the local records. They illustrate the rapid creation of a national Church during the Tudor era.

The most dramatic transformation in parish operations, however, occurred in the final area to be discussed here, 'social relief'. This category includes aid to orphans, the elderly, the sick, and the unemployed. Poor relief had been a traditional concern of the local community, but it drew increasingly larger sums from the parish, accounting for 20 per cent of all expenditures under James I.[62] Furthermore, parochial philanthropy dealt increasingly with orphans and vagabonds in the late sixteenth century. The impetus to these changes came from demographic and social conditions which produced larger numbers of destitute men and women on the one hand and a moral conviction that the parish had an obligation to provide organised charity. The growth in unemployment among the able-bodied perplexed contemporaries, but was pressing enough that the government took action. Parliamentary legislation and civic ordinances began to appear early in the sixteenth century, usually identifying the parish as the institution best suited to oversee poor relief. Since so many of the destitute migrated to the city to find refuge, London often led the rest of the nation in such new endeavours.[63]

In 1514 and 1524 the London authorities required beggars to obtain a badge or licence in order to beg within the City walls. Violators were to be branded or whipped, the common penalties for illicit begging throughout the era.[64] Such stringent measures did not address the fundamental causes of poverty in the sixteenth century and therefore failed to do more than harass and punish the vagrants – and to keep them wandering. Attempts to regulate and discipline the poor with badges and whippings were fraught with difficulty, and the usual problems of enforcement were exacerbated by theft, loss, or forgery of badges.[65] The

---

60 Cox, *Churchwardens' Accounts*, ch. 1.
61 GL, MS 4457/2.
62 This figure is somewhat skewed by the parish of St Bartholomew Exchange, which gave unusually large sums of money for poor relief. If the parish is left out of consideration, the number would be closer to 15 per cent.
63 John Pound, *Poverty and Vagrancy in Tudor England* (London, 1971), p. 58. For a recent national survey see P. Slack, *Poverty and Policy in Tudor and Stuart England* (London, New York, 1988).
64 Pound, *Poverty*, p. 59, and John Hadwin, 'The problems of poverty in early modern England', in Thomas Riis (ed.), *Aspects of Poverty in Early Modern Europe* (Stuttgart, 1981), p. 227.
65 Michel Mollat, *The Poor in the Middle Ages*, trans. Arthur Goldhammer (New Haven, London, 1978), pp. 251–93.

aim of the whole system was simply to isolate the deserving from the undeserving, since society commonly considered the able-bodied unemployed as victims of their own sloth.[66] In short, the measure did nothing to address the basic problem and vagrancy continued to grow.

By 1533 City officials sought to stop all casual distribution of alms by making parish masters – the more honest and more discreet members of the parish elite – responsible for poor relief. Money was to be collected at the church door or by way of a poor box and administered deliberately to the needy of the community.[67] A parliamentary Act of 1536 ordered the parish to care for orphans and foundlings and to provide them with a trade for their future well-being.[68] Compulsory poor rates were established in the City in 1547.[69] Until the passing of the final version of the Elizabethan poor laws in 1598 and 1601, this was largely the system of poor relief for the last half of the sixteenth century.

Besides those legal stipulations poor relief had been an important part of parish life, at least in the form of individual bequests administered by the churchwardens, for centuries.[70] St Mary at Hill distributed 'bread and ale and cheese to the poor people of the parish' in 1492.[71] In 1430 William Estfield, alderman, provided £100 to the parish of St Mary the Virgin Aldermanbury for poor relief.[72] In 1560 the same parish received £3 from Lady Gresham for the same purpose and Alderman Rowland Hill provided coal for the needy during the winter.[73] Midway through the sixteenth century St Michael Cornhill regularly distributed money 'to the poor of [the] parish in the alleys and in the street side and in the churchyard'.[74] In 1555 5s. was 'paid and given unto Robert Dickenson in Harpe Alley when his wife was brought to bed of two children by the consent of the Masters of the Parish'.[75] About the same time in the parish

66 'The magistrates of London who had to deal with the intensification of poverty in their city came in the year 1552 to [this] conclusion: "after due examination had, we evidently perceived that the cause of all this misery and beggary was idleness: and the mean and remedy to cure the same must be by its contrary, which is labour".' See Robert Jütte, 'Poor relief and social discipline in sixteenth-century Europe', *European Studies Review*, 11 (1981), 31.
67 Hadwin, 'Problem of poverty', p. 228.
68 *Ibid.*, p. 229.
69 First administered through ecclesiastical courts, but taken over by secular courts in 1563. See *ibid.*, pp. 229–30.
70 See A. L. Beier, 'Social problems in Elizabethan London', *Journal of Interdisciplinary History*, 9 (1978), 203–21, and Valerie Pearl, 'Social policy in early modern London', in Hugh Lloyd-Jones et al. (eds), *History and Imagination* (New York, 1982), pp. 115–31.
71 Littlehales (ed.), *Mary at Hill*, i. 192.
72 C. W. F. Goss, 'History of the parish of St Mary the Virgin Aldermanbury', *Transactions of the London and Middlesex Archaeological Society*, NS (1944–47), 159.
73 *Ibid.*
74 Overall and Waterlow (eds), *Michael Cornhill*, pp. 109–10.
75 *Ibid.*, p. 125.

of St Peter Westcheap an old woman named Mother Wotten was given free lodging in a chamber 'by the consent of the parish'.[76] Similarly a blind woman named Alice Howson lived at the expense of the parish of All Hallows Staining in the first decade of the seventeenth century. The parish allowed her free lodging in her infirm old age and occasionally gave her a few shillings for food and other essentials.[77] Philanthropy was an essential part of parish operations, but it faced increased demands as the century passed.

An obvious but important characteristic of London's system of poor relief was that richer parishes possessed greater resources to help the poor. Wealthy communities received higher levels of charitable donations and benefited from more substantial rate revenues. A wealthy church such as St Bartholomew Exchange certainly had its poor inhabitants huddled in various alleyways, but the total number of poor there could only have been a fraction of those residing in the very large peripheral parishes. In the early seventeenth century St Bartholomew's had over £100 in legacies to help the poor, while All Hallows Staining held only two legacies, worth £3 annually.[78] In 1602–03 St Bartholomew's parish distributed over £52 to the poor of the parish, paid over £10 for the care of orphaned or abandoned children, donated money to Christ's Hospital, and doled out a great number of additional alms.[79] All Hallows' parish could not match such largesse, yet it possessed greater need.

It is thus not surprising that large numbers of strangers had to be escorted from the parish of St Bartholomew Exchange. The many poor people, especially pregnant women, removed from its area were probably trying to settle there. The fact that it was a very wealthy church must have been common knowledge among the poor and thus they tried their chances at penetrating into the parish community. But acceptance was not easy. The masters of St Bartholomew's kept a record of the poor inhabitants who lived in the parish and those records acted as a sort of census, allowing the elites to monitor the poorer population.[80] Parishioners were anxious about the potential demands on their resources and began to monitor their relief operations more closely. Vagrants had to be excluded, especially pregnant women, whose children would burden the parish for years.

76 GL, MS 645.
77 GL, MS 4956/2.
78 One legacy, worth £1 *per annum*, was recorded in the CWA, see GL, MS 4956/2. Additionally the parish of All Hallows Staining also received £2 annually for poor relief from a bequest by one John Parrott of St James Garlickhythe. This legacy was sometimes recorded in the CWA, but was also kept separately. See the 'Sacramental account and brief book of the parish of All Hallows Staining': GL, MS 4959, 1585–1664.
79 Freshfield (ed.), *St Bartholomew Exchange*, pp. 18–21.
80 *Ibid.*, pp. 10–12.

The leading men of St Bartholomew Exchange agreed upon the proper method of food distribution and care of the sick at vestry meetings and parishioners were obliged to conform to those methods or forfeit all rights to future aid. After 1577 the poor were assigned places at the rear of the church, where they received bread every Sunday after divine service; a method which lessened chances of fraud. Elderly women who received parish pensions were required to nurse the sick of the community or lose their income.[81] Nightly warding of the parish helped keep rogues and vagabonds out.[82] Parishioners, both wealthy and poor, recognised the fragility of their system and sought to protect it from too great a demand. They did not always succeed in sealing off their parish borders against the homeless. The sad logic behind the action of the mother who left her child on the doorstep of the Royal Exchange on the night of 21 February 1579 is obvious.[83] And it succeeded; the churchwardens of the parish assumed responsibility for the child and paid for its care and upbringing.

Other prosperous central parishes had to deal with similar problems. In 1589 the vestry at St Dunstan in the East tried to control migration to the parish by limiting 'visitors' to only six days. This action was directed towards the poorer residents of the community, who often took in kith and kin. Their failure to comply with the new parish ordinance resulted in a loss of all right to future parish aid.[84] St Mary Magdalen Milk Street recognised civic obligation by collecting money for welfare purposes, paying the burial expenses of several poor families, and raising orphans.[85] When their best efforts to ward against the itinerant poor failed, they also met their obligations, paying 'the poor woman that was delivered of a child in the street 9s. 3d'. [86] The parish masters at St Mary the Virgin Aldermanbury spent 2s. in 1586, and 4s. in 1592, in order to identify the mothers of two foundlings.[87] But even they realised that abandoned children needed attention, and by 1655 the parish was spending over £23 on orphan care.[88]

The parishes of London were increasingly under siege by the indigent from the 1570s. Across the City established residents watched vigilantly for transients, hoping to expel them from their neighbourhood as quickly as possible. Sometimes the poor received some money before

81 Edwin Freshfield (ed.), *The Vestry Minute Books of the Parish of St Bartholomew Exchange in the City of London 1567–1676* (London, 1890), p. 5.
82 *Ibid.*, p. 6.
83 *Ibid.*, p. 10.
84 CWA of St Dunstan in the East: GL, MS 4887, 1494–1509.
85 GL, MS 2596/1.
86 *Ibid.*, 1605–06.
87 Goss, 'St Mary', 147.
88 *Ibid.*

being sent on their way.[89] But such help needed adequate funding. The poorer the parish, the rarer the largesse. St Stephen Coleman Street had more impoverished residents than it could handle in the early Stuart era. Thus the wandering poor were required to continue on their travels without much in the way of alms. In 1602 the wardens paid six of its own women 3*d*. each to convey a poor woman out of the parish, while a 'rogue' was whipped and sent on his way.[90] In 1604 2*s*. was paid to the constable for his efforts in removing vagabonds from the parish.[91] Throughout London rich and poor inhabitants, the powerful and the powerless, united to protect their neighbourhoods. Since poor relief to established parishioners was contingent upon their co-operation in limiting the number of such obligations, the community as a whole worked at defining itself and expelling intruders.

A coalescence of community action and solidarity against the threatened influx of impoverished migrants was clearly at work. Poor or pregnant outsiders were not welcomed. Contemporaries recognised their limited means. Thus they tried to care for their own and urged the rest to move on. 'Their own' was defined by the parish. That was part of the cultural continuity of the Tudor era. However, as stated before, Jacobean parish masters pursued duties quite different from their fifteenth-century predecessors and the changes appear most sharply in a comparative analysis of Tudor churchwardens' accounts. Gone were chantries, relics, shrines, anchorites. Prayers for the dead had been replaced by alms for the living, private masses had given way to public sermons, and devotion to saints had been replaced by service to king and country.

89 As in the case at St Margaret Pattens in 1620: 'Item paid to wandering poor at several times ... £1 2*s*. 10*d*. Paid to diverse poor and impotent men and women travelling by passport ... £1 17*s*. 4*d*.' See GL, MS 4570/1, 2.
90 GL, MS 4457/2.
91 *Ibid.*

Reformation and resistance in Thames/ Severn parishes: the dramatic witness

Dost thou think because thou art virtuous there shall be no more cakes and ale?

[*Twelfth Night*, II, iii. 108–10]

In 1572–73 the churchwardens of St Laurence's, Reading, recorded what was apparently a decision of a parish meeting to regulate the rental of pews because:

the Colleccions or gatheringes heretofore Accostomably vsed for and towardes the mayntenaunce of the Church As well on the feast of All saintes, The feast of the Byrthe of our Lord god As on Hocke Monday & Hocke Tewesdaye; Maye Daye And at the feast of Penticost commonly called Whytsontyde togyther With the Chauntery Landes ar lefte of and cleane taken from the Churche to the great Impoverishement therof, the which heretofore Dyd muche healpe the same ...[1]

This entry comes at a curious place in the account book of the wardens of St Laurence. All evidence of activities 'Accostomably vsed' had disappeared from the book in 1558–59, fourteen years before, and the wardens had been renting pews since at least 1441–42. Edmund Guest, Bishop of Salisbury, made two visits to St Laurence's in the early 1570s – one in 1571, the other in 1573. The recording of this parish decision in the official book of the wardens in 1572 may have been an attempt to assure the bishop that they were conforming to the injunctions.[2]

Yet with its combination of regret and practicality this entry encapsulates the reality of the changes that took place in the life of the parishes of the Thames/Severn watersheds during the sixteenth century. Faced with the necessity of maintaining both their ancient buildings and their churchyards, wardens of most of these locations had exploited the money-making potential of parochial customs for generations. Yet the religious and political changes of the century forced a fundamental transformation in the way these parishes supported themselves. This study attempts to

---

1 Berkshire RO, D/P 97 5/2, p. 349. In this and all subsequent quotations from original documents we have followed guidelines for transcriptions established for the Records of Early English Drama (REED) series. Expansions are indicated by italics and record office abbreviations refer to the List of abbreviations supplied above.
2 Register of Edmund Guest, Wiltshire RO, Diocese of Salisbury, fos 1–15.

chart the progress of reform in this region, reform that was eagerly embraced in some locations, but in others resisted through a potent combination of economic awareness, conviction, and nostalgia. The reasons why the parishes did or did not conform to the ecclesiastical or civil edicts during this period are varied. For some the proximity to Protestant urban authorities at London or Bristol was the greatest influence. For others it was the religious and political persuasion of a powerful local landowner. For many it was the relative fervour with which the ecclesiastical authorities enforced the injunctions, especially for those tucked away deep in the countryside, where there may have seemed no other practical way to meet the costs of the parish.

We have based our survey primarily on churchwardens' accounts surviving as originals or in antiquarian extracts from seven counties centred in the Thames and Severn Valley watersheds – Surrey, Middlesex, Berkshire, Buckinghamshire, Oxfordshire, Gloucestershire, and Bristol, a county in its own right after 1373 (see Fig. 10.1).[3] The sources vary significantly in their coverage of the period before 1600. There are detailed accounts for St Mary's, Lambeth, in Surrey, St Laurence's, Reading, in Berkshire, Thame, Oxfordshire, and St Ewen's, Bristol. Other books such as those from Wing and Ludgershall in Buckinghamshire, Wantage, Stanford in the Vale, and Thatcham in Berkshire, and Marston and Pyrton in Oxfordshire are less carefully kept but nevertheless more detailed than purely summary accounts. Most of the rest are partial or erratic: Middlesex, for example, has but one set of accounts antedating the Elizabethan era and even these, from St Botolph's Aldgate, begin at the end of Henry VIII's reign. The very interesting accounts from St Mary the Virgin's, Tewkesbury, start late, in 1563, and they furnish the primary evidence for parish dramatic activity in Gloucestershire; the seven other sets of churchwardens' accounts are mostly summary and only three predate 1560.

We are fortunate to have a variety of pre-1560 records for Berkshire, Bristol, Oxfordshire, and Surrey, but it should be noted that some of these are known only from idiosyncratic antiquarian extracts. Others have frustrating gaps: the detailed accounts for All Saints, Kingston upon Thames, range from 1503 to 1681, but there is a book missing for the important transitional period 1539–61.

---

3 For a detailed list of these sources see Appendix 10.1. We follow here the pre-1642 county boundaries. Drawing upon research recently completed by ourselves and others for the Thames/Severn Valley region, this survey is the first stage of a larger study of provincial entertainment in England before 1642. We are grateful to the Social Sciences and Humanities Research Council of Canada for their ongoing support of our work.

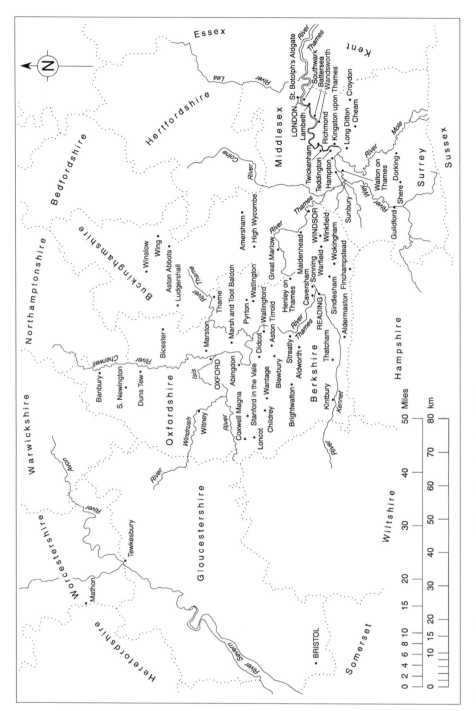

Figure 10.1 Thames/Severn parishes with mimetic activities.

I

The Thames/Severn watersheds provide us with some of the most detailed and important pre-Reformation evidence for dramatic and related mimetic activity in English parishes.[4] Twenty-three sets of churchwardens' accounts survive from before 1536. Of these, fifteen contain entries of interest for this study. When references to activity from twenty-three other parishes with other documentary and antiquarian sources are added, we have evidence from thirty-eight parishes. Four (Kingston upon Thames, Thame, St Laurence, Reading, and Henley) record the production of single episode biblical plays that included Old Testament themes – Jacob and his brothers at Thame (1481), Creation and Cain and Abel at St Laurence (1512 and 1516), the three kings at St Laurence (1499) and Thame (1522) – as well as Easter plays at all four parishes. The latter were recurring events at Thame and Reading, while the play is mentioned only once at Henley (1511) and Kingston (1520); all, however, clearly took the Easter celebrations beyond traditional festive liturgical observances.[5] These four parishes are important witnesses in our growing understanding of the nature of biblical drama in medieval England, since they provide evidence for single episode biblical presentations that contrast with the multi-episode cycles of York, Chester, and Coventry.[6]

More equivocal evidence attests to a Thames Valley tradition of plays on the lives of saints. St Margaret, Southwark, seems to have performed plays for St Margaret's and St Lucy's feast days during the mid-fifteenth century. Thame records a St George play in one year only (1482–83) and a 'box play' (1488–89) portraying the story of SS Fabine and Sabine in 1464. A play on the subject of Amys and Amylon associated with the miracles of the Virgin was performed for the prior of Bicester, Oxfordshire, by what appear to have been players from the local parish in 1424–25.[7]

According to the late fifteenth-century description by the Bristol clerk, Robert Ricart, the religious gild of St Katherine sponsored some sort of play door-to-door for civic officials and prominent citizens on the eve of that saint's festival (25 November).[8] It seems likely that the word 'play' is used here more broadly to refer to a traditional gathering custom

4 We have chosen 1536 as the beginning of the Reformation for our purposes, because the dissolution of the monasteries had a significant impact on several parishes in this study.

5 See Sally-Beth MacLean, 'Festive liturgy and the dramatic connection: a study of Thames Valley parish ceremonial', *Medieval and Renaissance Drama in England*, 8 (1996), 49–62.

6 See A. F. Johnston, 'The Continental connection: a reconsideration', in Alan Knight (ed.), *The Stage as Mirror: Civic Theatre in Late Medieval Europe* (Woodbridge, forthcoming).

7 See A. F. Johnston, '"Amys and Amylon" at Bicester Priory', *REED Newsletter*, 18/2 (1993), 15–18.

8 The 1478–79 entry comes from Ricart's Calendar: Bristol RO, 04720(1)a, f. 160v.

featuring the saint with her followers exacting ritual submission and a
fee from members of the community. St Katherine was the patron saint
of the important Weavers' gild, which had been granted indulgences for
a chapel dedicated to her in Temple Church in the late fourteenth century,
so it is reasonable to assume that the Weavers – possibly with their wives
prominently featured – participated in the mimetic custom associated
with her festival.[9] There is also early evidence from Abingdon of Robert
Neville, Bishop of Salisbury, rebuking the gild of the Holy Cross of St
Helen's parish for having masked men and carrying the devil in effigy
in procession.[10]

Though these plays sometimes brought in small profits for the
parish, they could also incur production costs for making costumes and
constructing stages. More important as assured money raisers for these
Thames Valley parishes and their smaller neighbours were the ubiquitous
summer church ales. They often featured a variety of events such as king
plays or games, when summer kings and queens (mock lords and ladies)
were chosen to preside over festivities that could include Robin Hood
and his followers in attendance, morris dancers, maypoles, and bowers
to shelter the feasters.[11] The remarkably detailed first book of churchwardens' accounts from Kingston upon Thames gives us a vivid picture
of the largest of these summer games. During the early decades of the
sixteenth century its size and spectacle attracted as many as 2,000 people
to this market town. Celebrations went on for a full week at Whitsuntide
in conjunction with the town's Whitsun fair and involved the selling of
'liveries' or paper badges to indicate that the purchaser had paid for the
privilege of joining the party.[12] Payments by the parish to the king game
at other smaller places along the river suggest that Kingston's summer
lord also went in progress, probably by barge, to the parishes of Twicken-
ham, Teddington, Hampton, Long Ditton, West Molesey, Walton on
Thames, and Sunbury.[13] This tour of Kingston's hinterland may have

9 For further insightful discussion of the customs relating to the feasts of St
    Katherine and St Clement (two days earlier) in Bristol, their underlying ritual
    purpose, and sixteenth-century decline see David Harris Sacks, *The Widening
    Gate: Bristol and the Atlantic Economy 1450–1700* (Berkeley, 1991), pp. 140–3. St
    Katherine was the patron saint of young women as well as of spinners and other
    crafts, so festive activities in her honour typically featured women as key par-
    ticipants.
10 Wiltshire RO, D1/2/9, f. 109v.
11 For further detail see A. F. Johnston, 'Summer festivals in the Thames Valley
    counties', in Thomas Pettit and Leif Sondergaard (eds), *Custom, Culture and
    Community*, Proceedings of the 17th International Symposium of the Centre for
    the Study of Vernacular Languages (Odense, 1994), pp. 37–56.
12 For further analysis of Kingston's Whitsun game see Sally-Beth MacLean, 'King
    games and Robin Hood: play and profit at Kingston upon Thames', *Research
    Opportunities in Renaissance Drama*, 29 (1986–87), 85–93.
13 There are separate receipts from Robin Hood's gathering at inland Croydon
    in 1514 and a perhaps related payment for a taborer (drum-player) to go to

called to mind for onlookers genuine royal progresses along the Thames to favoured residences at nearby Richmond and Hampton Court. Intriguingly, a royal household payment at Richmond in May 1505 to the players of Kingston towards the rebuilding of the parish church steeple suggests that the parish troupe included the royal palace in their tour in this year at least, so that local community and royalty encountered each other directly in festive celebration.[14]

Similar events containing various of these festive elements within the context of a king play were held in the two Reading parishes of St Laurence and St Giles as well as at Henley and Thame in Oxfordshire. The Oxford parish of St Aldate had a maypole and hired minstrels without the general framework of a king game. There is also evidence from Amersham for an independent Robin Hood gathering.[15]

Although summer game customs were clearly extraordinarily popular in the Thames Valley, there is only one parish at the other end of our area of study which is known to have sponsored a king game and Robin Hood performance. The limited antiquarian transcripts from the accounts of St Nicholas, Bristol, note in passing payments for May Day 1520 to entertain the summer king, queen, and entourage with minstrels, food, and wine. Costume expenses for Robin Hood and Little John in 1526 show that Bristol, at least in the early sixteenth century, had one parish in the city which featured popular folk characters more typically associated with less urban centres.

Also popular in the Thames Valley – there is no evidence of the custom from Gloucestershire or Bristol – were Hocktide collections or 'gatherings'.[16] Celebrated on the second Monday and Tuesday after Easter, hocking appears to have been a free-spirited inversion-of-order ceremony, a time when women took the lead, binding men who passed by and extracting often substantial dues before releasing them. The men responded in kind, but with less apparent profit on an adjacent

Cheam in 1511. For a later example of reciprocal visits by summer lords see the 1601 evidence from South Kyme in Lincolnshire cited by Ronald Hutton, *The Rise and Fall of Merry England: The Ritual Year 1400–1700* (Oxford, 1994), p. 117.

14 See the Household Book of Henry VII: BL, Add. MS 21480, f. 16.

15 Buckinghamshire RO, PR 4/5/1, p. 1. David Wiles, *The Early Plays of Robin Hood* (Cambridge, 1981), p. 7, citing *Records of Buckinghamshire*, vol. 7 (1892), p. 44, suggests that Robin Hood and the summer lord in Amersham were the same figure. His argument is based on the antiquarian misreading of a 1539–40 entry 'of the lades for Robyn hode' as 'of the lordes of Robyn hode' (misdated 1529–30). This source was unfortunately used also by Hutton, who has enshrined the misdating in his appendix (*Rise and Fall of Merry England*, pp. 32–3, 265).

16 Two studies of the hocktide custom were published in 1996: Sally-Beth MacLean's 'Hocktide: a reassessment of a popular pre-Reformation festival' in Meg Twycross (ed.), *Festive Drama* (Woodbridge, 1996), pp. 233–41, and Katherine French, 'To free them from binding: women in the late medieval English parish', *Journal of Interdisciplinary History*, 27 (1997), 387–412.

day.[17] While other late medieval customs fell from favour in the mid-sixteenth century, hocking remained entrenched as the most constant money-raiser in many Thames Valley parishes even after the Reformation. For example, when the Kingston accounts resume upon the accession of Elizabeth I, only hocking remained of the elaborate parish festivities (at least until 1578). Evidence for a variant on the Hocktide customs comes from Wallingford, where in 1538–39 the town council brought to an end an ancient custom of dancing on Hock Tuesday with sumptuous borrowed costumes.[18]

Although most of the mimetic activities in these parishes occurred during the festive seasons of Eastertide and Whitsuntide, there are a few to be noted at other times during the liturgical calendar.[19] Ceremonial dancing, possibly in the context of liturgical processions through their communities, occurred in two parishes at opposite ends of our area of investigation, both in or near large cities. At St Ewen's, Bristol, both young men and women danced on the dedication day of their parish, and at St Margaret's, Southwark, the young women danced on the patronal festival (20 July). Unlike urban Salisbury, where such ceremonial dancing remained a notable feature of community celebration until 1624, we only see such dancing in Bristol and Southwark for a few years during the second half of the fifteenth century.[20] By the Reformation era it would seem to have been long gone.

Beyond the traditional decoration of the church with boughs and ivy, there were few mimetic customs at Christmastide. Players' garments for an unspecified Christmas event are accounted for at St Peter in the East, Oxford, in 1488–89 and 1495–96. Thanks to prohibitions recorded by Ricart, we know that mumming or disguising must have occurred in Bristol in the late fifteenth century, but whether it had a parish connection is unclear.[21] However, Ricart does describe with considerable relish a

17 Hocking is on record at St Margaret, Southwark, until the early sixteenth century and elsewhere in pre-Reformation Surrey at Guildford, Lambeth, and Shere. West through the Thames Valley it occurred routinely at St Giles and St Laurence, Reading, in Berkshire, at Amersham and Wing in Buckinghamshire, and at Henley, Thame, and St Aldate, St Martin, St Michael, St Peter in the East, and St Peter le Bayly, Oxford.

18 Wallingford Town Minute Book: Berkshire RO, W/ACa 1, f. 55v.

19 The Thames/Severn Valley parishes do not fit neatly into the outline of 'ritualistic' and secular halves of the year posited by Charles Phythian-Adams in his influential study, 'Ceremony and the citizen: the communal year at Coventry 1450–1550', in Peter Clark and Paul Slack (eds), *Crisis and Order in English Towns 1500–1700: Essays in Urban History* (London, 1972), pp. 57–85. For discussion of the variations see MacLean, 'Festive liturgy and the dramatic connection', 51–4.

20 For the enduring Salisbury tradition see Audrey Douglas, '"Owre Thanssynge Day": parish dance and procession in Salisbury', *Folk Music Journal*, 6/5 (1994), 600–16.

21 The 1478–79 entry is in Ricart's Calendar: Bristol RO, 04720(1)a, f. 164.

Bristol version of the traditional boy bishop ceremony usually associated with cathedrals, collegiate churches, religious houses, and schools. The boy's mock episcopacy usually began on St Nicholas's Day (6 December) or at the feast of the Holy Innocents (28 December). In late fifteenth-century Bristol the patronal feast of St Nicholas Church had special observances involving a boy bishop, with the mayor and civic officials in attendance for his sermon and mass. An intriguing civic extension of the bishop's brief episcopacy involved his visit to and blessing of a symbolic dice game played by the mayor, sheriff, and other officials, followed by the sharing of bread and wine before all returned to the church for evensong.[22] As the churchwardens' accounts for the parish do not survive beyond very partial antiquarian extracts, we cannot trace the continuation of this custom up to the Reformation. Nor do we know whether the children whose vestments were noted in a 1485 inventory at St Margaret, Southwark, participated in more than a passing trend at the church, which had notably rich musical resources in that period.[23] The only other church known to have had a boy bishop before the Reformation was St Mary, Lambeth, across the river from Westminster and adjacent to the archbishop's palace on the south bank of the Thames.[24]

Finally, players identified as coming from parishes are recorded in the accounts of other parishes, towns, or patrons in the region. In most instances these sources do not reveal the nature of their performance, only the reward given, and it is typical to have no corresponding churchwardens' accounts surviving from the parishes whose players toured locally. The converse is true of Kingston, where we have evidence in the home church records, but no parallel accounts from the eight host parishes that the summer lord visited. We are probably safe to assume that that most august of patrons, Henry VII, rewarded Kingston's summer lord, or his cohort Robin Hood, at Richmond in 1505, but the royal payment at Greenwich in the Christmas season of 1494 to another troupe of parish players from High Wycombe in Buckinghamshire is less transparent.[25] The Reading gild merchant rewarded players from six neighbouring parishes in the late fourteenth and fifteenth centuries, while

22 For further analysis of this Bristol custom see David Harris Sacks, 'Celebrating authority in Bristol 1475–1640', in Susan Zimmerman and Ronald F. E. Weissman (eds), *Urban Life in the Renaissance* (Newark, N.J., 1989), pp. 198–201.

23 Sally-Beth MacLean and Alan H. Nelson are collaborating on a study of John Medwall and his activities as organist of St Margaret's during the second half of the fifteenth century as part of an essay tentatively entitled 'New light on Henry Medwall'. The St Margaret inventory is held at the Greater London RO, P92/SAV/24, f. 6v.

24 The festivity is noted only in a single year, 1522, when the bishop made a profitable gathering on the eve and feast of St Nicholas.

25 For the Kingston players see above. The High Wycombe players were also paid by the king for performances at Christmastide 1497 and 1498 (see W. R. Streitberger, *Court Revels 1485–1559* (Toronto, 1994), pp. 241, 428).

the Robin Hood troupe of Henley visited St Laurence, Reading, in 1504–05 and the troupe from Finchamstead the next year. Sir Edward Don, sheriff of Buckinghamshire in the early sixteenth century, rewarded players from Watlington, Oxfordshire, and Windsor, Berkshire.[26] In Gloucestershire such evidence comes only at the early date of 1420–21, a year for which accounts survive from the household of Elizabeth Berkeley, Countess of Warwick. From this chance survival we know that local players from the neighbouring parishes of Slimbridge and Wotton under Edge visited Berkeley Castle during the Christmas season.[27]

The range of activity recorded here, although it is derived from only a partial collection of witnesses, testifies to a parish life rich in communal activities linked with the liturgical year and the passing seasons during the opening decades of the sixteenth century. Parishes do not appear to have felt confined to their own boundaries, but seem to have made common cause with their neighbours (sometimes at a considerable distance) to promote the financial and broader community interests of the parish. It is worth noting, however, that there appears to have been some erosion of traditional mimetic customs in the urban centres of Bristol and London, including Southwark on the south bank, by midway through the reign of Henry VIII.[28] Economic development, increases in population, and new religious ideas from local radicals or Continental thinkers influenced the movement towards more secular entertainment in both London and Bristol, as well as the way their parishes raised funds.[29] This trend is distinct from the maintenance of traditional patterns of communal life observable in the parish accounts from market towns and smaller villages in the Thames Valley up to the period of Henrician reforms.[30]

26 The rewards are as follows: Henley and Aldermaston (1382–83) and Wokingham (1385–86) to be found in W. D. Macray, 'The manuscripts of the corporation of Reading', Historical MSS Commission, *Eleventh Report* (London, 1888), App. 7; Sindlesham and Sonning (1421–22), in Berkshire RO, R/FCa 2/11, and Wokingham (1423–24 and 1427–28) in Berkshire RO, R/FCa 2/13, 2/17. The Don household book reference is Warwickshire RO, CR 895/106, fos 200, 235.

27 See Peter Greenfield's edition of this account in Audrey Douglas and Peter Greenfield (eds), *Cumberland/Westmorland/Gloucestershire*, REED (Toronto, 1986), p. 347.

28 For a stimulating analysis of the complex factors underlying the early change in Bristol's ceremonial communal life see Sacks, *The Widening Gate*, pp. 131–59.

29 St Margaret, Southwark, for example, moved away from traditional hocktide activities in the early sixteenth century in favour of rate-paying by the three neighbourhoods in the parish. For the influx of immigrants and other Protestant influences on Southwark from the Continent in the early sixteenth century see Ida Darlington, 'The Reformation in Southwark', *Proceedings of the Huguenot Society of London*, 19 (1955), 66–8.

30 Clive Burgess and Beat Kümin have recently studied such variations from an economic perspective in their essay 'Penitential bequests and parish regimes in late medieval England', *JEH*, 44 (1993), 610–30; see especially 626–30.

II

Henrician reforms brought significant changes to the way parishes marked out their liturgical year. The last recorded Easter play in the Thames Valley was at Thame in 1539, while St Laurence, Reading, had stopped its celebrations the year before. These antedate the first surviving injunction against plays and play-making, from Edmund Bonner, Bishop of London, in 1542: 'That no parsons, vicars, no curates permit or suffer any manner of common plays, games or interludes, to be played, set forth, or declared, within their churches or chapels, where the blessed Sacrament of the altar is, or any other sacrament administered, or Divine service said or sung ...'[31] It is perhaps significant that during the last years of the Easter plays the communities of Reading and Thame were suffering the major loss of their monasteries. Both had grown up under the shadow of their abbeys and the disestablishment of those houses and the sale of the property to families that would become highly influential in local affairs are important threads in this study.

The dissolution of the Benedictine house in Reading in 1539 was central to its urban development. Until Henry granted the town incorporation in 1542, there was no real tradition of civic independence outside matters of markets and trade.[32] The abbot had been the lord of the manor, and as part of his manorial function he nominated the master of the gild merchant each year to act as chief burgess. The last abbot, Hugh Faringdon, was accused of financially supporting the northern rebels, summarily tried, and executed in Reading with two of his monks in 1539.[33] This action is unlikely to have found favour locally, since Coverdale had implied in the spring of that year that 'the area from Newbury ... to Henley-on-Thames was deep in Popery'.[34] There must have been profound repercussions, particularly in neighbouring St Laurence. Backing on to the abbey grounds, the parish had no churchyard, and there are frequent references to the use of the 'Forbury', a space against the abbey wall, for the performance of the parish plays. The accounts record none of the customary activities for two years after the dissolution. In 1541, however, the parish resumed its king play and repeated it in the next two years. In 1542 the wardens paid one of their priests 5s. for his expenses 'to play the play in thabbay'.[35] Whether this was for a strictly parish event

31 Cited from W. H. Frere and W. M. Kennedy (eds), *Visitation Articles and Injunctions of the Period of the Reformation* (3 vols, London, 1910), ii. 88.
32 See Macray, 'The manuscripts of the corporation of Reading', Appendix 7, pp. 168, 179.
33 *DNB*, pp. 1070–1. Abbot since 1520, he rented a pew for his mother in St Laurence's in 1521 (Berkshire RO, D/P 97 5/2, p. 136).
34 Eamon Duffy, *The Stripping of the Altars* (New Haven, 1992), p. 418, citing Myles Coverdale, *Remains*.
35 Berkshire RO, D/P 97 5/2, p. 27.

or for a performance for the resident king's commissioners is impossible to tell.

The Edwardian injunctions (with Bonner's prohibitions still in place) turned their attention to behaviour in and around churches. Ridley's injunctions for the diocese of London in 1550 and Hooper's articles for Worcester targeted rowdiness during service time. Hooper specifically singled out 'plays, games, sports, dancing and such like'.[36] A letter from the king's commissioners to the Bishop of Wells dated 1 November 1547 is more direct. All archdeacons are urged 'to give commaundment unto the churche wardeans and other parishioners, from henceforth to surcease from kepinge any churche ales, because it hath byn declared unto us that many inconveniences hath come by them'. The commissioners recognised the financial importance of the ales in the next sentence, requiring 'yerely collection for the reparacion of their churchies'.[37] This letter highlights a crucial tension of the Reformation's local impact – the insistence that the parish must maintain its own fabric while prohibiting an age-old method of fund-raising. Under such pressure almost all the folk drama and other community activity discussed above also came to an abrupt halt in the Thames/Severn region. In Protestant-minded Bristol, parish evidence suggests that dramatic or related customary activity had already ceased altogether. Furthermore, most biblical plays in the region did not survive beyond the reign of Henry VIII. Although the thirty-five extant churchwardens' accounts could have recorded such activities, only five (from Berkshire, Buckinghamshire, Oxfordshire) maintained their church ales during Edward's reign and only Wing records a continuing tradition of customary activity in the form of hocking.[38]

During the Marian period evidence from forty-three parishes survives. There is an excited sense of revived customary activity from many of these locations. In Thame, where the Edwardian entries (perhaps concealing more extensive festive activity) had given evidence only of a continuing ale, the churchwardens responded to the new regime with exuberance, paying their summer lord 6s. 6d. for his expenses at Whitsun 1554 and hiring a taborer from London for the event. Hock gatherings resumed at Lambeth, all three Reading parishes, Wing, and St Martin, St Michael, and St Peter le Bayly, Oxford, while new evidence for the custom begins at St Botolph, Middlesex, however briefly (1554–55), and St Mary Magdalen and St Mary the Virgin, Oxford.

Parishes energetically renewed their summer games, the other central celebratory and fund-raising event of the post-Easter season. An

36 Frere and Kennedy (eds), *Visitation Articles and Injunctions*, ii. 234, 277–8.
37 W. H. B. Bird and W. P. Baildon (eds), *Calendar of the Manuscripts of the Dean and Chapter of Wells* (London, 1914), ii. 265.
38 The five were Winkfield in Berkshire, Thame, Pyrton, and Marsdon in Oxfordshire, and Wing in Buckinghamshire.

undated Henley account (which internal evidence suggests is from the mid-1550s) has a list of expenses for the refurbishing of the morris costumes, the repairing of the garters of bells, and rewards to one man for playing 'the fool' at Whitsuntide and another for playing his tabor. In Reading the biggest event under Mary was also a revival of the Whitsun games mounted by two parishes. The more lavish of the two would seem to have been organised by St Mary's. At Whitsun 1555 it raised £6 9s. 7d. at its ale, which also incurred expenses for the summer lord's costume, minstrels, liveries, and three dozen bells for the dancers. The next year St Mary's held events on both May Day and Whitsun. This time expenses included a hobby horse, the making of morris costumes, shoes for the dancers, and four dozen more bells as well as payment to minstrels. These festivities continued until 1559.

A number of other Thames Valley parishes record renewed summer games during this period, although in less detail. Guildford's summer lord reigned once more in the North Downs, while the rural parishes of Stanford in the Vale, Berkshire, and Pyrton, Oxfordshire, raised summer poles for their ales. Morris dancers are typically associated with such games, but another account for this period from the large parish of St Olave's, Southwark, illustrates that they could appear in other contexts. St Olave's showed evident enthusiasm for the revival of its rich liturgical celebrations – its patronal feast in late July 1558 is notable for its special features: London waits, clerks from St Magnus' church across the river, and morris dancers were hired to augment this occasion, the last of its kind on the south bank.

No records of customary activity survive from the Severn watershed in the Marian period and the churchwardens' accounts for Kingston parish, former producer of the most ambitious of Whitsun games, are missing between the significant transitional years 1539–60.

III

On 14 January 1559 Sir Francis Knollys, recently returned from exile in Germany, was appointed Elizabeth's vice-chamberlain. From then until his death in 1596 Knollys was one of the leading spokesmen within Elizabeth's government for the Protestant cause. Over the next fifteen years he and his sons acquired considerable property on both sides of the Thames near Reading, including the land once occupied by Reading Abbey. His sixth son, another Sir Francis, became a parishioner of St Laurence.[39] It should not come as a surprise, therefore, that all customary activities came to an end in the Reading parishes. St Laurence's hock gatherings ended in 1558, while St Giles held its last king game in 1556

---

39 Charles Kerry, *A History of the Municipal Church of St Lawrence, Reading* (Reading, 1883), p. 81. For the Knollys family see P. W. Hasler (ed.), *The House of Commons 1558–1603* (London, 1981), ii. 409–20.

and its last hock gathering in 1557. Even St Mary brought its newly refurbished Whitsun event to a close in 1560. From being a centre of such activity in the early years of the century, Reading became one of the first towns in the Thames Valley to stop it altogether.

The disappearance of the customary activities in Reading marks it as a town under the influence of a Protestant landowner. The reformers within the Church once again became hostile to parish customary activity. For example, Archbishop Grindal issued a far-reaching set of injunctions in 1571 while he was at York which included the forbidding of:

anye lordes of misrule or summerr Lordes or ladyes or anye disguised persons or others in christmasse or at may gammes or anye minstrels morrie dauncers or others at Ryshebearinges or at any other tymes to come vnreverentlye into anye churche or chappell or churchyeard ...[40]

Yet considerable tolerance for some traditional forms of entertainment continued in many parts of the Thames/Severn watershed. Churchwardens' accounts survive in original or antiquarian sources from seventy-one parishes from the Elizabethan period. Of these, thirty begin after the queen's accession. In all there is mimetic evidence in this period for forty-one parishes, when we include ecclesiastical court records and other notices.[41]

There are no further records of customary activity in Bristol, Gloucester, or the Middlesex parishes, but in other locations some of the most popular and lucrative forms endured. The once widespread tradition of hock gathering survived into the 1560s at Battersea and Guildford and until 1578 at Kingston in Surrey. The custom also continued at Windsor (Berkshire), Wing and Ludgershall (Buckinghamshire), and St Mary the Virgin, Oxford, until the mid-1580s, while it carried on, remarkably, to the end of the century at St Martin, Oxford, and well into the next century at St Mary Magdalen, St Michael, St Peter le Bayly, and St Peter in the East in the same city.

Evidence of summer festivals exists for several parishes, with records of the increasingly controversial figure of Robin Hood reduced to Abingdon in the 1560s. On the other hand, maypoles continue to be recorded later under Elizabeth in the upper Thames Valley counties at Aston Abbots, Wantage, Wing, Marsh and Toot Baldon, Pyrton, and Thame. The last was taken down at Wing in 1595–96. The Surrey parish of

---

40 See Alexandra F. Johnston and Margaret Rogerson (eds), *York*, REED (Toronto, 1979), i. 358.

41 Evidence of survival of mimetic customs is found in the CWA for thirty-one parishes – five in Surrey, five in Buckinghamshire, ten in Berkshire, ten in Oxfordshire, and one in Gloucestershire. Ecclesiastical court records provide evidence for one further parish in Buckinghamshire, seven in Berkshire, and one in Oxfordshire, with a further entry from a neighbouring parish's accounts adding another parish to Berkshire's total.

Wandsworth's wardens paid to have their pole taken down twice, in 1566–67 and again in 1575–76. Battersea and Wandsworth in Surrey and Abingdon and Wantage in Berkshire record morris dancing before 1570. The last mention of morris in Thatcham comes in 1577–78 and in Thame in 1590–91. In the last decade of the century Great Marlow's accounts provide evidence not only of its own vigorous morris troupe, but also (in the form of payment received for hiring out its morris gear) of dancing in the Berkshire parish of Maidenhead across the river (1593–95).[42]

Another very traditional feature of the summer celebrations, the king game, still appears in the 1560s at Shere in Surrey (1565) and at Henley in Oxfordshire (1563–64); St Mary Magdalen, Oxford, gives evidence of the end of this tradition when it sells its lord's coat in 1562. Summer bowers for these events are recorded relatively late at Thatcham (1574–75) and Wantage (1592–93) in Berkshire and at Marsh and Toot Baldon (1588–89) in Oxfordshire. Wing provides the most extensive and interesting evidence we have for the continuation of the custom of choosing the summer lord and lady. The leading parishioner was Sir William Dormer, whose family, although staunch Catholic sympathisers, continued to be involved in the life of the parish. In 1565 Sir William and two of his neighbours, with the consent of the churchwardens, agreed that any young man once chosen should pay the parish 3*s*. 4*d*. if he did not serve; a young woman chosen and defaulting was to pay 20*d*. For almost every summer for the next fifteen years the names of the lords and ladies of the festival are recorded. They are invariably described as servants: for example, in 1568 Richard Cooke, servant of Sir William Dormer, and two years later Sir William's footman. Wing's summer festival ended in 1600–01 after a prolonged struggle with the Bishop of Lincoln.[43]

The story of the attempts of the parish of Wantage in Berkshire to balance the need to maintain its income with the growing hostility to customary practice is particularly interesting. A remote parish in the Vale of the White Horse away from the busy waterway of the Thames and the roads that followed its course, it was a peculiar of the dean and canons of Windsor, who were at some distance and seem to have had only intermittent interest in its affairs. A substantial parish, Wantage had potential income from a variety of sources. Although, unlike smaller parishes, the income generated from customary activity was not its only significant income, the summer festivals and their attendant mimetic

---

42 For the custom of renting morris gear see Michael Heaney, 'Kingston to Kenilworth: early plebeian morris', *Folklore*, 100/1 (1989), 88–104.

43 See Buckinghamshire RO, PR 234 5/1, fos 87–104. From 1588 until his death in 1616 Sir Robert Dormer, Sir William Dormer's son, made a significant financial contribution to the parish, after which his widow took up the obligation. She 'was living, a Papist', 29 September 1623 (*Complete Peerage*, ii. 412).

celebrations provided the margin of safety, the cushion against the ever present danger of a leaking roof or crumbling foundations. The accounts begin in 1565 and it is clear that this was a community that celebrated the Whitsun festival with enthusiasm. In the first of the surviving documents we learn of morris dancing during the event the parishioners call their 'revel'. In 1581–82 they hired minstrels from outside the parish and paid the substantial sum of 6s. 6d. for their board, which suggests an event of more than one day's duration. There is also evidence that the revel continued as an annual event until 1582–83. In that year the wardens record 40s. proceeds from their revel. However, under expenses we find 6d. paid out for a book of injunctions and 1s. for the Ten Commandments. There is no evidence for customary activity for the next nine years. It seems clear that the parish had been called to account in a visitation from the officials of the dean of Windsor and told to find alternative ways to finance themselves. For almost a decade they struggled to make ends meet and by 1591–92 the income from all sources had dropped to a mere 12s. In that year the customary activities were revived. The wardens recorded £5 4s. 3d. 'of the church ale and other gatherings' with expenses for liveries, a summoner to spread news of the event in the neighbourhood, and payments to the 'vice' and John Rowland, a taborer. Revels income is again recorded in 1592–93, with extra receipts from the sale of the wood from the temporary maypole and the bower. Although there does not seem to have been a summer festival in 1594–95, it returns again in 1595–96 and 1596–97, with Rowland again playing the tabor. The wardens of Wantage could have maintained their financial margin of safety by increasing parish levies or renting pews, but they chose to defy the injunctions of the Church and the hostility of the state, preferring to continue in the old ways. The community seemed, then, to have had a strong sense of nostalgia for traditional methods of generating income. To do this while enjoying the customary Whitsun games and the pleasure of drinking in the company of friends was preferable to the imposition of yet another tax that had the potential to exacerbate community relations rather than enhance them.

Other kinds of records also attest to continuing customary activity well into Elizabeth's reign. A heated controversy swirled around the taking down of the Banbury maypole in Oxfordshire in 1589, with the defendant pleading: 'As for Whitsonales & morisdaunces (beinge in all the Townes about me) I haue restrayned none ...'[44] Other evidence comes from ecclesiastical court proceedings surviving for Berkshire parishes in the diocese of Salisbury. The Sonning churchwardens were cited for holding an ale with a maypole in 1576. Four years later the Didcot churchwarden

---

44 PRO, SP 12/224, f. 97.

vigorously defended himself against the charge of stealing the church cloth, saying it had been the morris dancers who took it.[45]

Several early Elizabethan citations for dancing in service time come from remote areas of Berkshire such as Aston Tirrold on the Berkshire Downs (1560) and Longcot in the Vale of the White Horse (1564). The wardens of Blewbury on the Downs confessed to dancing in 1576, but those from Aldworth five years later claimed it was 'strangers' who disturbed the parson. Even later, the wardens of Streatley on the edge of the Downs were cited for dancing in 1593 but claimed they were present only to stop the rowdiness. Finally, a case against several young people dancing in Coxwell Magna near Wantage was recorded in 1599.[46]

The only ecclesiastical court evidence that is not from Berkshire provides unusual witness to the survival of dramatic activity at the parish level. Parishioners of Winslow in Buckinghamshire were several times cited in the ecclesiastical courts for mimetic activity originating in the parish. In 1575 six men pleaded guilty to 'momery' using the communion cup at Christmas.[47] Five years later the wardens were cited for holding 'in ther church a godly enterlude' and again in 1595 a churchwarden had to defend himself against a similar charge.[48] The wardens of Duns Tew in Oxfordshire were cited in 1584 for having a play in their church. This they admitted but said that 'they did not know whose men they weare'.[49] A similar event took place in Great Marlow in 1593 when the wardens rented the church loft to players. These last two references are clearly to travelling players using the churches as such troupes had done elsewhere. We cannot know for sure what they were playing, any more than we can know what was meant by a 'godly interlude' in Winslow in 1580.

Even at this late date drama could be used as a political statement supporting one side or the other of the religious divide. If Winslow may be an example of a Protestant parish still inclined to play-making with a reformed purpose, there were others with lingering sympathies for the old ways. Intriguingly, perhaps the most surprising information about parish-based drama comes from the otherwise enigmatic county of Gloucestershire. Although there is no evidence extant of parish mimetic activities from the county town of Gloucester, the churchwardens' accounts

45 Wiltshire RO, Dean's Presentments 9, unfoliated (Sonning); Berkshire RO, D/A2/c. 16, f. 89 (Didcot).

46 Berkshire RO, D/A2 c. 5, fos 16, 256v (Aston Tirrold and Longcot); Wiltshire RO, Dean's Presentments 4, unfoliated (Blewbury); Berkshire RO, D/A2 c. 5, f. 168 (Aldworth); Berkshire RO, D/A2 c. 32, f. 93 (Streatley); Berkshire RO, D/A2 c. 42, fos 153–153v, 174–174v, 194 (Coxwell Magna).

47 Archdeacon of St Albans Court Book: Hertfordshire RO, ASA 7/10, fos 35v, 38.

48 *Ibid.*, f. 277v; Archdeacon of St Albans Court Book: Hertfordshire RO, ASA 7/17, f. 27.

49 Oxfordshire Archdeaconry Papers: OA, MS Oxon. c. 7, f. 121.

for Tewkesbury provide important entries on the maintenance of a biblical play or plays that we think indicates the conservative inclinations of this town parish. Tewkesbury had preserved its church fabric as well as some of its more elaborate vestments longer than average into the Elizabethan period. Although the Lady chapel was torn down at the dissolution, the town's purchase of the church allowed protection of lovely effigies and seven medieval painted glass windows, including three representations of the Coronation of the Virgin. Tewkesbury's high altar was removed but not destroyed and is now the largest ancient English altar in existence.[50] Vestments, images, and an old Bible were still being sold in 1576–77, while the 1585 inventory lists 'the best coope of Tynsell with redd roses' among other items.[51]

Frustratingly, the churchwardens' accounts only begin in 1563, but by 1567 we start to pick up a steady stream of receipts for play gear 'loaned' or hired out, apparently to local men, or for renewal of costumes or repair of seats broken at a performance in the church. The last entries of this kind occur in the 1580s accounts and are uncharacteristically for hirings beyond the town. In two years two men from Mathon, eleven miles away in Worcestershire (1583–85), and a 'person of hyllchurche' paid for the loan of play gear at Christmastime, 1584–85.[52] It is apparent both from the list of costumes renewed in 1577–78 and from an inventory of church goods in 1585 that the play (or plays) was based on a New Testament subject, featuring Christ, the Apostles, and the devil. In one year the time of the costume rental is specified as Midsummer Eve, so local performances may have typically occurred at this time. A detailed late account of extraordinary expenses in 1600 also relates to three summer season performances of a play or plays mounted as part of an extended Whitsun ale intended to raise much needed funds for rebuilding the battlement on the tower of the former abbey church. The subject of the play, perhaps prudently, is not mentioned in the account and the need for the enterprise is carefully justified:

Also these Churchewardens vndertooke to sett a battlem*en*t of stone vppon the topp of the tower as now it standeth where before was none, but stoode as it was at the fall of the spier of leade, w*h*ich happened on Easterdeye in the first yeere of the Quenes ma*ie*stis raigne on w*h*ich was a beautifull wooden battlement.[53]

50 See Lionel Gough, *A Short Guide to the Abbey Church of St. Mary the Virgin at Tewkesbury* (5th edn, Tewkesbury, 1991).
51 GRO, P329 CW 2/1, pp. 55, 87.
52 See Greenfield and Douglas (eds), *Cumberland/Westmorland/Gloucestershire*, pp. 335–9.
53 *Ibid.*, pp. 340–2. For further analyis of Tewkesbury's response to Elizabethan reforms see an essay forthcoming by Caroline Litzenberger, 'The coming of Protestantism to Elizabethan Tewkesbury', in Patrick Collinson and John Craig (eds), *The Reformation in English Towns 1500–1640*.

The Tewkesbury example illustrates the value of tracing not only the fate of liturgical practice and church furnishings but also mimetic activities of parishes through post-Reformation churchwardens' accounts. Although parishes were frequently forced to comply with official regulations of their liturgy earlier than they may have liked, their lingering attachment to the extra-liturgical customs of the old church calendar can help us to identify conservative habits of mind.

The rate of progress of the Reformation in the Thames/Severn parishes was undoubtedly affected by the zeal or lassitude of the various bishops of the eight dioceses involved. Unfortunately, the survival of the visitation records and the proceedings of the ecclesiastical courts for these regions is patchy and, for the most part, very late. The Bishops of Lincoln for the Elizabethan period, Cooper, Wickham, and Chaderton, were all firmly of the Puritan persuasion. After Cooper had been translated to Winchester in 1584 he wrote 'to the ministers and chief gentry of his diocese ... to stop morris dancers and similar "heathenish and ungodly customs"'.[54] In light of this opinion, the general paucity of evidence from Buckinghamshire (with a few notable exceptions) should not surprise us. Cooper's predecessors shared his reforming attitude at Winchester, a diocese which included the archdeaconry of Surrey, where traditional activities had an early demise.[55]

Jewell and Guest, the first two Elizabethan Bishops of Salisbury who had jurisdiction over Berkshire, were central figures in the emerging Elizabethan settlement, but the extent of customary activities that flourished in the county suggests that their preoccupations may not have been with the parishes under their care. The visitation books for Salisbury survive in significant numbers from the episcopacy of the third Elizabethan Bishop of Salisbury, John Piers (1577–89). Under Piers, and his successors Coldwell and Cotton, the diocesan officials began to tighten their control over the parish entertainments.[56]

The situation in Oxford was entirely anomalous. Robert King, the first bishop, died in 1557. His successor, Hugh Curen, was not named until 1567 and he died the next year. The see was again vacant until 1589, when it was filled for three more years by John Bridges. For all but four years of the forty-five year reign of Elizabeth, the diocese of Oxford was vacant and the parishes continued their traditional practices unhindered.[57]

54 As cited by Ronald Hutton, *Merry England*, p. 126.
55 See further Darlington, 'The Reformation in Southwark', 65–81. The bishops of Winchester had one of their principal residences in Southwark, so they exercised a more than usually potent influence in the area.
56 See Maurice Powicke and E. B. Fryde (eds), *Handbook of British Chronology* (London, 1961), p. 252. See also *DNB*, pp. 815–19 (Jewell), pp. 1155–6 (Piers), and p. 719 (Coldwell). There is no *DNB* entry for Cotton.
57 See Powicke and Fryde (eds), *Handbook of British Chronology*, p. 244.

Neglect undoubtedly played a role in the diocese of Gloucester as well. Although the Edwardian Bishop Hooper had been vigilant in implementing reforms, his Elizabethan successors were less so. In fact, 'the 1570s saw the ecclesiastical discipline in the diocese reduced practically to the point of collapse, the majority of offenders either refusing to attend when cited or neglecting to obey orders given'.[58] Richard Cheyney, the bishop concerned (1562–79), was more Lutheran than Calvinist and therefore more attendant to troublemaking Puritans than to the conservatives, many of whom were of the gentry class in this county and those on its northern borders.[59] It is into this context that we must place the interesting example of Tewkesbury, at some distance from the Protestant end of the county in the Severn estuary near Bristol.

But the bishops were not the only figures of influence. We have also shown how Reformation and resistance at the parish level were constantly influenced by the coincidence of official policy and local power. In the urban and suburban areas examined, some mimetic customs died long before the Reformation took hold, and few customs survived the reign of Edward. The proximity to the national government in London, at the eastern end of our survey, and the presence of strong Protestant civic rule in Bristol in the west ensured that official policy would be enforced. However, powerful local landowners also influenced customary practice. In the market town of Reading the presence of the Knollys family seems to have been instrumental in bringing the multi-faceted celebrations in all three parishes to an early end. On the other hand, the strong conservative presence of the Dormer family in the life of the parish of Wing seems to have increased its determination to hold to the old customs.

The parish that stands apart from any general conclusion is Thame. Nothing seems to have disturbed its traditional activities. There are two possible reasons for this. At the Reformation it was sequestered from the new diocese of Oxford and with three neighbouring parishes became an independent peculiar free of episcopal jurisdiction. The parish was also made up of two villages – Old and New Thame, with each village holding its own celebration at Whitsun away from the parish church. There was, therefore, never any reason for them to be cited for unlawful activity in the church or the churchyard. The combination of lax ecclesiastical control and local custom protected them from prosecution.

Eleven of the parishes we have been studying – Stanford in the Vale, Thatcham, and Wantage in Berkshire, Thame in Oxfordshire, and, remarkably, all seven parishes in the city of Oxford – continued their traditional activity beyond 1600. But the temper of the times had changed.

---

58 F. Douglas Price, 'Gloucestershire diocese under Bishop Hooper 1551–3', *TBGAS*, 60 (1938), 150.
59 Patrick McGrath, 'Gloucestershire and the Counter-Reformation in the reign of Elizabeth I', *ibid.*, 86 (1969), 5–28.

The festivals were no longer reconciling community events celebrating a widespread common culture as was the case in the pre-Reformation period. The economic imperative seems to loom larger in the parish accounts and, although the customs had not become as politically charged as they would in the Stuart period, the potential for using them as a way of presenting causes in issues of contention in the ever-widening ideological gulf in the country is apparent. What had been celebrations enjoyed by all were to become bitterly disputed partisan activities – but that is another story.

Appendix 10.1 Churchwardens' accounts used

Listed below are all the Reformation era churchwardens' accounts surveyed in manuscript for this study. Where originals do not survive we have used the earliest or most complete antiquarian transcript available, listing the printed source used below. MSS with relevant entries are indicated by an asterisk. Further evidence from other parish, town, or judicial documents is cited in full in the notes.

We would like to acknowledge, gratefully, the extensive research work done by Marianne Briscoe (Oxfordshire), Mark C. Pilkinton (Bristol), and Mary Erler (Middlesex) for their forthcoming editions in the REED series. We have been fortunate to have access to their research reports, transcriptions, and MSS reproductions, at present on deposit at the Records of Early English Drama headquarters in Toronto.

Berkshire

*St Helen, Abingdon: antiquarian extracts printed in A. J. Ward, 'Extracts from the church-wardens accompts of the parish of St Helen's in Abingdon, Berkshire, from the first year of the reign of Philip and Mary to the thirty fourth of Elizabeth, now in the possession of the Reverend Mr G. Benson, with some observations upon them', *Archaeologia*, 1 (1770), 11–23.

Brightwalton 1481–1867: Berkshire RO, D/P 24 5/1.

*Childrey 1568–1688: Berkshire RO, D/P 35 5/1.

*Kintbury 1582–1849: Berkshire RO, D/P 78 5/1.

*Reading:

    *St Giles 1518–1808: Berkshire RO, D/P 96 5/1.

    *St Laurence 1433–58 (fragmentary): Berkshire RO, D/P 97 5/1; 1499–1626: Berkshire RO, D/P 97 5/2.

    *St Mary 1547–1907: Berkshire RO, D/P 98 5/1.

*Stanford in the Vale 1552–1725: Berkshire RO, D/P 118 5/1.

*Thatcham 1561–1633: Berkshire RO, D/P 130 5/1A.

*Wantage 1565–1665: Berkshire RO, D/P 143 5/1.

Warfield, undated fragments: Berkshire RO, D/P 144 5/1; 1586–1728: Berkshire RO, D/P 144 5/2.

*Windsor 1531–84: Berkshire RO, D/EX 554.
Winkfield 1521–1606: Berkshire RO, D/P 151 5/1.

Bristol

All Saints 1407–81, 1446–1662: Bristol RO, P/AS/ChW/1,3(a).
Christ Church 1531–99: Bristol RO, P/XCh/ChW/la.
*St Ewen 1454–1632: Bristol RO, P/StE/ChW/1–2.
St James 1566–1623: Bristol RO, P/StJ/ChW/1 (a).
St John Baptist 1469–1581: Bristol RO, P/StJB/ChW1(a).
St Mary Redcliffe *c*. 1530: PRO, STAC 2/6/90–2; 1548–1600: Bristol RO, P/StMR/ChW/1(a), (b).
*St Nicholas (destroyed in World War II): extracts (1385–1629) printed by E. G. Cuthbert F. Atchley, 'On the mediaeval parish records of the church of St Nicholas, Bristol', *Transactions of the St Paul's Ecclesiological Society*, 6 (1906–10), 35–67, and John Taylor, 'St Nicholas Crypt, Bristol,' *Journal of the British Archaeological Association*, 31 (1875), 374.
St Philip and St Jacob 1562–1783: Bristol RO, P/StP and J/ChW/3a.
St Thomas 1544–1642: Bristol RO, P/StT/ChW/1–75.
Temple 1582–1642: Bristol RO, Temple Records Ca 2(1), Ca 2(2), Ca 6(1).

Buckinghamshire

*Amersham 1539–41, 1597–1607, 1646: Buckinghamshire RO, PR 4 5/1.
*Aston Abbots 1562–1669: Buckinghamshire RO, PR 7 5/1.
*Great Marlow 1593–1674: Buckinghamshire RO, PR 140 5/1.
*Ludgershall 1565–1799: Buckinghamshire RO, PR 138 5/1.
*Wing 1527–1723: Buckinghamshire RO, PR 234 5/1.
Wingrave 1575–1695: Buckinghamshire RO, PR 235 5/1.

Gloucestershire

Dursley 1566–1738: GRO, P 124/CW2/4.
Gloucester:
    St Aldate 1563–1683: GRO, P 154/6/CW1–2.
    St Michael 1546–91: GRO, P 154/14/1.
    St Mary de Crypt 1576–1649: GRO, P 154/11 CW2/1.
Lechlade 1567–70: GRO, P 197/CW2/1.
Minchinhampton 1555–1693: GRO, P 217/CW2/1.
*St Mary the Virgin, Tewkesbury 1563–1703: GRO, P 329/CW2/1.
Tetbury 1589–1703: Tetbury Parish Church.

Middlesex

*St Andrew Holborn 1492+: Bentley Register, late sixteenth-century antiquarian compilation including extracts: GL, MS 4249.

*St Botolph, Aldgate 1547–1690: GL, MS 9235/1–2.

Chelsea 1594–1670: antiquarian extracts in Daniel Lysons, *The Environs of London*, vol. 2 (London, 1792).

East Bedfont 1593–1629: Greater London RO, DRO 84/35.

Oxfordshire

Ambrosden 1550–1686: OA, MS DD Par. Ambrosden c. 6.

Epwell 1594–1680: OA, MS DD Par. Epwell b. 5.

*Henley 1395–1563: OA, Borough Minute Books MSS DD Henley A V/1–4; Church and Bridge Accounts MSS DD Henley C I/1, /4, /7, /36/1, /4; A XII/11/173–4, /183; A V/22, /30.

*Marsh and Toot Baldon 1551–1715: OA, MS FC III/I.

*Marston 1540–1610: OA, MS DD Par. Marston c. 2.

North Leigh 1587–1609 (antiquarian compilation): Bodleian Library, MS Top. Oxon. f. 36.

*Oxford

   *St Aldate 1410, 1536, 1573–1642: OA, MSS DD Par. Oxford St Aldate c. 15–16, b. 17.

   *St Martin 1540–1680: OA, MS DD Par. Oxford St Martin a. 1.

   *St Mary the Virgin 1553–1628: OA, MSS DD Par. Oxford St Mary the Virgin c. 1–2.

   *St Mary Magdalen 1560–1650: OA, MSS DD Par. Oxford St Mary Magdalen a. 1–15, b. 5–41, b. 57–65, c. 58–63, d. 8–9.

   *St Michael 1404–1659: OA, MSS DD Par. Oxford St Michael a. 1–3.

   *St Peter in the East 1443–1546, 1581–1685: OA, MSS DD Par. St Peter in the East a. 1–2, d. 1.

   *St Peter le Bayly 1453–1642: OA, MSS DD Par. Oxford St Peter le Bayly b. 1–3.

*Pyrton 1547–1689: OA, MS DD Par. Pyrton c. 1.

South Newington 1553–1682: OA, MS DD Par. South Newington a. 1.

Spelsbury 1525–1705: OA, MS DD Par. Spelsbury d. 5.

*Thame 1443–1524, 1527–1912: OA, MSS DD Par. Thame c. 5, b. 2.

Warborough, late sixteenth-century (?) fragment: OA, MS DD Par. Warborough c. 3.

Witney 1538–1718: OA, MSS DD Par. Witney d. 1, c. 9.

Surrey

*Battersea 1559–1647: Battersea Local Studies Library.

Bermondsey 1598–1628: Southwark Local Studies Library, MS YJ 852 S

Bletchingley 1546–c. 1553: Folger Shakespeare Library, MS L. b. 84.

Cobham 1588–1839: GMR, PSH/COB/5/1.

Compton 1570–1638: GMR, PSH/COM/6/1.

East Clandon 1590–1755: GMR, PSH/CL. E/7/1/1.

Elstead 1591–1658: GMR, PSH/EL/6/1.

*Holy Trinity, Guildford 1509–73: antiquarian Symmes's extracts included in BL, Add. MS 6167, fos 239–41.

Horley 1507–1702: BL, Add. MS 6173.

*Kingston upon Thames 1503–38, 1561–6, 1567–1681: Surrey RO, KG2/2/1–3.

*Lambeth 1504–1646: Minet Library, Lambeth: P/1/1.

Leigh 1582–1703 (included in parish register): Surrey RO, P19/1/1.

Mortlake 1578–1656 (with vestry minutes): Surrey RO, 2414/4/1.

Seale 1559–1723: GMR, PSH/SEA/2/1.

*Shere 1500–1612: GMR, PSH/SHER/10/1.

*St Margaret's, Southwark 1444–1540: Greater London RO, P92/SAV/1–22.

*St Olave's, Southwark 1546–1610: Southwark Local Studies Library, Southwark Archives 1635.

St Saviour's, Southwark 1552–1605: Greater London RO, P92/SAV/591–2.

*Wandsworth 1545–83, 1590–1654: Greater London RO, P95/ALL 1/43–4.

PART IV

Groups within the parish

Marginality and the assimilation of foreigners in the lay parish community: the case of Sandwich

Francis Gunsales saw the dawn of the sixteenth century in the port of Sandwich on England's south-east coast. He was one of the more powerful, affluent men of the town and served in its government for more than thirty years.[1] While living in the parish of St Clement's he both represented St Clement's on the Common Council and served as one of the church-wardens; he occupied the same offices after he moved to the nearby parish of St Peter's.[2] Gunsales was assessed by Exchequer officials as owning goods worth £20, and he employed at least four servants.[3] What is surprising about this prosperous, successful townsman is that he was not a native Englishman, but a Fleming.[4]

How can the positions of public authority achieved by Gunsales be reconciled with his foreign nationality? Sylvia Thrupp has observed that the problem of assimilation is one of the most interesting aspects of late medieval immigration. She argues that its implications can be understood only by tracing the lives of individuals and their relationship with host communities.[5] This study attempts to pursue that suggestion; it considers the experience of assimilation and exclusion of aliens in the parish communities of Sandwich, Kent, during the late fifteenth and the sixteenth century. Additionally, this chapter relates their experience to that of other 'marginal' groups in the community.

---

1 Gunsales is first listed as a member of the Common Council in the account of 1494–95 and he continued to serve until the account of 1532–33. He never held any other type of town office: CKS West, Sa/AC, 2 and 3.
2 Gunsales appears in the diocesan visitation records as a churchwarden of St Clement's in 1498 and of St Peter's in 1508, 1515, and 1521: CKS East, X 8/2, f. 9r; Z 3/2, f. 100r; Z 3/3, f. 36v, Z 3/4, f. 39r.
3 Gunsales was listed as owning £20 worth of goods in the lay subsidy records: PRO, E 179/124/196 (1523/24). Earlier, in a taxation register kept by the town of Sandwich, he had been assessed as owning goods worth fifty marks: BL, Add. MS 33511 (1513). The latter also listed his four servants: Frances Alien, Alice Mener, Nene Markes, and Frances his boy, who may have been the son of the first servant or of Gunsales himself; the servants were collectively taxed 1s.
4 Both tax documents cited in note 3 label Gunsales an alien; the former describes him as a 'Flemyng'.
5 Sylvia Thrupp, 'A survey of the alien population of England in 1440', in R. Grew and N. H. Steneck (eds), *Society and History: Essays by Sylvia Thrupp* (Ann Arbor, 1977), p. 143.

Kent provides a convenient case study because it had an appreciable alien presence. Although the extent of international migration during the Middle Ages is not precisely known, a national tax of aliens in England in the early 1440s suggests that less than 1 per cent of the population had immigrated from abroad. In Kent, however, the proportion was significantly higher; it had one of the largest alien populations in England.[6]

The town of Sandwich experienced remarkable economic and cultural vitality in the High Middle Ages, but was in a slump in the fifteenth century. The economy operated at a reduced level and malaise characterised town life. Before the fifteenth-century stagnation and decline, the town, one of the principal Cinque Ports, had founded three parishes, three hospitals, and a Carmelite friary. But its population dwindled, and the number of households shrank from 810 in the late fourteenth century to a mere 200 by the mid-sixteenth century.[7] Several factors led to the town's decay. Perhaps the most important were the changes in the geography of the coastline that depleted trade. Although the town was not located directly on the coast, a portion of the river Stour known as Sandwich Haven had provided a safe anchorage.[8] This situation changed in 1287 when a terrible storm struck the coast of Kent, resulting in the formation of sandbanks which narrowed the eastern entrance of the estuary.[9] The subsequent silting of the harbour was a slow process, becoming especially noticeable to the inhabitants during the fifteenth century, when it coincided with the extensive use of larger ships.[10] By the end of the fifteenth century, the days of Sandwich as a major port were over.

Another factor in the town's woes was the intermittent French invasions from the thirteenth to the fifteenth century. Sandwich was burnt in one such attack in 1216, while a second attempt the following year was defeated. The citizens rebuilt and recovered; the town flourished again.[11] However, a French force of 4,000 men invaded in August 1457 and left the town devastated. It was a hit-and-run raid, lasting less than twenty-four hours, but it resulted in the destruction of much of the town and the death of the mayor. The worst devastation hit the two outer parishes, St Mary's

---

6 Thrupp, 'Alien population', pp. 133–8.
7 The best introduction to the history of Sandwich may be found in Dorothy Gardiner, *Historic Haven: The Story of Sandwich* (Derby, 1954). For a history of the Cinque Ports see Katherine Murray, *The Constitutional History of the Cinque Ports* (Manchester, 1953). The former population figure is drawn from Murray, p. 210, the latter from Communicant Lists: BL, Harl. MS 594 (1563). See also *Sandwich, Ancient Town and Cinque Port: Official Guide* (Sandwich, n. d.), p. 17.
8 Edward Hinings, *History, People and Places of the Cinque Ports* (Bourne End, 1975), pp. 44–5.
9 Peter Brandon and Brian Short, *The South East from A.D. 1000* (London, New York, 1990), pp. 74–81.
10 Murray, *Cinque Ports*, p. 209; Gardiner, *Historic Haven*, pp. 195–211.
11 *Ibid.*, pp. 15–18.

and St Peter's, while most of the town centre was preserved.[12] Sandwich never fully recovered from the attack of 1457. Nearly a century later the magistrates issued a declaration that large parts of the town were still uninhabited and that its population was generally impoverished.[13]

In spite of these troubles the town persevered and a substantial number of foreigners continued to reside there. Throughout the first half of the sixteenth century the town treasurers' rolls and lay subsidy records yield clear proof of foreigners living and doing business within its boundaries.[14] These documents are far from comprehensive, but some definite patterns emerge. For example, the alien shopkeepers originated primarily from Scotland, France, and the Low Countries. These national identifications were made in the sources by the use of terms such as 'Scott', 'Brytan', 'Frenchman', 'Dutchman', 'Fleming', and 'Pycard'. This evidence both supports and augments the work of Sylvia Thrupp which asserted that the Kentish alien population was comprised largely of people from France and the Low Countries. That assessment is true, but many had also come from Scotland.[15]

The treasurers' rolls also indicate that, although many of the aliens worked as servants, other occupations were open to them as well. Henry Maister, for example, was described as a brewer, a man named Adrian as a cooper, and one Martyn as a smith.[16] According to the lay subsidy rolls, some foreign nationals had servants of their own. Francis Gunsales did, James Tailor had a servant named Edward, and a 'Widow Adran' employed a servant named Margaret.[17] In short, the economic status of foreign nationals may have been even more precarious than that of their English neighbours, but many prospered and flourished.

Most important, these documents reveal that the aliens lived throughout the town, not in an isolated area within a single parish. Although they sometimes chose to board together, as exemplified by the entry 'a Flemyng in the cornmarket which dwelleth at Olyver Stumble' (Stumbyll also being foreign), it was also quite common for foreigners to share a residence with a local English family.[18] In many cases, the living

---

12 *Ibid.*, pp. 137–40; Brandon and Short, *South East*, pp. 74–81.
13 Peter Clark, 'Reformation and radicalism in Kentish towns *c.* 1500–53', in H. J. Mommsen (ed.), *The Urban Classes, the Nobility and the Reformation: Studies on the Social History of the Reformation in England and Germany* (Stuttgart, 1979), pp. 108–9.
14 The treasurers' rolls had a separate listing for foreigners: CKS West, Sa/FAt (hereafter Treasurers' Rolls). Sandwich also kept internal records of its lay subsidy collections; these are more informative than the official lists in the PRO because they are grouped by household. They also indicated foreign nationals: BL, Add. MS 33511. Neither of these sources may be considered a full listing, but together they constitute a substantial register of the alien population.
15 She also found a number of Irish immigrants: 'Alien population', p. 139.
16 Treasurers' Rolls, 1533–34, 1518–19, 1519–20.
17 BL, Add. MS 33511 (1513).
18 Treasurers' Rolls, 1537–38.

arrangements reflected an occupational situation in which the alien national was a servant. Such was the case of John Van Colyn, working for
William Crips, and of Gerard Tilman, servant of Thomas Petyman.[19] In
other cases the relationship between the foreigner and the native resident
was more ambiguous. For example, 'Dericke Flemynge wt M Piham' and
'a Scot dwelling wt Robert Broke'.[20] These entries may reflect alien
nationals living as boarders with local families. Whatever the actual situation was, their dispersed settlement pattern was apparently common in
medieval England. Sylvia Thrupp concluded from the addresses of aliens
given in the lay subsidy rolls that foreigners were not segregated from
the English and did not cling together physically in national groups.[21]
Instead of having 'alien parishes', a situation which would emerge during
the reign of Elizabeth I, the foreign residents of late medieval Sandwich
lived among the native English and shared with them membership of the
local parishes.[22] While resident strangers must surely have experienced
the occasional xenophobic incident and heard nationalist sentiments, their
dispersed living arrangements indicate a large degree of tolerance and
'openness' in late medieval English culture.

For these foreign nationals, like their English neighbours, the parish
culture and community contained complex and vibrant spiritual and
secular interests, duties, and organisations. Under canon law, lay parishioners bore the collective obligation of maintaining the fabric of the nave
and the ornaments of the church.[23] To meet these managerial and
financial responsibilities, each parish chose two or more churchwardens
to serve as chief administrators for a year or more, and many parishes
also had vestries, groups of senior members of the community, who
audited the accounts and discussed church affairs.[24] Most employed full
or part-time workers such as scribes, carpenters, or additional clergy.
Funds to carry out work and pay salaries were obtained in a variety of
ways, from simple bequests to intricate property investments. The financial

19 BL, Add. MS 33511 (1513).
20 Treasurers' Rolls, 1533–34.
21 Thrupp, 'Alien population', p. 143.
22 Gardiner, *Historic Haven*, p. 175.
23 The custom that parishioners were responsible for the nave while the parson
    or rector was responsible for the chancel probably dates to the early thirteenth
    century. It was formalised at the Synod of Exeter in 1287. See J. H. Bettey,
    Church and Parish: A Guide for Local Historians, Batsford Local History Series
    (London, 1987), p. 39, Ralph Houlbrooke, *Church Courts and the People During
    the English Reformation 1520–1570* (Oxford, 1979), p. 151, and Charles Drew,
    Early Parochial Organisation in England: The Origins of the Office of Churchwarden
    (York, 1954).
24 According to J. Charles Cox, the use of the word 'vestry' to describe these groups
    of auditors and advisers came into general use only in the second half of the
    sixteenth century: *Churchwardens' Accounts from the Fourteenth Century to the Close
    of the Seventeenth Century* (London, 1913), p. 10.

organisation of the parish alone could be very complex.[25] There was, in addition, a social component. Most lay parochial organisations had at least one general meeting each year; many also had ales, feasts, processions, plays, games, and other events to promote Christian charity and a community identity among the parishioners. Moreover, the hierarchy of authority within the lay parish community was intricately connected with secular political and economic status. In short, parochial organisation closely reflected the social network which shaped and mediated relationships within local village and neighbourhood societies.

Given its avowed religious and charitable nature, it would be natural to assume that the parish acted as one of the primary avenues of assimilation open to aliens in medieval England. The Sandwich evidence suggests that the reality may have been more complicated. It is clear that the parish community did not exclude foreigners from activities and services.[26] A good example is the Scotsman Robert Hunter.[27] In the fiscal year 1511–12 the churchwardens of St Mary's granted him a twenty-year lease on a garden.[28] In 1529–30 Hunter paid to have his wife 'churched' in the same church, that is, he reimbursed the wardens for providing a taper when she returned to church for a clerical blessing after absenting herself following the delivery of her child.[29] Robert Hunter was even permitted, after the passage of many years, to join the small parish gild which carried the statue of the patronal saint, the Virgin Mary, in procession and collected alms.[30] This sign of approbation must have been

25 See Chapters 7 and 9 in this volume and B. Kümin, *The Shaping of a Community: The Rise and Reformation of the English Parish c.1400–1560* (Aldershot, 1996).

26 St Mary's is the only one of the three parishes in Sandwich for which the medieval CWA are extant, so most information about the participation of foreigners in the lay parish community is drawn from there: CKS East, U3/11/5/1 (hereafter St Mary's CWA).

27 Robert Hunter was taxed as an alien in the Sandwich treasurers' rolls, 1527–28, 1533–34 and 1537–38. In all three entries he is called a Scot; the last two place him in St Mary's parish.

28 The lease, which appears along with other deeds as a memorandum in the CWA, allocated the garden next to William Crips (a native English parishioner of St Mary's) to Robert Hunter for an annual payment of 16*d*. due on the feast of St Michael the Archangel and required him to make all repairs to the grounds and fence: St Mary's CWA, 1511–12. Subsequent accounts record his rent payments.

29 The cost was 2*d*., which was standard in St Mary's at that time: *ibid.*, 1529–30.

30 No charters or gild accounts are extant for this organisation, but some information may be pieced together from two memoranda in the CWA. The first names a current warden and records the election of a new warden for the next term; this information indicates at least a rudimentary gild organisation. The second notes that money was collected at 'the gaderyng of owr Ladys beryng', which implies that there was an image carried in procession; it also reveals that the gild owned two 'great spits', which suggests that it may have held feasts: St Mary's CWA, folios between the account of 1519–20 and 1520–21, and 1527–28.

near the end of his life; the account which records Hunter's participation in the gild is the last in which he appears.[31]

In the same documents there are numerous instances of foreigners making donations and buying services from the lay parish community, from the most costly and exclusive to the most inexpensive and anonymous. The latter seems more common, which is not surprising in light of the number of aliens who worked as servants. As early as 1448–49, just a few years prior to the devastating raid by the French, the church-wardens of St Mary's recorded that a French woman left a bequest of 12*d.*, and that a Dutch woman donated 6*d.* to buy a wainscot for the church.[32] Such interaction continued beyond the French attack. St Mary's account book of 1522–23 notes that 20d. was given to the church by 'Strangers' on Assumption Day, while that of 1530–31 shows 'a Flemyngs wyfes chyrcheyng' although no payment was registered.[33] These examples suggest that foreigners were involved in their parish and identified with it. The same impression emerges form a consideration of the more affluent members of the stranger community.

Jerome Penell, a Fleming, made at least three donations to St Mary's church and also arranged to have his wife buried within the building in 1509–10.[34] The latter was a privilege accorded to the affluent. Most people were buried in the graveyard and only the well-to-do could afford the expense of interment indoors.[35] This choice represented the ultimate identification of the individual with the church fabric. The tombs of the very wealthy were identified in several ways; their names were inscribed on the monuments and their effigies were sculpted there as well. Even the brass plates marking the graves of the moderately prosperous carried both names and images. Such devices no doubt served to remind the parishioners who the donors were and to reinforce the social standing of their families.[36] There is no evidence to indicate how the Penell grave looked, but the family were clearly affluent. They were not alone; other

---

31 *Ibid.*, 1527.

32 *Ibid.*, 1448–49.

33 *Ibid.*, 1522–23, 1530–31.

34 Penell was labelled a Fleming in the lay subsidy lists: PRO, E 179/124/196 (1523–24). The parish activity is recorded in the CWA, undated account (*c.* 1497–1500), 1507–08, 1509–10, 1510–11.

35 R. C. Finucane, 'Sacred corpse, profane carrion: social ideals and death rituals in the later Middle Ages', in Joachim Whaley (ed.), *Mirrors of Mortality: Studies in the Social History of Death* (London, 1981), pp. 43–4.

36 Christine Carpenter describes these tombs and grave markers: 'The members of the family would be remembered in stone or in brass, as they wished to look for posterity: often surrounded by children, to show how effectively they reproduced their line, perhaps in a judge's robe, like Richard Bingham of Middleton, or more often, in full armour (all ready to take the kingdom of heaven by storm) …'. See her 'The religion of the gentry of fifteenth-century England', in Daniel Williams (ed.), *England in the Fifteenth Century* (Woodbridge, 1987), pp. 69–70.

foreigners arranged for similar burials in St Mary's. For example, Oliver Stumyll, also foreign, had his wife interred within the church building in 1531.[37]

In spite of the availability of services to foreigners, and their active choice to take advantage of them, there are indications that the parish was not necessarily the first institution to make them welcome. Consider the cases of three foreign nationals who achieved positions of public authority: John Bryan, Richard Christmas, and Francis Gunsales. As mentioned earlier, Gunsales, though Flemish, served as both churchwarden and common councillor. The chronology of his office-holding is very interesting. Gunsales first appears as a councillor for St Peter's in 1494–95, as a churchwarden there in 1498, then as a representative to the Common Council for St Clement's in 1502–03, and finally as a churchwarden of the same parish in 1508.[38] In both cases he achieved a distinguished position of public authority in the secular government before holding office within his parish.

Richard Christmas was a shoemaker of an unknown foreign nationality.[39] He became a member of the Common Council in 1537–38 as a representative from St Mary's parish and served on the council for the next nine years.[40] Christmas served the town government in other capacities as well; he was constable for five years and treasurer for one.[41] He became churchwarden of St Mary's parish, but only in 1542, after he had been on the Common Council for five years and had served as both constable and treasurer.[42]

John Bryan, a Scot, also lived in St Mary's parish.[43] He was a wealthy man: in 1513 his goods were assessed at £50, twice the worth of Francis Gunsales.[44] Bryan first served on the Common Council in 1510–11 and as treasurer in the same year. He remained on the council for seven years, serving two terms as constable during the same time.[45] In 1517–18 two important events occurred. One was the death of Bryan's wife. He had her elaborately interred in the church of St Mary's with a stone marker purchased from the parish for her grave; the parish was paid to

---

37 Stumyll appears as an alien in the Sandwich treasurers' rolls twice: 1518–19 and 1519–20. The payment for burial is recorded in the CWA of 1531.
38 See notes 1–2 above. The Common Council of Sandwich, created in 1454–55, was an advisory body to the mayor. Its members were sometimes grouped under their parish in the Year Books, but at other times all listed together. For a discussion of the development of the Common Council see Gardiner, *Historic Haven*, pp. 148–60.
39 Treasurers' Rolls, 1533–34.
40 CKS West, Sa/AC.
41 *Ibid.*
42 St Mary's CWA, 1542–44.
43 Treasurers' Rolls, 1518–19, 1537–38.
44 BL, Add. MS 33511 (1513).
45 CKS West, Sa/AC.

toll the 'knell bell' for her.[46] The ringing of the knell was quite exclusive and normally reserved for the memory of the clergy and very wealthy parishioners. These funerary arrangements no doubt indicated Bryan's esteem for his late wife, but they also undoubtedly served to express and solidify the family's leading role in the community. The second event was Bryan's first term as baron-jurat, a municipal position second only to the mayor.[47] Indeed, the elaborate funeral arrangements Bryan made for his wife may have been expected by the community of someone who held that rank of public office.

Despite John Bryan's wealth and political position, he never achieved the office of churchwarden. The highest parochial office he held was as a member of the committee which 'heard' or audited the accounts, a proto-vestry.[48] For St Mary's, his situation was unusual. It is unlikely that he considered the position of churchwarden beneath him, despite his wealth. Although men of very elevated social positions, such as knights, did not normally take parish office, the class of men who worked their way up through the ranks of the town government almost always did. Moreover, Bryan does not appear to have been indifferent to the lay community of St Mary's: he contributed generously to both a general collection for a rood loft and one to buy new portable organs.[49] His failure to become churchwarden was more likely due to his neighbours' reluctance to elect him than to an unwillingness to serve. Foreigners in Sandwich thus appear to have been admitted into positions of authority in the parish cautiously and only after they had proved themselves in town government.

The overlap of town and parochial office-holding exhibited by these men was not exclusive to the foreign-born in Sandwich but part of a *cursus honorum* of public positions in which the secular and religious were intermeshed.[50] Generally, men who held only the lowest of town offices, such as bailiff, wardman, or member of the Council of Thirty-seven, did not attain office in their lay parish community. For those who moved up in rank, membership of the Common Council was usually achieved prior to, or in the same year as, the office of churchwarden. The great majority of Englishmen who held the highest offices in Sandwich, such as the barons-jurat and mayors, had previously served as churchwardens in their

46 St Mary's CWA, 1517–18.
47 CKS West, Sa/AC.
48 St Mary's CWA, 1512–13.
49 *Ibid.*, 1509–10, 1510–11.
50 There are other examples of religious institutions forming part of a *cursus honorum* to civic office: e.g. the Corpus Christi and Holy Trinity gilds in Coventry: J. R. Lander, *Government and Community: England 1450–1509* (London, 1980), p. 21; see also Charles Phythian-Adams, 'Ceremony and the citizen: the communal year at Coventry 1450–1550', in P. Clark and P. Slack (eds), *Crisis and Order in English Towns 1500–1700* (London, 1972), pp. 57–85.

parish.[51] It appears that the foreigners who held public office were accepted into parish office more slowly, but that both native and foreign-born were expected to have attained a degree of secular authority before gaining admittance to the ranks of parochial authority. Their experience is indicative of a greater pattern of limited access exhibited by medieval parishes.

Given that an unequal distribution of civic power characterised the division between officeholders and other members of the parish community, can an image of spiritual brotherhood be maintained? The concept of a disparate company of parishioners practising social equality on the basis of an assumed spiritual equality in Christ has been severely criticised in recent studies of late medieval England. In a recent article Miri Rubin has challenged even the use of the word 'community' by medieval historians, objecting that it obscures real tensions that existed between individuals. She argues that, while people lived, worked, and played in groups, and while they trusted and helped one another, they did so in a conscious and considered manner, choosing communities when they could or negotiating their place within them in accordance with their own priorities.[52] Even Eamon Duffy, who expressed more optimism about the concept, has asserted that membership of the parish was not so uncomplicatedly all-inclusive as has sometimes been suggested.[53]

Without rejecting the concept of community completely, it is necessary to acknowledge that the late medieval parish was far from egalitarian. While Christians of all nationalities who lived within the boundaries were parishioners according to canon law, they displayed varying degrees of association with their parish church. People who grudgingly paid their tithes and fulfilled only the minimum sacramental requirements, without ever becoming involved in any of the non-compulsory aspects of parochial life, might be called marginal members. Those who constantly did more than was required formed part of the active core, while in between were those whose voluntary activities remained occasional.

Equally important for an understanding of lay parish communities is the observation that the degree of membership experienced by an individual was not determined entirely by choice. The cultural construction of the 'parish community' was fundamentally conservative; it incorporated those preconceptions which fifteenth- and sixteenth-century men and women brought to any social organisation. Certain groups within

---

51 Judy Ann Ford, 'The Community of the Parish in Late Medieval Kent' (Ph.D., Fordham University, 1994), pp. 98–104 and Appendix 2.

52 Miri Rubin, 'Small groups: identity and solidarity in the late Middle Ages', in J. Kermode (ed.), *Enterprise and Individuals in Fifteenth-Century England* (Dover, N.H., 1991), pp. 132–50.

53 Eamon Duffy, *The Stripping of the Altars: Traditional Religion in England c. 1400–c. 1580* (New Haven, London, 1992), pp. 153–4.

the parish found their opportunities for participation restricted by a secular bias, most notably women and the poor.

As an urban environment long past its prime Sandwich had its fair share of poor residents who did not find the parish a place where Christian brotherhood erased social differences among neighbours. While the everyday experience of less affluent parishioners is somewhat difficult to determine, it is clear that they had fewer opportunities for involvement in local religious life. Several parochial services offered an attractive combination of piety and social ostentation, but at a price only few could afford. One example already discussed was burial inside the church building. Another was the foundation of an obit administered by parish officers. These annual observances which re-enacted the funeral services in the parish church not only encouraged intercessory prayer but also enhanced the social standing of the family of the deceased.[54] Their establishment was more common among the well-to-do than among the poor.[55]

Similarly a greater percentage of the affluent bequeathed ornaments, statues, stained glass, and other religious art to their parish church than did those of average or lesser wealth.[56] Individuals who donated money for church ornaments could dictate their design, and it was not uncommon to request that their names and those of kin be displayed on the new items. For example, William Brok of St Peter's, Sandwich, requested in his will that a velvet chasuble, two copes, and an embroidered altar cloth be made and embellished with angels or eagles of gold and 'a scripton uppon every of them to be made of my fadder name my moders and myn'.[57] Eamon Duffy points out that the donor's symbolic proximity to the spiritual center of the community's self-awareness was even more important.[58] Through these bequests wealthy parishioners were able to shape the physical environment of their community's place of worship and symbolically associate themselves with their favourite aspect of religious belief or the cult of a particular saint. Such practices allowed affluent individuals to have a profound influence on parish worship.

Another benefit available only to those able to make generous gifts to the church was inscription on the parish 'bede roll' or list of benefactors. A fragmentary copy of the bede roll of St Mary's, Sandwich, survives from the mid-fifteenth century, complete with names, donations, and sometimes the exact monetary value. For example, one entry reads, 'Also for the

54 See Clive Burgess, '"By quick and by dead": wills and pious provision in late medieval Bristol', *EHR*, 102 (1987), 847–9, and P. W. Fleming, 'Charity, faith and the gentry of Kent 1422–1529', in Tony Pollard (ed.), *Property and Politics: Essays in Later Medieval English History* (New York, 1984).

55 Duffy, *Stripping of the Altars*, p. 136.

56 Ford, 'Community of the Parish', pp. 113–16.

57 CKS West, PRC 17/9/311 (1506).

58 Duffy, *Stripping of the Altars*, pp. 128–9.

sawlys of John Colwy & of hys wyff the whyche gaf be ther lyf days the best cross of sylver & gylt wy a staf of laton and gylt ther to the wyche cost xxv li.'[59] According to the churchwardens' accounts of this parish, the bede roll was read by the priest to the congregation every Sunday, for which he received a small payment from parish funds.[60] The primary purpose of this custom was to encourage prayers for the benefactors, but it also provided a means through which parishioners could create a potent reminder of their wealth and generosity before a captive audience, no doubt enhancing their standing in the community. The fact that some individuals chose to make their donation and have their name inscribed while they still lived is an indication that temporal recognition was a part of the exercise.[61]

In light of the degree of access that the parish community reserved for the wealthy, it is not surprising that only 20 per cent of the poorest testators in Sandwich bequeathed anything to the common fund support-ing the church fabric.[62] This pattern of bequests strongly suggests that economic status was a major determinant of an individual's type of involvement in the parish. The poorest testators were simply unable to afford many of the options available to the more affluent parishioners. The poor of the parish participated in other ways, such as prayers, worship, and the receipt of alms. In fact Christian tradition had always maintained the efficacy of sincere prayers by the poor and the parish elite always encouraged them. Yet participation in Christian worship cannot be judged as identical with participation in the activities developed and maintained by the power elite of a given parish, and the poor often found themselves excluded from the latter.

The correlation between socio-economic status and type of member-ship in a parish community was not always as strong as it was in Sandwich. Duffy argues that the social distance between rich and poor was not as great in rural parishes as in urban ones, because the former were less inclined to emphasise the contributions of wealthy parishioners.[63] But this gap between rich and poor was particularly significant in Sandwich, where, according to Peter Clark, the economic contraction of the town during the late Middle Ages aggravated and increased social polarisation.[64]

---

59 CKS East, U3/173/6/5.
60 The first such entry appears in St Mary's CWA, 1456. The Ashburton accounts also record that the lay community paid the priest to read the bede roll from the pulpit: Robert Whiting, *The Blind Devotion of the People: Popular Religion and the English Reformation* (Cambridge, 1989), pp. 19–20.
61 See Duffy, *Stripping of the Altars*, pp. 153–4, 335–6.
62 Testators who bequeathed less than 1s. for 'forgotten tithes' were classified as 'poor': Ford, 'Community of the Parish', p. 115 and Appendix 2.
63 Duffy, *Stripping of the Altars*, pp. 334–5.
64 Peter Clark, *English Provincial Society from the Reformation to the Revolution: Religion, Politics and Society in Kent 1500–1640* (Hassocks, 1977), p. 8.

The role played by women in the parishes of Sandwich is not a mirror image of that of the poor, but there are resonances of similar exclusion. Here, as elsewhere, women mainly performed menial labour: cleaning the church and its ornaments, or mending altar cloths and vestments. Women were, however, also involved in the funding of their parish communities through bequests and donations, and their contributions to collections. Nevertheless, their economic transactions with the parish community were not without complications. The majority of married men who left wills named their wives as executrices, which turned many widows into debtors to their parish, often for unpaid rent as well as bequests.[65] Characteristic is the case of the widow of John Browning, who remained in debt to St Mary's for rent her former husband owed the parish for a house in the butchery, as well as for his bequest, through the course of twenty years and two successive marriages.[66]

The most conspicuous aspect of the position held by women in parochial communities was their exclusion from formal administrative involvement. No woman held parochial office in Sandwich during the late Middle Ages, nor did women serve as clerks, sextons, or scribes, nor were they ever included among the parishioners recorded as attending parish visitations. In short, the offices and occupations of responsibility and authority were reserved to men. There were very few female churchwardens throughout medieval England and those few usually served under unusual circumstances. For example, Lady Isabel Newton served as a churchwarden in Yatton, Somerset, in the 1490s, but she was a recent widow whose husband had bequeathed a substantial endowment to the parish to fund an intercessory foundation; she no doubt wished to administer the bequest.[67] In most cases women were barred from serving in explicitly authoritative positions in secular society, such as town and village offices, and this restriction seems to have extended to parish communities as well. The latter were clearly not as receptive to the participation of women as they were to that of men: parochial organisations almost universally excluded women from access to office, and hence from the exercise of authority in the decisions made and the actions taken by the laity as a parish community.

The parishioners of Sandwich thus developed parochial organisations

---

65 Clive Burgess, 'Late medieval wills and pious convention: testamentary evidence reconsidered', in Michael Hicks (ed.), *Profit, Piety and the Professions in Later Medieval England* (Gloucester, 1990), p. 21.

66 Her subsequent husbands were Thomas Koc, whom she had married by at least 1456–57, and John Goff, whom she had married by at least 1459–60: St Mary's CWA, 1443–44 to 1463–64.

67 Edmund Hobhouse (ed.), *Churchwardens' Accounts of Croscombe, Pilton, Yatton, Tintinhull, Morebath, and St Michael's Bath*, Somerset Record Society 4 (London, 1890), pp. xi, xx–xxi. Other historians have noted the presence of women parish officers: see Cox, *Churchwardens' Accounts*, p. 11.

principally in tune with conventional cultural expectations and supportive of the existing social order. Women and the poor, whose sphere of activity was always restricted in the secular world, found themselves similarly limited in the ways in which they could participate in their parish community.

In light of parochial attitudes to culturally marginalised groups it is not surprising that foreigners were not sought out by medieval lay parish organisations either. Those aliens who rose above the rank of the servant class had to prove their stature in secular office before being admitted to positions of authority within the parish. In this town secular government was the arena in which social validation was conferred; parochial office merely confirmed what had already been achieved. Francis Gunsales's tenure as churchwarden, remarkable as it may appear, represents not the triumph of Christian brotherhood over real temporal divisions but the ordinary acquisition of public authority by men of wealth in medieval urban environments.

The degree of inclusion of foreigners displayed by parishes in Sandwich during the late fifteenth and early sixteenth centuries was not to remain constant over time; there is evidence of a change in attitude towards them during the late sixteenth century.[68] In 1561 there was a sudden influx of foreigners into the town. Queen Elizabeth I had granted asylum to certain Flemish Protestants who were fleeing religious persecution by the Spanish, and the government of Sandwich petitioned her to send a number of refugees to settle in the town. The hope of both the urban and the royal government was that this resettlement would revitalise Sandwich's flagging economy. Naturally, restrictions were placed upon the newcomers: they were to pay higher taxes and to follow only those occupations not sufficiently filled by native English workers. In other words they were not supposed to compete with the native residents for jobs. Under these conditions approximately 250 aliens, mostly Flemish, moved to Sandwich.[69]

This time the newly arrived foreigners were not integrated into the existing parochial communities. A Dutch consistory was given supervisory authority to discipline the religious and moral behaviour of the 'Strangers'. All the Flemings were required to join the consistory within a month of their arrival; if they did not, they faced banishment and heavy fines.[70] They had their own minister, their own deacons, their own lay council, and, after 1564, they were confined to St Peter's church.[71] In the 1570s a group of Walloons also settled in town, but they were not permitted to

---

68 See Chapter fourteen in this volume.
69 Gardiner, *Historic Haven*, pp. 174–5.
70 *Ibid.*, pp. 175.
71 *Ibid.*, pp. 177–8.

organise religious meetings and had to travel more than ten miles to Canterbury every Sunday for their services.[72]

Why were these newcomers marginalised by parishes to a greater degree than the earlier immigrants? Segregation was not due to respect for different rites, for the 'Strangers' were gradually compelled to change their practices to conform with English custom. For example, the Flemish resisted the convention of choosing godparents for infants who were to be baptised, but they were forced to conform on pain of excommunication. In 1575 the foreign community at Sandwich was required to swear to the articles of faith and to uphold the government of the Church of England.[73] In the course of a century, the experience of Sandwich's resident aliens had completely changed. English national identity and religious sensibilities were more clearly defined and more exclusionary. The confessional age had created distinct groups who did not wish to be merged or assimilated.[74] The national Church, with its English 'Supreme Governor' and English articles of faith, no longer viewed foreigners as fellow believers, but as possible sources of error and 'religious pollution'. The foreigners were now even more marginal, and participation in parish life was forgotten. Their only path to assimilation lay in the larger arenas of Westminster and Canterbury.

72 Walloons were French-speaking inhabitants of the Netherland coast, whose lands were also under Spanish rule: *ibid.*, pp. 175–9.
73 *Ibid.*, p. 178.
74 See Heinz Schilling, *Religion, Political Culture, and the Emergence of Early Modern Society: Essays in German and Dutch History* (Kinderhook, 1992).

Religious policy and parish 'conformity': Cratfield's lands in the sixteenth century

The rural parish of Cratfield, in eastern Suffolk, has been the subject of much scholarly attention, owing to its rich documentation dating from the late fifteenth century. The records, however, are not as conclusive as one might wish.[1] Historians have used the churchwardens' accounts to demonstrate that Cratfield was a rapidly reformed parish by the mid-1540s and also that it displayed conservative tendencies until the Elizabethan period.[2] It is highly unlikely that the two views are compatible, and a more balanced narrative of the Reformation has to rely on further pieces of evidence.

The strength of the surviving accounts lies in the detailed lists of revenues deriving from real estate. This information can be used in conjunction with the large number of deeds and manorial sources relating to parish lands.[3] There were two manors in the area covered by Cratfield church: Cratfield manor, under the lordship of the Earl of Sussex, the accounts of which survive, and the manor of Cratfield Roos, probably belonging to St Neot's priory. This chapter will consider how the parish received its property, how the rents were used in the pre- and post-Reformation periods, and how individual trustees and wardens managed to ensure a period of relative financial stability during the Reformation. The latter was a remarkable achievement, given the devastating impact of the religious changes on parochial budgets elsewhere:[4] as a result of official attacks on the maintenance of lights before images in 1538 many religious gilds no longer met (depriving churchwardens of valuable contributions),[5]

1 Cratfield CWA: Suffolk RO, Ipswich (SROI), FC62/E1/1 (1490–1502), FC62/E1/2 (1507–15), FC62/E1/3 (1533–1709); loose sheets, FC62/A6/1–50 (1533–70).
2 A. E. Nichols, 'Broken up or restored away: iconoclasm in a Suffolk parish', in C. Davidson and A. E. Nichols (eds), *Iconoclasm versus Art and Drama* (Kalamazoo, 1989), pp. 164–96; E. Duffy, *The Stripping of the Altars: Traditional Religion in England c. 1400–c. 1580* (London, New Haven, 1992), p. 569.
3 Cratfield deeds: SROI, FC62/C1/1, FC62/L1/1–25, FC62/N1/1–5; Cratfield manor rolls: CUL, Vanneck MSS, 1402–1652.
4 See the stark assessments in R. Whiting, *The Blind Devotion of the People: Popular Religion and the English Reformation* (Cambridge, 1989), esp. pp. 95–101, and Duffy, *The Stripping of the Altars*, pp. 497–502. On financial regimes in general see C. Burgess and B. Kümin, 'Penitential bequests and parish regimes in late medieval England', *JEH*, 44 (1993), 610–30; B. Kümin, *The Shaping of a Community: The Rise and Reformation of the English Parish c. 1400–1560* (Aldershot, 1996), esp. pp. 103–25 and 205–16 on parish income.
5 Duffy, *Stripping of the Altars*, p. 149.

the abolition of feasts reduced the number of potential collection days, and the two Chantries Acts of 1545 and 1547 removed from the parishes all property relating to gilds, chantries, anniversaries, and other so-called 'superstitious' endowments.

So how did the Cratfield wardens avoid financial ruin? In the main the answer seems to lie in the concealment of property from the Crown from the mid-1530s. Whilst this strategy is of interest in itself,[6] it should also provide some clues as to what may have happened in the country at large had the chantry land been used for charitable purposes – as in some areas of Lutheran Germany – instead of being confiscated for the use of the Crown.[7] The evidence for concealment may tell us little about the parishioners' attitude towards religious change, but it does say something about their willingness to defy the state's desire to appropriate their property. In what follows we shall (I) examine the origin and composition of the parish's landed estate, (II) sketch a profile of the early trustees and wardens, (III) investigate the development of the churchwardens' accounts up to the late sixteenth century, and finally (IV) compare the characteristics of the later parish officers with those of their predecessors.

I

Cratfield parish owned nine major properties and several smaller plots of land on the eve of the Reformation.[8] The rents from some of them, although nominally received for the benefit of the church, actually helped to fund a priest employed by the parish gild of St Thomas the Martyr. The gild itself owned very little land – as we shall see, not even the hall it used for its activities.[9]

By the sixteenth century it was increasingly common for parishes to hold land. Equity jurisdiction protected their tenurial claims in spite of the fact that they were not formally incorporated. The transfer of property in rural communities such as Cratfield, however, was more complex than in some urban contexts. Whereas freehold land could be permanently enfeoffed by its owner for the use of specific beneficiaries, copyhold property could not. Most of the Cratfield holdings belonged to the latter category and were thus subject to manorial custom. As a result

---

6 See, for instance, C. Kitching, 'The quest for concealed lands in the reign of Elizabeth I', *TRHS*, 5th Series 24 (1974), 63–78.

7 H. Cohn, 'Church property in the German Protestant principalities', in E. Kouri and T. Scott (eds), *Politics and Society in Reformation Europe* (London, 1987), pp. 158–87.

8 I am grateful to Dr Neil Jones for his explanation of the legal implications of the different forms of land tenure in this period.

9 On the gild see my 'A late medieval parish gild: the gild of St Thomas the Martyr in Cratfield c. 1470–1542', *Proceedings of the Suffolk Institute of Archaeology and History*, 38 (1995), 261–7.

land held for the use of the parish had to be surrendered in the lord's court before it could be regranted to a new set of trustees. In this chapter, then, the term 'feoffees' will be used only where the sources make it clear that the transaction involved an enfeoffment of freehold estate, while 'trustees' will be applied to those bodies who held copyhold land for the use of the parish.[10]

The parish's landed endowments came from a number of different sources. One of the first properties granted to the church was the house of Sir John Caryell, the parish priest from 1439 to 1444. The gift at once illustrates the ubiquitous problem of changing names. Caryell's house, and the grounds which came with it, were at one stage simply designated 'the town house and close' or 'the house at chancel end'.[11] However, Caryell's gift later became the schoolhouse, and the 'town house' label in the seventeenth century applied to a different property formerly known as Benselyns.[12] Few deeds relating to it have survived; the most important dates from 1553, when it was regranted to a group of trustees. Sixteen years earlier, in 1537, it had been transferred to John Thurketyll, probably as a ruse to prevent its seizure by the Crown.[13]

In the 1460s the parish acquired two more properties. One of them was the aforementioned Benselyns house and adjoining land, given by John Fyn in his will of 1461. Three regrants of the property survive, in 1510, 1533, and 1568.[14] The Benselyns property was substantial enough to have its own account, still mentioned by the churchwardens in the 1540s. Soon after this date, however, when the parish would have been well used to handling landed properties, the revenues were integrated into the main church accounts. The few extracts of the Benselyns' separate records indicate that the proceeds were used, in the 1530s at least, to pay for soldiers and poor relief.[15]

10 For the situation in urban communities cf. C. Burgess, 'Strategies for eternity: perpetual chantry foundation in late medieval Bristol', in C. Harper-Bill (ed.), *Religious Belief and Ecclesiastical Careers in Late Medieval England* (Woodbridge, 1991), pp. 1–33, and for parish landholding generally Kümin, *Shaping of a Community*, pp. 24–7. For the legal background: J. Baker, *An Introduction to English Legal History* (3rd edn, London, 1990), pp. 283ff, and G. H. Jones, *History of the Law of Charity* (Cambridge, 1969), pp. 43, 78.

11 See Cratfield deeds, FC62/L1/18. Caryell's house is the house at the chancel end and identified as the town house in SROI, FC62/A6/23.

12 The rent for the town house or chancel end house in CWA, FC62/A6/17 and 32, is identical to that for the schoolhouse in FC62/A6/36 and 37. I am grateful to Lynn Botelho for the information on Benselyns in the seventeenth century.

13 Deeds, FC62/L1/15.

14 Will of John Fyn 1461: Norfolk RO, NCC, Brosyard f. 258; deeds, FC62/N1/3, 1 and FC62/L1/18.

15 The Benselyns income is notably absent from the first CWA book of 1490–1502, indicating that it was probably not used to subsidise general church expenditure. FC62/E1/3, account for 36 Henry VIII (there are no page or folio numbers in this volume); the opening sections contain the Benselyns accounts.

A second property, called the church house and close, was probably given at the same time. Whilst it was normally called the church house, one entry in 1510 and another in 1537 refer to a property known as 'Flyntards' being rented out for the same return.[16] Interestingly the first reference to a church house occurs in the manorial records of 1462, two years after the death of one John Flyntard. His will contains no further information, but the transfer may have been arranged by his executors, namely his son Thomas and the clergyman John Church.[17]

One property, still surviving with something like the appearance it must have had in the late fifteenth century, is the gildhall situated just south of the church. The building, plus grounds of one acre and one rood (a local measure, usually of between thirty-six and forty-eight square yards), were given by the priest John Rusale in 1502. Rusale actually left the property to the town, by which he probably meant the trustees of the other church lands, for the use of the gild. The hall was not recorded as being rented out, and repairs on it were carried out by the churchwardens. In 1537, whilst the gild was still functioning, the hall and the neighbouring town house passed to John Thurketyll. Both were returned in 1553, when the former became an almshouse and the latter a schoolhouse.[18]

The largest group of donations to the parish, however, dates from the last years of the fifteenth century. Having inherited the family lands from her parents John and Rose after the death of her brother Thomas, Elizabeth Baret and her husband Richard Roberts gradually alienated all their holdings to the use of the parish.[19] A tenement called Barretts was among the first of this group to be granted to the church in 1498. It remained in its possession throughout the sixteenth century, being re-enfeoffed in 1532, 1584, 1590, and again in 1606.[20] Five years later, in 1503, a property known as Swan comprising three acres and three roods accrued to the parish, having initially (and illegally, since the land was not surrendered in the manorial court) been given to the gild. It, too, remained in the hands of the wardens throughout the century.[21] A third property acquired in the same year was called Rose Larks, probably after Rose Baret. It became the most important landed resource for the support of the gild chaplain and was regranted to the church in 1538, 1556, and 1568.[22]

16 CWA, FC62/E1/2, f. 5v; FC62/E1/3, account for 29 Henry VIII.
17 Cratfield manor rolls, Friday after the feast of All Saints 2 Edward IV; will of John Flyntard 1460: SROI, IC/AA2/2/53.
18 Will of John Rusale 1502: NCC, Popy f. 113; CWA, FC62/E1/2, f. 6r, FC62/E1/3, account for 25 Henry VIII (repairs by churchwardens) and Cratfield deeds, FC62/L1/15.
19 Family history traced *ibid.*, FC62/C1/1.
20 *Ibid.*, FC62/C1/1, FC62/L1/2, 7, and 25–7.
21 *Ibid.*, FC62/L1/4/1–2; illegal grant in Cratfield manor rolls, Saturday after the feast of Corpus Christi 17 Henry VII.
22 Deeds, FC62/L1/3, FC62/N1/4–5, FC62/L1/18; Farnhill, 'Parish gild', 262–3.

Cratfield parish thus received the vast majority of its properties in the second half of the fifteenth century. The donors, it would appear, were orthodox Catholics, giving properties for the benefit of their souls. Significantly, however, in view of the later Chantries Acts, the surviving deeds specify no 'superstitious' use for the land, such as a chantry or an anniversary. The churchwardens' accounts suggest that the profits simply augmented parochial income, which offered the community greater financial flexibility. Government legislation, furthermore, posed no real threat to the property: mortmain statutes do not seem to have applied to copyhold land and charitable endowments escaped the clamp-down on uses in the 1530s.[23]

II

Given the gradual accumulation of real estate, the churchwardens and parish trustees played an ever increasing role in Cratfield's history. Fortunately the extensive manorial records allow us to construct a biographical profile of some of these individuals.[24] The group studied here acted for the parish in the period 1490–1510 and can serve as a basis for comparison with the officers of the Reformation period.[25]

Henry Franceys held the churchwardenship one year before his death in 1508. In 1498 he was involved in the illegal alienation of the Swan tenement by Richard Roberts and Elizabeth his wife. He transferred a property known as Tonges, possibly another parish possession, to a new set of trustees in 1507, and acted as one of the feoffees of Barretts in 1502. His age at the time of death is impossible to determine, but he clearly lived longer than he had expected. In 1493 he surrendered over thirty-one acres to fulfil his will, followed by a further six and a half acres a year later. From 1466 Franceys regularly attended the court leet. Only twice, in 1489 and 1493, did he complain against a fellow parishioner, once over debt against John Baret (possibly the formal written record of a loan), and once against William Clerk. No resolution of either case was recorded in the court rolls.[26] He was elected messor (rent collector) in 1499 and surrendered land on behalf of Henry Everard and Elizabeth Smith in 1496. In 1504 and 1506 he faced the charge of illegally alienating land. In a second will of 1509 Franceys left money to nine local parish churches (including £12 for new vestments to Cratfield) and smaller sums to the friars in Orford, Dunwich, and Norwich. He also provided for a tabernacle to house the images of St Margaret and St Anthony and

23 Cf. note 10 above.
24 For the workings of manorial courts see M. K. McIntosh, *Autonomy and Community: The Royal Manor of Havering 1200–1500* (Cambridge, 1986), pp. 181–220.
25 The biographies were compiled from the sources in notes 1 and 3.
26 McIntosh, *Autonomy and Community*, p. 198, suggests that loans were often recorded as debts in manorial records in order to obtain an official record.

requested that a priest sing for him, his wife, and his son John for one year.[27]

John Everard, churchwarden in 1508 and 1510, formed part of a group of senior parishioners noted in 1507. Everard was also a feoffee of the Barretts property and trustee of Rose Larks, Swan, and the fourteen acres of Benselyns. His frequent appearances as a juror at both court leet and court baron between 1500 and 1508 were overshadowed by his numerous offences, chief amongst which was failure to look after his own properties, and a tendency to alienate copyhold land without going to the manor court. On seven separate occasions presentment juries accused Everard of being party to an illegal transfer of property.[28] He was fined in 1499 for failing to cut back some branches which blocked the road, repeatedly instructed to clear out his ditches, and, in 1517 and 1518, charged three times with failing to repair one of his houses. In 1519 he refused to rebuild a fire-damaged property. More serious still were the charges of theft brought against him in 1503, when he was accused of stealing a horse and four cows. In the same year he caused an affray in John Bole's house, while in 1504 Bole accused him of theft. What makes Everard so remarkable is his simultaneous involvement in church and gild business. His various offences do not seem to have ruled him out as a parish trustee, not even those which related to poor maintenance of property.

Robert Smith became churchwarden shortly before he died in 1508. He had been a trustee of Rose Larks and Swan as well as a feoffee of Barretts since the turn of the century and – along with Franceys – one of the recipients of the lands given by Richard and Elizabeth Roberts in 1498. His first appearance in the manor records dates from 1483, when he was a leet juror, and he then regularly served in one of the two courts up to his death. He also acted as ale taster in 1502, as messor in 1503, and as executor of the wills of Thomas Flyntard in 1494, John Crispe in 1496, and Geoffrey Wyott in 1503. In 1496 Smith inherited land from his mother, who had appointed Henry Franceys her executor. His land dealings were extremely rare, and almost wholly restricted to the execution of John Crispe's will: in 1497 he was charged with leaving a tenement called Gowyn's, owned by Crispe, in a poor state of repair, and the accusation reappeared the year after. In 1508, the year of his death, he received some land from Henry Franceys, in an attempt to protect it by means of enfeoffment between Franceys's death and the proving of his will. In his own testament of 4 December Robert Smith left 6s. 8d. to Cratfield church, as well as money to the neighbouring churches of

---

27 Will of Henry Franceys 1509: SROI, IC/AA2/5/50.
28 See, for example, Cratfield manor rolls, Saturday after the feast of Corpus Christi 17 Henry VII. Of course, we only know of the instances when Everard was caught; he may have successfully concealed his actions on other occasions.

Ubbeston and Huntingfield. The latter also received a sum for tithes forgotten, indicating that he probably owned land there.[29]

The Cratfield officers, then, were of similar standing in the parish, all being substantial manorial tenants and conspicuous figures in the seigneurial courts. Their local prestige seems to have influenced the choice of them as officeholders in the church, not least because of their ability to advance money for communal activities. However, the practices of some of them, such as illegally transferring lands, may have cast doubt on their suitability as trustees. Not all of them, of course, proved equally good at the job.

III

Although Cratfield already possessed a number of properties at the time of the first surviving churchwardens' account of 1490, no revenues from them are recorded there. The second account book, from 1507 to 1515, includes the rents of the church house, Barretts, and of Benselyns, but not those of the other tenements. It is only from 1533 that the real impact of the properties on the church becomes clear: the emphasis on landed revenue provides a stark contrast to the first account book, where income had been dominated by ales, legacies, and gifts.[30] From 1533 the church let out around half a dozen properties; some were initially administered by the gild, but after 1542 the churchwardens assumed control over the entire range. As exemplified above, it is often difficult to tell the various holdings apart. Only rarely are they referred to explicitly, and clues have to be retrieved from the sums due or the name of the tenant. Not all the problems, however, can be eliminated: the steep and sudden increase in the rent of Rose Larks in 1566, for instance, may seem unrealistic, particularly when contrasted with the steadier development of revenue from a property such as Benselyns. Can we assume, then, that a much larger rent received for a property in one account actually relates to the same premises as in previous years?

There are some indicators that we can: the tenants of the parish properties in Cratfield are nearly always the same, implying that they retained the same holdings throughout the period. In addition it seems that the church leased its properties for a limited time only. At the end of one agreement a new one was drawn up with a more realistic, inflation-adjusted rent. The respective deeds, made with John Duke in 1538, survive for a property known as Heringfield. The lease extended over seven years, and in 1545 the property was duly returned.[31] Furthermore

29 Will of Robert Smith 1508: SROI, IC/AA2/5/31.
30 The lack of references to lands in the first CWA book, covering the period 1490 to 1502, suggests that they were earmarked for specific purposes and accounted for separately. The largest properties, furthermore, were not in the hands of the parish feoffees until after 1502; for what follows see CWA, FC62/E1/3, *passim*.
31 Cratfield deeds, FC62/L1/8 and 12.

all the rent rises noted for Benselyns, recurring at regular five-year intervals, coincided with a change of tenant.[32] The parish had thus found a way to make the most of its assets, and the rapid rise in inflation over the sixteenth century explains the size of the rent increases.

Landed revenue in the first complete churchwardens' account amounted to a mere 21s. 2d. In addition, however, Benselyns was worth £1 6s. 8d., and Rose Larks and Tonges, administered by the gild, yielded £8 2s. Allowing for some fluctuations in revenue due to property repairs and some poor accounting, this remained unchanged until the demise of the gild in 1542. Afterwards church rents exploded from 17s. 8d. in the previous year to £8 18s. 2d., an increase due almost entirely to the revenues from Rose Larks and Benselyns appearing in the same, single account. In due course more and more money accrued to the parish. In 1545 the Benselyns rent was raised by £1, bringing the total to over £10. Two similar increases, in 1550 and 1556, together with a rise in the rent for the town house and close from 9s. to 15s., boosted the overall receipts to over £12.[33] In the Elizabethan period yet more serious rises were noted in the accounts. The rent of Benselyns reached £5 and, for the first time in thirty years, Rose Larks' rent was increased, from £6 12s. to £11. By 1561 rent revenues stood at £17 12s. 8d. and ten years later at over £20, almost double the revenue received in 1533.[34]

There are two obvious consequences of the parish's ownership of so much property: first, rents came to dominate the accounts and completely changed the fund-raising regime adopted by the parish, and second, the extent of land ownership allowed the wardens to provide more elaborate charitable benefits for parishioners than might have otherwise been the case.

The most striking characteristic of the early accounts is the impression they give of a typical rural parish in the late medieval period.[35] Receipts came from several ales held during the year, various collections, and legacies. The money raised was spent on the fabric of the church and its images. The churchwardens' accounts from the 1530s, however, are entirely different. Receipts for ales are no longer recorded (except for 1536 and 1539) and the two final Plough Monday celebrations appear in 1544 and 1546. Thereafter revenues derived almost exclusively from rents or the sale of trees from church lands. Of course this does not mean

32 Rises in the rent for Rose Larks from 1562 also coincided with new tenants.
33 The town close was actually an orchard.
34 During the same period the price index for a basic basket of consumables rose from 169 (1533) to 265 (1571), i.e. considerably less: E. H. Phelps-Brown and S. V. Hopkins, 'Seven centuries of the prices of consumables', *Economica*, 23 (1956), 312.
35 See CWA, FC62/E1/1; Burgess and Kümin, 'Parish regimes', 617–19. But see SROI, FC62/E4/1 (inventory of 1527), which reveals remarkably expensive provision for church worship.

that church ales or plough celebrations had actually vanished, but it suggests that they were no longer of financial importance to the parish.[36] As a result Cratfield was spared a financial crisis in the mid-century, when traditional forms of fund-raising were either officially discouraged or banned.[37]

In addition to providing a steady source of income the land revenues allowed the parishioners of Cratfield to broaden their horizons in terms of religious or charitable provision. Few village or even market town gilds could employ a full-time priest like Cratfield's St Thomas the Martyr. Following its dissolution two charitable institutions benefited from the parish lands: the almshouse on the one hand,[38] and the school on the other.

Rural schools in the later Middle Ages often amounted to no more than a priest being paid to teach children in his spare time.[39] Cratfield was probably neither large nor wealthy enough to support a school in the pre-Reformation period, but there seem to have been a number of educational efforts. John Warne, for example, who died in 1540, asked his wife, Agnes, to arrange reading and writing tuition for their two sons.[40] More institutional provision eventually emerged in Mary's reign, when a schoolmaster was paid 20s. a quarter in 1559 and 30s. in 1562. The latter is almost identical to the receipts of the gild priest in the 1530s.[41]

The fact that rents from parish lands were still used to benefit parishioners after the dismantling of traditional religious practices raises one important question: how did the church manage to retain so much of its property? The rent receipts make it clear that the church lost no land to the Crown at any stage of the Reformation. In theory this ought not to have been possible. One property, standing immediately south of the church, was called the gildhall, several deeds linked other tenements with the same institution, and the accounts show quite clearly that, even

36 Ceremonial life is described in detail in R. Hutton, *The Rise and Fall of Merry England: The Ritual Year 1400–1700* (Oxford, 1994), pp. 5–48.

37 Kümin, *Shaping of a Community*, p. 214: 'Under Edward [VI], ales were in sharp decline and other fundraising methods not yet established; this worst-case scenario was a reality for many parish communities.'

38 Later accounts are littered with payments for the elderly: L. Botelho, 'Accommodation for the aged poor of Cratfield in the late Tudor and early Stuart period', *Suffolk Review*, NS 24 (1995), 19–31, and 'Provisions for the Elderly in two Early Modern Suffolk Communities' (Ph.D., University of Cambridge, 1996).

39 N. Orme, *Education in the West of England 1066–1548* (Exeter, 1976), pp. 93–109, surveys unendowed schools in the West Country. See also K. Farnhill, 'Religious Gilds and the Parish Community in Late Medieval East Anglia *c.* 1470–1550' (Ph.D., University of Cambridge, forthcoming), chs 2 and 3, for two unendowed Norfolk schools.

40 They were to acquire these skills in preparation for an apprenticeship: Cratfield manor rolls, Wednesday after the feast of the Exaltation of the Holy Cross 31 Henry VIII.

41 CWA, FC62/A6/35 and 37.

if the fraternity did not actually own all the properties, landed revenue
was used to provide for its priest. So how did these assets remain in the
parish's possession?

As indicated above, the parishioners of Cratfield resorted to concealment from the early 1530s. The most obvious asset, the gildhall, was
handed over to a single owner, for fear that a formal enfeoffment or a
renewed grant to trustees would have to specify its actual use. Other
properties named in the gild accounts came to be known as the town
lands, probably in an attempt to deflect any hostile enquiries about their
religious connections.

The parish possessions as such did not require concealment. Neither
deeds nor accounts explicitly specify 'superstitious' uses for them, and
they passed from generation to generation without infringing the Chantries Acts of 1545 or 1547. The 1532 requirement that all uses for the
benefit of parish churches of over twenty years' duration should revert
to the feudal lord, although in practice restricted to superstitious possessions, was preventively circumvented by frequent re-enfeoffment or
regrant.[42] The parishioners of Cratfield, then, concealed what had to be
kept hidden, preserved the endowments which could not be contested,
and thus succeeded in retaining the entire stock of land given to the
parish in the fifteenth and early sixteenth centuries.

This cautious policy seems to have continued well into Elizabeth's
reign. A deed of 1568, which involved the surrender to Simon Smith, lord
of the manor of Cratfield Roos, of all the lands held by the parish in his
manor, followed by his regrant of them for £70, indicates some unease
within the parish about the security of its tenure. The bargain may have
been prompted by news of Crown-licensed investigations into concealed
'chantry' lands or may have been simply the final part of a long-term
strategy.[43] Whatever the precise motivation, it indicates that the lands
were considered to be vulnerable. The 1568 deed marked the final stage
of the parish's efforts to preserve its lands and its financial viability.

IV

We have already examined the kind of people who served as churchwardens and trustees on the eve of the Reformation, when the parish
received much of its land. It is clear from the court records that they did
little to endear themselves to the lord with their cavalier attitude to
manorial discipline. We have also observed, however, that their successors
were astute in the measures they took to preserve the parish lands in the

---

42 On the relevant legislation see S. Raban, *Mortmain Legislation and the English
Church 1279–1500* (Cambridge, 1982), p. 170; E. W. Ives, 'The genesis of the
Statute of Uses', *EHR*, 82 (1967), 673–97; Kümin, *Shaping of a Community*,
pp. 207–8.
43 Cratfield deeds, FC62/L1/18; Kitching, 'Concealed lands'.

1530s and 1540s. This chapter will conclude with a closer examination of three of the later officers and an attempt to illustrate the many links between the major Cratfield families.[44]

William Crispe served as churchwarden from 1545 until 1547, together with Richard Brodbank, himself a figure of some importance in the community, and Richard Baldry. Crispe was also a trustee of Rose Larks from 1538, and parish tenant of the Common Fine Meadow from 1539 until his death in 1557. He had married his wife, Elizabeth, prior to the keeping of parish registers in 1539, and at William's death the couple had three surviving children. Elizabeth died almost exactly one year after her husband in October 1558, and their son John inherited the family lands.[45] Crispe was a regular attender at the manor courts from 1527, when he served as a juror at the leet court. He quarrelled with a relation, Thomas Crispe, a little over a year later about the rights to some property which the latter claimed he had inherited but which William continued to occupy. He served as subconstable in 1542 and as keeper of stray animals in 1550, surrendered land to John Warne in 1540 and Edmund Mellys in 1545, and witnessed the respective transactions of Thomas Smith in 1529 and John Smith of the Hill in 1547.[46]

John Dousing served as churchwarden five times before his death in 1557. He became a trustee of the Swan property in 1539 and a feoffee of Barretts in 1532. Like William Crispe he had married before the parish registers began and named three children in his will.[47] All of them married into two of Cratfield's leading families: Elizabeth became the wife of George Rous in 1555, and William married Elizabeth Brodbank in 1553. By way of cementing that alliance Dousing's other daughter, Margaret, married Edmund Brodbank in 1554. John Dousing's appearances in the manorial records, once disentangled from those of his father and namesake, make the most interesting reading of any of his contemporaries. One of the first references dates from 1533, when Nicholas Ive claimed ownership of the property surrendered by William Fisk one year earlier to Dousing. The demand was reiterated in 1536 by Johanna Ive, former wife of the deceased Augustus Fisk. It would appear that Ive was contesting the dispersal of her husband's estate by one of his relatives. In 1536, however, Dousing compurgated himself by producing six men to back his claim to the land. Four years later he was declared its rightful owner.

---

44 The sources for the biographies are listed in notes 1 and 3. Also used is a microfilmed transcript of the parish registers from 1539: Suffolk RO, Lowestoft, M44/25A.

45 Will of William Crispe 1558: NCC, Veysye f. 306.

46 He also presented Henry Fisk's excuses for his absence from the manorial court in 1535 and witnessed the wills of John Warne in 1538 and John Dousing in 1557. Will of John Warne 1538: SROI, IC/AA2/13/83; will of John Dousing 1557: NCC, Hustinges f. 301.

47 Will of John Dousing 1557: *ibid.*

This episode marks a shift in family allegiances. John Dousing senior had presented Thomas Fisk's excuses for his absence from the manor court in 1509 and surrendered land for two other Fisks, John and Simon, in 1517 and 1530. Before the dispute involving his son, however, Dousing senior seems to have enjoyed good relations with Nicholas Ive as well, presenting the latter's excuses for his absence from court in 1515 and requesting permission to sub-let land from him in 1524. The dispute, then, effectively ended the good relations between the Ives and the Dousings, whilst reinforcing that between the Dousings and the Fisks. John Dousing senior surrendered most of his lands to his son in the early 1540s, after which John Dousing junior, identified as a free tenant in 1547, regularly appeared as a juror at the manorial courts. He served as subconstable once, in 1550, and surrendered land on behalf of John Smith of the Hill in 1547, having been made executor of Smith's will two years earlier. He died in September 1557, leaving most of his lands to his son and heir, William.[48]

John Newson, finally, served as churchwarden with William Orford in 1569 and 1570. Together with John Stubbard he occupied Benselyns from 1544 to 1548, and he had acted as trustee of Swan from 1539, Rose Larks from 1538, and the Cratfield Roos lands from 1568. His marriage to Alice Aldhous in 1546 produced at least two daughters, Mary and Elizabeth. In the manorial records Newson appears as a juror in the leet court from 1547 and as subconstable the year after. In 1555 he presented John Dousing's excuses for his absence from the manor court and three years later witnessed the transfer of lands by William Warne for Richard Aldhous to William Aldhous, the latter two probably relations of his wife. Although accused of failing to maintain properties in 1564 and 1567, he continued to serve on leet court juries until 1582.

The profile of these trustees and wardens is remarkably similar to that of their early sixteenth-century predecessors, apart perhaps from improved adherence to manorial discipline. The fact that some appear more often in secular activities may in part be due to the survival of the records from only one of the two manors of Cratfield. What is most remarkable about this group is the closeness of the relations between them, revealed by the parish registers. Newson, Crispe, and Dousing all had some connections between them, a number cemented by marriage, and both Dousing and another feoffee and warden, William Warne, were linked with the Brodbanks, a family of some importance in Cratfield.[49] Although not by any means a clique, there were strong ties between the

---

48 *Ibid.*
49 A biography of Richard Brodbank is contained in Farnhill, 'Parish gild', 265. For a similarly intertwined village elite in the late Middle Ages see, for instance, E. B. Dewindt, *Land and People in Holywell-cum-Needleworth* (Toronto, 1972), esp. pp. 162–275.

leading families of Cratfield, whose reputation can only have been enhanced by their success in keeping the parish lands in the hands of the
local community.

The study of parochial landholding in Cratfield sheds little light on the
progress of the Reformation or the convictions of the protagonists, but
it offers important insights into the local impact of religious change. What
is clear, for instance, is that the Reformation was no financial disaster for
this particular community. To a large extent it had become immune to
the pecuniary consequences of the attack on church ales, plough gatherings, and other celebrations on which so many other churches relied.
Equally, the confiscation of land held for so-called superstitious purposes
seems not to have affected the parish at all. This was above all an
achievement of its officers. The wardens, trustees, and feoffees, otherwise
increasingly law-abiding, skilfully obscured the extent to which the lands
had been used to fund traditional religious activities and prevented their
confiscation by the Crown. As a result of this lack of conformity Cratfield
was able to redirect its landed income to the support of a school and an
almshouse. The case provides a stark reminder of what would have been
possible in the country at large.[50] More extensive charitable provision,
without recourse to compulsory rates, would surely have been the consequence of a less rapacious government policy towards pre-Reformation
parish endowments.

---

50 On criticism of the Crown's seizure of chantry lands see J.J. Scarisbrick, *The
   Reformation and the English People* (Oxford, 1984), pp. 90–3.

St Michael's, Gloucester, 1540–80: the cost of conformity in sixteenth-century England

In the summer of 1551 the churchwardens of St Michael's, Gloucester, paid two labourers 4s. 'for the cariege of yerthe owte of the churche' to lower the floor where the new communion table was to stand. Three years later they hired a haulier to put it back, and soon after the accession of Elizabeth I they removed it yet again.[1] This pattern suggests a high degree of conformity to the religious preferences of successive Tudor monarchs: radical forms of Protestantism under Edward VI, a Catholic restoration by his sister Mary I, and renewed emphasis on reformed worship under Elizabeth I. But how can we make sense of the evidence from St Michael's? Did the religious convictions of parishioners really change in line with those of their monarchs? Or was it rather, as revisionists have suggested, an inevitable consequence of a well governed state with massive powers of enforcement?[2] This chapter proposes to look for explanations within the parish itself. It will sketch the peculiar context and social composition of a city-centre community in order to arrive at a better understanding of what motivated religious conformity in the mid-Tudor period.

I

The antiquarian John Leland described the city of Gloucester in 1540 as 'antient, well builded of tymbre, and large, ... strongly defended with walles, where it is not well fortified with the deepe stream of Severne Water ... The beauty of the towne lyeth in .2. [*sic*] crossing streets.'[3] St Michael's was situated at the point where those streets crossed, the highest point in the town and the geographical and economic heart of the city. The church building was large, with a chancel, a south aisle, and a south chapel (which had served as the Lady chapel prior to the Reformation). It also had a

---

1 CWA of St Michael's, Gloucester: GRO, P154/14 CW 1/5, 1/7, 1/21.
2 Cf. Christopher Haigh, *English Reformations: Religion, Politics, and Society under the Tudors* (Oxford, 1993); Ronald Hutton, 'The local impact of the Tudor Reformations', in C. Haigh (ed.), *The English Reformation Revised* (Cambridge, 1987), pp. 114–38.
3 John Leland, *The Itinerary of John Leland the Antiquary*, ed. Thomas Hearne (Oxford, 1744), iv/2. 74.

porch and a large square tower containing six bells.[4] In addition, before the abolition of the chantries and lights, the parish was home to 'the fraternytie or company of the crafte of wevers, otherwise called Seynt Annes Service', and a second fraternity 'of certain brethern and sisters' dedicated to St John Baptist which also had a light before the rood and a light dedicated to St Katherine.[5] One of eleven parishes in Gloucester, its boundaries extended to the east along both sides of Eastgate Street to the city wall, and also included a fairly large area outside the gate. Both the market area and the guildhall were located within the parish. As a result of its location, the parish seems to have seen itself as a religious role model, and it counted among its members a high proportion of the city's elite, some aldermen even serving as churchwardens. In addition, city officials were among those whose purchases of church goods and generous gifts assisted the parish in meeting the major expenses of religious conformity.

One such prominent individual was William Bond, who served as sheriff of the city in 1547 and 1554 and as mayor in 1540 and again in 1556 and 1561.[6] During his second term as sheriff he was one of the first to greet the ardently Protestant former Edwardian bishop of the diocese of Gloucester, John Hooper. As a consequence of the Marian restoration of Catholicism, Hooper had been escorted back to the city to be burned at the stake for his religion within sight of his former cathedral. In greeting him, Bond very publicly declined to stand with those who were enforcing the new religious policy. Hooper was most appreciative of the gesture.[7] The same year, 1554, Bond sold back to St Michael's a 'vestemente of redde velvett', a bell (presumably the sacring bell), and 'a patente of a chales of sylver and gilte', all items which he had probably purchased in 1550–51 when St Michael's divested itself of such 'superstitious goods'.[8] Now the parish needed the items once again in order to restore traditional worship to the parish. Also, just a few months before Hooper's death, Bond had paid a debt of 5s. owed to the parish by the previous rector, Nicholas Oldsworth, who had been deprived for marriage, another effect of the Marian ecclesiastical policies.[9] It is difficult to discern Bond's

---

4 A. R. Jurica, 'Churches and chapels', in N. M. Herbert (ed.), *The History of the County of Gloucester* (London, 1988), iv. 307.

5 J. MacLean (ed.), 'Chantry certificates, Gloucestershire (Roll 22)', *TBGAS*, 8 (1883–84), 255; 'History of Gloucester': GRO, D327, Furney MS, p. 426.

6 'History of Gloucester', p. 22.

7 John Foxe, *The Acts and Monuments of John Foxe*, ed. G. Townsend (London, 1846), vi. 655.

8 The accounts for that year do not always indicate the purchaser of the item sold: CWA, 1/5, 1/7.

9 CWA, 1/6. Oldsworth, who had been instituted as rector on 6 September 1550, was deprived for marriage in April 1554. The policy against clerical marriage was one of the most consistently enforced of all the Marian religious policies. Hockaday Abstracts: Gloucester City Library, vol. 219, 1550, unpaginated; GDR: GRO, vol. 1b, p. 13.

personal religious preferences. His purchase of church goods and support for Oldsworth, along with his hospitality toward Bishop Hooper, could be interpreted as signs of his support for the new religion. After all, Protestantism brought with it the need for the parish to alter its worship space and purchase new books, both of which required funding which probably came in part from the sale of those church goods. Furthermore, when Bond paid Oldsworth's debt he may have been supporting his fellow Protestant. But why had Bond kept those church goods, rather than destroying them? That seems more in keeping with the hope of the return of Catholicism. On the other hand, Bond's actions may have been motivated more by civic responsibility than by religious belief, that is, by a desire to assist the parish in responding promptly and completely to official religious policy. In any case he was characteristic of the more prominent members of the parish in that he was always ready to step forward with his ample financial resources to provide needed and timely support. A careful reading of the sources reveals other similarly active individuals, including the alderman John Webley, who also bought and then sold back church goods, and a number of other aldermen and sometime mayors, such as William Hassard, Thomas Seames, and Richard Cugley, who contributed funds more directly to the ongoing operations of the parish.[10]

In April 1557 Bond married another prominent and generous parishioner, the widow Margaret Fawkner, who not only participated in the financial leadership of the parish but additionally, like her male counterparts, led by example in her charitable giving. Margaret's first husband, John Fawkner, had also served as alderman and mayor in the 1530s and early 1540s, while Margaret, too, had purchased church goods in 1550–51. Two years later she was one of those who assumed the responsibility of 'finding' (that is, funding) the parish clerk one day each week for a year.[11] William Bond died on 8 June 1565 and in his will he declared his assurance in his salvation by Christ's death and passion, 'not dowtinge that throughe the deathe of the same my God and savyor I have remyssion of my syns and ever shall have the fruycion of that which he the same God hath soe dearely boughte', thus affirming his Protestant faith. He went on to leave £20 and twelve black gowns to the needy.[12] Margaret died just two months later and left both money and rents from specified lands to the poor.[13]

The Bonds' wills also begin to reveal a leadership network within

10 CWA, *passim*.
11 Parish Register of St Michael's, Gloucester: GRO, P154/14 IN 1/116; 'History of Gloucester', p. 21; PRO, PROB 11/30, fos 283–4; CWA, 1/6.
12 Gloucester Corporation Records: GRO, B2/1, f. 29v; Parish Register: IN 1/171; Gloucestershire Wills: GRO, 1565/116.
13 Parish Register: IN 1/171; Gloucestershire Wills, 1565–66.

the parish which overlapped with that of the city aldermen and included other prominent families in Gloucester.[14] They contain connections with aldermen Richard Cugley senior, Bryan Fayrfaxe, John Celye, Thomas Lane, and Thomas Seames. Richard Cugley senior, in turn, was linked with prominent parishioners such as Richard and Jone Goldeston and John Restall. In their wills the Goldestons mentioned Richard Pate, the city clerk and MP, and the following prominent parishioners: Agnes Restall (wife of John and widow of William Webbe, churchwarden), John Webley, Richard senior, Richard junior and Thomas Cugley, William Walkeley, and Humphrey Taylor. Similarly linked by common responsibilities, friendship, and marriage, the whole parish leadership network consisted of approximately forty-five families.

This key group provided the individuals who assumed both leadership roles and special financial responsibilities in support of the parish. It supplied most of the churchwardens and most of those funding the position of parish clerk. In the thirty-six years from 1545 to 1580 thirty-five different individuals were churchwardens, serving two-year terms in pairs. The network of the parish elite contributed twenty-seven of these men (over 75 per cent), including one father–son combination (Richard and William Wayte) and two pairs of brothers: Richard and William Goldeston as well as Robert and William Walkeley. An additional fraternal pairing may have been John Taylor alias Coke and Henry Taylor junior, each of whom served a term as churchwarden. Most wardens stayed in office for one term, spreading the duties and responsibilities among the parish's prominent families. Only one person, Richard Cugley senior, served twice.[15]

Funding the clerk with its concomitant financial burden necessarily involved a much larger number of individuals. In order to spread the expense seven people were chosen annually, each being responsible for paying the clerk's wages. The magisterial community all contributed to the parish in this manner, as did some equally well connected women. This group also included relatives of former churchwardens, as is illustrated by the Webbe family. William Webbe is the earliest churchwarden listed in the surviving records. The same year he occupied the office, his brother, Thomas, was one of those responsible for funding the clerk. Following William's death, his widow, Agnes, took on the same responsibility for a year. Richard Cugley's two sons each served in that capacity for at least one year, and the brothers of two other churchwardens also

14 The parish leadership network was identified by developing nominal linkages between individuals and families based on the following records: CWA, 1/1–1/31; Parish Register: IN 1/5–1/28, 1/113–1/129, 1/163–1/187; Gloucester Corporation Records: B2/1, B3/1; 'History of Gloucester'; Gloucestershire Wills; PRO, PROB 11; Episcopal and Archiepiscopal Visitation Records: GDR, vols 20, 26, 29, 40.
15 CWA, 1/1–1/31, *passim*.

took their turn. Henry Taylor and Humphrey Walkeley, fathers of church-wardens, served as well.[16] The task seems to have been a prerequisite for acting as churchwarden.[17] However, many more people were needed: sixty-four parishioners who helped to fund the clerk never became church-wardens, but only twelve of them were from the leadership network.[18]

Even though a parish elite can be clearly identified, the responsi-bilities of funding and running the church were spread among an even larger part of the congregation. This in turn provided a broad base of support for the parish during the difficult times of the mid-sixteenth century. For instance, funding the clerk also provided an opportunity for some women, albeit all widows, to be involved in the leadership of the parish. In addition to Agnes Webbe and Margaret Fawkner, mentioned above, two other women also served in that capacity. Jone Edwards, a widow and the mother of Richard and Elizabeth, helped out in 1556–57, and Katherine Messyngers, widow of Robert, in 1559–60.[19] In each case the woman's participation seems to have been limited to providing fin-ancial support. There were no female churchwardens during this period and one gets the sense that more active involvement would not have been tolerated.

One of the predominant characteristics of St Michael's was its strong sense of accord and community. Only two parishioners appear in the records for failing to conform between 1541 and 1580; however, a more probable explanation may be found by considering the cohesive nature of the parish leadership network and its close ties with the civic elite. The actions of others may have been concealed from the authorities to preserve an image of compliance. Hugh Dorington refused to honour the sacra-ment in 1556 and was required to perform his penance while standing 'under the pulpitte in the tyme of the priestes beinge at the beades and

---

16 Thomas Webbe served again in that capacity nine years later. John Sandes acted as churchwarden in 1549–50 and 1550–51, while his brother, William, was one of those responsible for funding the clerk in 1562–63. Richard Smythe, who served in 1570–71, may have been the brother of John Smythe, brewer and churchwarden in 1566–67 and 1567–68. CWA, 1/1–1/31, *passim*.

17 Only William Webbe (1545–46), the Walkeley brothers, the Taylors, and William Gybbes (1578–79 and 1579–80) served as churchwardens without having pre-viously been one of those responsible for funding the clerk for at least one year. Both responsibilities required some degree of individual affluence, so it is not surprising to find the two roles relying on the same group of people. The churchwarden would often be expected to meet a shortfall in parish finances from his own pocket, while those funding the clerk were also using their own resources.

18 This may have been the 'shallow lower slope' of the leadership pyramid described for Chester parishes. Nicholas Alldridge, 'Loyalty and identity in Chester par-ishes 1540–1640', in S. Wright (ed.), *Parish, Church and People: Local Studies in Lay Religion 1350–1750* (London, 1988), p. 107.

19 CWA, 1/2, 1/6, 1/8, 1/11; Parish Register, IN 1/116. Margaret Fawkner also purchased a chair from the parish in 1550–51: CWA, 1/5.

there ... [to read] certen werdes to be written unto him'. Some sixteen years later, in 1572, John Stevens was presented for failing to receive communion.[20] The scarcity of cases concerning nonconformity at St Michael's could indicate that the parish did indeed adapt uniformly and immediately to each new set of directives. However, those in charge may have preferred to present a public image of unanimity and accord, given their prominence within the city; they may have privately disciplined nonconformists themselves to preserve harmony. With no strife, resistance, or dissension apparent within their ranks, they would have been able to maintain the parish's claim to set a standard for others to follow, a standard characterised by conscientious religious conformity and a beautifully adorned, well maintained edifice.

II

St Michael's parish funds were also managed in a coherent and uniform manner, despite the heavy, sporadic demands on the parish chest between 1545 and 1580 (see Table 13.1 and Fig. 13.1 for expense details).[21] Many items and activities which had been supported by other sources, such as communion bread and wine (previously paid for by the clergy), appeared as parish expenses for the first time in Mary's reign and then increased substantially after Elizabeth's accession.[22] Some more traditional categories, such as visitation expenses, now increased significantly. In addition to the cost of preparing the requisite bill of presentment, for instance, the parish now had to pay the apparitor and diocesan registrar several pence each for their services in exhibiting the bill and the wardens were often required to give the archdeacon or bishop several shillings 'for his procurations' as well. From 1561–62 the parish also began providing food and drink on the day of the visitation for those who were to represent the parish before the diocesan representative.[23]

In response to these and other increased demands for funds St Michael's developed new fund-raising devices and assigned old forms of revenue to new uses (see Table 13.2 and Fig. 13.2 for revenue details). Beginning in 1557 a rate was assessed on the more affluent parishioners, apparently in lieu of the tithe previously collected by the rector. Then,

20 GDR, vol. 26, p. 63; vol. 11, p. 205. Stevens appeared in court on 4 October 1572 and said that he had received in the cathedral. The case was adjourned: *ibid.*, vol. 29, p. 85.

21 CWA, *passim*.

22 The cost of bread and wine purchased with parish funds increased from 4s. 6d. to £1 6s. 3d. during the period from 1555 to 1577 before dropping to 16s. 9d. in 1580. While this general increase may have been due in part to inflation, it may also indicate that St Michael's parishioners were conforming to the requirement that they should receive communion three times a year, rather than just at Easter as in the past. (There is no indication as to why the amount spent decreased in 1580.) CWA, 1/8–1/31, *passim*.

23 *Ibid.*, 1/13–1/31, *passim*.

Table 13.1 *St Michael's Gloucester: total annual expenses by category (in old pence)*

Year	Fabric	Liturgy	Visit.	Misc.[a]	Totals
1546	374	386	2	283	1,045
1547	705	434	4	245	1,388
1548					
1549	303	169	2	71	545
1550	653	171			824
1551	6,348	341		113	6,802
1552	2,000	22	30	195	2,247
1553					
1554	729	2,142		254	3,125
1555					
1556	1,407	721	16	62	2,206
1557	577	373	26	35	1,011
1558	654	741	21	49	1,465
1559	584	630	40	72	1,326
1560	635	1,054	7	6	1,702
1561	6,672	238	65	19	6,994
1562	1,713	120	9	20	1,862
1563	874	202	94	738	1,908
1564	502	222	16	32	772
1565	1,809	515	82	259	2,665
1566	988	248	116	43	1,395
1567	2,066	225	119	79	2,489
1568	424	120		90	634
1569	991	523	589	59	2,162
1570	1,447	844	51	98	2,440
1571	1,588	340	52	54	2,034
1572					
1573	647	481	47	644	1,819
1574	3,261	386	53	159	4,159
1575	843	324	82	78	1,327
1576	2,100	394	72	262	2,828
1577	718	351	32	112	1,213
1578	929	363	122	88	1,502
1579	432	230	68	100	830
1580	571	276	112	142	1,101
Totals	43,544	13,586	1,929	4,761	63,820

Note
a 'Misc.' expenses include payments for obits, subsidies, priests' wages, writing the accounts, paper, Pentecost money, repairs of rental houses, etc.
Source CWA of St Michael's, Gloucester: GRO, P154/14 CW 1/1–1/31.

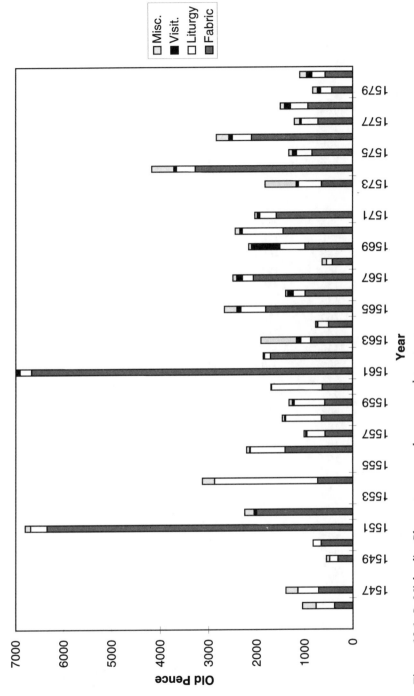

Figure 13.1 St Michael's, Gloucester: annual expenses, by category.

Table 13.2 *St Michael's, Gloucester: total annual revenue by category of income (in old pence)*

Year	Seats	Easter	Rents	Sales [a]	Misc. [b]	Totals
1546	234	138	632		20	1,024
1547	176	78	632		152	1,038
1548						
1549	165		512		172	849
1550	193		512		6	711
1551	159		512	6,510	800	7,981
1552	212		512	6	2	732
1553						
1554			512	60		572
1555						
1556	288	204	516	16	52	1,076
1557	196	170	516	960	690	2,532
1558	192	168	516		252	1,128
1559	180	124	516		2,015	2,835
1560	132	652	516		40	1,340
1561	132	624	708	2,147	326	3,937
1562	160	726	324		621	1,831
1563	186	888	516		500	2,090
1564	156	600	516		24	1,296
1565	200	930	532		144	1,806
1566	218	965	532		120	1,835
1567	244	1,042	532		116	1,934
1568	208	1,052	532		89	1,881
1569	168	1,020	532	132	244	2,096
1570	198	1,036	532		40	1,806
1571	192	1,034	532	240		1,998
1572						
1573	216		564		40	820
1574	196		844			1,040
1575	209		272		120	601
1576	196		564		18	778
1577	209		564		53	826
1578	208		564		68	840
1579	192		564		320	1,076
1580	193	223	564		144	1,124
Totals	5,808	11,674	16,692	10,071	7,188	51,433

Notes
a 'Sales' refers to receipts from the sale of church goods.
b 'Misc.' revenues includes receipts from church rates and debts owed to the parish, and for lights, knells, gravestones, burials, churchings of women, etc.
Source CWA of St Michael's: GRO, P154/14 CW 1/1–1/31.

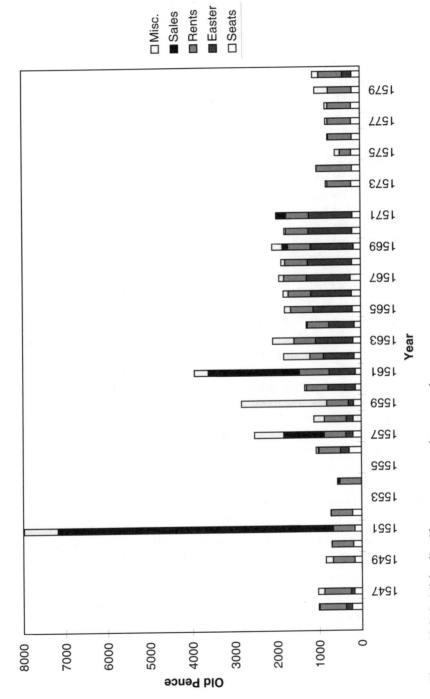

Figure 13.2 St Michael's, Gloucester: annual revenue, by category.

too, Easter money, which had long been a regular source of income and had traditionally provided the funds for the Easter taper, reappeared in Mary's reign (it had lapsed during Edward VI's reign, since the taper was no longer permitted). Again, following Elizabeth's accession, the taper was eliminated; however, in the early 1560s Easter money was put to a new use, and the amount collected was considerable. As was the case in Chester and probably in other parishes across England, receipts from this source were to be put toward the priest's wages, but at St Michael's this assessment was selective rather than comprehensive.[24] It was gathered from 'those parishioners there that doth not contribute to the pryest wayges', probably an indication that St Michael's no longer had a resident rector.[25] The parish was in the gift of the Crown, but the latter seems to have neglected its duty to appoint a clergyman. Lacking adequate provision for either a rector or a curate from that quarter, the parish had found it necessary to hire its own priest. In this way the churchwardens were able to assess the poorer members of the parish, those who were not paying the regular parish rate. This reliance on receipts from rates and other assessments on parishioners to fund their parish priest was not unique to St Michael's. For instance, some parishes in nearby Bristol also lacked resident rectors and raised money to pay their priests in a similar manner.[26] Additionally they looked for ways to spread their income-gathering net to include those beyond the confines of the parish, an option which was more difficult for urban than for rural parishes. The latter traditionally raised funds from non-parishioners by holding church ales which attracted people from the surrounding countryside, but such events were held much less frequently in the cities.[27] Lacking that option, St Michael's resorted to charging outsiders for services provided free to parishioners. In 1545–46 it had decreed 'that for every knell range within the said parishe, beying not for any of the inhabitauntes ther shall pay xij d'.[28] Thirty years later, in the mid-1570s, they increased the figure

24 It appears to have been comprehensive in Chester: Alldridge, 'Chester parishes', p. 92.

25 The amount collected in 1562, for instance, was £3 0s. 6d. and it increased significantly each year until it was discontinued in the early 1570s. When it was reinstituted in 1580 to pay for communion bread and wine the sums collected were much smaller: CWA, 1/14, 1/15, 1/31.

26 Martha C. Skeeters, *Community and Clergy: Bristol and the Reformation c. 1530–c. 1570* (Oxford, 1993), pp. 105, 113.

27 The records of the parishes of Tewkesbury and Minchinhampton, each the only parish in a relatively small town, contain substantial revenues from church ales to fund parish expenses, while that source is never mentioned in St Michael's accounts. See also Judith M. Bennett, 'Conviviality and charity in medieval and early modern England', *PaP*, 134 (1992), 19–41; and Clive Burgess and Beat Kümin, 'Penitential bequests and parish regimes in late medieval England', *JEH*, 44 (1993), 610–30.

28 CWA, 1/1.

to 20*d*. and additionally levied a charge of 4*d*. on every household 'absent from the compte [account]', very possibly another way of referring to those who had not contributed to the priest's wages.[29] Meanwhile the two sources of income typically gathered from parishioners, seat money and rents, remained at a fairly constant level throughout the period, providing an average of approximately £4 per year to the parish chest.[30]

By means such as these additional levies St Michael's seems to have steered a steady course through the series of major religious changes which characterised the mid-sixteenth century (see Fig. 13.3 for a comparison of annual revenues and expenses). While income was not always sufficient to meet all the commitments, the leadership consistently responded in a positive manner to each new set of directives and maintained the parish's sound financial condition while simultaneously preserving the quality of both their worship and their building, each of which made substantial demands on parish funds.

III

During the last years of the reign of Henry VIII parish worship in Gloucestershire was largely unchanged from its pre-Reformation form, although St Michael's location in the diocese of Worcester would have exposed it to Bishop Latimer's early reforming initiatives, such as the requirement that the priests under his authority should 'not admit any young man or woman to receive the sacrament of the altar, until that he or she openly in the church, after mass or evensong, upon the holiday, do recite in English the *Pater*'.[31] By the early 1540s some holy days were no longer celebrated (though restrictions seem to have been slow to take effect) and some churches had procured the requisite Bible.[32] However, the basic liturgical practices and visual symbols of parish worship appear

---

29 *Ibid.*, 1/28.
30 Rental income accruing to the parish seems to have been separate from rents which supported chantries at St Michael's. The former was fairly constant throughout the period of this study, while the latter were confiscated in 1549 and the endowments given to Thomas Chamberlain and Richard Pate (Chamberlain was a member of a wealthy merchant family from London which had also acquired lands in Gloucestershire following the dissolution of the monasteries, while Pate was recorder of Gloucester and sometime MP for the city): Hockaday Abstracts, vol. 219, 1549.
31 'Injunctions given by the Bishop of Worcester in his visitation of his diocese [1535]', in G. E. Corrie (ed.), *The Works of Hugh Latimer* (Cambridge, 1845), ii. 243. For information on Bishop Latimer see A. G. Chester, *Hugh Latimer: Apostle to the English* (Philadelphia, 1954), and S. R. Wabuda, 'The Provision for Preaching during the Early English Reformation with Special Reference to Itineration *c.* 1530 to 1547' (Ph.D., University of Cambridge, 1992).
32 Eamon Duffy, *The Stripping of the Altars* (New Haven, 1992), pp. 222, 394–6, 499; Robert Whiting, *The Blind Devotion of the People: Popular Religion and the English Reformation* (Cambridge, 1989), pp. 190–1.

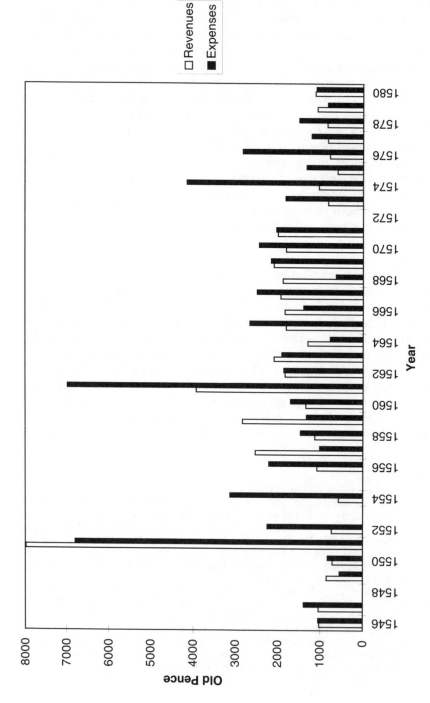

Figure 13.3 St Michael's, Gloucester: total annual revenue and expenditure.

to have remained unchanged until after Henry's death.[33] The bells, clock, and locks were repaired, ornaments were washed, and the 'brasen egle' was scoured. The churchwardens mended the albs, gave money for lights, said obits, purchased coals for Easter, and erected and watched the Easter sepulchre.[34] However, it is remarkable that only one extant parish will from this period included the traditional provision for masses for the dead, and that testator, John Fawkner, alderman and husband of Margaret, was also the only testator to make a generous charitable bequest. He left an endowment of £40 to be distributed to the poor, in addition to the black gowns for twelve men who were to attend his burial and pray for him for twelve months.[35] Little changed in terms of liturgical practices and religious beliefs among the parishioners of St Michael's prior to the accession of Edward VI.

Innovations came to St Michael's at the end of the decade. In 1548, the clergy probably began to administer the communion in both kinds as required by the royal injunctions of that year, using the English words of administration published in the Order of Communion. The next year brought a more significant change. As a result of the Chantries Act of 1547 two chantries were dissolved, their endowments confiscated, and their priests left without positions. They also were no longer available to assist the rector in ministering to the parish, as they had probably done previously.[36] Also in 1549 the churchwardens purchased several psalters and, more significantly, the 'boke of the communyon', that is, the Book of Common Prayer, in which the entire liturgy was in English. No longer would the words of worship be uttered in Latin, although vestments, priestly actions, and church decoration had probably not changed. In fact, it appears that the parish leadership did not innovate beyond the dictates of official religious policy. For instance, they again purchased holy oil at Easter, as they had done in the past.[37]

More substantial changes in the fabric and worship of St Michael's parish appear to have come in 1550–51. In that year the churchwardens brought worship in line with the latest set of acceptable reformed practices, as directed by the Crown and administered by the new Bishop of Gloucester, John Hooper. Church goods were sold (see Figure 13.2), and the interior of the church was modified. The churchwardens realised over

33 W. H. Frere and W. M. Kennedy (eds), *Visitation Articles and Injunctions of the Period of the Reformation* (London, New York, 1910), ii. 9, 35–6; P. L. Hughes and J. F. Larkin (eds), *Tudor Royal Proclamations* (New Haven, 1964), i. 297, 301–2; A. Wilkins (ed.), *Concilia Magnae Britanniae et Hiberniae ab anno MDXLVI ad annum MDCCXVII* (London, 1727), iii. 823–4.
34 CWA, 1/1–1/2.
35 PRO, PROB 11/30, f. 283. The gift of gowns to poor people in exchange for prayers for the soul of the benefactor was a very traditional provision.
36 Hockaday Abstracts, vol. 219, 1548, 1549.
37 CWA, 1/3, 1/4.

£27 from the sale of such items as a silver spoon, copes, the timber 'abowght Saynct Annes Chapell', 'the Lentyne clothe', 'the timber that was of the rode lofte', and a chapel.[38] This was also – as we have seen – the time when the churchwardens lowered the level of the floor where the altar had stood and installed a communion table, probably in response to Bishop John Hooper's visitation articles.[39] Additionally, the walls were whitewashed (to cover forbidden images), while new pews and a new pulpit appeared as well, with the old pulpit being sold for 6*d.*, perhaps an indication that preaching was increasing in importance. Workers also removed the rood loft and it was sold as well. The parish purchased a Bible and a copy of Erasmus's *Paraphrases*, as required. Meanwhile, normal maintenance continued, including some major repair work (see Table 13.1). The following year the west tower was given a new lead roof, gutters were repaired, and the west end of the church received some needed attention. At the same time, the new pews and pulpit were finished, and a desk was constructed to hold the *Paraphrases*. In aggregate the changes to the church fabric indicate the transformation of the church from a centre of traditional worship to a centre of the Reformed tradition. However, the alterations had hardly been completed before new demands were made.[40]

The accession of Mary, with its concomitant restoration of Catholicism, brought a whole new set of modifications to the parish. Now it was necessary to undo what had been done during the previous three years. The churchwardens' accounts for 1553–54 show expenditures for the construction of a new altar, including hauling dirt into the church to return the altar to its previous level, and six parishioners sold vestments and communion vessels back to the parish. In addition the parish purchased tapers, a number of service books, and a cross fashioned from copper and gilt, constructed a new Easter sepulchre, mended a cope, and made a new alb.[41] Meanwhile the normal maintenance of the fabric of the building

38 William Whitingame purchased the chapel for 13*s.* on 3 June 1551. Other buyers included Margaret Fawkner, Thomas Davis, Abell Hariett, Robert Ingrame, Hugh Evans, and William Hassarde: *ibid.*, 1/5.

39 Bishop Hooper's visitation articles of 1551 called for the setting up of 'the Lords board after the forme of an honest table' in place of the altar in all churches of the diocese, to 'turne the simple from the old superstitious opinions of the Popish Mass and to the right use of the Lord's Supper', and to 'take down and abolish all altars': London, Dr Williams's Library, Morice MS 31/L, p. 6. In urging this action Hooper, along with Nicholas Ridley, Bishop of London, was anticipating future policy. Susan Brigden reports that in London by the end of 1550 altars had been replaced by communion tables in all parishes: *London and the Reformation* (Oxford, 1989), p. 468.

40 CWA, 1/1, 1/5, 1/6.

41 In addition to the transactions with William Bond discussed above Mr Payne received 52*s.* 8*d.* for 'a tynekell of laten' and two ropes, one of velvet and the other silk. By 1556, most of the ornaments and plate were back in the possession of the parish. An inventory of church goods, dated 14 February 1556, recorded

continued, if at a slightly reduced level. Two years later the Catholic restoration continued with gifts of a processional and a torch from parishioners as well as with the purchase of a blue velvet cushion and 'a pece of fringe for the banner cloth and for the cloth before the hye aulter and redde threade and the settinge on'. That same year the churchwardens also purchased a copy of 'a homelye bocke' from the diocesan summoner and two unspecified books from another parishioner.[42]

As was their usual fashion the parish leaders at St Michael's conformed to official policy, but the Marian changes occurred more slowly than the previous ones, probably owing to the more serious financial implications. The requisite books, vestments, sacramental vessels, ornaments, and other decorations were just too expensive. In 1556–57 a special rate was assessed to augment regular revenues and fund the continuing restoration process. Between October 1556 and September 1557 a collect was purchased from the summoner, William Sandes was paid 1d. 'for the puttynge up of a [painted] clothe on a Rodde' (to provide temporary images of Mary and John), 'a chesable of redde velvett' was obtained from the former churchwarden and dyer John Webley, and work was begun on the carving of Mary and John for the permanent rood.[43] Then in 1557–58, shortly before Mary's death, another mass book and a tabernacle were purchased and the statues of John and Mary painted and put in place.[44]

The fact that financial constraints rather than religious fervour were responsible for the slow response to the Catholic restoration is further illustrated by the events of 1558–60. St Michael's responded even more slowly to Elizabeth's accession and the official return to Protestantism than it had to the previous changes in religious policy. Easter was observed in the traditional fashion in 1559; the Easter sepulchre was repaired and the paschal taper paid for. Then Parliament approved the new Act of Uniformity and on 24 June the new Book of Common Prayer came into use.[45] By the end of September 1559 St Michael's had purchased a new service book and psalter, and the rood, completed just the year before, had been removed.[46] The following year the parish leaders

that William Hassarde, draper, had the Our Lady service, while 'all and singular the [other] ornaments ... remaynethe unsold' (Hockaday Abstracts vol. 38, 1556; CWA, 1/5, 1/7). The service books included three 'antiphoners', a mass book, two 'grayles', two processionals, a noted manual, and a hymnal. Following the initial restoration work, the proctor of York visited 'for the reedyfyenge of ther churche': *ibid.*, 1/7.

42 *Ibid.*, 1/8.
43 *Ibid.*, 1/9.
44 *Ibid.*, 1/10.
45 Henry Gee, *The Elizabethan Clergy and the Settlement of Religion 1558–1564* (Oxford, 1898), p. xviii.
46 Two carpenters were paid 14d. to remove the rood. As with the other changes having to do with images at St Michael's, the rood was removed professionally, rather than being torn down or burned: CWA, 1/1, 1/11.

devoted a majority of the parish's resources to rebuilding the tower, but in 1560–61 they once again turned their attention to alterations in worship. The churchwardens disposed of unwanted church goods by selling them to parishioners (see Table 13.2) and again hired men to whitewash the interior of the church to cover offending images. In addition the churchwardens also had to contend with some extraordinary expenses. They were forced to use funds from the parish chest to pay the priest 'at a certaine time when some of the parishe refused to paie', they had to buy extra bread and wine 'for communion on three occasions when a greate number of the parishe receaved', and that year, for the first time, they paid for 'ringinge the bell at sundrie sermondes'.[47] However, once again the parish leaders did not shirk their responsibility for building maintenance. They seem to have been determined to make sure that the fabric of the church did not suffer in the face of the continued drain on the parish coffers due to religious change. In the midst of all the new and exceptional costs, they still saw to the repair of the chancel (see Table 13.1).

After 1560–61 parish life at St Michael's seems to have settled back into its normal rhythm. Once the need for grand change had ceased, minor upkeep and repairs dominated the churchwardens' attention. They made sure the ornaments were washed and the brass eagle was scoured. Bells had to be repaired, tiles needed replacing, and surplices were mended. They also purchased new communion books and the new set of homilies as well as small books of special prayers against the plague and the Turks. Then in 1566–67 the church porch received a major renovation.[48]

And yet religious change continued to influence some activities and expenditures through the 1560s and 1570s. The interior of the church was whitewashed on two occasions.[49] Then in 1568–69 the proceeds from the sale of a chalice funded the purchase of a communion cup, an action which illustrates one of the ways in which St Michael's took the lead in implementing Elizabethan Protestantism in the shire as well as in the city of Gloucester. It would be another six years before most Gloucestershire parishes purchased communion cups and even then some still refused to relinquish their chalices.[50] The next year the wardens paid for a desk below the pulpit to hold the Bible and in 1572–73 the communion table was carpeted. Another dramatic alteration occurred in

---

47 Those Sundays were 24 November, 14 January, and the first Sunday in Lent. A quart of wine and a corresponding quantity of bread were purchased each time: *ibid.*, 1/13.

48 *Ibid.*, 1/13–1/19.

49 In 1566–67 and 1573–74: *ibid.*, 1/19, 1/25.

50 *Ibid.*, 1/21; David Verey, *Gloucestershire: The Vale and the Forest of Dean* (2nd edn, Harmondsworth, 1976), *passim*; David Verey, *Gloucestershire: The Cotswolds* (Harmondsworth, 1970), *passim*; GDR, vols 40, 47, *passim*.

1573–74 when a communion seat was built near the communion table for those who were to receive the sacrament, and texts (probably the Ten Commandments, the Creed, and the Lord's Prayer) were painted on the freshly whitewashed walls.[51] These most recent modifications reflected the increasingly obvious Protestant sympathies of parish leaders which were in harmony with general trends in official policy, although neither of those changes was specifically required at that time. They also provide evidence that the new religion had gained a stronger following among St Michael's parishioners than was generally the case in Gloucestershire. This impression is strengthened by an examination of the wills of parishioners dating from that decade. While most of the county's testators either clung to their traditional beliefs or opted for ambiguous statements of faith in their wills, beliefs declared by testators from St Michael's included a number of expressions of Protestantism. The number of extant wills from the parish is too small to be statistically reliable, but of the fourteen extant wills four express beliefs consistent with the new religion.[52]

There were also some difficulties within the parish community at the end of the 1560s, perhaps indicating that even a model parish might find the demands of nearly constant religious change overwhelming. In 1569 the St Michael's churchwardens were accused in consistory court of lacking both a curate and the *Paraphrases* of Erasmus. They appeared on 15 December and certified that they had made the appropriate corrections.[53] Soon thereafter the curate, David Walter, was brought before the same court for not administering the sacraments according to the injunctions, a point of significant confusion in the Elizabethan Church. In all likelihood he was using common bread in conformity with the rubric in the Book of Common Prayer of 1559 rather than the communion wafers prescribed by the royal injunctions of the same year. This transgression was often overlooked, but he had the misfortune of serving under Bishop Richard Cheyney, who would not tolerate the use of ordinary bread.[54] The presentment against the parishioner John Stevens for not having received the

---

51 There is no record of the building of the communion table. Perhaps the Edwardian table had been stored during Mary's reign and just had to be moved back into the church: CWA, 1/24, 1/25.

52 Most Gloucestershire wills from 1570 to 1580 employed ambiguous religious preambles (88 per cent), while 5 per cent reflected traditional beliefs and 7 per cent espoused Protestant assurance in salvation. A Protestant consensus may have emerged in some portions of the realm by the 1570s, but that did not happen in Gloucestershire. (In contrast, nearly 30 per cent of the wills from St Michael's during that decade include Protestant statements of faith.) Gloucestershire Wills, 1570–80, *passim*; PRO, PROB 11/52–63, *passim*.

53 GDR, vol. 26, p. 63.

54 *Ibid.*, vol. 24, pp. 709, 722; John E. Booty (ed.), *The Book of Common Prayer 1559: The Elizabethan Prayer Book* (Charlottesville, 1976), p. 267; Gee, *The Elizabethan Clergy*, p. 64.

holy communion 'this ij yeres' came in 1572.[55] Despite these temporary lapses in some of the details of religious conformity, there is no doubt that the parish steered an especially orthodox course, in terms of both liturgy and fabric maintenance.

In the 1570s St Michael's elite continued its tradition of charitable giving. William, Richard, and Jone Goldeston were most notable. William had served as churchwarden from 1558 to 1560 and his will dates from August 1569. After a very ambiguous soul bequest, he left several parcels of land to the use of St Bartholomew's Hospital, Gloucester, as well as providing bread for the poor at his burial. His brother, Richard, a carpenter, had also served a term as churchwarden. In his will, written in April 1574, Richard declared that he trusted 'to be savid by no other meanes savinge only by and throughe the meryghtes of Christ's passion', a decidedly Protestant declaration. He then designated the rents from eight tenements in the city to be used to fund annual gifts to the poor in the nearby hospitals. His wife, Jone, wrote her will four years later. In it she bequeathed her soul more equivocally 'into the handes of the Allmightie God my onely saviour and redemer' and left £20 as an endowment for wood and coal to be distributed to the poor annually. In each of these cases the testator either declared his or her Protestant faith or resorted to a religious preamble which did not disclose a clear religious preference. Furthermore, none of these testators specifically asked the poor to pray for the dead; rather they seem to have been acting out of a belief in their own responsibility for the welfare of their humbler neighbours, combined with a sense of civic duty, the very same motivations which more generally seem to have prompted the leadership of St Michael's to respond so conscientiously to the twin demands of religious change and parochial administration.[56]

IV

Strengthened and motivated by their sense of community, St Michael's strove to conform during the period of great religious upheaval from 1540 to 1580. It consistently presented an image of a healthy and vital institution, dedicated to fulfilling its mission of spreading God's word and maintaining a physical presence at the centre of the city, a mission which spoke eloquently of the responsible stewardship of God's bounty. In this fashion, St Michael's was a model Tudor parish. Simple state enforcement and individual religious preference do not fully explain why St Michael's churchwardens followed official policy so obediently. 'Religious conformity', although displayed less and less speedily in successive instances, was a strategy employed by a close-knit, coherent parish elite to retain their

55 GDR, vol. 29, p. 85.
56 Gloucestershire Wills, 1569/156, 1574/143, 1579/107.

church's prominent position in the city and to preserve it from further disruption and harmful inner division. Stability and continuity, visible also in the management of parish finances, were clearly priorities, whatever the current religious and political circumstances.

Women and the London parishes 1500–1620

Historians have long studied and argued about the vast series of cultural and religious transformations which cumulatively make up the 'English Reformations'.[1] But only recently have a few historians turned their attention to the issue of gender and spirituality, seeking information on how these tumultuous times affected men and women.[2] The relative paucity of women in the sources often leads historians to ignore the particular ways in which gender informed parish involvement. This chapter will outline how the legislated and popular 'Reformations' of the sixteenth century affected the lives of women in the City of London. These changes did not affect women in all the same ways. The Reformation introduced new responsibilities, but curtailed traditions that surely had been an enriching part of women's experiences, and redefined the public roles of rich and poor women. Beyond a doubt the spiritual and social lives of women in the reign of Henry VII were vastly different from those of women a century later.

Some historians have argued for a brief golden age for women in the late medieval period, when the economic and demographic repercussions of the plague created a range of new opportunities.[3] By contrast historians of the English family argue for an improvement in the status of women after the Reformation as Protestantism emphasised marriage and women's 'new' role as helpmates.[4] However, the subversive potential

---

1 To use Haigh's phrase: C. Haigh, *English Reformations: Religion, Politics, and Society under the Tudors* (Oxford, 1993); E. Duffy, *The Stripping of the Altars: Traditional Religion in England 1400–1580* (New Haven, 1992); B. Kümin, *The Shaping of a Community: The Rise and Reformation of the English Parish c. 1400–1560* (Aldershot, 1996); S. Wabuda, 'Revising the Reformation', *Journal of British Studies*, 35 (1996), 257–62.

2 P. Crawford, *Women and Religion in England 1500–1720* (New York, 1993); L. Roper, *The Holy Household: Women and Morals in Reformation Augsburg* (Oxford, 1989); M. E. Wiesner, *Women and Gender in Early Modern Europe* (Cambridge, 1994); S. K. Cohn, *Death and Property in Siena* (Baltimore, 1988); C. Cross, 'The religious life of women in sixteenth-century Yorkshire', in W. J. Sheils and D. Wood (eds), *Women in the Church*, SCH 27 (Oxford, 1990), pp. 307–24; S. Wabuda, 'Shunamites and nurses of the English Reformation: the activities of Mary Glover, niece of Hugh Latimer', in *ibid.*, pp. 335–44.

3 P. J. P. Goldberg, 'Women's work, women's role in the late medieval north', in M. Hicks (ed.), *Profit, Piety and the Professions in Later Medieval England* (Gloucester, 1990), p. 34. Cf. J. Bennett, 'Medieval women, modern women: across the gender divide', in D. Aers (ed.), *Culture and History* (Detroit, 1992).

4 L. Stone, *The Family, Sex, and Marriage in England 1500–1800* (New York, 1979).

in these reforms led to an Act of 1543 prohibiting Bible reading by women, apprentices, servants, and others of low degree, leaving in doubt the 'liberalising' impulses of reform. The Reformation, alongside the inflation and economic crises of the sixteenth century, reconfigured the economic and cultural participation of women and ultimately their status.

One way of looking at the effects of religious change on women is to focus attention at the parish level. This chapter uses churchwardens' accounts, vestry minutes, and wills from four London parishes of varied wealth and size, from within and without the walls: St Botolph Aldersgate, St Mary Woolnoth, St Michael Cornhill, and St Stephen Walbrook. Reading these sources with an emphasis on gender issues helps to show the similarities and differences between men's and women's parish activities. Analysing the changing ideas of parish support and oversight over the course of the Reformation illustrates women's shifting position within the parish. Three phases provide the framework for the chapter: (I) the early part of the sixteenth century, (II) the period of the major Reformation changes, and (III) the construction of a national Church.

The parish served as the focus of political, social, cultural, and economic life in the City of London both before and after the Reformation.[5] The relations between women and this crucial communal unit thus shed light on developments in London society as a whole. The loss of some opportunities for women and the parishes' new preoccupations with order and control resulted in a number of significant transformations which will be explored below. In the end this study will show that by trying to enforce a new religious ideology, and in fulfilling new political roles, the parish expressed and reinforced shifting gender roles that limited women's opportunities and involvement in the parish. While the Reformation may have elevated the condition of marriage within the Church, it challenged women's ability to articulate their own spiritual needs and act both within and without the confines of marriage.

I

Prior to the Reformation women had alternatives to marriage. The religious life of a nun or anchorite offered them a forum of intellectual and spiritual endeavour, an independence from men not easily found in secular life, and a holy example of celibacy. Scholars debate how attractive these alternatives were to women in the late Middle Ages.[6] After 1500

---

5 C. M. Barron, 'The parish fraternities of medieval London', in C. M. Barron and C. Harper-Bill (eds), *The Church in Pre-Reformation Society: Essays in Honour of F. R. H. Du Boulay* (Woodbridge, 1985), pp. 13–37; I. Archer, *Pursuit of Stability: Social Relations in Elizabethan London* (Cambridge, 1991), pp. 63–74.

6 N. Z. Davis, 'City women and religious change', in her *Society and Culture in Early Modern France* (Stanford, 1975; orig. 1965), pp. 65–95; B. Harris, 'A new look at the Reformation: aristocratic women and nunneries 1450–1540', *Journal of British Studies*, 32 (1993), 89–113.

support for nunneries in London wills declined and in only a few did testators note family members living in them.[7] Instead inhabitants left bequests to their parishes for a variety of purposes, including the 'church fabric' (maintenance and ornamentation), burial, and memorials. The trend away from endowing nunneries suggests that parishes attracted greater participation by women and fostered pious behaviour through a variety of services and foundations.

In 1535 the chronicler Charles Wriothesley described the Virgin Mary's girdle among other relics removed from churches during the early Reformation:

Our Ladies girdell at Westminster, which women with chield were wont to girde with, and Sainct Elizabethes girdell, and in Poules a relixque of Our Ladies milke, which was broken and founde but a peece of chalke, with other reliques in divers places which they used for covetousnes in deceaphing the people.[8]

The reformers sought to alter people's religious attitudes, but some of these 'deceived' women were reluctant to give up their beliefs associated with childbirth and pregnancy. The prominence of churching ceremonies and the midwife's ability to baptise children created special roles for women within the parish. Henry Machyn described the alderman's wife in 1560 who preserved the neighbourly and celebratory function of churching by organising her own ceremony, with a dinner to follow, since her priest would perform the service only at six in the morning, if it was to be held in the church.[9] Historians disagree whether the service was for purification or thanksgiving; contemporaries argued over whether it was superstitious or pious.[10] Importantly in the sixteenth century this rite retained its popularity among many women, perhaps in reflection of its origins in popular practice rather than in church ceremony.[11]

Surviving wills offer one of the most obvious ways of seeing how parishioners supported their communities. The testaments used in this study were written by individuals who identified themselves with a particular parish, commonly by burial or by the bequest for forgotten tithes before the Reformation and by parish death records or other references

---

7 Before the dissolution a mere 12.66 per cent (239) of 1887 pious bequests from men and women in this sample (cf. note 12 below) were earmarked for religious houses.

8 *A Chronicle of England during the Reigns of the Tudors, from AD 1485 to 1559*, ed. W. D. Hamilton, Camden Society (London, 1875), p. 31.

9 J. G. Nichols (ed.), *The Diary of Henry Machyn, Citizen and Merchant-Taylor of London, from AD 1550 to AD 1563*, Camden Society (London, 1848), p. 249.

10 W. Coster, 'Purity, profanity, and Puritanism: the churching of women 1500–1700', in Sheils and Wood (eds), *Women in the Church*, pp. 377–87; D. Cressy, 'Purification, thanksgiving and the churching of women in post-Reformation England', *PaP*, 141 (November 1993), 106–46.

11 Coster, 'Purity, profanity, and Puritanism', p. 377.

after the religious changes. The wills total 685, with 84 per cent (576) left by men and 16 per cent (109) by women. These wills were analysed in database files arranged by 'pious' and 'non-pious' categories, though 'non-pious' bequests often carried a pious purpose or default accounted for in the database.[12] Nearly all testators left bequests to the high altar for tithes forgotten, a customary bequest to their local church, and many remembered parishes in which they had previously resided. This frequent support of church works and repairs illustrated parishioners' attachment to their (home, former, and birth) parishes. There were also large numbers of gifts in support of the cult of saints and other popular devotions that would not survive the Edwardian reforms.[13]

Before 1538 women's and men's patterns of pious bequests were quite similar, suggesting a fair degree of overlap in their religious interests.[14] The cult of saints, for instance, offered protection and models of piety to both. In a study of late medieval rood screens Eamon Duffy has found a 'striking preoccupation with women saints and female sanctity', with half the screen frequently devoted to their images.[15] These heroic figures were admired by men and women for their virtue and steadfastness in the face of often violent persecution, while throughout Europe women invoked female saints, such as St Margaret and the Virgin, as patrons in pregnancy and childbirth. In London, St Mildred the Virgin had a shrine in her own church. Peter Cave of St Michael Cornhill requested a tomb in the wall or window before St Margaret in memory of himself, his wife, and his children, with a further £10 to make and gild her image. Additionally he left £5 for a similar statue in his birthplace.[16] Elizabeth Massey

---

12 Despite complications arising from lifetime provisions, formulaic structures, and the controversies about using preambles to test Protestantism, wills still shed light on pious intent and cultural expectations. Cf. C. Burgess, '"By Quick and by Dead": wills and pious provision in late medieval Bristol', *EHR*, 405 (1987), 837–58, and his 'Late medieval wills and pious convention: testamentary evidence reconsidered', in Hicks (ed.), *Profit, Piety and the Professions*, pp. 14–33; Duffy, *Stripping of the Altars*, pp. 504–23; Haigh, *English Reformations*, pp. 199–203; the wills in this sample (191 from St Botolph; 101 from St Mary; 173 from St Michael; 77 from St Stephen; 143 unspecified, but linked with these parishes) are located in the prerogative court at Canterbury and London's commissary and archdeaconry courts.

13 Duffy, *Stripping of the Altars*, p. 161.

14 43.44 per cent (371) of women's bequests benefited pious ends, compared with 46.70 per cent (1,516) of men's.

15 On the appeal of female saints to men and women see C. W. Bynum, '"... And Woman his Humanity": female imagery in the religious writing of the later Middle Ages', in C. W. Bynum, S. Harrell, and P. Richman (eds), *Gender and Religion: On the Complexity of Symbols* (Boston, Mass., 1986), pp. 257–88; cf. J. J. Scarisbrick, *Reformation and the English People* (Oxford, 1984), p. 171; Duffy, 'Holy maydens, holy wyfes: the cult of women saints in fifteenth- and sixteenth-century England', in Sheils and Wood (eds), *Women in the Church*, pp. 175–96, quote from p. 176.

16 PRO, PROB 11/25, fos 162R–163L.

remembered images of Our Lady at Walsingham, Dunaste (Dodnash?), Northampton, and Coosforpe (Coxford?) and Canterbury shrines.[17] The widow Maude Gowsell in 1523 provided for fifteen children to carry fifteen tapers to her burial in the cloister of St Mary, where the tapers would burn to honour God, Mary, and the saints.[18] In 1528 Joseph Shukburgh gave to every poor woman with child or in Our Lady's Bands in St Michael Cornhill 12*d*. 'to her comfort'.[19] Another man left the 'best' red wine to priests to celebrate mass, requiring that women with children and the sick should also benefit from the select drink.[20]

Parish gilds provided another manifestation of the cult of saints. Within these gilds or fraternities members offered prayers, memorialised the dead, held masses, venerated saints, and gave mutual aid to each other.[21] Women, unusually for the period, joined as full members of most gilds in their own right. In some associations outside the capital they even served as officers, but apparently not in London itself.[22] The Edwardian Reformation, through the abolition of the cult of saints and the dissolution of fraternities, deprived them – at a stroke – of potential patrons, role models, intercessors, and opportunities for membership of sometimes very important voluntary associations.[23] The end of fraternities and purgatory thus had a far greater impact on final testaments than the dissolution of religious houses.

Those with sufficient wealth could also endow chantries. In the four London parishes surveyed in this chapter women endowed chantries less frequently than men, but this clearly reflected the distribution of property in contemporary society.[24] Lifetime discussions of pious legacies between husbands and wives possibly guaranteed that his endowment also reflected her wishes, or that she followed his orders carefully when executing his will. Although she asked for no 'pompe or pride of the world' Elizabeth Berrell of St Stephen Walbrook left 40*s*. for an annuity to sustain a chantry in 1500.[25] As if in imitation of a chantry, Viscountess

---

17 PRO, PROB 11/17, f. 262R.
18 GL, MS 9171/10, f. 47.
19 *Ibid.*, f. 116v.
20 PRO, PROB 11/28, f. 140L.
21 Scarisbrick, *Reformation*, p. 20; on the importance of purgatory: C. Burgess, '"A fond thing vainly invented"', in S. Wright (ed.), *Parish, Church, and People* (London, 1988), pp. 56–84.
22 Scarisbrick, *Reformation*, pp. 25, 166; for London see Barron, 'Parish fraternities', p. 31.
23 S. Brigden, 'Religion and social obligation in early sixteenth-century London', *PaP*, 103 (May 1984), 67–112, esp. 98–9; C. Barron, 'Parish fraternities', p. 30.
24 This database shows only six provisions for chantries, five of them made by men. Men provided for eighty-three obits, women for seventeen, a total of 100 (4.85 per cent) pious bequests before the prohibition of purgatory, although obits included many separate, smaller bequests.
25 PRO, PROB 11/12, fos 27R, 28R.

Lisle funded a five-year obit in the chapel of Our Lady and St Katherine in St Michael Cornhill, a chapel dedicated to significant female saints and associated with her lifetime piety, 'where I am wonte to knele'.[26] With £5 a year for the event, the obit included a devout mass of Our Lady, with children of the choir, organs, and bell-ringing beginning at eight o'clock. Her elaborate will provided for her own and her husband's soul with thousands of masses and bequests to lazar houses, prisons, hospitals, and the poor and also remembered her children, servants, and knighted executor. Lisle clearly represented the possibilities available to an elite pre-Reformation widow. Her will, while unusual in the magnitude of her bequests, nonetheless typifies women's support of intercessory institutions.

Despite the provision for masses and obits, Lisle eschewed other forms of funereal or memorial extravagance in accord with stirrings against excessive self-display. She commanded:

I will and charge myn executors that they shall in nowise doo hold or kepe for me any solempne moneth mynde in manner and forme as it is accustomed to be don in makyng of grete dyners drynkyngs ... don only to the pompe and vaynglory of the world.[27]

The forgone expenditure went to 'deeds and werks of pitie almesse deeds and charities for the helth and comforte of my soule and of the other soules afternamed'.[28] Dame Thomasyn Percivale's gift of torches, costing twenty marks, for the Corpus Christi procession in St Mary Woolnoth highlighted the potential for social display and tension in religious rituals intended to unite the Christian community.[29] While problems of social disunity haunted elaborate pious provisions, the prominence of women in setting and supporting pious trends and in maintaining the whole church fabric emphasises unity of purpose within the parish. Percivale's gift also marked the opportunity for women's social and religious action beyond the altar. In a similar action she founded a free grammar school in Cornwall, her birthplace, requiring students' prayers, perhaps the first such endowment by a non-noble woman.[30]

Charity to the poor clearly represented another form of public piety in the parish. Prisons remained a consistent, if small, target of charity as testators linked their own desire for cleansing in purgatory with the relief

---

26 *Ibid.*, f. 72L.
27 *Ibid.*
28 *Ibid.*, fos 72L–72R.
29 PRO, PROB 11/17, f. 221R; on political and social tensions in Corpus Christi see M. Rubin, *Corpus Christi: The Eucharist in Late Medieval Culture* (Cambridge, 1987), p. 248.
30 M. Davies, 'Thomasyne Percivale, "The Maid of the Week" (d. 1512)', in C. M. Barron and A. F. Sutton (eds), *Medieval London Widows 1300–1500* (London, 1994), pp. 202–3.

of prisoners suffering earthly misery about London.[31] Dame Percivale, besides helping poor prisoners, solicited the prayers of the poor: she provided for sick householders to say prayers for her in their own homes and for her corpse's attendants to sit, stand, or kneel, depending on their physical abilities. She hired more poor householders, and 'such of them as can' to say selected prayers.[32] For Dame Percivale, the efficacy of the poor in her eventual salvation required their presence and acceptance of her charity. Need, impotence, and old age determined those deserving of informal charity or aid well before the Reformation and the Elizabethan poor law. The support of poor householders and 'pour persones lame blind bedered impotent por maidens mariages to be maried in the Church of St Mighell' eased a soul out of Purgatory.[33] By the late sixteenth century, in contrast, the godliness of recipients would become paramount in the plans of many donors.[34]

Within their parish church, men and women sat separately, but both seem to have utilised similar avenues of social and religious self-expression.[35] Representations of female saints about the church, for instance, served both male and female piety, in contrast to the post-Reformation church, in which male parish officers and male preachers were not offset by female examples of holiness.

II

The middle years of the century (1548–1580) – the years of uncertainty surrounding Edward's radical reforms, Mary's restoration of Catholic practice, and Elizabeth's early settlement – brought changes in the character of parish life. The churchwardens' accounts show the parish removing, reinstating, and removing again the artefacts of Catholic services.[36] The new message of Protestantism did not cause an abrupt break with the past; rather, new ideas often appeared in old forms. Similarly, the wills show a continuity of purpose in settling last affairs and providing for services and prayers through donations to the church fabric and to the poor. In this period testators, including women, wavered over their bequests, stipulating contingency plans should the law not allow chantries, obits, or prayers. Without fraternities and 'superstitious' devotions, and

---

31 Before 1538, 7 per cent (twenty-six) of women's pious gifts and 5.9 per cent (ninety) of men's reached prisons or prisoners; between 1580 and 1601 the figures are 4 per cent (fourteen) and 5.24 per cent (thirty-seven).
32 PRO, PROB 11/17, f. 219L.
33 PRO, PROB 11/21, f. 317L.
34 Paul Slack, *Poverty and Policy in Tudor and Stuart England* (London, 1988), pp. 25–7.
35 M. Aston, 'Segregation in church', in Sheils and Wood (eds), *Women in the Church*, pp. 237–94.
36 R. Hutton, 'The local impact of the Tudor Reformations', in C. Haigh (ed.), *The English Reformation Revised* (Cambridge, 1987), pp. 114–38.

with restrictions on funeral and burial 'extravagance', how did women participate in the life of the parish?

Whereas pre-Reformation rites had brought rich and poor together, at least in an ideal exchange of mutual benefit and temporary union in common services, after the Reformation such unions would become more difficult.[37] Testators continued to provide for the distribution of spice bread at their burials, such as the widow who charged her executor with the 'custom', 'as well amonge the poore as the Riche'.[38] The first Act punishing vagabonds and beggars in 1531 allowed doles connected with burials and obits, but legislation in 1536 attempted to replace doles with the Poor Box. Reformers linked the former with indiscriminate Catholic charity to beggars (conflated with vagabonds) who progressed noisily from funeral dole to funeral dole across parish boundaries. This older habit of face-to-face charity, based on 'mutual amity' rather than donations 'readily articulated in monetary terms', did not die with the Reformation, nor did its decline begin there.[39] The dichotomy of deserving and undeserving poor and the literal and metaphorical separation of the respectable and the poor evolved from late medieval piety. Its implementation, however, changed with the parish's new roles in an England that was becoming reformed.

Parishioners still supported their parishes, but in different ways. Instead of expressing piety through the veneration of saints and lavish funerals, testators in this middle period increasingly endowed sermons. While all the (male) preachers glorified God, edified the congregation, and memorialised the donor, they also articulated a Protestant message which, as we shall see, contributed to the creation of new roles for women in the parish. Before 1548 only a handful of bequests for sermons surfaced in wills,[40] but between 1549 and 1552 twenty-one can be found in these four London parishes. Between 1558 and 1580, testators left seventy-two pious bequests for sermons, after which the number declined.[41] Before the 1570s, parishes had not implemented full control of lectureships, sermons, and readers. St Botolph first mentioned a reader in the accounts of 1569–70.[42]

---

37 P. Collinson, *The Birthpangs of Protestant England: Religious and Cultural Change in the Sixteenth Century* (New York, 1988), p. 31.

38 PRO, PROB 11/35, f. 127L.

39 Felicity Heal, *Hospitality in Early Modern England* (Oxford, 1990), pp. 15–16, 33. On pre-Reformation change see M. Rubin, *Charity and Community in Medieval Cambridge* (Cambridge, 1987); on rogue literature: A. L. Beier, *Masterless Men: The Vagrancy Problem in England 1560–1640* (London, 1985); on poverty and the poor: Slack, *Poverty and Policy*.

40 J. Stow, *A Survey of London*, ed. W. J. Thomas, Camden Society (London, 1842), p. 75; PRO, PROB 11/27, f. 149R.

41 6.69 per cent of all pious bequests 1549–52 and 9.41 per cent 1558–80. Two per cent (nineteen) of pious bequests between 1581 and 1601 endowed sermons, down to 1 per cent (eleven) between 1602 and 1620.

42 GL, MS 1454, Roll 72; P. Seaver, *The Puritan Lectureships* (Stanford, 1970).

In 1588 St Michael's vestry ordered the churchwardens to collect for the Friday and Sunday lectures and in 1590 instructed the parson and church-wardens to go house to house through the parish to draw on the 'good will' and 'benevolence' of parishioners for the same.[43] Lifetime bequests and 'donations', not to mention the apparent success of reform by 1570, obviated the need for testamentary support.

Early provision for sermons combined desire for reform with pious bequests. Testators tried to merge the old and new ways by drawing on numerical symbolism from 'popish' practice – hence creating Catholic 'survivals' in the sixteenth century.[44] Elizabeth Stevyns played on the numerology of 'five' by asking her preacher, or another learned one, to make one sermon at her burial and four on the following Sundays in St Mary Woolnoth.[45] Even in 1579 a woman asked for thirty sermons in the year following her death, a nod toward the former practice of a trental of masses.[46] In their own wills, women asked for prominent preachers or learned men by name or description. With the parish's growing oversight of sermons after 1570 or so, and women's minimal role in parish leader-ship, women may have had less to say directly about the choice of preachers, readers, or lecturers. After all, men seem to have monopolised the office of churchwarden and the membership of vestries in the capital.[47]

The Reformation brought other changes in how women served the parish. In the late fifteenth and early sixteenth centuries St Botolph's paid a succession of women for washing and mending the 'church clothes', for making tapers, and for 'scouring'. In the same parish between 1511 and 1513 two widows each gave two altar cloths to the church, while expenses continued for washing and mending.[48] Later in the century, however, sextons or clerks assumed more responsibility for these types of job to scrape together an income. By one account, parish clergy and officials experienced a decline in the real value of their wages which they attempted to remedy through extra work in the parish.[49]

After the Reformation, parishes took increasing responsibility for reforming social and sexual behaviour. Again they called on old practices to help in a new cause. Poor women in need of support were often in charge of controlling behaviour during worship. In St Botolph Aldersgate

43 GL, MS 4072/1, Part 1, fos 43v, 50.
44 R. Binion, *After Christianity: Christian Survivals in Post-Christian Culture* (Durango, 1986).
45 PRO, PROB 11/34, f. 47L ('five' represented the popular devotion to Christ's five wounds).
46 PRO, PROB 11/62, f. 111R.
47 Maryan (?) Gerens may have been a female warden at St Andrew Hubbard in 1508–09: Kümin, *Shaping of a Community*, p. 40.
48 GL, MS 1454, Rolls 18, 20, 34, among others; for altar cloths *ibid.*, Rolls 32, 33.
49 G. Gibbs, 'Parish Finance and the Urban Community in London 1450–1620' (Ph.D., University of Virginia, 1990), p. 349.

beginning in 1571–72 a blind woman and another living in 'greate necessitye and wante' oversaw the young men's and maidens' galleries to enforce orderly and regular church attendance.[50] In 1576 St Michael's made seats available in the choir, behind the preacher, for poor folk and servants and later allowed maidservants' places near the 'womans pues' and in the quire.[51] Segregation by rank and sex, in continuation of medieval practice, coincided with enforcing 'good' public behaviour.

Parishioners involved their less prosperous neighbours in the relief and discipline of other poor in return for employment or benefits, inter- weaving solutions to the problems of the aged and the young poor. These tasks reflected larger societal gender roles: older men searched for parents of abandoned children, watched church doors, whipped dogs out of church and churchyard, performed minor offices such as sexton, and cleaned out churches and churchyards.[52] Women earned money for work centred around gritty charitable or medical tasks such as nursing children and the sick as well as searching for plague victims.[53] In St Stephen Walbrook in 1573 the churchwardens paid a Mrs Warfelie for keeping a child until it was sent to 'the hospitall'.[54] In 1583/84 St Stephen's hired William Dickinson to search for the parents of an abandoned child, while some years later Mrs Dickinson, quite possibly his widow, paid reduced rent to the parish and watched the maidens' pew.[55]

The domestication of religion meant that women influenced reform and parish matters from within the household. Their wills often make their concerns evident. Moral strictures such as the proviso that their children should lead 'godly and decent' lives appeared more frequently after the initial Reformation impact. Dame Margaret Van Lichetervilde, stranger widow from Flanders, asked that her children be brought up 'trusting in the true religion and for no thinge in the worlde to send them unto the low countries by their kinsfolke for to be instructed in papysei for it were better to suffer them to goe begging their bread than to have such bringing up'.[56] Her will functioned as a private document to provide for her children and her long-suffering servant Jacqueline, who remained through 'all my afflictions'.[57] At the same time, the source could in fact have been read and used as a 'public' document, at least

50 GL, MS 1454, Roll 94.
51 GL, MS 4072/1, Part 1, fos 20v, 28.
52 T. Wales, 'Poverty, poor relief and the life-cycle: some evidence from seven- teenth-century Norfolk', in R. M. Smith (ed.), *Land, Kinship and Life-Cycle* (Cambridge, 1984), pp. 351–404.
53 D. Willen, 'Women in the public sphere in early modern England: the case of the urban working poor', *Sixteenth Century Journal* 19/4 (1988), 559–75.
54 GL, MS 593/2, f. 62.
55 *Ibid.*, f. 72.
56 GL, MS 9051/5, f. 13.
57 *Ibid.*, f. 13v.

within her own circle, attesting to the 'evils' of popery.[58] In another form of exercising influence through domestic activities, Susan Wabuda has shown, women extended hospitality to preachers and thereby assisted (or impeded) reform by increasing sermons and supporting certain beliefs. For this, the preachers paid them public thanks even as the women stretched their traditional roles as nurses and mistresses of households.[59]

The nurses who supported Protestant reform and the women who provided hospitality to recusant priests after 1560 utilised their gender roles to participate in religious life. The latter used family networks to support the Catholic cause and left their husbands to preserve public respectability, while they undermined the emerging national Church.[60] During the reign of Mary, in turn, Protestant women opposing restoration were equally active: John Foxe related numerous letters written between male martyrs and female supporters and memorialised female martyrs. The martyr John Careles reassured Agnes Glascocke of God's forgiveness despite her 'fals and backslidings'. She had been led to mass by her husband, though 'doubtles he may be sory for it'.[61] In this sense the Reformation increased women's authority within the household as they gradually took over the instruction of children and servants and some direction of their own spirituality.[62] Thus women encountered religious and social conflict in their family roles as wives, mothers, and sisters.

Within this context of the household as a religious unit and the parish as a moral arbiter we begin to see greater differences emerge between men's and women's pious giving. Women split their pious bequests more evenly among men, women, and gender-neutral targets than did men.[63] Women were also more likely to remember poor women in their wills than men. Between 1558 and 1580, 34 per cent (122) of women's pious bequests went to other women, whereas men left only 2 per cent (seven) for the same purpose.[64] The greater number of bequests left to women by women may have represented an attempt to retain some

---

58 J. Craig and C. Litzenberger, 'Wills as religious propaganda: the testament of William Tracy', *JEH*, 44 (1993), 415–31.

59 Wabuda, 'Shunamites and nurses', pp. 335–44.

60 M. B. Rowlands, 'Recusant women 1560–1640', in M. Prior (ed.), *Women in English Society 1500–1800* (London, 1985), pp. 149–80.

61 J. Foxe, *Acts and Monuments* (London, 1610), ii. 1753–4.

62 M. McIntosh, *A Community Transformed: The Manor and Liberty of Havering 1500–1620* (Cambridge, 1991), p. 292; Roper, *Holy Household*, p. 3.

63 Between 1500 and 1620 women left 417 (30.96 per cent) pious bequests to women, 344 to men (25.54 per cent), and 467 (34.67 per cent) to 'neutral' foundations or outlets. By contrast, men left 150 (3.87 per cent) to women, 1,720 to men (44.38 per cent), and 1,599 (41.25 per cent) to others.

64 After 1580 the figure for women rose to 76.02 per cent (260), while that for men dropped to 1.76 per cent (twenty-four). Before 1558 testators left few gifts to women: 5.86 per cent from women and 5.91 per cent from men. For non-pious bequests to women (family, friends) the figures are not so disparate.

of the pious control and female solidarity they had enjoyed in the gilds and traditional rites. The men's bias towards male beneficiaries, however, was related to their preference for longer funeral processions, for which they tended to hire members of their own sex as mourners.

The Reformation ushered in visible changes in women's parochial roles. Poorer and older women worked for the parish, helping to impose discipline and administer charity, while other women used their household authority to further reform agendas. Yet while many women embraced these changes, their pious bequests hint at a desire for a more prominent role within the public view of the parish.

III

The regulatory activities marking the years 1580–1620 sprang from economic, demographic, and cultural causes. The 1590s marked a time of inflation and unemployment in England that left contemporaries believing in a significant downturn, though historians debate the severity of the crisis.[65] A 1598 statute reinforced provisions for apprenticing poor children and setting the adult poor to work, and called for the whipping of rogues, vagabonds, and sturdy beggars and returning them to their birthplace. Some of those punished by the statute are likely to have migrated to London looking for work. One critic remembered the deserving poor, those 'poore Neighbours' impoverished by 'Haglers, Hawkers, Huxters, and Wanderers', and charged the Lord Mayor and aldermen with remedying the situation.[66] Strain on parish resources coupled with parishioners' perceptions of the poor conjured up an unprecedented crisis.[67]

In the midst of economic and demographic instability, relative stability had been achieved in religion. The combination of factors and new religious values that discouraged indiscriminate charity led churchwardens to devote more attention to social problems. This in turn stiffened attitudes toward the poor and further defined proper roles for women with respect to the parish, even as parishes continued to relieve the destitute.[68] Greater

---

65 Cf. S. Rappaport, *Worlds within Worlds: Structures of Life in Sixteenth-Century London* (Cambridge, 1989), p. 13, and Archer, *Pursuit of Stability*, p. 12.

66 I. Archer, C. Barron, and V. Harding (eds), *Hugh Alley's Caveat: The Markets of London in 1598* (London, 1988), p. 47.

67 'Crisis' in religion: Haigh, *English Reformations*, p. 181; C. Burgess and B. Kümin, 'Penitential bequests and parish regimes in late medieval England', *JEH*, 44 (1993), 610–30, esp. 630. On the importance of perceptions of hardship see G. Himmelfarb, *The Idea of Poverty: England in the Early Industrial Age* (New York, 1985).

68 B. Pullan, 'Catholics and the poor in early modern Europe', *TRHS*, 5th Series 26 (1976), 15–34; M. Spufford, 'Puritanism and social control?', in A. Fletcher and J. Stevenson (eds), *Order and Disorder in Early Modern England* (Cambridge, 1985), pp. 41–57; R. von Friedeburg, 'Reformation of manners and the social composition of offenders in an East Anglian cloth village: Earls Colne, Essex, 1531–1642', *Journal of British Studies*, 29 (1990), 347–85.

discrimination in charity and poor relief further stigmatised poor women by judging the morality of their behaviour and, perhaps most significantly, its cost to parish and city. Thus Protestant or Puritan sexual reform meshed easily with economic exigencies as parishes sought to curb parochial responsibilities.[69] Residence became a key factor in discriminating between the deserving and undeserving poor; hence parishes discouraged poor pregnant women or 'idle' young couples from settling or having children in the parish. As part of an effort to limit expenditure on relief, churchwardens began accounting for the care of abandoned children and their removal from parish expense.[70]

Targeting poor women, whether of an age to bring children or grandchildren on to the parish rolls, became an ever more prominent feature of local government.[71] As a poorer, suburban parish, St Botolph Aldersgate experienced problems associated with overcrowding and disorder, including the abandonment of children.[72] After a succession of such cases a vestry passed the following order to stem the number of illegitimate or abandoned children depending on the parish's financial support.

The said daie and yeare [20 June 1596] it is ordered by consent of the whole p'rishe that if any inhabitant dwelling within this p'rishe doe receave or take into his or her howse any woman with childe, or Inmate whereby any suche woman shalbe delyv'ed of childe, whereby any charge may growe to the p'rishe as before this tyme is hathe ben very chargeable to the p'rishe or if any suche p'son shall receave any childe whereby the like charge may growe to the said p'rishe, that then every suche p'son shall stande charged w'th the kepinge of ev'y suche woman & childe and shall have no releif of the p'rishe towards the same.[73]

Despite this proclamation, nursing of foundlings and lame children and searching out the mothers, or sometimes parents, of abandoned children continued. In 1606 St Botolph's extended its prohibitions against inmates and lodgers to include the 'children sonnes or daughters eyther married or marriageable' within the homes of any poor man or woman receiving a pension or alms from the parish.[74]

---

69 Cf. Stone, *The Family, Sex, and Marriage*, and M. Ingram, 'The reform of popular culture? Sex and marriage in early modern England', in Barry Reay (ed.), *Popular Culture in Seventeenth-Century England* (London, 1985), p. 159; S. Amussen, *An Ordered Society: Gender and Class in Early Modern England* (Oxford, 1988).

70 The years 1581–1640 marked a high point of illegitimacy before the eighteenth century, 3.8 per cent of births being illegitimate: P. Laslett, *Family Life and Illicit Love in Earlier Generations: Essays in Historical Sociology* (Cambridge, 1977), pp. 133–5. For one example out of many see GL, MS 593/2, f. 126v.

71 Cf. M. Roberts, 'Women and work', p. 96.

72 On the poor in extra-mural parishes see Archer, *Pursuit of Stability*, pp. 12–3.

73 GL, MS 1454, Roll 96.

74 GL, MS 1453/1, f. 3.

From the parish's point of view relief had already been stretched thin without having to support young and presumably able-bodied (and therefore undeserving) poor. In addition married or marriageable sons and daughters could increase the parish rolls further. Without the removal of inmates or children the respective tenants were threatened with removal themselves, as at St Michael Cornhill in 1573; in 1616 the vestry threatened to negate a widow's pension if she did not send her son and his wife out of her rooms, and the parish as a whole.[75] Thus defining the deserving poor could clash with the role of mother and domestic provider that was promoted in other aspects of religious reform.

All parishes tried to limit their responsibility for sick, abandoned, and poor women. Parishes petitioned Bridewell, the hospital in London that became a house of correction, to take in poor sick or fallen women in the early seventeenth century and paid for warrants to carry destitute women delivered of children to Bridewell.[76] St Stephen's carried a woman there as she was about to give birth.[77] Occasionally, before pregnancy and its spectre of two poor charges on the parish, churchwardens took pre-emptive action, as in handing 1s. 'to a poore woeman to gett hir out of the pish'.[78] In a sense parishes already considered themselves free of moral responsibility by condemning the idleness or ungodliness of the poor, hence reinforcing the impression of social and gender differentiation among those living in or migrating to certain parishes. Limits to concealment of pregnancy and reproductive roles made women at once an easy and potent target of this form of social control; sometimes the parish searched for and had arrested only the mother. The crowded nature of life in London, especially in the later part of the sixteenth century, enabled parishioners to inform searchers about possible suspects and abandoned children.[79]

In 1597–98 the churchwardens of St Mary Woolnoth recorded outlays for the poor in bread, coals, and money to the parish and ward. Collections for maimed soldiers, Christ's Hospital, and the year's lecture rested alongside payment to a carpenter for stocks built at the church door, including the pavement and hinges. The parish also paid Mr Samwell for 'findinge out the woman that laide the childe in our street lately'. The stocks at the church door provided a visual reminder of the limits of behaviour and benevolence, and the distinction between those deserving and undeserving of parish aid.[80] The pew for the collectors for

75 GL, MS 4072/1, Part 1, fos 16v–17; f. 110.
76 GL, MS 1454, Roll 96.
77 GL, MS 593/2, f. 137.
78 *Ibid.*, f. 131v. On fear of 'masterless' women see Mack, *Visionary Women*, p. 95.
79 Archer, *Pursuit of Stability*, p. 77.
80 GL, MS 1002/1A, fos 305–10.

the poor may have been just inside the church door – far from the godly space of the pulpit and the prestigious place of the more expensive pews.[81]

This kind of attention to the behaviour of the poor, and their descent from the 'poor in Christ' to the disorderly poor, cut across age and gender. While parishes seemed to sense the conjuncture of factors – the death of a spouse, a number of children, or no employment – that left many widows economically fragile, they were most likely to help those who had lived in the parish long enough to show their character and to shore up sympathy.[82] Widows or 'goodwives' hired by parishes, or paying reduced rent or receiving a pension, had often lived long in the parish or had been married to men once employed there.[83] For example, St Stephen's supported the Howe family past John Howe's days as a famous organ maker in the parish and around London. By virtue of their long history of service to and residence in the parish, parishioners supported the Howes, paying for his grave in 1571 and paying Mrs Howe 52s., her husband's salary, as her 'exhibition' and pension in 1576 until her death in 1585.[84]

Another widow in the same parish also benefited from her husband's previous service, although the parish attempted to spread responsibility for her care. In 1574 churchwardens began sustaining Andrew Ludford, the former parson. Beginning in 1581, after his death, Widow Ludford collected £5 4s. yearly for her pension, to which the Grocers contributed, starting in 1586. The churchwardens specified her costs, including articles of clothing and ready money. Some time between 1586 and 1587 Widow Ludford entered Bedlam, but her pension continued to pass from the Grocers through the parish to the hospital. Her son took over her care for at least part of the year in 1588.[85] She died near the end of 1604. This effort signified both the potential expense of caring for a long-lived person and the number of parties enlisted to help.

While much recent scholarship on poverty casts the widow as the most deserving of the poor, impressions from parish records suggest that she was often treated with little sympathy.[86] One churchwarden recorded

---

81 GL, MS 1454, Roll 72.
82 V. Brodsky, 'Widows in late Elizabethan London: remarriage, economic opportunity and family orientations', in L. Bonfield, R. M. Smith, and K. Wrightson (eds), *The World we have Gained: Histories of Population and Social Structure* (Oxford, 1986), p. 124.
83 On residence outside London see B. Wilkinson, '"The poore of the parish"', *Local Historian*, 16 (1984), 21–3.
84 GL, MS 593/2, fos 60, 65.
85 *Ibid.*, fos 75, 76–76v, 78v.
86 Brodsky, 'Widows in late Elizabethan London', pp. 123–4; A. Erickson, *Women and Property in Early Modern England* (London, 1993), pp. 203, 227; Wales, 'Poverty, poor relief and the life-cycle', p. 364; M. McIntosh, 'Networks of care in Elizabethan English towns: the example of Hadleigh, Suffolk', in P. Horden and R. Smith (eds), *The Locus of Care: Families, Communities, and Institutions in History* (London, forthcoming).

a financial incentive of 20s. 'given to wydowe pteriche' to encourage her to leave the parish.[87] Widows were also mercilessly entered on lists of parishioners in arrears for clerks' wages and parsonage expenses, although fastidious churchwardens may have been primarily accounting for uncollected funds.[88] Parishes might try to collect arrears, however, once a widow remarried; William Olyver refused payment of his wife's 10s. debt for rent to the parish.[89] Deserving widows waited for the deaths of others to secure their own entrances to hospitals, rooms, tenements, and pensions, and competed for limited relief, as seen in petitions to St Michael's in the 1590s. In one vestry, two widows petitioned for the churchyard house formerly occupied by another 'goodwife', while another petitioned for her pension.[90] Parishes frequently restricted widows from remarrying while in parish tenements or on a pension and granted living space as long as 'none shall come into her house during her life to be chargeable to the p'rish'.[91] But parishes often allowed, or encouraged, widows and other women (not called 'widow' or 'goodwife' in the sources) to occupy houses together, creating a 'subculture of widows' in the lower orders.[92]

A parish's attention to status and character was not limited to the poor. Pews in post-Reformation London delineated social and economic status, as well as age and gender.[93] In addition to their petitions and makeshift arrangements, other public signs, such as where widows sat in church during services, demonstrated their social and economic positions. The fact that – to 'avoyd futuere trouble' – St Stephen's officers had to defend the seats of two elder widows in the 'uppermoste pewes' for the rest of their lives against the challenges of male parishioners illustrates not only the social dislocation experienced by widows, but also the damaging after-effects on parish harmony.[94] The arrangement of the women in the same church in 1607 appeared to antagonise age and communal status: women whose husbands had been churchwardens sat in privileged positions, behind whom sat other women, 'nott displasinge any whoe were formerly sett be for ther Ancientts'.[95] The vestry of 27 March 1612 'agreed that the wyfe of Cazar Brambele shalbee removed out of her seate in the church & placed in some inferior place alone at the discretion of the

---

87 GL, MS 1002/1A, f. 169.
88 GL, MS 1454, Roll 68.
89 *Ibid.*, Rolls 60–1.
90 GL, MS 4072/1, Part 1, f. 76.
91 *Ibid.*, Part 1, f. 76.
92 Brodsky, 'Widows in late Elizabethan London', p. 124.
93 Scarisbrick, *Reformation*, pp. 173–4; Aston, 'Segregation in church'.
94 GL, MS 594/1, f. 88.
95 *Ibid.*, f. 64.

churchwardens before Easter day'.[96] In this fluctuating world one woman still left clothing to 'my puefellowe'.[97]

Other changes in the expectations parishes had of women limited their participation in parish life. While husbands in London most often named their wives as executrices in the sixteenth century after a medieval high of 88 per cent, the practice went into some decline about 1580.[98] Between 1548 and 1552 74 per cent (twenty-three) of wills of married men designated wives as executrices. Between 1580 and 1601 the number had declined to 60 per cent (sixty). This change lessened widows' direct control over their husbands' estates and increased the control exercised by male churchwardens over bequests. In one case the widow did not attend the distribution of her husband's bequest and instead sent a male representative.[99]

St Michael's made a 'Table of Remembrance' of parishioners' 'charitable benevolences' in 1608 intended for 'suche others as shall here after accordinge to their good examples bestowe any further charitable benevolences to the releif of the poore Inhabitants of this p'rishe'.[100] In another parish in 1614, however, the 'charitye & liberalitye of a gentlewoman who suppresseth her name' provided for building shops to create an annuity for sermons and doles.[101] This may have been a simple case of selfless charity, but it might be taken as a symbol of how much more problematic public female charity could become after the Reformation. Dame Percivale had confidently made bequests without too many qualifications in an earlier age; now restrictions in wills reflected growing regulation of almsgiving and closer supervision of testamentary and lifetime bequests.

Thus the parish remained central to the experiences of Londoners during the era of plainer services and plainer interiors. Pew arrangements, charity, and office distribution worked to marginalise poor women and to redefine the public roles of wealthier women. At the same time, women's giving in last wills diverged from men's, suggesting the exercise of private influence with public consequences for reform. By the mid-seventeenth century, a reaction against the spiritual restraints and tighter moral discipline surfaced, albeit for a short period of time. The proliferation of female prophets and the exceptional behaviour of women and especially London women temporarily overthrew constraints on the pious activity of lay women imposed by the Reformation.[102]

96 GL, MS 1453/1, f. 5.
97 GL, MS 9171/13, f. 20v.
98 R. A. Wood, 'Poor widows *c.* 1393–1415', in Barron and Sutton (eds), *Medieval London Widows*, p. 55.
99 GL, MS 4072/1, Part 1, f. 110v.
100 *Ibid.*, f. 100v.
101 GL, MS 1453/1, f. 8.
102 Scarisbrick, *Reformation*, p. 39; Mack, *Visionary Women*, p. 49; cf. Cross, 'The religious life of women', p. 324.

IV

The now familiar revision of the Reformation has questioned notions of a passive laity following the medieval Church and of an active laity in the post-Reformation Church.[103] Gifts to gilds, lights, obits, and other services continued until the last moments of those institutions that supported the doctrine of Purgatory. Thereafter the removal of outlets for pious observance and lay control of services and devotions radically reoriented women's and men's relationship with the church and their status within the parish. As the century wore on, testators' reliance on the male-run parish, specifically the churchwardens and vestry, to oversee disbursement of the estate reduced the opportunities for women's public involvement in charity. The pious participation of men and women in the ritual life of the parish had become more marked by gender lines by the reign of the Stuarts. Mainstream parish life had no more room for mixed-sex voluntary associations such as gilds or for prominently displayed examples of female holiness. Men had grander funerals, and older or widowed women moved to lesser places within the church. Parish accounts focused more clearly on the wayward behaviour of disorderly poor women. The oversight of women servants, the dogged pursuit of mothers of foundlings, and the attempts to restrict pregnant women's temporary residence in parishes attested to efforts to control inappropriate female behaviour that cost the parish dearly.

The restriction of English lay religious options in the parish resembled a similar trend within Counter-Reformation churches. Episcopal supervision of Italian confraternities increased in the later sixteenth century and reduced lay autonomy and initiative. On the other hand, more individual devotion encouraged greater lay involvement, especially among women, in Counter-Reformation cults dedicated to the rosary and Eucharist.[104] Despite changes in the extent or even intensity of lay devotion over the course of the Reformation, the parish remained central to the lives of male and female Londoners.

The enthusiastic embrace of sects by some lay women in the mid-seventeenth century allowed them to challenge restraints on their devotion and control.[105] The behaviour of women in this period attempted to negate the social and gender divisions that ran through the sixteenth-century parish. Less emphasis on spiritually strong female figures and the formalisation of seating for the poor, the young, and women curtailed

---

103 Haigh, *English Reformations*; Duffy, *Stripping of the Altars*; Kümin, *Shaping of a Community*.

104 C. Black, *Italian Confraternities in the Sixteenth Century* (Cambridge, 1989), pp. 273–4.; R. Weissman, *Ritual Brotherhood in Renaissance Florence* (New York, 1982); Cohn, *Death and Property*.

105 Mack, *Visionary Women*, p. 49; Scarisbrick, *Reformation*; A. Laurence, 'A priesthood of she-believers: women and congregations in mid-seventeenth-century England', in Sheils and Wood (eds), *Women in the Church*, pp. 345–63.

the participation of women in the parish. At the same time, however, they supported reform and counter-reform in their homes, testaments, and eventually in separate congregations by adopting biblical precedents. The change in women's participation in the parish suggests that, by the 1590s, English society had become yet more stratified and the room for female public involvement yet more limited.[106]

---

106 Cf. 'Parish congregations went to church: they prayed again to their God, learned again how to be good, and went off home once more. That was how it had been in 1530; that was how it was in 1590': Haigh, *English Reformations*, p. 295.

Index

This is primarily a subject index. Major cities are included, but other place names appear only if they are mentioned several times (see the respective counties), and there are no entries for individual parishes or parishioners. References to illustrations are given in italics.